Nuclear Weapons and International Law

— from the London Nuclear Warfare Tribunal via the International Court of Justice Advisory Opinion to contemporary developments
2nd edition

A SHORT HISTORY LESSON: 1945

August 6th:
Dropped atomic bomb
On civilians
At Hiroshima.

August 8th:
Agreed to hold
War crimes trials
For Nazis.

August 9th:
Dropped atomic bomb
On civilians
At Nagasaki.

David Krieger

Nuclear Weapons and International Law

— from the London Nuclear Warfare Tribunal via the International Court of Justice Advisory Opinion to contemporary developments

Geoffrey Darnton

Foreword and Contribution by Richard Falk and David Krieger

PEACE ANALYTICS ™

Copyright © 1989, 2015 Geoffrey Darnton

All rights reserved. No part of this work which is copyright may be reproduced or used in any form or by any means — graphic, electronic, or mechanical, including photocopying, recording, taping or information storage and retrieval systems — without the written permission of the Publisher, except in accordance with the provisions of the UK Copyright Designs and Patents Act 1988.

Whilst the Publisher has taken all reasonable care in the preparation of this book, neither the Author nor the Publisher makes any representation, express or implied, with regard to the accuracy of the information contained in this book and cannot accept any legal responsibility or liability for any errors or omissions from the book or the consequences thereof. Information in the book is provided solely to facilitate choices and decisions by the reader.

Products and services that are referred to in this book may be either trademarks and/or registered trademarks of their respective owners. The Publisher and Author make no claim to these trademarks other than trademarks owned by the Author.

First edition published 1989 ISBN 91-87396-09-2 by Alva and Gunnar Myrdal Foundation & Swedish Lawyers Against Nuclear Arms.

Second edition 2015 Published by:
Requirements Analytics, for Peace Analytics
Suite 59
2 Lansdowne Crescent
Bournemouth, BH1 1SA
UK

https://nwil.xyz/ and https://peaceanalytics.com/

ISBN: 978-1-909231-06-1 (paperback)
       978-1-909231-07-8 (hardback)
       978-1-909231-08-5 (eBook)

Contents

Foreword to 2nd Edition **xi**
Preface to 2nd Edition **xvii**
Acknowledgements **xxi**
Foreword to 1st Edition **xxiii**
Preface to 1st Edition **xxvii**
Back Cover Text from Original Edition **xxxii**

Chapter 1
Introduction

1.1 The Relevance of International Law. ... 1
1.2 Substantive Foundations ... 4
   1.2.1 Just War Doctrine ... 4
   1.2.2 Customary Norms of International Law ... 4
   1.2.3 Treaty Rules and Principles ... 6
   1.2.4 Supplementary Norms with Legal Force ... 10
1.3 Method of Inquiry ... 11
1.4 Overview of Tribunal Scope ... 12
   1.4.1 Evidence before the Tribunal ... 12

Chapter 2
Relevant International Law

2.1 Lawfulness of Nuclear Weapons - Position of Nuclear States ... 13
2.2 Sources of International Law ... 14
2.3 Relevant Treaties, Declarations and Conventions ... 14
   2.3.1 The St Petersberg Declaration 1868 ... 14
   2.3.2 The Hague Conventions of 1907 ... 15
   2.3.3 Geneva Gas Protocol 1925 ... 16
   2.3.4 United Nations Charter ... 16
   2.3.5 Nuremberg Judgment ... 16
   2.3.6 Genocide Convention 1948 ... 16
   2.3.7 Geneva Conventions 1949 ... 17
   2.3.8 Nuremberg Principles 1950 ... 17
   2.3.9 McCloy Zorin Accords 1961 ... 18

2.3.10 Test–Ban Treaty 1963 ... 18
2.3.11 Non–Proliferation Treaty 1968 ... 18
2.3.12 Biological Weapons Convention 1972 ... 19
2.3.13 Geneva Protocols I and II 1977 ... 19
2.3.14 Conventional Weapons Convention 1981 ... 21
2.4 Additional Treaties and Conventions ... 21

Chapter 3
Use of Nuclear Weapons

3.1 General Effects of Nuclear Weapons ... 23
3.2 Medical and Environmental Effects of Nuclear War ... 25
    3.2.1 Atomic Bomb Effects on Hiroshima and Nagasaki ... 25
    3.2.2 Consequences of Nuclear Attack on the UK ... 28
    3.2.3 Nuclear War and the Provision of Health Services ... 31
    3.2.4 Longer Term Effects of Low-Level Radiation ... 33
    3.2.5 Long-Term Effects on the Global Ecosphere ... 34
    3.2.6 Tribunal Conclusions on Global Ecosphere Effects ... 36
3.3 Nuclear Weapons and Strategy ... 37
    3.3.1 Detonation of a Single Weapon ... 37
    3.3.2 Detonation of Single Weapon in Water ... 37
    3.3.3 Use of Single Weapon on Land ... 37
    3.3.4 Use of Single Weapon as Demonstration ... 38
    3.3.5 Tendency of Weaponry and Strategies Towards Use ... 38
3.4 Lawful Use of Nuclear Weapons - Is It Conceivable? ... 40

Chapter 4
Possession of Nuclear Weapons

4.1 General Evidence on Possession ... 43
4.2 Deterrence and the Evolution of Technology ... 46
4.3 Change of Governmental Policies ... 47
4.4 Strategic Defence Initiative (SDI) ... 51
4.5 Military Manuals and a Soldier's Duty ... 52
4.6 Sovereignty ... 54
    4.6.1 The Loss of Constitutional Powers ... 55
    4.6.2 Loss of Sovereignty of Members of Alliances ... 55
4.7 Neutrality ... 56
4.8 Unlawfulness of Possession of Nuclear Weapons ... 58

Chapter 5

Public Conscience

5.1 Morality and Dictates of the Public Conscience **67**
5.2 Mass Movements against Nuclear Weapons **71**
5.3 Individual Responsibility and Nuclear Weapons **72**
5.4 Legal Challenges to Nuclear Weapons **73**
5.5 Mass Movements and The Military **74**
5.6 The United Nations and Nuclear Weapons **74**

Chapter 6

Value of International Law

6.1 General Evidence on Value of International Law **77**
6.2 Interpretation of International Law **80**
6.3 General Remarks on the Evidence **82**

Chapter 7

Judgment and Recommendations

7.1 Preamble **85**
7.2 Judgment of the Tribunal **86**
    7.2.1 Implications for Governments **88**
    7.2.2 Implications for Statesmen, Policy-Makers, Strategists, Advisors, Scientists, Engineers, Military Commanders in Nuclear Weapons States and their Allies **88**
    7.2.3 Implications for Dissenters, Protesters, Resisters, and Ordinary Citizens **89**
7.3 Recommendations of the Tribunal **89**

Chapter 8

World Court Project

8.1 LNWT Recommendation 5 .... **91**
8.2 The Birth of the World Court Project (WCP) **92**
8.3 Scope of the World Court Project (WCP) **92**
8.4 ICJ Judicial Recognition of WCP **95**
8.5 Final Comments **96**

Chapter 9

International Court of Justice

9.1 Advisory Opinions from the ICJ 97
9.2 Requests for Advisory Opinions about Nuclear Weapons 97
9.3 Additional Comments by Judges 102
9.4 Decision to Give an Advisory Opinion 103
9.5 Declarations by Judges 103
9.6 Separate Opinions by Judges 107
9.7 Dissenting Opinions by Judges 108
9.8 Voting 111
9.9 Commentary on the Advisory Opinion 112
9.10 Other Commentaries 113
9.10 Preamble and Advisory Opinion - Full Text 113

Chapter 10

Dissenting Opinion of Judge Weeramantry

Table of Contents (see the book table of contents for page numbers) 149
   Preliminary Observations on the Opinion of the Court ... 152
   (a) Reasons for Dissent 152
   (b) The Positive Aspects of the Court's Opinion 152
   (c) Particular Comments on the Final Paragraph 153
      (i) Paragraph 2B — (11 votes to 3) 153
      (ii) Paragraph 2E — (7 votes to 7. Casting vote in favour by the President) 153
      (iii) Paragraph 2A — (Unanimous) 154
      (iv) Paragraph 2C — (Unanimous) 154
      (v) Paragraph 2D — (Unanimous) 154
      (vi) Paragraph 2F — (Unanimous) 154
      (vii) Paragraph 1 — (13 votes to 1) 155
I. Introduction 155
   1. Fundamental Importance of Issue before the Court 155
   2. Submissions to the Court 157
   3. Some Preliminary Observations on the United Nations Charter 157
   4. The Law Relevant to Nuclear Weapons 159
   5. Introductory Observations on Humanitarian Law 159
   6. Linkage between Humanitarian Law and the Realities of War 160

7. The Limit Situation Created by Nuclear Weapons ... 162
8. Possession and Use ... 162
9. Differing Attitudes of States Supporting Legality ... 163
10. The Importance of a Clarification of the Law ... 163
II. Nature and Effects of Nuclear Weapons ... 164
   1. The Nature of the Nuclear Weapon ... 164
   2. Euphemisms Concealing the Realities of Nuclear War ... 164
   3. The Effects of the Nuclear Weapon ... 165
      (a) Damage to the environment and the ecosystem. ... 166
      (b) Damage to future generations ... 167
      (c) Damage to civilian populations ... 168
      (d) The nuclear winter ... 168
      (e) Loss of life ... 169
      (f) Medical effects of radiation ... 169
      (g) Heat and blast ... 171
      (h) Congenital deformities ... 171
      (i) Transnational damage ... 173
      (j) Potential to destroy all civilization ... 173
      (k) The electromagnetic pulse ... 175
      (l) Damage to nuclear reactors ... 176
      (m) Damage to food productivity ... 176
      (n) Multiple nuclear explosions resulting from self-defence ... 177
      (o) "The shadow of the mushroom cloud" ... 177
   4. The Uniqueness of Nuclear Weapons ... 178
   5. The Differences in Scientific Knowledge between the Present Time and 1945 ... 179
   6. Do Hiroshima and Nagasaki Show that Nuclear War Is Survivable? ... 180
   7. A Perspective from the Past ... 180
III. Humanitarian Law ... 181
   1. "Elementary Considerations of Humanity" ... 182
   2. Multicultural Background to the Humanitarian Laws of War ... 183
   3. Outline of Humanitarian Law ... 186
   4. Acceptance by States of the Martens Clause ... 188
   5. "The Dictates of Public Conscience" ... 189
   6. Impact of the United Nations Charter and Human Rights on "Considerations of Humanity" and "Dictates of Public Conscience ... 191
   7. The Argument that "Collateral Damage" Is Unintended ... 192
   8. Illegality Exists Independently of Specific Prohibitions ... 192
   9. The "Lotus" Decision ... 194

- 10. Specific Rules of the Humanitarian Law of War 195
  - (a) The prohibition against causing unnecessary suffering 196
  - (b) The principle of proportionality 197
  - (c) The principle of discrimination 197
  - (d) Respect for non-belligerent States 198
  - (e) The prohibition against genocide 199
  - (f) The prohibition against environmental damage 199
  - (g) Human rights law 202
- 11. Juristic Opinion 203
- 12. The 1925 Geneva Gas Protocol 204
  - (i) Is radiation poisonous? 204
  - (ii) Does radiation involve contact of the body with "materials"? 205
- 13. Article 23 (a) of the Hague Regulations 206

IV. Self-Defence 206
- 1. Unnecessary Suffering 208
- 2. Proportionality/Error 208
- 3. Discrimination 209
- 4. Non-belligerent States 209
- 5. Genocide 210
- 6. Environmental Damage 210
- 7. Human Rights 210

V. Some General Considerations 212
- 1. Two Philosophical Perspectives 212
- 2. The Aims of War 214
- 3. The Concept of a "Threat of Force" under the United Nations Charter 215
- 4. Equality in the Texture of the Laws of War 216
- 5. The Logical Contradiction of a Dual Regime in the Laws of War 217
- 6. Nuclear Decision-Making 218

VI. The Attitude of the International Community Towards Nuclear Weapons 219
- 1.. The Universality of the Ultimate Goal of Complete Elimination 219
- 2. Overwhelming Majorities in Support of Total Abolition 220
- 3. World Public Opinion 221
- 4. Current Prohibitions 221
- 5. Partial Bans 222
- 6. Who Are the States Most Specially Concerned ? 222
- 7. Have States, by Participating in Regional Treaties, Recognized Nuclear Weapons as Lawful ? 223

VII. Some Special Aspects ... 223
  1. The Non-Proliferation Treaty ... 223
  2. Deterrence ... 224
    (i) Meaning of deterrence ... 224
    (ii) Deterrence — from what ? ... 224
    (iii) The degrees of deterrence ... 225
    (iv) Minimum deterrence ... 225
    (v) The problem of credibility ... 226
    (vi) Deterrence distinguished from possession ... 226
    (vii) The legal problem of intention ... 226
    (viii) The temptation to use the weapons maintained for deterrence ... 227
    (ix) Deterrence and sovereign equality ... 227
    (x) Conflict with the St. Petersburg principle ... 227
  3. Reprisals ... 227
  4. Internal Wars ... 229
  5. The Doctrine of Necessity ... 229
  6. Limited or Tactical or Battlefield Nuclear Weapons ... 230
VIII. Some Arguments against the Grant of an Advisory Opinion ... 232
  1. The Advisory Opinion Would be Devoid of Practical Effects ... 232
  2. Nuclear Weapons Have Preserved World Peace ... 233
IX. Conclusion ... 234
  1. The Task before the Court ... 234
  2. The Alternatives before Humanity ... 235
Comparison of the Effects of Bombs ... 236

Chapter 11

Initiatives Since ICJ Advisory Opinions

11.1 International Criminal Court ... 239
11.2 Trident and Scotland ... 239
11.3 ICAN, NAPF, Mayors for Peace and PICAT ... 244
  11.3.1 ICAN ... 244
  11.3.2 NAPF ... 245
  11.3.3 Mayors for Peace ... 245
  11.3.4 PICAT ... 246
11.4 Humanitarian Pledge ... 247
11.5 Marshall Islands Cases Before the ICJ - the Nuclear Zero Lawsuits ... 249
11.6 UK Renewal of Trident ... 250

viii

11.7 Application Instituting Proceedings against the United Kingdom ... 251
I. Introduction and Summary ... 251
II. Facts ... 256
    A. The Five Nuclear Weapon States Parties to the NPT ... 256
    B. The Nine States Possessing Nuclear Weapons ... 256
    C. The UK and the Nuclear Arms Race ... 258
        1. Early Nuclear History ... 258
        2. The UK's Current Nuclear Arsenal ... 259
        3. Nuclear Policy, Doctrine and Expenditure ... 262
        4. Current Plans for Modernization and Qualitative Improvements of the UK's Nuclear Arsenal ... 264
    D. The UK and Nuclear Disarmament ... 268
        1. History and General Policy Regarding Negotiation of Nuclear Disarmament ... 268
        2. Opposition to Negotiation of a Nuclear Weapons Convention ... 271
III. The Law ... 274
    A. Article VI of the NPT ... 274
    B. Customary International Law ... 275
    C. Good Faith ... 276
IV. Obligations Breached By the UK ... 278
    A. Breach of Article VI of the NPT ... 278
    B. Breach of Customary International Law ... 280
    C. Breach of the Obligation to Perform its Obligations in Good Faith ... 280
V. Jurisdiction of the Court ... 281
VI. Final Observations ... 281

Chapter 12

Falk and Krieger Dialogue

Nuclear Weapons and International Law ... 285

Chapter 13

Epilogue

13.1 Nuclear Weapons - and their Effects ... 307
13.2 Tokyo Tribunal ... 308
13.3 Alternatives to deterrence ... 309
13.4 Peace and War ... 310
13.5 Religion and Morality ... 310

13.6 More legal Commentary ... 311
13.7 Psychological and Sociological State of Mass Murder Killers ... 311
13.8 Taking this Book Forward ... 312
13.9 Register of Nuclear Weapons Advocates, Decision-Takers, etc. ... 312
13.10 Errors, Omissions, and, Comments ... 312

Appendix A
Nuremberg Principles 313

Appendix B
McCloy-Zorin Accords 315

Appendix C
Baden Consultation 319

Appendix D
Interim Declaration 320

Appendix E
Judges 325

Appendix F
Tribunal Supporting Organizations 328

Appendix G
Convenors of the Tribunal 329

Appendix H
List of Evidence before the Tribunal 330

H.1 Moral Issues ... 330
H.2 Medical and Environmental Effects ... 331
H.3 Current Weaponry and Strategy ... 332
H.4 Legal Implications ... 333
H.5 Books Submitted to the Tribunal ... 335

References 329

Index 339

Foreword

When the London Nuclear Warfare Tribunal was convened in 1985, the Cold War set the tone of international relations. Beyond this, Ronald Reagan was the most anti-Communist and belligerent American leader since the end of World War II. There was every reason to be worried that the risks of nuclear war had become unacceptable from the outlook of political prudence additional to their dubious moral and legal status. In this atmosphere the London Tribunal sought an authoritative assessment of the status of nuclear weapons and warfare under international law with the hope that this might move the political debate toward the embrace of nuclear disarmament.

Now 30 years later, the Cold War is over and Barack Obama, the current American leader declared in 2009 his resolve to work toward achieving a world without nuclear weapons. This message of hope and commitment was reinforced at the time by four prominent American political figures with strong realist credentials (Henry Kissinger, George Shultz, Sam Nunn, and William Perry) who present the case for nuclear disarmament to avoid the further spread of nuclear weaponry. Yet as we reflect upon these issues in 2015 we note that there is not present among the nuclear weapons states the existence of a political will to place nuclear disarmament on the global policy agenda, much less evidence of a willingness by non-nuclear states to exert meaningful pressures.

Despite important shifts in conflict patterns, which make it more dangerous than ever that nuclear weapons will get into the hands of non-state political actors that would be inclined to disregard the horrifying consequences of use, there are no serious initiatives proposed by governments or through the United Nations to address this menacing challenge. What we find in 2015, instead of a sense of urgency, is a shared mood of complacency on the part of governments, international institutions, and international public opinion. Without the Cold War, and considering the absence of any use of such a weapon since 1945 at Nagasaki, there is a false sense of security, even as anxieties rise to fever pitch when contemplating the prospect of

Iran armed with nuclear weapons. Indeed, the evident present priority of nuclear weapons states is to invest heavily in the modernization and further development of their existing arsenal of nuclear weapons, as well in the pseudo-stability of the nonproliferation regime.

And thus, even more so than in 1985, it would seem that it will be up to civil society activism to create the kind of climate of opinion that will force the hand of governmental actors. One step in this direction is to remind the people of the world that from the perspective of international law, nuclear weapons are unlawful, making their threat or use, crimes of utmost magnitude. In this regard, the material gathered in this volume is an invaluable resource for citizen activism on the basis of expecting governments in the 21st century to pursue security within the framework of the global rule of law. The clarity and authoritativeness of the conclusions of the London Tribunal are reinforced by the Advisory Opinion of the International Court of Justice rendered in 1996, and especially by the historic dissent of Judge Christopher Weeramantry that is also included in this volume.

In 1986 there were some 70,000 nuclear weapons in the world. Since then, the number has fallen to approximately 16,000. It is a dramatic quantitative drop, but remains far from the only safe number, which is zero. Over 90 percent of the weapons are in the arsenals of the US and Russia, and their negotiations for further reductions have stalled while they engage in military posturing, including nuclear posturing over the conflict in Ukraine. The US and Russia still maintain some 1,800 nuclear weapons between them on hair-trigger alert, ready to be fired within moments of an order to do so. Neither country has a commitment to No First Use of its nuclear arsenal, leaving open the threat of a preemptive attack, or other initiating use of the sort sometimes suggested as the best means to destroy Iran's underground nuclear facilities.

The United States unilaterally withdrew from the Anti-Ballistic Missile Treaty in 2002 under Bush II, a treaty that was designed to limit the number of missile defense deployments in order to discourage defensive-offensive escalation cycles. This US withdrawal from the treaty coupled with the subsequent deployment of missile defense installations near the Russian borders has generated Russian anxiety about a possible US first strike, which increases tensions between the two countries and makes more nervous the fingers on the nuclear buttons.

In addition to the US and Russia, seven other countries possess nuclear weapons: the UK, France, China, Israel, India, Pakistan and North Korea. All of them have joined the US and Russia in modernizing their nuclear arsenals. Each of these arsenals is a source of nuclear danger, as are those of the US and Russia. Atmospheric scientists found through modelling studies that a relatively small nuclear exchange between India and Pakistan using 50 Hiroshima-size nuclear weapons each on the other side's cities would put enough soot into the upper stratosphere to block warming sunlight from reaching the Earth, reduce temperatures on the planet to the lowest levels in 1,000 years, shorten growing seasons, cause crop failures and result in nuclear famine that could take two billion lives of the most vulnerable people on the planet. A larger exchange of nuclear weapons between the US and Russia could send the world tumbling into a new ice age, destroy civilization and annihilate the human species and most complex forms of life on the planet.

Article VI of the 1970 Nuclear Non-Proliferation Treaty obligates the parties to the NPT to negotiate in good faith on effective measures for a cessation of the nuclear arms race and an early date and for nuclear disarmament. These negotiations have never taken place, despite the unanimous legal support of the Article VI obligations in the 1996 ICJ Advisory Opinion: "There exists an obligation to pursue in good faith and bring to a conclusion negotiations leading to nuclear disarmament in all its aspects under strict and effective international control."

In 2014, one of the smallest countries on the planet, the Republic of the Marshall Islands (RMI), took a bold action to enforce the Article VI obligations and the customary international law obligations that derive from them. The RMI brought lawsuits against the nine nuclear-armed countries in the ICJ, seeking declaratory judgments that they are in breach of their nuclear disarmament obligations and injunctive relief ordering them to commence the required negotiations within one year. Because only three of the nine nuclear-armed countries accept the compulsory jurisdiction of the ICJ, only the cases against the UK, Pakistan and India are currently going forward at the ICJ. The other six countries would have had to affirmatively accept the jurisdiction of the ICJ to have their cases go forward and none have chosen to do so.

The Marshall Islands also brought a separate lawsuit against the

US in a US federal court, due to the pivotal position of the US in terms of its leadership on nuclear issues. That case was dismissed by the lower court and is currently being appealed in the Ninth Circuit Court of Appeals. The cases are drawing interest throughout the world and currently over ninety civil society organizations, including the World Council of Churches, Greenpeace International and the Nobel Women's Initiative, have joined a consortium headed by the Nuclear Age Peace Foundation in support of the RMI's Nuclear Zero lawsuits (see www.nuclearzero.org).

The Marshall Islands acts with great moral authority, as their territory was used as a site of US nuclear testing in the early years of the Nuclear Age. The US conducted 67 nuclear tests in the RMI between 1946 and 1958, with the equivalent explosive power of having tested 1.6 nuclear Hiroshima bombs daily for 12 years. The Marshall Islanders suffered cancers, leukemia, stillbirths, birth defects and other radiation-induced illnesses. Some of their islands still remain uninhabitable, and they have never been adequately compensated for their pain, suffering, premature deaths and the loss of their lands.

In addition to the Nuclear Zero lawsuits by the Marshall Islands, one other positive initiative in relation to nuclear weapons is the series of inter-governmental conferences on the humanitarian impacts of nuclear weapons that have taken place in recent years in Oslo, Nayarit (Mexico), and Vienna. At the Vienna conference in December 2014, the Austrian government made an Austrian Pledge to work to close the legal gap to achieve the prohibition and elimination of nuclear weapons. Since then, over 100 other states have joined Austria in taking this pledge, now known as the Humanitarian Pledge. The hope is that one or more of these countries will convene a meeting of states to initiate a Nuclear Ban Treaty, similar to the Ottawa Conference that was convened to create a Landmine Ban Treaty. This can be done with or without the initial participation of the nuclear-armed countries.

This year (2015) marks the 70th anniversaries of the bombings of Hiroshima and Nagasaki. The survivors of those bombings, the hibakusha, have been outspoken in their calls to abolish nuclear weapons so that their past does not become someone else's future. Every year, every day, that this advice is not heeded, increases the danger to the human future. This is a legal issue, as this book makes clear, but it is also a moral issue, a security issue and, ultimately, a spiritual issue. Humankind must step back from the nuclear abyss now, before it is too late.

Richard Falk & David Krieger*
July 2015

* President, Nuclear Age Peace Foundation

Editorial Note: Some of the key themes of this book have been discussed in a dialogue between Richard Falk and David Krieger in their book *The Path to Zero: Dialogues on Nuclear Dangers* (Falk and Krieger, 2012) published by Paradigm Publishers. The dialogue, in Chapter 7 of their book, is the substance of Chapter 12 of this book, and serves as a very helpful extension to this Foreword.

[this page is left blank intentionally]

Preface to 2nd Edition

This book is the 2nd edition of the book 'The Bomb and the Law' (Darnton, 1989), which presented a summary of legal argument, evidence, and Judgment of the London Nuclear Warfare Tribunal (LNWT) held in London, January 1985.

There is a great deal of material available about public international law, particularly humanitarian law as it applies to warfare. This book has as its focus, nuclear weapons. A great deal has also been written about nuclear weapons. So, why another book?

The original book has been out of print for some considerable time, and over the years I have received many requests for copies, and reprinting if possible. Therefore, this book re-issues the contents of the original LNWT book (with some minor edits). In doing so, I had to ask the question if the material in the original book is still valid? The core legal material in the original book remains as valid as it was more than quarter of a century ago.

However, some very interesting things have happened since the Tribunal hearings in 1985. Therefore, in making the LNWT book easily available again, I have taken the opportunity to add a substantial amount of additional material, to cover important events along that road to today.

Millions of people all over the world are deeply troubled about nuclear weapons, and seriously concerned that 70 years have gone by since the first use of nuclear weapons on Hiroshima and Nagasaki, the nuclear weapons states have made solemn promises to negotiate in good faith for nuclear disarmament, but the nuclear weapons states have cynically avoided serious discussions with any reasonable prospect of nuclear disarmament. There has also been a steady 'creep' of nuclear weapons to states beyond the original nuclear weapons states, notwithstanding the 1968 Non-Proliferation Treaty — nuclear weapons have proliferated, and without serious moves towards disarmament, are likely to continue proliferating. The world is in mortal danger, and that danger is increasing.

In the face of such cynical failures by governments to negotiate in good faith for world nuclear disarmament, there is urgent need for members of civil society to fill the void by relevant actions and activities, and make very clear the dictates of the public conscience.

This book is published to remember the 70th anniversaries of the bombings of Hiroshima (6th August 1945) and Nagasaki (9th August 1945), and the signing of the Nuremberg Charter (which, with incredible irony and substantial cynicism, was signed in between those bombings of Hiroshima and Nagasaki — 8th August 1945, in London — initially by four states that would become nuclear states). That Charter reaffirms the basis of the tribunals to be held as crimes against peace, war crimes, and crimes against humanity. These were subsequently accepted by the United Nations. They were printed in Appendix A of the first edition of this book, and hence appear also as Appendix A to this book.

Between 1945 and 2015 there has been, on the one hand, the cynical disregard for international law by the initial nuclear weapons states, compounded by a creeping proliferation of nuclear weapons to more states, and on the other hand, activities by a *majority* of nation states and *millions* of individuals protesting against nuclear weapons and calling for total nuclear disarmament.

This book does not attempt to cover the long road from 1945 to 2015 of demands for nuclear disarmament; it covers some important events between 1985 and 2015 concerning international and humanitarian law as they apply to nuclear weapons. However, in doing so, let us not forget those millions of people, and non-governmental organizations, that have worked and protested tirelessly for nuclear disarmament. Many of those NGOs and individuals have worked independently of each other; there has been no over-arching organization bringing individuals and NGOs together. It is an absolutely remarkable story of so many people wanting expressions of the public conscience to impact the cynical government officials who are content to breach international law on an existentialist scale. At present, the worst perpetrators of terrorism are people who are able to manipulate nation states. Do not allow nation states to get away with this by a simplistic narrative that the worst perpetrators of terrorism are non-state actors; in 2015, the worst perpetrators of terrorism are state actors.

In this book you will find detail or pointers to virtually all aspects of judicial, legal scholar, practitioner, and individual legal argument about the law as it applies to nuclear weapons — in one place at low cost.

The overwhelming conclusion of all that debate about the lawfulness or otherwise of the possession, threat, or use of nuclear weapons was summed up very precisely by Judge Weeramantry of the International Court of Justice, when he states: "...the use or threat of use of nuclear weapons is illegal *in any circumstances whatsoever*" (see the very detailed reasoning of this later in the book).

Decision takers, take note — the law is clear right down to individual and personal responsibility: if you do anything to promote, procure, deploy, or use nuclear weapons, you render yourself liable to indictment before any competent legal enforcement mechanism on those very matters set out in the Nuremberg Charter: crimes against peace, war crimes, and crimes against humanity. If you are asked to take part in any decision making (for example voting on the renewal of Trident), you need to read this book. Make sure you are not seduced by the rhetoric of 'deterrence' — it is devoid of any available legal defence — so is "I'm just following orders". You are on your own with your own personal legal liability whatever anyone else tells you. Individuals have already been executed and sentenced to long periods of imprisonment for such individual responsibility for breaches of international law. The nuclear weapons states will resist for as long as they can, but ultimately they will be called to account — it is only a matter of time. The best and only mitigation available to them now is to enter into negotiations in good faith, and ensure that there is total and effective nuclear disarmament.

That journey from 1985 to 2015 described in this book had its humble beginnings in 1982-84 with various individuals and organizations contemplating the idea of a Tribunal to be held in London. A push by the Ecology Party helped to coalesce the convenors and supporting organizations to organize the London Nuclear Warfare Tribunal. The LNWT was held in London, January 1985. It was organized extremely well, with eminent judges, witnesses, and some very competent lawyers and counsel to conduct the case and cross-examine the witnesses. A summary of the Tribunal was the first edition of this book. The legal arguments and Judgment remain as valid today as they were then. Some of the other material about convenors, supporting organizations, and witnesses is included for historical record. I was one of the Convenors.

Following on from the LNWT, several participating organizations and individuals (and others not involved in the LNWT) went on to set up the World Court Project (WCP). That is discussed briefly in a new chapter for this book.

The WCP was a remarkable story in itself, with what can be described as spectacular results: The World Health Organization and the UN General Assembly were both persuaded to request Advisory Opinions from the International Court of Justice.

The WHO request did not make much progress, but the UN General Assembly request did. Additional chapters for this book discuss the

ICJ cases, and present the full text of the ICJ Advisory Opinion for the UN General Assembly. Many of the Judges accompanied the Advisory Opinion with declarations, separate opinions and dissenting opinions. Collectively, they provide a solid summary of all the legal arguments likely to be raised in relation to the possession and use of nuclear weapons. The most comprehensive discussion is the Dissenting Opinion of Judge Weeramantry, so that is included in full also in this book.

Finally, there is a new chapter discussing recent and current events. Trident and Scotland are discussed, including the 'Trident Three' along with the state response in the Lord Advocate's Reference. The particularly interesting activity of legal relevance, going on right now (August 2015) is the cases of the Republic of the Marshall Islands (RMI) against the nuclear weapons states in the International Court of Justice. The Application in the case of RMI v UK is included in this book because it presents a helpful summary of UK policy with respect to nuclear weapons, and allegations of ways in which the UK has avoided its legal obligations, particularly with respect to the Non-Proliferation Treaty. Other current activity involves NGOs, and there is brief discussion (with pointers) to ICAN (International Campaign to Abolish Nuclear Weapons), NAPF (Nuclear Age Peace Foundation) and Mayors for Peace. PICAT (Public Interest Case Against Trident) is a very new initiative. There are other initiatives by other NGOs and individuals, which I have not been able to include.

I am very fortunate to be able to include a new Foreword written by Richard Falk and David Krieger. Richard was one of the Judges at the LNWT, and is a very eminent scholar of international law in his own right, known to very many people. David is President of the Nuclear Age Peace Foundation (discussed later). Together they span the legal and civil society serious concerns about nuclear weapons. Their Forword is continued by means of a dialogue between them, which is included as Chapter 12. The original Foreword from the 1st edition of this book was provided by Sean MacBride who was Chairman of the LNWT (among other things, he was a Nobel Peace Prize winner, an Assistant Secretary General of the United Nations and one of the founders of Amnesty International). What he said in 1985 remains relevant and up-to-date today, so it is also included.

Geoffrey Darnton
Bournemouth,
8th August, 2015
(70th Anniversary of the first signing of the Nuremberg Principles)

Acknowledgements

First, it is important to say that I feel very humbled producing this book. I'm only producing the book. Over the years, hundreds, if not thousands of years, many people have struggled against the tyranny of those who wield power over others — a small minority wielding power over the majority, to be able to force that majority to fight wars for them. Nuclear weapons present a new and very serious existential challenge to mankind, put in place by governments who do not seem to understand their fundamental obligations to their own people, let alone the rest of the world.

Since 1945, countless millions of people, and hundreds of NGOs around the world have made their contribution to bringing reminders about the folly of nuclear weapons before the governments of the nuclear weapons states. Much of that activity has helped to influence the direction of this book and its underpinnings in law.

As far as this particular book is concerned, acknowledgments are still due to those who organized and sponsored the first LNWT - the Judges, lawyers, witnesses and participants who made this happen. Many are identified in the appendices to the 1st edition of the book, and repeated in this 2nd edition.

This edition draws extensively on formal documents of the International Court of Justice. Acknowledgements and thanks are due to the ICJ for their confirmation that those documents can be used in this book.

Contact was established with several prominent members of the World Court Project, and people concerned with and affected by the 'Trident Three' cases and their aftermath. Thanks are due for the various suggestions and encouragement provided in the course of discussions.

Thanks are due also to those who have been directly involved in some way with the RMI cases in the ICJ against the nuclear weapons states.

People who have commented, or encouraged, or contributed ideas and information include: Colin Archer of the International Peace Bureau, Kate Dewes, Rob Green, Nick Grief, Rebecca Johnson, Brian Larkin of the Edinburgh Peace and Justice Centre, Alyn Ware, Angie Zelter. Of course, responsibility for what was or not included in the book, and the way information has been presented, remains my own personal responsibility.

Thanks are due also to Carey Sublette and Gregory Walker for confirmation that they expect their websites about nuclear weapons to be available for years to come.

Special thanks go to Richard Falk and David Krieger for their Foreword to the new edition, and the contributed Chapter 12. Richard Falk has been there since the beginning, as one of the London Nuclear Warfare Tribunal Judges. Some of David's poetry is included also.

The book cover design was an interesting project, as my own design capabilities are very limited indeed. I decided to use crowd sourcing via Design Crowd to obtain ideas for the book cover. Eventually, the core design concept produced by Maple Producciones was adopted. My thanks go to all those who helped me to select by voting in my design polls. Of course, my thanks and apologies also go to all those designers who offered designs but were not selected. It was one of those unfortunate situations where I could only accept one design, and many excellent designs were turned down.

Finally, my thanks for support and understanding go to my family, relatives, and friends who have been sorely neglected on occasions during very intensive periods of working on the book.

What is from the 1st Edition, and what is New?

The material from the 1st edition included in this edition (with some minor editorial corrections) is:

- Preface and Foreword (by Sean MacBride) to the 1st edition
- Chapters 1 - 7 (inclusive)
- Appendices A - H (inclusive)

What is new to this 2nd edition is:

- New Preface and Acknowledgements
- New Foreword (by Richard Falk and David Krieger)
- Chapters 8 - 13 (inclusive)
- References

Of course, the Contents and Index from the first edition have been updated substantially.

Foreword to 1st Edition by Sean MacBride

The aims of the International Peace Bureau, which was founded in 1892, are "to serve the cause of peace by the promotion of international cooperation and nonviolent solution of international problems" and "to serve the independent peace movements of the world". It is the oldest international peace organisation in the world and has its headquarters in Geneva. It is a federation of peace organisations from all parts of the world. The International Peace Bureau does not see peace merely in economic or political terms. It seeks to spread the conviction that a life of dignity and justice is the inalienable right of all men and women and that it is capable of realisation only on the basis of peace.

Shortly after its foundation, the International Peace Bureau became engaged in the promotion of the first Hague Peace Conference which was convened on 18th May 1899 and which adopted two important international conventions namely:

a. The Convention for the Pacific Settlement of International Disputes
b. The Convention for the Respect of the Laws and Customs of War on Land.

In recognition of its work at the Hague Peace Conference of 1899, the International Peace Bureau was in 1900 awarded the Grand Prix at the Paris Exhibition of 1900. The International Peace Bureau continued its work and supported the 1906 Geneva Convention on Wounded Persons and also the Second Hague Conference of 1907. At the Second Hague Conference, thirteen Conventions were adopted, all aimed at restricting and limiting the use of force in international relations.

In 1910 the International Peace Bureau was awarded the Nobel Peace Prize for "Serving as a channel of communication between Governments and the Peace Movements".

After World War I, the International Peace Bureau in collaboration with the Society of Friends worked actively on the preparation and adoption of the 1925 Protocol for the Prohibition of the Use of Asphyxiating, Poisonous and other Gases. It also worked for the adoption of the General Treaty for the Renunciation of War in 1928 known as the "Treaty of Paris". It is well to recall at this stage the first two articles of this important Treaty which provided:

Article 1 — "The High Contracting Parties solemnly declare.. that they condemn recourse to war for the solution of international controversies and renounce it as an instrument of national policy in their relations with one another".

Article 2 - "The High Contracting Parties agree that the settlement or solution of all disputes or conflicts of whatever nature or whatever origin they may be which may arise among them, shall never be sought except through pacific means".

Ineffective as the Treaty of Paris was to prevent the Second World War it is of some importance in that most of the judgments of the Nuremberg Tribunal were based on the provisions of the Treaty of Paris. The Nuremberg Tribunal in 1946 laid it down that:

"...the solemn renunciation of war as an instrument of national policy necessarily involves the proposition that such a war is illegal in international law; and that those who plan and wage such a war, with its inevitable and terrible consequences, are committing a crime in so doing".

The Charter of the United Nations signed in San Francisco came into force on 24 October 1945 and its Preamble proclaimed:

"WE THE PEOPLES OF THE UNITED NATIONS determined to save succeeding generations from the scourge of war, which twice in our lifetime has brought untold sorrow to mankind, and to reaffirm faith in fundamental human rights, in the dignity and worth of the human person, in the equal rights of men and women and of nations large and small, and to establish conditions under which justice and respect for the obligations arising from treaties and other sources of international law can be maintained, and to promote social progress and better standards of life in larger freedom, and for these ends to practice tolerance and live together in peace with one another as good neighbours, and to unite our strength to maintain international peace and security, and to ensure, by the acceptance of principles and the institution of methods that armed force shall not be used, save in the common interest, and to employ international machinery for the promotion of the economic and social advancement of all peoples, have resolved to combine our efforts to accomplish these aims".

In Article 1 of the Charter, the purposes and the principles of the United Nations are set forth:

"1. To maintain international peace and security, and to that end: to take effective collective measures for the prevention and removal of threats to the peace, and for the suppression of acts of aggression or other breaches of the peace, and to bring about by peaceful means and in conformity with the principles of justice and international law, adjustment or settlement of international disputes or situations which might lead to a breach of the peace".

The Nuremberg Trials were open to criticism in that they were held under a retroactive law and were a trial of the vanquished by the victors. Subsequently, however, it was recognized that the principles upon which they were based should be applied in the future to all cases of crimes against humanity and of war crimes. Accordingly, on 11 September 1946 the General Assembly of the United Nations unanimously affirmed "the principles of international law recognized by the Charter of the Nuremberg Tribunal and the judgment of the Tribunal". Subsequently, the General Assembly entrusted the formulation of the Nuremberg Principles to the International Law Commission, an organ of the United Nations composed of experts in international law representing all the legal systems in the world and expected to promote the progressive development and codification of international law. It should be noted that the United States, the Soviet Union, France and Britain all took a leading role in the drafting of the Nuremberg Charter and the elaboration of the Nuremberg Principles. The Nuremberg Principles were formulated by the International Law Commission in 1950 and were finally unanimously adopted by the United Nations. For convenience, the full text of the Nuremberg Principles are reproduced in Appendix A, and they form part of international law.

From 1945 onwards all the world leaders worked closely together to ensure that there would be no further wars and that nuclear weapons would be outlawed; as a result, after several years of work the Soviet Union and the United States of America reached an agreement on 20 September 1961, known as the Zorin-McCloy Accords, which were submitted to the United Nations and unanimously adopted on the proposition of the Soviet Union and the United States on 13 December 1961. This agreement, unanimously adopted, was the biggest step forward ever taken to bring about General and Complete Disarmament. For convenience, the full text of the Accords as adopted is set forth in Appendix B.

On the moral plane both the Vatican and the World Council of Churches in the Consultation on 3-9 April 1970 at Baden, Austria laid down that the right of conscientious objection to participation in a war is extended to the right to refuse to participate in a conflict in which weapons of mass destruction might be used. The same stand was adopted by the World Conference for Religion and Peace held in Kyoto some months later in 1970. For convenience, the full text of the principles laid down by both these religious conferences, which encompassed all the religions in the world, are included in Appendix C.

At an international conference held in Bradford during 29 August-1st September 1974, convened by the International Peace Bureau, the call was issued to all the Governments of the World to proceed to implement the programme for General and Complete Disarmament adopted by the United Nations, on 13 December 1961. A million copies of this call, issued in the different languages of the United Nations were distributed throughout the world. From then onwards, conferences and consultations were organized by non-governmental organizations which ultimately led to the First Special Session of the United Nations General Assembly devoted to Disarmament in 1978. The First Special Session of the General Assembly on Disarmament again called for the achievement of General and Complete Disarmament and pointed out:

"Mankind today is confronted with an unprecedented threat of self—extinction arising from the massive and competitive accumulation of the most destructive weapons ever produced. Existing arsenals of nuclear weapons alone are more than sufficient to destroy all life on earth.... Removing the threat of a world war — a nuclear war — is the most acute and urgent task of the present day. Mankind is confronted with a choice: we must halt the arms race and proceed to Disarmament or face Annihilation".

At its General Conference held in Helsinki 4-6 September 1981, the International Peace Bureau decided to initiate studies and conferences as to the ethical morality and legality of the use of nuclear weapons. As a result, conferences of specialists in law, morality, and medicine have been held in most parts of the world and have come to the conclusion that nuclear weapons and other weapons of mass destruction or of social annihilation are indefensible morally and legally. Such conferences were sponsored either by the International Peace Bureau or by other non-governmental organizations of Jurists, of religious leaders or of medical scientists. In many countries organizations of lawyers have been formed such as Lawyers for Nuclear Disarmament (Britain) and the Lawyers Committee on Nuclear Policy (USA). On 24 June 1982 the International Peace Bureau presented to the Second Special Session of the General Assembly of the United Nations on Disarmament concrete proposals which had been adopted by an International Symposium sponsored by the Lawyers Committee on Nuclear Policy in the United States and the International Peace Bureau. These proposals contained a draft Convention for General and Complete Disarmament. Since then many important conferences of jurists, scientists and medical experts have been held in Geneva, Amsterdam, London, Helsinki, Tokyo, New York, Greece, and Moscow, all calling for the outlawing of Nuclear Weapons.

Finally, it was decided following an original initiative from the Green Party (previously known as the Ecology Party) of Great Britain and taken up by Lawyers for Nuclear Disarmament in Britain, in collaboration with the International Peace Bureau and a large number of supporting organizations, to create a Nuclear Warfare Tribunal that would sit in London to take evidence and report on the legality and morality or otherwise of nuclear weapons. The Tribunal, over which I had the honour to preside, sat in London from 2-6 January 1985. Particulars of my distinguished colleagues on this Tribunal and of the organizations which helped make it a success will be found later in this Report. To the members of the Tribunal, to all those who worked so selflessly at the preparation and conduct of the Tribunal, I would like to extend the most sincere and grateful thanks of the International Peace Bureau. The task of eliminating conflicts of societal destruction and doing away with nuclear weapons is no easy one. There are tremendously powerful and wealthy interests that are opposed to world disarmament. There are many military groups and many industrialists that profit from the scourge that war imposes upon humanity. Those that work for peace are voluntary workers that have little or no resources at their disposal. Therefore a great debt of gratitude is due by the public at large to all those who have been involved in this work.

Sean MacBride S.C.*
Chairman of the Tribunal

[*This Foreword was drafted and submitted by Sean MacBride before his death in 1988.]

Preface to 1st Edition

Very many people have made a *significant* contribution to this Tribunal; it is very sobering indeed to be putting the finishing touches to a document after so many eminent people have put in such effort. The Tribunal and work afterwards have been done on an entirely voluntary effort, and there were many times we thought the work would never be completed. However, we have now been able to reach a final version of this summary text.

While we were nearing final draft the Chairman of the Tribunal, Sean MacBride, died peacefully at his home in Dublin on 15th January 1988. This was a great loss, and of course set back the work of the Tribunal. In many ways this Tribunal was Sean's last major project, so we were even more determined to see it is carried forward.

The Tribunal itself would not have been possible without the efforts of the witnesses, the Organising Committee, the Tribunal Members, the Supporting Organisations, (who are all listed in the Appendices), and of course those who finally helped to put this document together.

It is over four years since the Tribunal was held and it has fallen to me to put together a final draft of this document. The material and underlying principles have not dated at all since the Tribunal. In many ways, publication now will have the benefit of a new momentum in international affairs which was simply not present for a few years after 1985 when publication may well have fallen on deaf ears.

Many people have contributed various sections of this document, and I have tried to weave them together in a coherent structure, trying not to lose too much of the detail of different drafters, and using the evidence and international law to fill in gaps where I thought necessary. In totality we had available a vast amount of evidence. It was a difficult editorial decision whether to produce a full and accurate account of the Tribunal and evidence, or whether to attempt a summary. In the end, time and resources prevailed and a summary has been produced. This inevitably means loss of detail and nuances for many witnesses. The selection or non-selection of material from particular witnesses should not be considered as an editorial statement of relative value; rather material has been selected primarily for illustrative purposes. Much very valuable work placed in evidence remains unpublished or dispersed. The editorial work has been to try and distil the essence of much of the evidence. Many people have helped in this process but I must accept personal editorial responsibility for this final version, and all errors of omission and commission must remain mine. I will, of course, be pleased to hear from anyone with corrections which should be made in future printings or editions.

It is always a problem picking out individuals to acknowledge assistance because I do not want to leave out others who have also made a valuable contribution. In terms of preparing this final version for publication, I would like to acknowledge in particular, the participation, support, encouragement and suggestions from Sean MacBride, Richard Falk, Francis Boyle, Ed Rees, Nick Kollerstrom, Philip Webber, Rainer Santi of the International Peace Bureau, Hans Koechler of the International Progress Organisation, Stig Gustafsson, Gertrud Ivri and the Swedish Lawyers who made first publication possible. It is fitting indeed that the launch of this publication coincides with the First World Congress of the International Association of Lawyers against Nuclear Arms (IALANA) held in the Hague where several of the foundations of international law affecting the conduct of war were established.

Finally, I would like to add some personal comments. I had started out this editorial task with a personal conviction that nuclear weapons are wrong, but I had no idea that in the course of going through the whole weight of evidence and legal argument I would realise the terrible indictment of unlawfulness against nuclear weapons states to be so extensive and devastating; it is difficult to imagine lawbreaking in any other way on such a vast scale. It is perhaps ironic that this lawlessness is by those who presume to set and enforce laws against their own citizens, and frequently issue vociferous condemnations of the lawlessness of others. Humanity today, as in the past, suffers dearly at the hands of governments and an international order which are of very poor quality and do not have the intellect, integrity or courage to deliver effective human rights and safeguards against arbitrary death, poverty, deprivation and loss of real freedoms and rights. This Tribunal addressed only the question of nuclear weapons.

The work of this Tribunal shows the possession, deployment and use of nuclear weapons to be profoundly unlawful. Humanity has the right and duty to demand urgent and immediate delivery from the existence of such weapons.

Geoffrey Darnton
Reading, England
July, 1989

Back Cover Text from Original Edition

The 1st edition of the book had the following text on the back cover, and is presented here to give some idea of thinking at the time. As can be seen, it is as relevant today as it was 30 years ago:

* * *

Since the Tribunal was convened in 1985 East-West tensions have diminished dramatically, but nuclear arms race goes on. New weapons systems, more accurate and with less reaction time available for political leaders for assessing threats and devising responses, are giving machines and computers an ever greater role in shaping human destiny. The militarization of space proceeds with new geopolitical visions of global dominance being nurtured, based on the viability of a communications and guidance grid capable of delivering smart weaponry, whether nuclear or non-nuclear, on target anywhere in the world. This is not a time for the peoples of the world to suppose that the nuclear war threat has safely slipped into history!

Pressure from civil society is indispensable. Without a peace movement that conveys the sense that nuclear weapons are illegal, immoral, and exceedingly dangerous, it seems likely that the present reality will remain more or less frozen. One important way to revive public concern about existing arrangements is to present the case that nuclear deterrence in doctrine and deployed capabilities violates international law and that the construction of First Strike weapons systems constitutes preparation for aggressive war, and as such, is itself a Crime against Peace in the full Nuremberg sense. We believe that the Judgment of the London Nuclear Warfare Tribunal establishes this conclusion in responsible and convincing fashion. We invite objective citizens to read this Judgment and come to their own conclusions.

Richard Falk

Chapter 1

Introduction

1.1 The Relevance of International Law.

At the outset, we are aware of public scepticism. Many citizens and public officials continue to query whether international law is *really* law in the absence of police mechanisms for enforcement and the absence of procedures for impartial interpretation. Our response here is that international law provides the underpinning for many varieties of transnational life that work so well we take it for granted. An effective legal order does not necessarily depend on central institutions for decision and enforcement. Law can be effective if the parties seek to make it so out of reasons of convenience, mutual benefit, a sense of right and respect, or even because they find value in a reputation of law-abidingness. These factors all operate to some extent in international life, varying from one substantive area to another, and from one kind of leadership to another.

Of course, all law is violated at times. Indeed, enforcement would be superfluous were compliance perfect. The special problem of international life arises because some violations are so totally disruptive and unacceptable in their effects. It is important to be clear that preventing a particular kind of violation is a different challenge to a legal order than a denial of its existence altogether.

There is no doubt that considerations of reciprocity which ensure a high degree of effectiveness for international law (e.g. upholding the immunity of foreign diplomats to reinforce the immunity of our own) are least operative in the context of war and peace where fundamental security, even survival, is at stake. Again, the wider context is important to appreciate. All law tends to bend and break in conditions of crisis, as is evident during periods of civil strife or economic privation.

Nevertheless, even governments have acknowledged over the centuries the great importance of bringing law to bear on decisions associated with *recourse to* and the *conduct of* war. From Grotius onward there has been a consensus to the effect that unrestrained warfare was a regression to barbarism, unacceptable as such. Especially in the last century or so there has been a dual series of developments: first of all, the technological innovations in warfare, culminating in the development and use of atomic bombs; secondly, an intensifying insistence on restricting the discretion of governments to wage war "legally".

There is no doubt that the possession of nuclear weapons underscores the tension between those political developments that give the modern state unconditional power over human destiny and those normative reactions by civil society that seek to impose limits upon what governments can do, even beneath the banners of military necessity and national security. There is no doubt also, that since 1945 the statists have prevailed in relation to warfare and weaponry of mass destruction. There have been many wars and relatively little success in resolving conflict by recourse to the procedures made available by international law and embodied in the United Nations Organisation.

The leading nuclear weapons states have claimed that their possession of such weaponry has probably prevented World War III, and that the only reliable method to sustain "peace" is to threaten the annihilation of a rival society in retaliation. This system of mutual threat is generally called deterrence, and its logic and probable effects are not reconcilable with most understandings of law and morality. This Tribunal proceeded on the assumption that such a departure from normative restraint is dangerous and unacceptable, and that it does entail a relapse into barbarism on the grandest imaginable scale.

This Tribunal takes cognizance of both sides of this modern dilemma. Firstly, the urgent need to replace deterrence with a system of international security responsive to law and morality. Secondly, the realisation that governments and their institutional creations, including the United Nations, are not sufficiently motivated or empowered to satisfy this most fundamental of international needs. In these regards, this Tribunal is filling a normative vacuum. It intends to mobilise public opinion throughout the world around the necessity to bring available law to bear on the nuclear weapons policy of governments.

It is, at the same time, important to realise that this Tribunal has not invented the legal framework it relies upon. This framework has been evolved over the years by governmental action responding to felt necessities and to the aspirations of the peoples of the world. We shall endeavour to demonstrate clearly that the international law interpreted and applied by this Tribunal is of a status that should be applied by governments themselves.

In this respect, the Tribunal was convened to fill a constitutional gap in the international political system of the present. Its existence is an enactment of the call for individual responsibility that is itself a signal achievement of modern international law and has been heralded as such by the main nuclear weapons states.

It is a startling irony that, aside from China, the other states that now acknowledge possession of nuclear weapons constituted the four prosecuting states at Nuremberg after World War II. In particular the two superpowers, the United States and the Soviet Union, were most insistent that German leaders at all levels of society be held criminally liable for their refusal to uphold international law in the context of war and peace.

The victorious governments were emphatic that their proceedings against the defeated governments of Germany and Japan would provide a framework for all political activities in international life. After the judgments had been given, a consensus among the victorious governments supported the effort to formulate the Nuremberg Principles as universally binding rules of international law. These Principles impose on governments and officials an unconditional duty to uphold international law regardless of state policy. This Tribunal believes that this duty serves the interests of all peoples, and that even the interest of one's own country is best upheld by assuring that its policies abroad conform to the rules of international law. It is then a matter of patriotic duty to insist on the application of the Nuremberg Principles, and most especially, in relation to the nuclear weaponry where so much is at stake and where it is too late to await an entire breakdown of order to establish the full evidence of a violative pattern of conduct.

It is true that, at the time of the Nuremberg Judgment, and ever since, critics have dismissed the whole enterprise as "victors' justice". There was a sombre truth to this contention. As the Indian member of the Tokyo Tribunal, Justice Pal, pointed out, it was unacceptably hypocritical to accuse Japanese war leaders of crimes but exempt from scrutiny the Western indiscriminate bombing of Japanese cities climaxing in the atomic attacks on Hiroshima and Nagasaki. This Tribunal acknowledges the imperfections in the legal precedents, but seeks to build upon them to complete their promise.

It can also be alleged that the nuclear weapons states have not clearly accepted the view that these weapons are illegal. This Tribunal carefully considered this allegation, but feels convinced by the evidence that international law exists with sufficient clarity to assess the policies of governments with respect to nuclear weapons. This Tribunal agrees that a comprehensive treaty of prohibition would be a contribution to the avoidance of nuclear war, but that even without such a document, existing treaties and customary rules of international law are clear on these matters.

1.2 Substantive Foundations

This Tribunal is not inventing law. It has relied upon the best available experts on the international law of war to ascertain the character of rules applicable to nuclear weapons policy. These experts were cross-examined by trained legal counsel and by the members of the Tribunal itself. To introduce the Judgment, a brief survey is provided of the sources of international law applicable here.

1.2.1 Just War Doctrine

Originating in theological discourse during the Middle Ages, the so-called Just War Doctrine was incorporated into positive international law. Drawing on still more ancient practices of political communities, the Just War Doctrine called upon participants in war to carry on combat with due respect for moral principles, including an overriding obligation to confine military attack to military targets, thereby avoiding any direct injury to civilians.

The application of the principles of the Just War Doctrine were left to each sovereign ruler, and amounted to an appeal to conscience. There was no higher authority aside from the questionable claim by the Roman Church that lost whatever overall validity it might have once possessed as a result of the fragmenting of Christendom due to the Reformation of the sixteenth century. In a sense, the Just War Doctrine was an instance of religious morality being converted into an applied ethics for international relations. It was borrowed and incorporated into international law at the inception of the state system.

1.2.2 Customary Norms of International Law

The lack of specificity in the Just War Doctrine was a shortcoming, as was the absence of any ritual of assent by which a sovereign authority acknowledged its duty to be bound in definite ways. International jurists collected the body of practices that governments accepted as binding upon themselves, and set forth these rules and principles beneath the label of customary international law. These rules and principles helped shape the direction of treaty law, and, as well, provided legally accepted yardsticks for measuring claims about the status of new weapons and tactics. Such rules and principles provide a normative background against which to evaluate the controversy about the lawfulness of nuclear weapons and about various doctrines governing their use.

o **Principle of Discrimination** - to be lawful, weapons and tactics must discriminate clearly between military and non-military targets, and be confined in their application to military targets. Indiscriminate warfare is per se illegal, although indirect damage to civilians and civilian targets is not necessarily so.

o **Principle of Proportionality** - to be lawful, weapons and tactics must be proportional to their military objective. Disproportionate weaponry and tactics are excessive, and as such, illegal.

o **Principal of Lawfulness** - to be lawful, weapons and tactics must not violate any treaty rule of international law binding as between the parties.

o **Principle of Necessity** - to be lawful, weapons and tactics involving the use of force must be reasonably necessary to the attainment of their military objective. No superfluous or excessive application of force is lawful, even if the damage done is confined to the environment.

o **Principle of Humanity** - to be lawful, no weapon or tactic can be relied upon that causes unnecessary suffering to its victims, whether by way of prolonged or painful death, or in a form that is calculated to cause severe terror or fright. For this reason, weapons and tactics that spread poison, disease, or do genetic damage are generally illegal *per se*, as being weapons with effects not confined in the place and time of damage to the battlefield. Such a prohibition, under contemporary circumstances, extends to ecological disruption in any form.

o **Principle of Neutrality** - to be lawful, no weapon or tactic can be relied upon that seems likely to do harm to human beings, property, or the natural environment in neutral countries. A country is neutral if its government declares itself to be so and if it pursues a policy of impartiality in relation to armed conflict, including the avoidance of any kind of alliance relationship.

1.2.3 Treaty Rules and Principles

Often it is assumed, wrongly, that international agreements in treaty form are the only valid source of international legal obligations. In some respects, written agreements, duly ratified, are preferable sources of guidance as to the requirements of international law. Written formulations can be more explicit and elaborate with respect to a given pattern of conduct. Furthermore, as far as governments are concerned, there is a tendency to accord greater respect to those legal obligations to which consent in explicit and constitutional form has been given, especially if the negotiation and ratification processes are recent, most particularly within the life span of the governmental leadership currently in power.

There are also limitations to the view that treaty rules are the only genuine source of international law, or even the more moderate view, that these formulations of law are necessarily the best source. Some general norms have not been reduced to treaty form. In other instances, some states are not bound by treaties, having withheld their consent. In still other instances, the content of the treaty rules is vague or subject to contradictory formulations, especially so in relation to the early efforts to codify war and peace, quite dramatically superseded by modern methods and styles of warfare, as well as by new military technologies and weapons systems. This Tribunal has applied international law by taking full account of both customary and treaty rules of international law.

There is an obvious problem of application with respect to nuclear weapons. The nuclear weapons states have so far refrained from entering into any serious negotiations towards a treaty, or even a declaration, acknowledging the unlawfulness of threats or uses of nuclear weapons. Such a deficiency is obviously not an oversight. Hence, to derive applicable rules of international law that add up to an unconditional prohibition of the use of this weaponry is bound to collide with the official security policies of major states, and to challenge the legitimacy of weapons capabilities and bureaucracies that command control over vast allocations of resources.

In the summary of Evidence before the Tribunal (see Chapter 2) the applicable Treaty rules are considered in detail, and are anticipated here. There are, however, certain broad efforts to reduce to treaty form agreed standards of behaviour that seem crucial here, especially because their generality suggests a relevance to any assessment of the lawful status of nuclear weapons and tactics. The important general treaties in this area were formulated at the Hague in 1899 and 1907 in a series of comprehensive conventions that summarised the pre-World War I levels of agreement as they existed between the governments playing a leading role in international life. The goal was not to eliminate war, but to regulate its conduct in accordance with the customary principles briefly set forth in the preceding paragraph. Especially important was the broad imperative embodied as a common article in the various Hague Conventions of 1899. Article 22 in the Annex to the Hague Convention IV (Regulations Respecting the Laws and Customs of War on Land) states:

"The right of belligerents to adopt means of injuring the enemy is not unlimited"

The apocalyptic implications of a major reliance on nuclear weapons gives this provision an obvious orienting relevance.

Also critical was the celebrated "de Martens clause" (named after the Belgian jurist Feodor de Martens) inserted in the 1907 Hague Conventions[1]:

"Until a more complete code of the laws of war has been issued, the high contracting Parties deem it expedient to declare that, in cases not included in the Regulations adopted by them, the inhabitants and belligerents remain under the protection and the rule of the principles of the law of nations, as they result from the usages established among civilised people, from the laws of humanity, and the dictates of the public conscience".

This resolve in international treaty law to base permissible action expressly on normative traditions and upon conscience is a significant basis of encouragement for the inquiry of this Tribunal. The "de Martens clause" definitely refutes the ultra-statist view that everything is permitted if it has not been expressly renounced by a formal manifestation of governmental authority.

International treaty law has successfully achieved a very widely endorsed prohibition of poison as a weapon and tactic of war. To date the most important treaty instrument, adopted in response to

---

[1] from the preamble to the 1907 Hague Convention IV Respecting the Laws and Customs of War on Land.

the menace of poison gas revealed in the trenches of World War I, is the 1925 Geneva Protocol for the Prohibition of the Use in War of Asphyxiating, Poisonous and other Gases, and of Biological methods of Warfare. At present a variety of negotiations and proposals seek to extend in more detailed form this prohibition on toxic weaponry. Unlike in the case of biological weapons, the current treaty law prohibits threat and use, but not development and possession. Hence, a deterrent approach to chemical weapons is not *per se* prohibited under contemporary international law.

Another significant line of effort in treaty law concerns the discretion to initiate war via acts of aggression. In the 1928 Pact of Paris, war is outlawed as an instrument of national policy, and legitimate force confined to circumstances of self-defence. This treaty norm provided a major basis for the war crimes prosecution at Nuremberg and Tokyo after World War II, giving rise to the category of offence known as "Crimes against Peace". The United Nations Charter, a multilateral treaty, carries forward in Articles 1(4), 33, and 51 the basic notion that there is no legal pretext for recourse to force in international relations except in self-defence against a prior armed attack. There is some controversy among international law specialists as to whether patterns of state practice have so consistently ignored this constraining legal framework as to suspend, or to draw into question, its continuing validity. At stake in the nuclear weapons setting is the critical issue as to whether the design and development of first-strike weaponry and supporting doctrine amounts to a *per se* act of aggression, as well as rendering officials liable for crimes against the peace. At Nuremberg it was definitely decided that planning for aggressive war is itself a crime even if the aggressive policy is never consummated. Does this prohibition pertain to those allegations that certain classes of nuclear weapons systems have first-strike properties and roles?

Another major treaty instrument was the Genocide Convention of 1948 that established the criminality of any course of deliberate state policy that intends to destroy, in whole or part, national, ethnic, religious, or racial groups. Nuclear weapons are aptly described as weapons of mass destruction, and their use in any sustained manner, seems genocidal in impact, as well as ecocidal. Indeed, the grim magnitude of such destruction suggests that beyond genocide lies the result of omnicide. Given the inability to apprehend after the event, this Tribunal seeks to examine whether the genocidal propensities of nuclear weapons, and doctrines governing their use, do not constitute sufficient ground to find governments and their leaders guilty of intentional violations of the Genocide Convention.

Ever since the nineteenth century there has been an effort complementary to that of the Law of the Hague dealing with weapons and tactics to codify international humanitarian law applicable during wartime, sometimes known as the Law of Geneva, because so many of the main treaty instruments were negotiated and signed at Geneva. The main elements of the Law of Geneva are the four Geneva Conventions of 1949 — for the protection of land forces, of sea forces, of prisoners of war, and of civilians. The attempt of these agreements is to give concrete application to the Principle of Humanity, by imposing obligations on belligerent states to respect the sanctity of such things as hospitals, cultural monuments etc., and to avoid any military action against the sick and wounded, or against those of the enemy who have laid down their arms and become prisoners of war.

These treaty rules suggest levels of respect for the limits of warfare that seem utterly inconsistent with any use of nuclear weapons. Again an issue for this Tribunal is whether this body of law can be considered superseded by contrary patterns of state practice. Efforts to extend this humanitarian approach to the explicit circumstances of nuclear weaponry have not been successful as yet. Both the United States and Britain made it clear that its participation in the negotiation of the Geneva Protocols I and II in 1977, to modernise the 1949 Conventions, was taking place on the assumption that nuclear weapons were not to be considered subject to the treaty norms, even in relation to Article 35 which explicitly deals with new weapons and methods of warfare. Is such an exclusion effective? This question is important for this Tribunal to address in its Judgment.

A final source of treaty guidance for this Tribunal arises from the legal duty imposed on the governments of nuclear states by such arms control agreements as the Limited Test Ban Treaty of 1963 and the Non-Proliferation Treaty of 1968, to negotiate in good faith an end to the nuclear arms race and to establish by stages or any reasonable process, secure arrangements for general and complete disarmament. This Tribunal needs to determine whether the failure to accept proposals for a comprehensive test ban and the continued preparation for nuclear warfare, including the development of new weapons systems with first-strike propensities, amount to violations of international treaty obligations

1.2.4 Supplementary Norms with Legal Force

The United Nations has itself contributed in a variety of respects to the development of international law. General Assembly resolutions have been claimed to have a limited legislative effect under certain conditions of their passage. The UN General Assembly has manifested its concern about the lawful status of nuclear weapons in a long series of widely endorsed resolutions going back to General Assembly Resolution 1653(XVI) which clearly supported the view that threats or uses of nuclear weapons were violations of the UN Charter and constituted Crimes against Humanity. The United States and its NATO allies voted against this and other subsequent resolutions on this subject matter. Does its opposition undermine or erode the legal force of General Assembly efforts in this area?

A closely related concern involves the status of initiating use of nuclear weapons. Both the Soviet Union and China made in 1981, a unilateral and unconditional commitment never to use nuclear weapons first. The Western nuclear powers have not acceded in any formal way to this no-first-use position. What status the no first use position has in contemporary international law is an important issue for this Tribunal to examine.

Natural law criteria of state behaviour are also applicable through a continued reliance on the de Martens clause, and its invocation of the "laws of humanity" and "the dictates of the public conscience". Such a moral outreach *within international law* makes it important and entirely appropriate to consider for *legal relevance* the great variety of statements by religious bodies describing their urgent concern and supporting reasoning about the irreconcilability of current doctrines pertaining to the use of nuclear weapons and the dictates of public conscience. Such an assessment is reinforced by a growing number of independent experts lending their professional judgment to the view that current policies of nuclear weapons states violate international law in flagrant and serious ways and to varying degrees. Such materials by religious bodies or international jurists are not law as such, but *evidence* as to the content of law, especially given the legal duty by governments to respect the dictates of public conscience in their war-making activities.

1.3 Method of Inquiry

This Tribunal is an informal body without any official mandate. At the same time, it is totally independent and no one connected with its activities received any kind of compensation for their efforts. The Judges were selected by the Convenors and listened to the evidence as presented by expert witnesses and in documentary submission. It sought arguments pro and contra the main issues in as effective form as was available. On its own the Tribunal examined additional materials as relevant for the discharge of its functions. Some background is more fully presented in the Foreword.

The Judgment will discuss the probable effects of nuclear weapons if they are ever used again, and rely on this analysis to infer the probable intentions of responsible civilian and military officials. As in domestic law, a person is held responsible for the probable effects of his actions whether or not a specific result is willed. Such accountability is even more appropriately imposed on a collective entity such as a government. This process of ascertaining and applying legal standards is especially appropriate where the burden of social policy is preventive rather than reactive. The circumstances posed by the nuclear arms race and the doctrine of deterrence make such a preventive emphasis in the law of decisive and overwhelming importance. After analyzing the evidence as carefully as possible the Tribunal will present its conclusions, followed by a set of policy recommendations. In a broad sense, this Tribunal is carrying on in the spirit of Nuremberg which above all else imposed on individual citizens the duty to safeguard international peace and security by making sure that governments upheld their obligations under international law. It is also trying to clarify "the dictates of public conscience" on the matter of legal duty pertaining to nuclear weaponry, and thereby responding to the call of the de Martens clause. And finally, it joins with such kindred entities as the Permanent People's Tribunal[2] to support the legitimacy and importance of societal initiatives to encourage adherence to international law in the war/peace area, and claims for itself authority to declare the character of legal obligations in relation to nuclear weapons that is owed by governments, officials, military officers, scientists and engineers, as well as by citizens occupying various roles in society. Some of these implications are spelled out in the Recommendations section of the Judgment shown in Chapter 7.

---

2 see for example, *A Crime of Silence: The Armenian Genocide* published giving the deliberations of the Permanent People's Tribunal on the question of Armenia.

1.4 Overview of Tribunal Scope

The primary enquiry of the Tribunal was *"An Examination of the Legality of Nuclear Weapons"*. As an acceptable standard of lawfulness they have taken the six principles identified above, namely:

1. Principle of Discrimination
2. Principle of Proportionality
3. Principle of Lawfulness
4. Principle of Necessity
5. Principle of Humanity
6. Principle of Neutrality

As part of that examination the Tribunal posed and endeavoured to answer two fundamental questions:

1. does international law forbid the use of nuclear weapons, and
2. does international law forbid the possession of nuclear weapons?

The Tribunal received evidence under four main headings:

1. The Medical and Environmental Effects of Nuclear Attack
2. Current Weaponry and Strategy
3. The Moral Implications
4. The Legal Implications

The task of the Tribunal was to make findings of fact on the evidence and in particular of the behaviour and intentions of the nuclear weapon states and of the likely effects of that behaviour and those intentions. Those findings have been compared with the standards set by the six principles.

1.4.1 Evidence before the Tribunal

The Tribunal had before it the oral and written evidence submitted by the witnesses listed in Appendix H, and the results of cross-examining those witnesses who appeared in person before the Tribunal.

Chapter 2

Relevant International Law

This section summarises the evidence from witnesses about International Law which is relevant to the possession and use of nuclear weapons.

2.1 Lawfulness of Nuclear Weapons - Position of Nuclear States

Professor Meyrowitz stated the US position as to the legal status of nuclear weapons under international law thus:

> "The official US position is that there is no expressed prohibition in international law or formal treaty or clause in a convention that prohibits the use of nuclear weapons."

The USSRs position was stated by Dr Vlasikhin as follows:

> "Although the existing instruments, conventions and Geneva protocols prohibit the weapons of mass destruction, and obviously nuclear arms fall under this category, still there is no specific prohibition of the nuclear arms."

The UK position was stated in correspondence from the UK Foreign Office, whilst declining the Tribunal's invitation to give evidence:

> "The Government's considered and firm view is that there is no aspect of current defence policy which is inconsistent with the United Kingdom's obligations under international law, including the laws of war. Britain and NATO possess nuclear weapons only to deter aggression. NATO leaders gave a solemn undertaking in Bonn in 1982, repeated in Brussels in December 1983, that no NATO weapon, be it conventional or nuclear, would ever be used except in response to aggression. NATO possesses nuclear weapons not to fight war but to prevent one ever occurring."

2.2 Sources of International Law

According to the evidence before the Tribunal, several sources of international law were identified by various witnesses and deponents, to include (this is not intended as an exhaustive list):

- the United Nations Charter (to which all nuclear weapons states are a party)
- other treaties and similar written documents
- customary international law
- highly qualified publicists of international law
- general principles of law recognized by civilised nations
- public conscience
- laws of humanity.

2.3 Relevant Treaties, Declarations and Conventions

This section surveys briefly several of the key treaties which affect the international law of war[1].

2.3.1 The St Petersberg Declaration 1868

The *St. Petersberg Declaration*[2] of 1868 is regarded as the first international legal instrument prohibiting weaponry. It was made following a conference convened by Czar Alexander II to deal with the recently invented explosive bullets. The preamble to the Declaration sets out the following two principles:

- the only legitimate object which states should endeavour to accomplish is to weaken the military forces of the enemy
- That for this purpose it is sufficient to disable the greatest possible number of men; That this object would be exceeded by the employment of arms which uselessly aggravate the sufferings of disabled men or render their deaths inevitable; That the employment of such arms, would therefore be contrary to humanity.

---

1 for a more detailed treatment see Singh and McWhinney, 1989
2 Declaration Renouncing the Use, in Time of War, of Explosive Projectiles Under 400 grammes Weight, St. Petersberg 1868.

2.3.2 The Hague Conventions of 1907

The preamble to the fourth Hague Convention of 1907 has become known as the de Martens clause, after its author. The clause has been duplicated and adopted in nearly all the major 20th century treaties of the laws of war. The nuclear weapons states consider themselves bound by the clause. It states as follows:

> "Until a more complete code of the laws of war has been issued, the high contracting Parties deem it expedient to declare that, in cases not included in the Regulations adopted by them, the inhabitants and belligerents remain under the protection and the rule of the principles of the law of nations, as they result from the usages established among civilised people, from the laws of humanity, and the dictates of the public conscience."

The main body of the Hague Conventions reaffirmed and expanded what is stated in the St. Petersberg Declaration in 1868:

- o that the right of a belligerent to adopt means of injury the enemy is not unlimited.

It expanded and forbade:

- o the employment of poison or poisoned weapons;
- o the killing or wounding treacherously of individuals belonging to the hostile state or army;
- o the employment of arms, projectiles or material calculated to cause unnecessary suffering;

It also went further by prohibiting:

- o the destruction or seizure of enemy property unless such destruction was necessary; and,
- o attacks on undefended villages and towns

The Hague Conventions reaffirmed that religious, artistic, scientific or charitable buildings should be spared as much as possible during a siege, as well as historical monuments and places where the sick and wounded are cared for.

By Hague Convention V, the territory of neutral powers was made inviolable[3].

2.3.3 Geneva Gas Protocol 1925

The law relating to poison was formally pronounced in the 1925 *Geneva Protocol for the Prohibition of the Use in War of Asphyxiating, poisonous or Other Gases, and of Bacteriological Methods of Warfare* which prohibited the use in war of asphyxiating, poisonous or other gases, and all analogous liquids, materials or devices including bacteriological warfare.

Between 1925 and World War II there were no major developments in the laws of war, apart from the Treaty of Paris mentioned earlier.

2.3.4 United Nations Charter

The *United Nations Charter* initially enacted in 1945 placed significant restrictions on the way nations can conduct themselves in terms of armed conflict. The Charter prohibits anything but self-defence in justification of conflict.

2.3.5 Nuremberg Judgment

The *Judgment of the International Military Tribunal for the Trial of German Major War Criminals* was delivered on 30th September and 1st October 1946. The impact of this is discussed elsewhere in this document. The Judgment was delivered by the Tribunal which was set up by a Treaty. The Treaty has annexed to it the set of legal principles to be applied, in what is known as the Nuremberg Charter.

2.3.6 Genocide Convention 1948

After World War II the *United Nations Convention on the Prevention and Punishment of the Crime of Genocide* was approved by the United Nations in 1948 and adopted by the international community. It defines Genocide, inter alia, as:

> "The killing or causing of serious bodily or mental harm to members of a national, ethnic, racial or religious group in whole or in part".

---

3 Article 1, Convention (V) Respecting the Rights and Duties of Neutral Powers and Persons in Case of War on Land.

Its intention was to protect a civilian population. It also gave rise to a concept previously elucidated at the Nuremberg Tribunal (1946), that of a crime against humanity.

The Genocide Convention intended to cover Hitler's policy of exterminating German Jews, who were German citizens. The Convention made sure that if ever something like that happened again, it would no longer be considered an internal matter, but a matter subject to international law.

2.3.7 *Geneva Conventions 1949*

The next developments were the *Geneva Conventions* of 1949, which provide protections for certain groups of people such as: wounded or sick civilians, chaplains, medical personnel, wounded or sick armed forces at sea and on land, prisoners of war and civilians.

It also specified areas of protection, such as churches and medical facilities.

This was the first time civilians as a group were given specific protection: i.e. those who find themselves in case of conflict or occupation in the hands of a party to the conflict or occupying power of which they are not nationals.

2.3.8 *Nuremberg Principles 1950*

The *Nuremberg Principles* were pronounced at the request of the General Assembly of the UN by the International Law Commission and adopted in a unanimous resolution in 1950. Thereafter these became rules of Customary International Law.

The Nuremberg Tribunal was conducted under a Charter which defined as a crime under international law, "planning, preparation, initiation or waging of a war of aggression, or a war in violation of international treaties, agreements or assurances or participation in a common plan or conspiracy for the accomplishment of any of the foregoing."[4]

The Charter for the Nuremberg trials defined and the Judgment affirmed a number of other principles, such as Crimes against Peace, Crimes against Humanity, War Crimes and personal criminal responsibilities for the commission thereof.

---

4 Article 6 of the Charter annexed to the Agreement establishing the Tribunal for the trial of War Criminals.

A copy of the Nuremberg Principles is annexed here as Appendix A.

2.3.9 McCloy Zorin Accords 1961

The McCloy-Zorin Accords have already been referenced and a copy is provided in Appendix B. It was a very significant agreement, subsequently used as a basis for the United Nations effort to commit to a program for general and complete disarmament.

2.3.10 Test–Ban Treaty 1963

The Test-Ban Treaty of 1963 is a treaty banning nuclear weapon tests in the atmosphere, in outer-space and under water, including territorial waters or high seas. Each party undertook to prohibit, to prevent, and not to carry out any nuclear weapon test explosion, or any other nuclear explosion, at any place under its jurisdiction or control.

The parties also proclaim their principal aim the speediest possible achievement of an agreement on general and complete disarmament.

2.3.11 Non–Proliferation Treaty 1968

The *Non-Proliferation Treaty* of 1968 was set up with three complementary sets of obligations:

1. nuclear weapons states undertook not to transfer to any recipient whatsoever nuclear weapons or other nuclear explosive devices or control over such weapons or explosive devices directly, or indirectly; and not in any way to assist, encourage or induce any non-nuclear weapon state to manufacture or otherwise acquire nuclear weapons or other nuclear explosive devices, or control over such weapons or explosive devices
2. non–nuclear states undertook not to receive the transfer from anybody of nuclear weapons or other nuclear explosive devices, or control over them, and not to manufacture or otherwise acquire nuclear weapons or other nuclear explosive devices and not to seek or receive any assistance in the manufacture of nuclear weapons or other nuclear explosive devices.
3. in addition to the prohibitions on the transfer of nuclear weapons technology, the Parties to the Treaty undertook to pursue negotiations in good faith on effective measures relating

to cessation of the nuclear arms race at an early date and to nuclear disarmament, and on a treaty on general and complete disarmament under strict and effective international control.

2.3.12 Biological Weapons Convention 1972

There have since been moves to prohibit the possession of bacteriological weapons, but not the possession or manufacture of chemical weapons. The 1972 Convention[5] Preamble also places the prohibition in the context of "achieving effective progress towards general and complete disarmament, including the prohibition and elimination of all types of weapons of mass destruction".

2.3.13 Geneva Protocols I and II 1977

In 1977 the Geneva Conventions of 1949 were amplified by the 1977 Protocols to those Conventions[6].

The provisions of the 1949 Conventions were restated, greatly amplified and extended in the Protocols by Geneva Protocol I as follows:

Article 35 section 3 says:- "It is prohibited to employ methods or means of warfare which are intended, or may be expected to cause, widespread long term and severe damage to the environment";

Article 36 provides that a party to the convention is under an obligation to determine the lawfulness of the use of new weapons yet to be invented;

Article 48 provides for respect and protection of the civilian population and civilian objects, and that parties to a conflict shall distinguish between the civilian population and combatants and civilian objects and military objects and accordingly shall direct their operations only against military objectives;

Article 51 provides further protection for individual civilians and the civilian population from dangers arising from military operations;

Indiscriminate attacks are prohibited and are identified as:

i those not directed at a specific military objective

---

5 *Convention on the Prohibition of the Development, Production, and Stockpiling of Bacteriological (biological) and Toxic Weapons and on Their Destruction, 1972..*
6 *Geneva Protocol I Additional to the Geneva Conventions of 12 August 1949, and Relating to the Protection of Victims of International Armed Conflicts, and, Geneva Protocol II Additional to the Geneva Conventions of 12 August 1949, and Relating to the Protection of Victims of Non-International Armed Conflicts, 1977.*

ii those which employ a method or means of combat which cannot be directed at a specific military objective, or
iii those that employ a method or means of combat the effects of which cannot be limited as required by this protocol; and consequently are of a nature to strike military objectives and civilians or civilian objects without distinction.
iv an attack by bombardment by any means which treats as a single military objective a number of clearly separated and distinct military objectives, located in a city, town, village or other area containing a similar concentration of civilian or civilian objects; and,
v an attack which may be expected to cause incidental loss of life, injury to civilians, damage to civilian objects, or a combination thereof, which would be excessive in relation to the concrete and direct military advantage anticipated.

Attacks against civilian populations or civilians by way of reprisals are prohibited.

Article 52 provides general protection to civilian objects and limits attacks to military objects as defined.

Article 53 provides protection for cultural objects and places of worship.

Article 54 provides protection to objects indispensable to the survival of civilians.

Article 55 provides that:
1. "care shall be taken in warfare to protect the natural environment against widespread long term and severe damage. This protection includes a prohibition of the use of methods or means of warfare which are intended or may be expected to cause such damage to the natural environment and thereby to prejudice the health or survival of the population"
2. "attacks against the environment by way of reprisals are prohibited"

Article 56 provides protection against attacks on dams, dikes and nuclear electrical generating stations even where these objectives are military objectives, "if such attack may cause the release of dangerous forces and consequent severe losses among the civilian population.

Article 59 provides that "It is prohibited for the Parties to the conflict to attack, by any means whatsoever, non-defended localities.

The Tribunal was interested to note that at the time of the 1977 Protocols, the issue was raised whether these were applicable to nuclear weapons.

The earlier history of these Protocols shows that they originated from concern about the fate of civilians in nuclear war and this had been reflected by the number of Resolutions of the General Assembly of the U.N.

In June 1977 the U.S. representative U.N. Ambassador Aldrich said, "We recognise that nuclear weapons are the subject of separate negotiations and agreements, and furthermore their use in warfare is governed by the present principles of International Law".

The US and UK adopted a reservation to the effect that "the 1977 protocols were not applicable to nuclear weapons ". The Tribunal did however note that no such reservation was made when it came to the Geneva Conventions of 1949, even though nuclear weapons were already in existence.

2.3.14 Conventional Weapons Convention 1981

The Tribunal noted that from the beginning of the 1970's, nuclear weapons began to be excluded from discussions at Geneva. Other meetings began and eventually led in 1981 to the "U.N. Convention on Conventional Weapons"[7]

This 1981 Convention does not explicitly state it is not applicable to nuclear weapons, and a consideration of the Convention terms simply reinforces the feeling that any attempt to exclude nuclear weapons from established principles of international law is merely a cynical attempt at manipulation by those involved. More details of this Convention can be found in Section 4.8.

2.4 Additional Treaties and Conventions

In addition to those treaties shown above there are several other treaties and conventions which have a bearing on the questions before this Tribunal and are referenced at different places in this text:
- o Outer Space Treaty 1967
- o Latin America Nuclear-Free Zone Treaty 1967
- o Vienna Convention on the Law of Treaties 1969
- o Bacteriological (Biological) and Toxin Weapons Treaty 1971
- o Nuclear Weapons, Sea-Bed and Ocean Floor Treaty 1971

---

7 *The United Nations Convention on the Prohibition or Restriction on the Use of Certain Conventional Weapons which may be Deemed to be Excessively Injurious or to Have Indiscriminate Effects.*

- Anti-Ballistic Missile Treaty (ABM), 1972 (Salt I)
- Treaty on the Limitation of Underground Nuclear Weapons Tests 1974
- Moon Treaty 1979
- Intermediate-Range Nuclear Forces (INF) Treaty, 1987

Chapter 3

Use of Nuclear Weapons

The fact that nuclear weapons are a subject of separate negotiations cannot be taken to exempt them from established international law.

It is obvious that the applicability of law to a nuclear setting requires consideration of the likely physical consequences of the use of nuclear weapons. Firstly, can it ever be possible to reconcile the use of nuclear weapons with the accepted principles identified in Chapter 1? In particular, is it possible to use nuclear weapons in a way which distinguishes between combatants and non-combatants, which represents proportionality of force, which can ever be selective or discriminating, and which does not violate the rights of neutral states?

The Tribunal heard much evidence to the effect that nuclear weapons are extremely destructive of both persons and property (Alcalay, Dawson, Greene, Haines, Iwasa, Myers, Percival, Sagan, Saito, Steadman, Thompson). The detonation of just one, one-megaton nuclear warhead over a major city would result in 900,000 immediate deaths primarily from blast and heat, and a further 900,000 from the effects of radiation, making a total of 1.8 million. The health and emergency services of the European countries could not cope with just one such detonation. Evidence from the British Medical Association indicated that the medical services would be completely overwhelmed by one such bomb.

3.1 General Effects of Nuclear Weapons

Potentially lethal and destructive effects such as fire and blast may extend over ten miles in radius from the centre (ground-zero) of a nuclear explosion, while lethal levels of radio-active fallout dust would be deposited as far as 50 to 100 miles down-wind depending upon wind speed and local precipitation. The highly destructive nature of the nuclear weapons means that it is extremely difficult, and in most cases impossible to hit military targets without also devastating civilian habitations and environments nearby or down-wind. Evidence from Hiroshima and Nagasaki in Japan and from US atomic bomb tests established that long-term (20 to 30 years later) effects include eye cataracts, cancers of various types and impaired reproductive ability.

Thus the detonation of just one weapon in the megaton range over or near to a civilian centre of population would be a breach of the law on the following counts, inter alia: indiscriminate, unnecessary suffering, disproportionate force and lack of protection to civilians or injured non-combatants.

The detonation of up to 200 nuclear weapons in the 10 to 100 kiloton range on purely military targets in central Europe would result in 5-14 million deaths, primarily of civilians. Civilian casualties would exceed military casualties by a factor of 16 to 1. It was noted that in areas such as the Middle East or most of Europe, the use of even relatively few nuclear weapons - less than 0.1% of the current nuclear arsenals - would result in very high casualties. This is because in such areas military and civilian targets are highly interspersed. The legal provisions to protect property, buildings and undefended cities could not be kept. The possible erection of a so-called Star Wars or SDI (Strategic Defence Initiative) shield as envisaged at present would also not achieve the aim of separating civil and military targets. In the final or 'terminal' phase of such a putative shield, nuclear weapons would have to be destroyed in the atmosphere above cities and military bases. If these weapons were 'salvage fused', that is if they detonated with a nuclear explosion if hit, a most likely response to SDI, these low endo-atmospheric explosions would still cause severe blast and heat damage to cities. Weapons intercepted in the mid-course or this final phase would still deposit large quantities of highly radio-active elements and isotopes upon their intended targets.

Thus a 'limited' nuclear exchange would lead to a breach of the law on all the counts above, with the addition of the following: devastation of the environment and violation of neutrality (by fallout and blast). Countries such as Switzerland, Sweden and Hungary would suffer casualties to their populations, disruption of trade and imports and the poisoning of tracts of land making movement hazardous for many weeks and farming for up to a year.

Once nuclear weapons are used in larger quantities, that is up to 1-2% of the current arsenals, or even possibly at the 'tactical' level, a further effect of nuclear weapons becomes important. The heat of the nuclear fire-balls will start many fires creating huge clouds of smoke. These smoke clouds will merge and reduce the levels of light and heat from the sun and furthermore create a 'greenhouse' effect as with normal water vapour clouds. The result will be a general reduction of local and northern hemispheric average temperatures. If sufficient weapons are detonated, the resultant smoke 'particles could lead to the so-called 'nuclear winter', in which light levels and land temperatures would be severely reduced for up to many months.

Causation of the nuclear winter would be an extreme violation of all the categories of the laws of war on every count. Countries very far removed from the theatres of war would suffer the most severe effects, leading to the starvation of estimated billions in the Third World as a result of crop and rains failure and world climatic catastrophe.

3.2 Medical and Environmental Effects of Nuclear War

The Tribunal heard much evidence about the medical and environmental effects of the use of nuclear weapons.

3.2.1 Atomic Bomb Effects on Hiroshima and Nagasaki

The atomic bombings on Japan in 1945 represent the only hostile use of nuclear weapons to date. The tribunal was therefore particularly interested in establishing the short-term and long-lasting effects of the Hiroshima and Nagasaki attacks even though the explosive yields of the two bombs (12.5 and 22 kilotons respectively) were substantially smaller than most present-day weapons with typical yields in the range of several hundred kilotons up to several megatons. The Japanese attacks were therefore equivalent to the use of only two small tactical nuclear warheads in modern terms which is conceivably the minimum level of use contemplated by modern field commanders in central Europe.

Evidence on the Japanese attacks was presented by Professor Iwasa (a survivor from Hiroshima) and by Dr. Saito a Japanese physician and authority on the physical injuries caused by the Hiroshima bomb.

Professor Iwasa who was the first witness to address the Tribunal recalled the grim scenes in Hiroshima on 6th August 1945. He read extracts from his report ("What Hibakusha Want") to the Tribunal:

> "I was in my garden about 1.2 kilometres from the point in Hiroshima where the bomb was dropped. At the moment of the explosion I felt as if I had been struck on the back of my head, and was knocked to the ground. I managed to rise a few seconds after that dreadful blast, and saw that all the

houses and other buildings of Hiroshima had vanished from before my eyes, and only bits of broken tiles and rubbish were left there. Great fires were sweeping everywhere.

My mother was trapped under the house, but even using all my strength (I was a sixteen-year-old boy at the time) I was unable to rescue her. I managed to get to the swimming pool of the nearby middle school, haunted by the voice of my mother chanting Hannya-Shin-Kyo' (a Buddhist scripture) in my ears. I prayed, 'Mum, please try to escape', but I could only watch the house burning, tears in my eyes.

What I saw were the terrible scenes of an earthly hell. A four-year-old girl in the next house was nearly dead, her neck split open, her bronchial tube sticking out. All around where our house had been were people injured by the blast, heat and radiation that swept all over us at once; people burnt all over their bodies by the intense heat had their skin hanging down like strips of rag, their bodies full of pieces of glass.

I saw some of the people covered with flames falling on the road after barely crawling out of the collapsed houses.

Everywhere near the blast centre where I went the next day, the burnt remains of people packed together in the water, some in a small tub where they had tried to escape the fire."

Professor Iwasa also pointed out that even those who escaped sudden death from the nuclear explosion and those who came into the city looking for family members after the attack also became victims.

Dr. Saito's evidence provided the Tribunal with more quantitative information on the Hiroshima attack. His written submission established that a total of 140,000 people had died in Hiroshima by the end of 1945. The total mortality rate standing at 56.5% of the population within 2km of ground-zero at that time. Dr. Saito's report detailed the immediate physical injury caused by the explosion:

"The first cause of death of these victims was atomic burns, called flash burns, plus external wounds caused by blast. The epidermis of A-bomb victims a short distance from the hypocentre was carbonized, and their internal organs vaporized instantly. Those who suffered serious burns within 1.0km where there was no shelter from radiation died within one week at a ratio of 90-100 per cent. Deaths from acute symptoms from the A-bombing occurred till around the end of 1945. But 90 per cent of the victims who suffered acute symptoms were dead within two weeks, and almost all the others died 8 weeks after the bombing. Another effect leading to death was the destruction of hematopoietic organs by radiation. The decrease of white blood corpuscles caused the following symptoms: nausea, vomiting, loss of energy and vitality, diarrhoea, and loss of hair. Victims within 500m from the hypocentre died on the day after medical examination or after the next day, because their white blood cells had decreased to 150-400 per cubic millimetre. Autopsies undertaken within 2 weeks after the bombing showed the disappearance of lymphocytes from the lymph nodes, and of hematopoietic cells from the bone marrow as common characteristics. It also showed bleeding of internal organs. The examination of people who entered the city soon after the bombing showed abnormality of white blood corpuscles".

Dr. Saito's evidence also examined the medium and long-term after-effects of atomic bomb injury. Within several months, many victims who had suffered thermal injury at a range of 2-3km developed grossly swollen scar tissue known as keloids. This effect is virtually unique amongst atomic bomb victims and occurred with a very high rate of incidence among the survivors. Surveys in 1946 and 1947 also revealed impaired sperm production and abnormal menstruation amongst victims. By 1948 cases of eye cataracts and leukaemia had been discovered in the victims. During the period 1950-55 the leukaemia rate peaked at 94.85 cases per 100,000 of the population amongst those who had been exposed to radiation doses in excess of 100 rads. The equivalent rate for non-victims stood at 1.04 cases per 100,000. Dr. Saito also referred to recent reports indicating that many Hibakusha (A-bomb survivors) are now suffering from cancers of the stomach, breasts and lungs at increased incidences compared to non-victims. Both Japanese witnesses agreed that the effects of the atomic bombings are still being felt today by many victims.

Besides the direct testimony of the two Japanese witnesses, the Tribunal received a further submission from the Japanese delegation giving more details on the physical and medical aspects of the attacks on Hiroshima and Nagasaki. In addition the attention of the Tribunal has been drawn to an eyewitness account of the atomic bomb attack on

Nagasaki and to a major compilation of scientific evidence on damage caused by the atomic bombs in the two Japanese cities (Ishikawa and Swain, 1981).

In weighing up the evidence from the Japanese experience the members of the Tribunal noted that many victims appear to have suffered from the complex synergistic effects of multiple sources of physical injury including flash burns, radiation and blast trauma. Although the total number of deaths attributable to the two atomic bombings is known fairly accurately up to the end of 1945 (140,000 plus or minus 10,000 dead in Hiroshima, 70,000 plus or minus 10,000 dead in Nagasaki) the total mortality rate since that time has been more difficult to establish as A-bomb effects cannot in all circumstances be isolated from other causes. Nevertheless the total number of attributable deaths by 1950 has been estimated at 340,000 for the two cities. It is certain that many hundreds if not thousands of people have died since that time through direct or indirect effects of the bombings (including for example the effects of psychological disturbances)

Although the Japanese evidence was invaluable to the Tribunal, it was noted that the casualty rates etc. cannot be directly extrapolated to possible present-day nuclear conflict scenarios on account of the special circumstances prevailing at the time, namely:

- o dual military and civilian targets were deliberately chosen by the Interim Committee of May 1945 which advised the US President on the use of the atomic bomb,
- o the explosions were both low-yield air-bursts generating little significant fall-out by present-day standards,
- o there was no warning of attack and many people were caught out of doors,
- o many buildings in both cities were of wooden construction,
- o the fabric of society in surrounding areas essentially remained intact permitting rescue attempts and rehabilitation of survivors.

3.2.2 Consequences of Nuclear Attack on the UK

Bearing in mind the special situations represented in the evidence from Japan, the Tribunal was anxious to establish the impact of a major nuclear attack on a modern and highly developed society using weapons currently existing in the arsenals of the major nuclear powers. Evidence was presented by Mr. Greene and Dr. Steadman of the Open University on the results of computer simulations of large scale nuclear attacks on the UK. Their evidence gave a detailed account of calculations of short-term effects, the numbers killed and injured, the extent of physical damage caused by blast and fire, and the extent of radioactive contamination by fall-out. These calculations are based primarily on direct evidence of the effects of modern weapons which are detailed in a recent joint US Department of Energy/Department of Defence report which provides the most comprehensive technical summary of nuclear explosion effects openly available (Glasstone and Dolan, 1977). The US report is based principally on the results of a large number of nuclear tests carried out by the United States during the 1950s and 1960s. Notably, results from British nuclear tests are still not openly available.

The Steadman and Greene evidence focused on assumed attack levels of 219 megatons and 348 megatons which are based on attacks covering (i) all major nuclear and conventional military bases including command centres, as well as power stations, oil and gas refineries, ports and a few heavy industrial plants and (ii) as in (i) but with a few general urban-industrial targets added as well. These attacks are regarded as primarily counterforce and countervalue attacks aimed at eliminating military forces and reducing industrial/economic recovery. Steadman and Greene assume that one-third to one-quarter of the nuclear warheads available to the Soviet Union in its Eurostrategic arsenal would be allocated for use against the United Kingdom on account of its key role within NATO and the high density of military targets and American nuclear bases. However only about one-third of these levels are used in their attack scenarios. Steadman and Greene also pointed out that up until 1981 the British Home Office made the assumption for the purposes of civil defence planning that an attack by the Soviet Union would be of roughly 200 megatons. More recently government spokesmen have been asserting that more limited attacks (e.g. of 50 megatons) are "more probable" than an all-out attack though this remains an issue of deep contention.

The effects of the two attack patterns presented by Steadman and Greene are given in Table 3-1. Both levels of attack which are not aimed principally at population centres generate substantial civilian casualty rates. The Tribunal interpret this as being indicative of the fact that it is impossible to distinguish between military and non-military targets with modern nuclear weaponry.

During his oral evidence, Dr. Steadman provided the Tribunal with estimates of the indirect effects of the attack scenarios on energy supply, agriculture, and the provision of food and water. He pointed out that the effects of blast damage, the electromagnetic pulse and radiation would seriously damage all public services and hamper if not eradicate all chance of post-attack recovery within a predictable or reasonable time-scale.

Mr. Greene was cross-examined at length on differences between their calculations and similar ones carried out by the UK Home Office which generated a casualty level of only 17 million. Mr. Greene pointed out that many independent scientists have been critical of assumptions in the Home Office models relating to the extent of blast damage and the radiation protection offered by damaged buildings.

Attack	A	B
Targets:	military plus a few industrial	military, industrial plus a few urban
Total yield:	219 MT	348 MT
Short-term casualties	37.5 million killed (79% of population)	42.5 million killed (90% of population)
Fire zones	66,000 sq. km	102,000 sq. km
Area contaminated by >450 rads (human LD 50)	120,000 sq. km.	120,000 sq. km
Blast damage zones:		
>12 psi (total destruction)	7,000 sq. km.	13,000 sq. km.
>5 psi (severe damage)	18,000 sq. km.	34,000 sq. km.
>2 psi (light housing damage)	49,000 sq. km.	80,000 sq. km. (*)
Total housing stock damaged or destroyed:	60%	80%
* approximately one half of the total UK land area		

Table 3–1: Effects of Two Nuclear Attacks on the UK

The members of the Tribunal noted with some concern that there appears to be substantial disagreement within the scientific community vis a vis the extent of blast damage from nuclear explosions, the protection factors for modern housing stock, and LDSO values for radiation injury. Nevertheless the Tribunal accepted that even allowing for the most optimistic assumptions the consequences of any nuclear attack against a nation would be extremely dire and that there could be no effective civil defence for whole populations particularly when long-term effects are taken into account.

The Tribunal noted that the UK Home Office had not been prepared to send representatives to the Tribunal to explain its own calculations and assumptions.

Finally Steadman and Greene presented the Tribunal with a publication outlining a number of other attack scenarios on the UK. Two other recent publications on British assessments of the effects of nuclear attack were also made available to the Tribunal, one dealing with an attack on London, the other with the detailed consequences for the British housing stock.

3.2.3 Nuclear War and the Provision of Health Services

In assessing the overall effects of nuclear war the Tribunal sought to identify more clearly the scale of physical and psychological damage to civilian populations and the ability of health services to provide for victims

The first witness to appear in this category was Dr. Dawson, Under Secretary of the British Medical Association. He presented the Tribunal with copies of the report by the BMA's Board of Science and Education on the medical effects of nuclear war as his prime proof of evidence (BMA, 1983).\ This report reviewed all the major studies on nuclear attacks on the UK and examined mortality rates and medical response. The BMA report establishes that in the UK there are approximately 160,000 acute beds available within the National Health Service (NHS) in peace-time. After a nuclear attack the majority of these would have been destroyed. Many victims would suffer from serious second and third degree burn injuries, orthopaedic, abdominal, spinal and thoracic injury from blast effects, as well as from the effects of high levels of radioactivity and infection. The report points out that substantial numbers of victims of nuclear attack even if they survive the first few days would require major surgery for blast trauma plus plasma and blood transfusions for burn and radiation injury. The majority of victims requiring such treatment (likely to be many millions) are certain to die. The report concludes (p124):

> "The explosion of a single nuclear bomb of the size used at Hiroshima over a major city in the UK is likely to produce so

many cases of trauma and burns requiring hospital treatment that the remaining medical services in the UK would be completely overwhelmed. An attack with, for example, 200 megatons represents an explosive power some 15,000 times greater than the Hiroshima bomb or the equivalent of forty (40) times all the conventional explosive used in the whole of the Second World War.

The NHS could not deal with the casualties that might be expected following the detonation of a single one megaton weapon over the UK. It follows that multiple nuclear explosions over several, possibly many, cities would force a breakdown in medical services across the country as a whole.

There is no possibility of increasing the production of certain drugs in a short period of tension before a war, and if it is wished to have large quantities of blood products available for transfusion purposes or the bulk of the present generation of medical practitioners in the country trained for certain eventualities, then all of these things would have to be done now and the country must exist on a more or less permanent emergency footing".

Dr. Dawson indicated that the BMA had taken the view in its study that the calculations performed by independent scientists on the effects of attacks on the UK were more realistic than those of the British Home Office. The members of the Tribunal note that regardless of who is right or wrong on this issue, the essential conclusions of the BMA report remain indisputable.

Additional evidence on the effects of nuclear war on the medical services was provided by Dr. Haines of the Department of Community Medicine at the Middlesex Hospital, London.

A third witness in this section, Dr Thompson, provided the Tribunal with useful information on the possible psychological reactions to nuclear disasters. Such evidence is based on observed reactions to past natural disasters and extrapolation to a post-nuclear society is difficult. Under examination Dr. Thompson expressed the view that approximately one half of the survivors of an attack would probably suffer from a 'disaster syndrome' in which people would feel 'dazed, stunned, bewildered, and apathetic and behave mechanically'. He estimated that a further 25% would be capable of reacting usefully but would suffer from a role conflict, i.e. family versus duty. The remaining 25% would be incapable of reacting. The Tribunal accepted that severe psychological disturbance was likely to be a major indirect effect of the use of nuclear weapons which would pose a serious threat to the continuing existence of initial survivors even at 'limited' scales of attack. The lack of a normal outside world would be a critical factor in amplifying the psychological effects.

The attention of the Tribunal was also drawn to a recent report by the International Committee of Experts in Medical Sciences and Public Health to the World Health Organization on the "Effects of nuclear War on Health and Health Services" (WHO, 1984) The report concludes that:

> "The immediate and the delayed loss of human and animal life would be enormous, and the effect on the fabric of civilization would be either to impede its recovery or make recovery impossible. The plight of survivors would be physically and psychologically appalling. The partial or complete disruption of the health services would deprive survivors of effective help. The committee is convinced that there is a sound professional basis for its conclusions that nuclear weapons constitute the greatest immediate threat to the health and welfare of mankind".

The members of the Tribunal believe this conclusion has significant legal implications.

3.2.4 Longer Term Effects of Low-Level Radiation

The Tribunal accepted evidence from several witnesses on the long–term effects of nuclear weapons in terms of low-level radiation and the human body. One, Dr. Glenn Alcalay, concentrated on long-term medical effects experienced by inhabitants of the Marshall Islands in the Pacific where a large number of American nuclear tests were conducted in the 1950's. This evidence was particularly revealing as it concerned the effects on populations who were not direct or intended victims of nuclear attack. In a written report, Dr. Alcalay revealed that on several occasions the Marshall Islanders were subjected to accidental radioactive contamination from fall-out. In one particular 15 megaton detonation, the BRAVO test of March 1954, a total of fourteen islands was affected. Three days after the explosion (at Bikini Atoll) the inhabitants of Kongelap Island were evacuated by the US

Navy. They were returned to the island in 1957 but began to experience medical problems. On several occasions women gave birth to "creatures like monkeys, some like octopi, and some like bunches of grapes". A few years later other islanders were found to be suffering from thyroid problems and leukaemia. Dr. Alcalay's report notes that the long-term effects on the islanders eventually included late-occurring thyroid effects including tumours and thyroid dysfunction with concomitant growth abnormalities, as well as blood changes and chromosome aberrations, adverse birth outcomes and the effects of ecosystem contamination and the uptake of radionuclides in the food-chain. The Tribunal noted with concern that his report indicated that data from the Marshall Islands suggests that low levels of ionising radiation may cause as much cancer as higher levels over a long period of time. A group exposed to a whole-body gamma dose of 14 rads (considered by many experts to be insignificant) appears to have experienced the same rate of thyroid cancer as a group exposed to 175 rads.

3.2.5 Long-Term Effects on the Global Ecosphere

Apart from examining the medical effects of nuclear weapons the Tribunal sought to address the recent and spectacular conclusions of a number of atmospheric and biological scientists who now believe that nuclear warfare can result in such drastic changes to the global climate that the continued existence of many life-forms would be questionable. The Tribunal recognised that the recent predictions of the so-called 'nuclear winter effect' needed special attention for three primary reasons:

    i   the nuclear winter theory is based largely, but not exclusively, on mathematical model predictions
    ii a nuclear winter would be the ultimate factor determining the eventual survival of the human race whether or not extensive civil defence provisions were available in the short-term
    iii the nuclear winter theory suggests that the global biosphere is at risk as the consequences of a nuclear exchange would be carried far beyond the nations involved directly in the military conflict. This has serious implications for the validity of the nuclear weapon as an instrument of war between nations.

The Tribunal received written evidence from four experts one of whom, Professor Ian Percival FRS of Queen Mary College London appeared before the Tribunal in person for cross-examination. The Tribunal was presented with papers from Professor Carl Sagan of Cornell University reporting the original research work which predicted a nuclear winter and the biological effects; a paper from Dr. Norman Myers on the environmental consequences; and a paper from Mr. Jonathon Porritt, also on the impact on the biosphere.

During the course of the oral proceedings Professor Percival outlined the main causes of the nuclear winter and its effects. He explained that one major effect of a nuclear war would be that dust and smoke from large fires would be carried high into the atmosphere where it would be carried around the globe acting as a barrier to sunlight causing darkness and extreme cold at the Earth's surface. He explained that if the dust and smoke reached the comparatively stable stratosphere as the computer models predicted then it could remain air-borne for many months and even up to one or two years resulting in severe biological consequences.

The precise nature of these consequences was outlined in some detail in the other written evidence. Basically the occurrence of very low light levels (down to a few percent of normal) combined with protracted periods of cold would effectively obliterate agriculture as plant photosynthesis would cease. In addition damage to the Earth's ozone layer caused by massive quantities of nitrogen oxides generated as a by-product of nuclear explosions would result in an increased level of ultraviolet light reaching the Earth once the dust had cleared, posing a further threat to any life-forms which might have survived the cold and the dark. In addition the Earth's surface and atmosphere may be contaminated not only with enhanced levels of long-lived radioactivity but also with hazardous chemical pollutants resulting from the combustion of plastics and other materials prevalent in a modern highly industrialized society.

If such predictions are correct then the consequences for human survivors are clear. With failing agriculture and no relief from the cold or dark the long term survival of the human race appears to be in some doubt on the basis of these startling scientific predictions.

The Tribunal attempted to ascertain what minimum level of nuclear exchange could give rise to the nuclear winter. Results from calculations by Professor Sagan and others indicate that sub-zero temperatures averaged over a hemisphere would exist for up to 3 months after only a 100 megaton city attack corresponding to a small 'theatre' exchange.

The Tribunal was also interested in assessing the certainty of the nuclear winter predictions or the lack of it. Under cross-examination Professor Percival accepted that the nuclear winter theory depends very much on estimates of the extent of fires, the amount of soot and smoke generated, the height to which soot and smoke particles rise, and the rates at which they fall out. Professor Percival accepted that there were many imponderables in the models but that the best judgment could be reached by examining a variety of studies.

3.2.6 Tribunal Conclusions on Global Ecosphere Effects

After careful consideration of all the evidence submitted on the nuclear winter the members of the Tribunal were drawn to a number of significant conclusions:

1. There appears to be genuine controversy within the scientific community on the certainty or severity of a nuclear winter after a nuclear exchange. However, a number of major computational studies carried out *independently* in the USA and USSR appear to come to the same conclusion: that a nuclear winter is a likely consequence of nuclear war.
2. Experimental evidence has shown that dust emitted by volcanoes can encircle the globe within 20 days and that there is an historical correlation between frost damage to tree rings and occurrences of major dust-creating volcanic eruptions.
3. A nuclear winter arising from a theatre or strategic nuclear exchange may render human life impossible in one or both hemispheres of the Earth on a long-term basis. This effect may far outweigh the short-term effects of nuclear weapons on civilians and combatants.
4. In view of the fact that the nuclear winter theory cannot be indisputably disproved short of a test in the form of a real war and that the evidence seems to point to it as a real and likely outcome of even a theatre nuclear war (e.g. limited to Europe), then it is apparent that the use of nuclear weapons within a limited scenario must be regarded as a grossly irresponsible act on a global scale having consequences far beyond any conceivable military objective within the theatre of use.

3.3 Nuclear Weapons and Strategy

In this section, the evidence which was presented about various categories of nuclear weapon use is summarised, along with summaries of perceived strategies employed by the nuclear superpowers.

Firstly were various scenarios for actual weapon usage, and then some overall policies.

3.3.1 Detonation of a Single Weapon

Such deliberate use takes the threat of use to its next logical conclusion. Such use is itself illegal for the various reasons examined in the cases given below, but in addition and more importantly such use is illegal if it is likely to bring about limited or general nuclear exchanges leading to a gross breach of all the principles of the laws of war as above.

3.3.2 Detonation of Single Weapon in Water

Use of a single, one kiloton nuclear warhead accurately targeted upon a surface ship even as large as an aircraft carrier would completely destroy it, with the probably loss of all hands. This would be in breach of the laws of war to the extent that disproportionate force would have been used. The same military objective could be achieved with the use of several successful torpedo or conventional missile attacks. If the weapon was detonated at very low altitude very substantial amounts of soluble radio-active isotopes would be generated and dispersed creating a large local environmental impact to the aquatic food-chains and a radioactive fallout plume lethal several miles downwind. Injection of radio-active material into the upper atmosphere would be unlikely. These effects would bring a further charge of unlawfulness to the extent that an area would be poisoned.

3.3.3 Use of Single Weapon on Land

Assuming that a small detonation was made in a remote pass before enemy troops could reach the area and that prevailing winds did not blow fallout over the territory of neighbouring countries the only breach of the law is that of poisoning of the environment. In reality it is very difficult to envisage all such eventualities being fulfilled and such use would be most likely to breach the neutrality of any neighbouring countries, to kill civilians, and to be indiscriminate use.

3.3.4 Use of Single Weapon as Demonstration

Such use would be a very explicit example of terroristic diplomacy and a very clear threat of further use on a possibly inhabited area or upon a military target.

3.3.5 Tendency of Weaponry and Strategies Towards Use

Here the Tribunal considered factors such as the disposition of various nuclear states to use nuclear weapons, cumulative tendencies to use nuclear weapons, crisis stability, specific technologies and strategies leading towards use and the likely influence of possible defensive components (e.g. SDI) in conjunction with the highly offensive nuclear weapons. A large body of evidence was presented and several specialist witnesses were cross-examined (Dando, Harbottle, Kaldor, Pentz, Prins, Rogers, Smith, Vlasikhin, Webber, Wilson).

Strong evidence was presented to the Tribunal that nuclear strategies currently in force, particularly western strategies, had detailed contingency plans for the first-use of nuclear weapons in response to conventional attack — known as 'extended' deterrence. Nuclear weapons were not seen as purely existing to make a devastating response to any nuclear attack. Soviet declared strategy differed in that the Soviets had made a unilateral pledge not to use nuclear weapons first, against non-nuclear states or neutrals. Despite this declared strategy, evidence was presented that the Soviet Union might in certain circumstances, such as in anticipation of an imminent nuclear attack by NATO, launch nuclear weapons first. Nevertheless the strategic trends were that NATO was more ready to threaten or actually to initiate nuclear weapons use than the Soviet Union. This was a clear asymmetry between the positions of the two superpowers.

Relating to the weapons themselves, the trend in weaponry is towards larger numbers of smaller and more accurate warheads. The accuracy of present-day warheads is far above that needed to target cities, which gives rise to the fear that these weapons are targeted upon other nuclear weapons in their silos and that they might be used in a nuclear 'first strike'. Neither side has sufficient weapons of sufficient accuracy to achieve such a disarming first strike over the other, also both sides possess submarine launched weapons whose positions were not sufficiently well-known to be hit. Nevertheless this trend in weaponry and in anti-submarine warfare was to increase the numbers of weapons systems potentially vulnerable to first-strike. The US was 5 to 10 years ahead of the Soviet Union in this technology.

New conventional weapons also 'fudge' the firebreak between nuclear and non-nuclear use for two reasons: (a) new dual-capable weapons systems are planned using cruise and Pershing type missiles to strike Warsaw Pact airfields and fixed targets, these launches would be indistinguishable from nuclear launches; (b) certain weapons such as the fuel-air explosion have explosive powers larger than the smallest nuclear weapons, others are intended to be just as destructive as neutron warheads to tank concentrations (MLRS Phase 3 warhead), others such as the cluster bomb can devastate large areas with withering blasts of shrapnel and deposit plastic minelets for area denial purposes.

Numerous witnesses referred to the Rand Study (Boyle, Meyrowitz) to support a proposition that more accurate and smaller weaponry could be an attempt to legitimise nuclear weaponry by reducing collateral damage. Evidence was presented that although individual warheads are smaller, intermixing of military and civilian targets would lead to inevitable and unlawful killing of civilians. Also increased forward basing of land-based weapons in highly populated areas such as Europe could only exacerbate the problem.

Both sides have deployed weapons which could be targeted upon the other's command and control networks and reaching them in 5 to 10 minutes from launch. These deployments were judged by the Tribunal to be diminishing stability in a crisis by reason of the very short flight times and the vulnerability of command and control networks. This trend represented, in the view of the Tribunal an increase in risk taking which was deemed to be both unnecessary and reckless endangerment.

The influence of possible future defensive measures was considered. The US SDI is defensive only insofar as its intention is to destroy incoming warheads. Both the US and the USSR possess large numbers of highly offensive weapons including long-range nuclear warheads. Such offensive capability in conjunction with a new defensive ability, would enhance both the defensive and the offensive capability of any power deploying an SDI system. If one side deploys SDI the result is simply a greater degree of threat to the side not possessing it, because as far as it is successful a certain proportion of the nuclear warheads of one's opponent are made useless. SDI could be interpreted as enhancing a possible first strike option because any response after first strike could be stopped by the shield. It can also be interpreted as removing the deterrent ability of the smaller nuclear powers. In both these respects it is destabilizing. SDI as presently envisaged cannot defend Europe, because tactical weapons do not go up into space, or defend against low-flying weapons of longer range. Anti-tactical Ballistic Missile (ATBM) systems are being considered for the point defence of US airfields in Europe. As far as SDI is successful and the belief that any retaliatory strike may be sufficiently blunted is enhanced, the likelihood of further unlawful and unethical risk-taking is increased.

Evidence was given to the effect that the nuclear state could only exist by means of excessive state security and was thus by its nature counter-democratic leading to a gradual erosion of human rights (Kaldor). The existence of nuclear weapons had led to a militarization of international relations since the Second World War. Successive nuclear threats were known to have been made by the US in Korea, but the effectiveness of these threats as a means of nuclear coercion or blackmail was severely questioned. It seemed that the only successful case of nuclear blackmail was by a small nuclear state (Israel) against the US.

The Tribunal found that the trends in weaponry and strategy made the unlawful use of nuclear weapons more likely, both the threat of use and the actual detonation of weapons. Many of the newer, smaller types of weapons particularly the US cruise missile, made verification of future treaties more difficult (cruise is outside existing arms control treaties such as SALT-2). This also applied to a lesser extent to mobile weapons such as the Soviet SS-20. Modern developments made the likelihood of escalation to all-out nuclear war from serious conventional conflicts almost inevitable and constituted an unlawful and unethical degree of risk taking. The US SDI initiative was seen as a further destabilizing development, particularly as an existing arms control treaty, the ABM treaty, was likely to be threatened.

One positive trend which emerged from the technology was that with the extremely high sensitivity of satellite monitoring operating at many different frequencies and new technologies for higher frequency seismic analysis — the transparency revolution — the possibility of any side cheating on any arms control agreements was more remote. This could not be used as a valid reason for not ratifying the Comprehensive Test Ban Treaty (CTBT) or a implementing a freeze on deployment, testing and development.

3.4 Lawful Use of Nuclear Weapons - Is It Conceivable?

In evidence before the Tribunal, Professor Meyrowitz stated that, of all those scholars who have expressly considered the topic, the substantial majority have concluded that the use of nuclear weapons would contravene international law. The minority opinion, predominantly American, is that the use of nuclear weapons would be lawful so long as their use complies with the standards of discrimination and proportionality. To be meaningful, this last assertion requires an answer to the question of whether the real (and not theoretical) use of nuclear weapons could be discriminating and proportionate. The Tribunal did not consider that the likely reality supports the assertion, and reached this conclusion based upon the evidence of the capabilities of existing nuclear weapons, the unlikelihood of a limited use of nuclear weapons and the medical and environmental consequences of their actual use.

Professor Boyle stated, "one might be able to conceive some totally insignificant situation in which a bomb could be blown off and perhaps not violate international law". Professor Griffith offered a few examples such as the use of a small 'clean' tactical weapon against an enemy ship in mid-ocean or against a small force in mid-desert. The Tribunal considered these examples to be unlikely.

In reality any major nuclear exchange would be an unprecedented human and environmental catastrophe proving a serious threat to the survival of all life on the planet. Even the use of a few tactical nuclear warheads would result in substantial incidental loss of civilian life and civilians would be subjected to unnecessary suffering far outweighing any immediate political or military objectives. There are the strongest religious and moral objections to the destruction of a society through the use of nuclear weapons. Indeed, it is difficult to identify any real value system that justifies their use. As for the rights of neutral states, missiles, which are not included within any of the treaties regulating air traffic, but which will inevitably fly over neutral territory are in breach of Article II of the fifth Hague Convention. The use of nuclear weapons would inflict considerable damage on neutral nations, most obviously upon Austria and Switzerland. It is the most extraordinary proposition that two warring states, engaged in a private conflict, may legitimately destroy their neutral neighbours.

Upon the evidence, the use of nuclear weapons cannot distinguish between combatants and non-combatants, that it does not represent a proportionate use of force, that it cannot be selective or discriminating, and that it violates the rights of neutral nations. In short, the use of nuclear weapons is unlawful. It is clear therefore that the use of nuclear weapons involves, inter alia, infringements the Charter of the United

Nations, the Hague Conventions of 1899 and 1907 on the Law of War, the Geneva Conventions of 1949 and the Geneva Protocols of 1977. It is also clear that mere possession (certainly in terms of testing nuclear weapons) has already involved quite unlawful actions against civilian populations and exposed certain populations to unacceptable risks and actual damage.

Chapter 4

Possession of Nuclear Weapons

4.1 General Evidence on Possession

After considering the consequences of using nuclear weapons the Tribunal concluded that they can never be used lawfully. More details of the conclusions are given at the end of this Chapter, and in the Judgment.

However, can they nevertheless exist as lawful weapons — weapons which it is lawful to possess but never to use? The answer to this question depends upon the absolute accuracy of the assertions that they will never be used, and that there exists no intention to use them under any circumstances.

The military, moral and legal justification for the existence of nuclear weapons is the same - the so-called "doctrine of deterrence". It is said that it is their very destructiveness which will deter anyone from ever using them[1]. Not only that, but it will deter anyone from serious acts of aggression against any state which possesses nuclear weapons. Accordingly, it is said that nuclear weapons have kept the peace for 40 years. 40 years is a very short time in the history of the world — it is necessary to consider the long term future of this planet.

The paradox within the so-called doctrine of deterrence is that, while its intention is to avoid the use of nuclear weapons by means of a threat, the effectiveness of the threat depends entirely on a real intention to use them. As the witness Dan Smith put it: "The commitment to use nuclear weapons, though conditional, must be unambiguously credible and irrevocable". Thus, in order to deter, the threat to use must be perceived by one's opponent as real and not mere bluff. Not only is this a theoretical strategy of high risk, but the real manifestations of nuclear credibility have led to a dangerously unstable military situation

The public imagination may believe that nuclear war means a senior politician, after mature and reasoned consideration, pressing a button

---
1 see for example the quotation from a British Foreign Office letter to this Tribunal, shown in Section 2.1.

launching slow inter-continental ballistic missiles on their way across the world. This is not the reality of modern nuclear technology and structures. Vast numbers of highly accurate weapons are deployed in the field ready to destroy entire societies within minutes. In the words of Professor Boyle: "What we have here today is the gun out of the pocket, pointed at the other fellow's head, and a firing mechanism is cocked and ready to pull".

The need to persuade the opponent of the credibility of one's willingness to strike hard and fast has led to actual weaponry and structures which are meant to and do reflect that willingness. Thus, of necessity, military personnel have had to be conditioned and trained to be willing to use nuclear weapons. In a war alert, the chain of nuclear command devolves from the politician to the officer in the field. Frequently in the case of so-called tactical nuclear weapons, this means soldiers below the rank of major; in the case of submarines, it means the submarine commander. There are two reasons for this devolution of command. Firstly, communications systems, based for example on vulnerable satellite and radio facilities, cannot be relied upon to convey commands to the field. Secondly because of the speed with which a nuclear strike can be delivered, there is not time to relay orders down the hierarchy of command. A further worrisome technological development is that of "launch on warning". This is a virtually automatic launch condition where once incoming missiles are detected a computer may give the order to fire. Thus, in time of a world crisis, which is bound to arise sooner or later, politicians may make the decision in principle that nuclear weapons may be used if necessary. The actual decision whether or not to use them will then have to be taken by military personnel in the field; personnel who are willing to use them and who believe that the opponent will use them. The entire history of warfare is riddled with errors of judgment and mistaken decisions made under stress. What is unique about the present situation is that decisions will have to be made within minutes which, if wrong, could escalate a nuclear exchange and destroy us all.

The USSR has sought agreement upon a treaty of no first use nuclear weapons. It was noted with dismay that NATO finds itself unable to agree to such a commitment. Further, the overall problem has been aggravated by the NATO strategy of "flexible response" first adumbrated in 1967. "Flexible response" allows for three options:
1. direct defence with conventional weapons;
2. escalation to first use of tactical nuclear weapons employed in a

selected and relatively limited geographical area (e.g. Europe);
3. general nuclear war of strategic nuclear exchange between the homelands of the United States and the USSR.

The idea of a limited nuclear exchange is dangerous nonsense. Professor Pentz represented that if we cannot avoid the start of a nuclear exchange then we have little hope of stopping or limiting one that has started. More to the point, however, the uncertainty inherent in NATO's declared policy to use nuclear weapons first, wholly undermines the balance of power. One argument in support of "flexible response" is that, because the USSR do not know at what point NATO would introduce nuclear weapons into a conflict, they would be less likely to risk any conflict at all. On the contrary, evidence suggested that it provides an inducement for the USSR to use nuclear weapons themselves. The Soviet witness, Professor Vlasikhin in cross-examination was adamant that the USSR would only use nuclear weapons if attacked with nuclear weapons. Other witnesses considered this to be an optimistic position on his part.

The USSR is faced with large numbers of missiles of phenomenal speed and accuracy. They can "decapitate" Soviet command positions and structures and destroy Soviet missile sites within minutes of launch. If the USSR does not launch its missiles before they are hit, it will have few left on land to launch. The difficulty facing the USSR is that there are no reliable radar systems for determining with absolute certainty whether one is under attack. Certainly no system can decide if NATO is about to attack. It follows, therefore, that in a war crisis, the USSR has to decide within minutes what NATO is about to do or is actually doing. In the face of NATO's commitment to first use, some witnesses did not accept Professor Vlasikhin's view that the USSR would wait and see — it cannot afford to. Similarly, Western Europe is faced with the nuclear weapons deployed by the Soviet Union.

The development of the strategic defence initiative (SDI) as a further dangerous ingredient in the overall equation. Robert Aldridge in his written paper described SDI as consisting of layered defence systems of interceptor missiles, electromagnetic guns, high energy lasers of various types, neutral particle beams and sensor systems. The claim underlying the development of SDI is that it could lead to an invulnerable defensive shield. If one side or the other were able to develop such a shield, it follows that they could start and finish a nuclear war with no fear of retaliation. The Tribunal however, does not accept the ability of either side to achieve such invulnerability in its defences. A more likely consequence is that such a system would simply reduce the number of missiles reaching their target. The obvious and regrettable response to this is that one's opponent is likely to increase the number of missiles deployed. One aspect of SDI that is, perhaps, achievable is its anti-satellite capability. This again reduces the ability to manage a war crisis and reinforce the need to devolve command to an even lower level, thereby increasing instability.

4.2 Deterrence and the Evolution of Technology

The problem with the deterrent system as it operates now is that one side seeks what it perceives as a significant strategic superiority in nuclear weapons systems because they don't feel safe until they are superior. The other side then reacts to this and seeks parity by taking counter measures. This reciprocal process is an *unstable system*.

This instability is enhanced by the data which each superpower gleans from the other side by surveillance activities. The interpretation which each puts upon it is a 'worst-case' one, usually the most pessimistic, since both sides are deeply suspicious of each other. This data is then used to justify further military expenditure.

This upward spiral did not surprise a number of the witnesses since the military traditionally have to prepare for the possibility of war. So faced with this prospect they take on board the newest and most complex weapons which are being produced by the research and development portion of the military industrial complex.

The Tribunal believe that one way out of this endless upward spiral is to move firstly towards a position of *minimum deterrence*. Even at this low level there is still risk, but this move should be part of a plan to ban nuclear weapons altogether.

The meaning, scope, objectives and effectiveness of "deterrence" are not clearly understood; that there has been no use of nuclear weapons in a war since 1945 is clear; that the non-use is due to "deterrence" is not clear. If nuclear weapons are supposed to deter war and aggression *per se*, they have clearly failed on a massive scale, on the simple fact that since 1945 *millions* of people have died as a direct consequence of war and armed conflict. Many of these *millions* have died by weapons used or supplied by the nuclear powers. All the nuclear powers have been involved in international armed conflict which was not prevented by the possession of nuclear weapons. *Millions* more have died in circumstances which could have been relieved by a small proportion of the resources which have been devoted to weapons of mass destruction. Therefore it is not clear at all what is being deterred or defended by the possession and deployment of nuclear weapons. As an instrument of national policy to prevent war and armed conflict, nuclear weapons have failed profoundly in the face of the fact of more deaths during the nuclear age due to armed conflict than deaths during the mainly conventional World War II.

4.3 Change of Governmental Policies

The rapid evolution of mass-destruction technology has been closely linked with Government policies. The stages in the evolution of the corresponding US policies have been summarised by Professor Boyle thus: "The United States government has experienced at least seven basic changes in the fundamental rationale underlying its official policy for the use and threat of nuclear weapons:

1. the Truman administration's utilitarian justification for the decision to drop the atomic bombs on Hiroshima and Nagasaki;
2. the Eisenhower administration's doctrine of "massive retaliation"
3. the Kennedy administration's doctrine of "mutually assured destruction" (MAD);
4. the Johnson administration's doctrine of "flexible response" for NATO;
5. the Nixon administration and its so-called "countervailing" strategy known as the Schlesinger doctrine;
6. the Carter administration's presidential Directive 59, that naively contemplated the possibility of America "fighting" a "limited" nuclear war; and,
7. under the Reagan administration, Secretary of Defence Casper Weinberger's 1982 Five-Year Defence Guidance Statement, that boldly proclaimed the incomprehensible objective of America "prevailing" in a "protracted" nuclear war.

The policy of MAD was gradually dropped as both NATO and WPO began to explore the possibilities of flexible response, which is the use of smaller quantities of nuclear weapons possibly stopping short of complete annihilation. This strategy was made conceivable by the existence of a complete range of nuclear weapons from low to high yield and of short to intercontinental range.

In the U.S. the Rand Corporation studied the legal implications of nuclear weapons. They concluded in 1981 that the U.S. *could not use nuclear weapons pursuant to MAD and be consistent with international law*. Its second conclusion was that one can use nuclear weapons in a more limited setting because of development in technology, targeting and weaponry sophistication.

This second RAND Report conclusion was strongly disputed by a number of witnesses who did not believe that these weapons can be used in a limited context, except in the most unlikely circumstances.

The Tribunal believe that once there has been a nuclear exchange, there are no reliable mechanisms to stop either side from increasing the number of missiles fired. In the escalating chaos of communications following even "limited" nuclear use and the escalation of crisis perceptions, use by mis-perception becomes highly likely.

Professor Meyrowitz stated that it may be theoretically possible to have such a limited war but in reality, the U.S. strategic doctrines do not envisage an isolated use, but a graduated increase. This he supported by quotations from General Rogers (Commander of NATO forces), General Jones (former Chairman of the joint Chiefs of Staff) and Robert Macnamara (former U.S. Defence Secretary).

Evidence was heard that the military had never liked MAD as a strategy since it negated the function of the military, viz to defend one's country. Under the policy they would neither defend nor defeat the opposition — their sole choice was between either holocaust or humiliation. It allowed the opposition to choose the time, place and manner of the attack.

The Tribunal believes that the U.S. feels the more precise a weapon is, the more usable it is, by reason of its controllability. The development of such weapons is against any principle of deterrence for which very accurate weapons are not needed, rather just ones capable of inflicting vast amounts of damage (and see Legge, 1983).

By reason of this it is possible and probable that the Soviets conclude that the U.S. intends to start and win any nuclear confrontation. The U.S. have a similar perception of the USSR.

The Tribunal sees that there are many seemingly good reasons for striking first. Taking the initiative is a military priority as one does not want to leave everything in the hands of the state which is an enemy. If one could make a sufficiently effective first strike, by which one reduces the retaliatory capability of ones adversary to an acceptable level, this would make a first strike an option.

Professor Pentz gave a detailed and disturbing analysis of the new generation of nuclear weapons such as Pershing II, MX, Cruise and Trident: these weapons could be directed against Soviet missiles silos which are 'hardened', heavily built, protected and thus able to withstand all but direct hits.

Also targeted are the Command and Control Centres, which are the military nervous system. As mentioned earlier, such targeting is called 'Decapitation'.

For these purposes Pershing II missiles based in West Germany are ideal and seen as offensive by the U.S.S.R. They are extremely fast and accurate, delivery time being 6—10 minutes from launch. This leaves very little time to react and they are thus seen as a considerable threat.

Philip Webber presented the book *Crisis Over Cruise* (Webber et al., 1983) as part of his evidence, in which is stated "Over three hundred SS-20s have now been deployed of which two thirds are targeted on Western Europe, and the remaining on China. They each carry three independently targeted warheads, and in total the force comprises enough warheads to strike at about 1000 separate targets within Europe or continental Asia. This force is far greater than that needed for deterrence against China and the European countries of NATO; it is also quite separate from the long—range intercontinental force targeted on the USA".

The accuracies attributed to the latest generations of weapons are between 5 and 10 times greater than those of the preceding generation of missiles. These missiles can be expected to land at most 120 metres from their designated target[2].

There is very little available information on the reliability of weapons, but in the past year there have been a number of well publicized failures of U.S. rockets and missiles.

It was stated that the purpose of improving the accuracy of delivery systems and numbers of independently targeted warheads has been to enable 'surgical strikes' against military targets to be carried out with greatly reduced 'collateral damage'. These promises have unfortunately not been borne out as there is now a trend to increase numbers, accuracy and yield even further.

The Tribunal's conclusion on first-strike capabilities is that at present the missiles deployed by both superpowers are too inaccurate and

---

2 editorial note: since the evidence before the Tribunal, the US and USSR have concluded the INF.Treaty 1987 *Treaty between the United States of America and the Union of Soviet Socialist Republics on the Elimination of their Intermediate-Range and Short-Range Missiles*, 8th December 1987.

unreliable to offer either side a credible first strike. This of course does not take into account the invulnerable submarine force and bombers, which make such a first strike even less credible and as such not a rational strategy.

The very rapid technological change resulting in greater accuracy, and the new weapons becoming operational, have far-reaching consequences for peace.

When both the U.S. and U.S.S.R. were prepared only for second strike retaliation, there was no danger that either side would intentionally strike first. The weapons were not accurate enough and thus a more stable condition existed at times of high international tension.

Today with the U.S. leading the technological advance towards a perceived first strike, it could conceivably motivate the Soviets to fire first, because of the fear that they would not be able to fire second. So advancing technology may provoke, not prevent, such a nuclear war. General Nino Pasti in his paper presented to the Tribunal stated: "Each of the two mightiest powers is finding itself with the enemy pointing a gun at its temple. Such a psychologically untenable position would be doomed to end with one power using its nuclear arms in order to free itself from the nightmare of a first strike launched by the enemy".

Dr Dando saw this change in technology leading to problems in a somewhat different way from the other witnesses. His concern was that of crisis management. In times of peace and stability decisions are made rationally, but in wartime when people are under pressure, they do not react rationally, nor do organizations, and misunderstanding arise easily. Errors are common. This assertion has been shown to be correct in a number of studies as well as in military exercise.

These problems limit the possibility of controlling a crisis and increase the danger of the crisis escalating, even if both sides do not desire war.

When a crisis is brewing there will come a point when if one's command and control systems are under threat one must delegate authority down to battlefield level; with the British army this means as low as a major.

A problem arises with this delegation to battlefield level of decision making. The technologically advanced conventional weapons are nowadays themselves very destructive - some more destructive than small nuclear weapons. It is very difficult to tell whether some weapons are nuclear or not. One must put oneself in the shoes of the person who has authority in the field. He may not know whether the weapons being fired are nuclear or not. One bomb in particular, the 'fuel air explosive', has a very similar blast signature to that of a nuclear weapon and the question arises if its use could inadvertently trigger a nuclear response. The firing of conventional cruise or standoff missiles could also provoke a nuclear response in error.

The Tribunal found that these advanced conventional weapons seriously blur the difference between nuclear and conventional war. The nuclear-conventional 'firebreak' has been eroded by advancing technology.

A further problem caused by advancing technology is that of 'launch on warning'. This is a virtually automatic launch condition where once incoming missiles are detected a computer may give the order. There have been many malfunctions of computers which are a cause for concern.

The Tribunal accepted that the time needed to manage crises is being diminished by the new technology. The time available to make a decision is less. So more mistakes are possible, moving us towards a hair trigger alert system.

The Reagan Administration have confronted this problem and as a result have updated the hotline between the superpowers. A crisis nowadays, however started, is becoming more difficult to manage.

The Tribunal also feel that if a nuclear war has actually started, the very fact that we were not clever enough to prevent the war commencing makes it extremely unlikely that once it has started anyone would be able to control it. The doctrine of 'decapitation' also makes this all the less likely since anyone who could have stopped the war would probably have been blown up.

4.4 Strategic Defence Initiative (SDI)

Robert Aldridge in his evidence described SDI as consisting of layered defence systems of interceptor missiles, both nuclear and non-nuclear, electromagnetic guns, high energy lasers of various types, neutral subatomic particle beams and sensor systems.

These systems are not seen as defensive by the Soviets, although they are presented to the world at large as such. The Soviets feel that they may negate any concept of deterrence since they could have the ability to intercept some of the Soviet missiles launched against the U.S.

When seen in conjunction with the various other technologically advanced weapons, one could come to the conclusion that a first strike is envisaged, with the SDI systems in the background to deal with any response.

This promotes even greater instability and concern. In times of severe international crisis the Kremlin decision makers would be guided by capacities, noting any pronounced U.S. intentions and would be therefore very predisposed to nuclear retaliation or even pre–emptive first strike.

The Tribunal observes that once one side has nuclear invulnerability it also has a nuclear monopoly and can therefore start and finish a nuclear war with impunity.

Professor Pentz stated that it was unlikely that SDI would ever be effective, but if the other side believed that it was capable of doing what it was designed to do, then it would upset any progress in East-West relations and agreements. If it was marginally effective there would be nothing to stop the other side from adding to its already vast arsenal, in order to preserve a second-strike capability.

The one aspect of SDI that is likely to be achievable is an anti-satellite capability. Satellites are the eyes and ears of the superpowers, as well as being in charge of navigation and control. The stability of world peace presently relies in part upon their remaining intact and not threatened with demolition.

The Tribunal expect that, if pursued, SDI will lead the world into a period of greater instability than the one we have lived through. It may oblige the Soviets to develop such a system within three to five years.

The US legal justification for SDI is derived from a traditional application of the rules of construction to the ABM Treaty[3] and Agreed Statement D annexed to the Treaty. However any testing of nuclear devices would violate the Moscow Test Ban Treaty of 1973. Secrecy over any activities in space or installations (details of all SDI space activities and installations should be placed in the public domain via the United Nations) contravenes the Outer Space Treaty 1967, as would any actual placement of nuclear weapons in space.

4.5 Military Manuals and a Soldier's Duty

The existence of such crimes and offences and the concept of personal criminal responsibility are recognised and affirmed by paragraph 498 of the U.S. Field Manual on the Laws of Land Warfare. The Navy

---
3 *Treaty on the Limitation of Anti-Ballistic Missile Systems, Moscow* 1972.

and Airforce have similar provisions. These manuals do also assert the non-unlawfulness of using nuclear weapons which is somewhat of a paradox.

The manuals expressly provide that "conspiracy, direct incitement, and attempts to commit, as well as complicity in the commission of crimes against peace, crimes against humanity and war crimes are punishable".

The Tribunal notes a remarkable inconsistency here between training and instructions. Officers are told that they cannot rely on the defence of "superior orders" and further that under U.S. military code, one is *under an obligation to refuse to obey* unlawful orders.

The manuals also blithely ignore the de Martens Clause which obliges a state to justify the use of a new weapon under the existing norms of the Laws of War. The manuals and the de Martens Clause are therefore irreconcilable.

Examples were presented to the Tribunal in which U.S. military personnel either refused to obey orders or asked to be relieved of their command as they did not feel they could carry out their orders.

In a pastoral letter of 1982, American Roman Catholic Bishops stated: "It is never permitted to direct nuclear or conventional weapons to the indiscriminate destruction of whole cities or vast areas of the population".

This does call into question whether or not orders would be followed; some apparently would not be. The military in the U.S. is composed of 30% Catholics. Does this bring into question the reliability of Catholics – should they be relieved from positions of command? Others, who are not religious, may also refuse to obey orders as they hold international law in high esteem.

Professor Boyle has spent a good deal of time with the military and believes that they are strong supporters of the laws of war. This is mainly because the laws of war were originally designed to protect them.

There is also a large amount of pride and self-esteem among the military that they are doing a worthwhile job defending their country; "a good job done professionally". To bomb cities indiscriminately would lead them to be regarded as butchers by civilians, on the scale of a Hitler or Stalin, not the 'honourable profession of a soldier'. This has greater importance than might otherwise be perceived in the light of the Vietnam experience when some military personnel became ashamed to wear uniforms.

Professor Boyle offered the evidence that although the US Army

Field Manual has been used many times to justify the proposition that the use of nuclear weapons can be legal, in fact in terms it never states as such. He quoted the US 1956 Army Field Manual: "The use of explosive "atomic weapons", whether by air, sea, or land forces, cannot as such be regarded as violative of international law in the absence of any customary rule of international law or international convention restricting their employment". He went on to point out that a close reading of this paragraph merely indicates that the use of nuclear weapons cannot be regarded as violative of international law solely because they are "atomic" as opposed to "conventional" weapons. In other words, there is no one conventional or customary rule of international law that specifically prohibits the use of "atomic" weapons by that name'. The quoted paragraph never states that the actual use of nuclear weapons would not be in violation of the international laws of humanitarian armed conflict and the laws of war. He also pointed out that even the similar statement in the US 1955 Navy Manual which made a grievous error by proclaiming "In the absence of express prohibition, the use of such weapons against enemy combatants and other military objectives is permitted", never went so far as to assert that nuclear weapons could be used lawfully against civilian population centres, as opposed to legitimate military targets. There is therefore the very interesting likelihood that most contemplated uses of nuclear weapons by US forces are illegal under their own field manuals, despite the cynical interpretation by some commentators.

4.6 Sovereignty

A number of witnesses expressed concern over the loss of sovereign power, which has been yielded by parliaments to the military; in the case of the NATO alliance, this includes loss of constitutional power and loss of sovereignty of neutrals.

Dealing with the sovereignty of neutrals, as defined previously, neutral states are concerned with (i) violation of neutrality by flying objects; (ii) the stationing of nuclear arms close to their borders; (iii) the direct threat of nuclear attack. All of these have been considered by the nuclear powers and the first two are a reality, it being unlikely that the missiles will be directed to fly around neutral territory and since bases are already stationed very close to neutral borders.

The direct threat of a nuclear attack is less probable but if one side believes that neutral territory is being used to shield offensive weapons, this becomes more of a possibility.

There has been considerable publicity and concern among neutral powers since the alleged infringement of Scandinavian national waters by a Soviet submarine. The response of their Governments was to depth charge the submarine but to no avail. The submarine was grounded on the rocks and exposed, and a great many diplomatic moves were made behind the scenes.

This sort of infringement could destroy neutral territorial rights as they came to be seen as a mere haven for such weapons and therefore become priority targets.

4.6.1 *The Loss of Constitutional Powers*

It was stated that nuclear weapons subvert the rule of law since they are represented to be entirely defence related and thus, of no concern to the public. An action was brought in the US Federal Court for an injunction on the deployment of Cruise missiles but the action was dropped as an Order could not be put into effect; it was considered by the Court as a matter purely for the US Government.

Being above the law not only subverts the rule of law, but also subverts the constitutional system of government which depends on the rule of law.

4.6.2 *Loss of Sovereignty of Members of Alliances*

It was accepted that to join in any alliance, one necessarily loses some of one's sovereignty. In joining an alliance, one is bound by rules and regulations which govern the treaty. The only way to regain control over sovereign power is to break the treaty.

Luciana Castellina was at pains to show that the NATO alliance has undermined the sovereign rights and constitutional norms, the democratic order of European Member States as well as the NATO Treaty itself.

The NATO Treaty is based upon an alliance of equal rights and the constitutions of European countries. The Italian and German constitutions do allow giving away some sovereign rights, but only to get into an alliance which recognizes completely the equality of all members.

The existence of both nuclear and non-nuclear members in NATO makes equal rights impossible. It has also been stated that the U.S. can, if there is no time to consult with allies, take the decision to launch nuclear weapons. General Pasti confirmed this and added that the use of nuclear weapons by NATO would be an exclusive American decision when European governments would have no possibility of intervention. The NATO official policy is that consultation will take place among NATO allies *only when time and circumstances permit.*

The rules of the Italian Constitution require that, before war can be declared, a measure be approved by the two Chambers and ratified by the President of the Republic.

It is also stated that the final decision on use is the preserve of those countries which possess nuclear weapons; This is a violation of both the NATO Treaty and the Constitutions mentioned.

NATO can in theory only implement measures which have been approved by national institutions according to constitutional procedures. These measures are now in fact introduced through 'simplified agreements', which do not need approval of the national institutions. Examples of such violations were given, such as in 1959 in Italy, nuclear weapons were deployed in the country without any discussion at all. In 1972, an American base in Sardinia took possession of nuclear ~missiles. No discussion took place in the Italian Parliament. It came to light that as it was a US base, not a NATO base, the Americans could do as they pleased. It was also recently discovered that Cruise missiles had been sited on the base without informing the Italian Parliament.

In Germany, chemical weapons were introduced in the 1950s without asking the German Government. It is the belief of Mr. Akamatsu that such weapons are already deployed in Japan.

In times of international crisis, American forces based in Europe will be warned of a state of alert known as Defence Condition III several hours before any other forces. Thus war could have been declared without the European forces being informed.

In Canada, an umbrella agreement was signed with the US in 1983. It was never formally approved by the Canadian Parliament and was in fact only a cabinet decision — an action contrary to the Canadian Constitution.

It was also considered most likely that there has been a similar serious loss of sovereignty and democratic processes in member states of the Warsaw Pact, due in part to the possession of nuclear weapons.

4.7 Neutrality

One of the most fundamental features, and perhaps the most profound, of the world order today is the way it is organised into sovereign states. International Law as expressed in treaties only recognises sovereign states as capable of executing and implementing treaties.

In terms of the laws of war, a neutral state is one which is not taking part in a war. Early treaties dealing with neutrality are the 1907 Hague Conventions and the 1928 Havana Convention on maritime neutrality. For example the 1907 Hague Convention V states "Article 1 - The territory of neutral powers is inviolable. Article 2 - Belligerents are forbidden to move troops or convoys of either munitions of war or supplies across the territory of a neutral power".

Convention XIII states "Belligerents are bound to respect the sovereign rights of neutral Powers and to abstain, in neutral territory or neutral waters, from any act which would if knowingly permitted by any Power, constitute a violation of neutrality".

The traditional laws of war relating to neutral powers are based in part upon a duty to respect the expression of a sovereign state to opt out of a war. The principle of sovereign equality is inherent in the United Nations Charter, and Members of the United Nations "…shall refrain in their international relations from the threat or use of force against the territorial integrity or political independence of any state, or in any other manner inconsistent with the Purposes of the United Nations".

Traditionally, when the territorial rights of a neutral power are violated, it has a right to demand reparation, which it may or may not do so, but when the rights are violated by a belligerent in wartime there is a duty to try and prevent violation and demand reparation if appropriate in order to remain impartial. It is abundantly clear that in the event of nuclear war affecting neutral powers, reparations would be ineffective, if not irrelevant.

A specific international assertion of sovereignty by nonnuclear powers wishing to be free from the effects of nuclear weapons can be found in the Latin-America Nuclear-Free Zone Treaty.

Nuclear testing as part of the development and deployment of nuclear weapons systems has dispersed radioactivity generally affecting nuclear and non-nuclear powers alike.

The nuclear weapons states are unable to discriminate between belligerents and non-belligerents in all effects of the use of nuclear weapons. It is a strange proposition indeed that states may indiscriminately destroy non-belligerents in furtherance of a nuclear weapons policy, particularly where those non-belligerents have declared their neutrality with respect to any nuclear conflict. Such a proposition in an outrageous breach of established laws and customs of war, constitutes a grave intention to y~age aggressive war, and is a crime against humanity.

In evidence was the proposition that under the present circumstances of an essentially illegal international security system by nuclear powers, neutral powers have a duty to fulfil the universal entitlement to stop the commission of crimes of State by giving a legal competence to act against such unlawfulness. As a minimum, non-nuclear states should establish and encourage widespread adherence to, a treaty based upon a formal consensus of the illegality of nuclear weapons plans, construction, testing, deployment and possible use.

It is instructive to note that United Nations General Assembly Resolution 38/68 on the Non-use of Nuclear Weapons and Prevention of Nuclear War of 15th December 1983 was passed with 141 in favour, 0 against and 6 abstentions, to the effect that the General Assembly "Recommends that the Conference on Disarmament should continue negotiation with a view to reaching early agreement and concluding effective international arrangements to assure non-nuclear weapon states against the use or threat of use of nuclear weapons, taking into account the widespread support for the conclusion of an international convention and giving consideration to any other proposals designed to secure the same objective"(SIPRI, 1984)

4.8 Unlawfulness of Possession of Nuclear Weapons

The question of whether mere possession of nuclear weapons is unlawful under international law is of great significance, and presents more complexities for jurisprudence than the use of nuclear weapons.

Professor Griffith presented a very well constructed argument for its unlawfulness, based upon the unlawfulness of use of these weapons and the Judgment of the Nuremberg Tribunal.

Nuremberg Charter Article 6(a) defines the term "crime against peace", as "the planning, preparation, initiation or waging of a war of aggression, or a war in violation of international treaties or agreements or assurances or participation in a common plan or conspiracy, for the accomplishment of any of the foregoing".

Nuremberg Charter Article 6(b) defines the term "War Crimes" to include murder, ill-treatment or deportation to slave labour or for any other purpose of civilian population of or in occupied territory, murder or ill treatment of prisoners of war or persons on the seas, killing of hostages, plunder of public or private property, wanton destruction of cities, towns or villages, or devastation not justified by military necessity.

Nuremberg Charter Article 6(c) defines the term "Crimes against Humanity" to include "murder, extermination, enslavement, deportation, and other inhumane acts committed against any civilian population..".

Article 6 also provides that leaders, organizers, instigators and accomplices participating in the formulation or execution of a common plan or conspiracy to commit crimes against peace, crimes against humanity and war crimes are responsible for all acts performed by any persons in execution of such plan.

Nuremberg Charter Article 7 demonstrates the applicability of the "act of state defence" to those who have committed such heinous crimes, by making it clear that their official position "shall not be considered as freeing them from responsibility or mitigating punishment".

Nuremberg Charter Article 8 also provides that, although an individual acted pursuant to an order of his government or of a superior that fact should not free the individual from responsibility but may be considered in mitigation of punishment if justice so requires.

Having stated the relevant Articles it is apparent that on the assumption that use of nuclear weapons is unlawful, the planning and preparation in breach of such treaties is also unlawful.

For this aspect of the question of unlawfulness, it is irrelevant whether there is or not an *intention to use* the weapons.

When one is considering the lawfulness of the possession of nuclear weapons one is not considering their abstract existence. One is considering a possession of weapons whose power, speed, accuracy, deployment and targeting taken together make it necessary for the protagonists in a potential crisis to take the nuclear initiative. In the case of the West, one is considering a declared policy to take that initiative, whether or not they are threatened with nuclear attack. The ability to manage a nuclear crisis has been reduced rather than enhanced by the development of technology. The risk of accidental or ill-judged nuclear exchange is becoming a certainty. One assesses the possession of nuclear weapons on the basis that it means possession combined with a willingness to use under certain circumstances, accidental or deliberate.

All legal systems endeavour not merely to punish crime but also to prevent it. Obviously, it is a rather ineffectual .system which can only deal with crime once its effects have been felt. Accordingly, in all criminal jurisdictions intentional preparation to commit crime is itself a crime. In common law systems, one has the example of conspiracy, incitement and attempt. A particularly pertinent example from English law is the offence of possession of an offensive weapon - it is a crime to carry with one any weapon with an intention to cause injury, whether or not the weapon is to be used only in self defence.

The laws of war are no exception. Thus, it is repeated that Article 6(a) of the Nuremberg Charter (Nuremberg, 1945) defines the term "crime against peace" as "the planning, preparation, initiation or waging of a war of aggression, or a war in violation of international treaties or agreements or assurances or participation in a common plan or conspiracy for the accomplishment of any of the foregoing". As stated above, the Article goes on to provide that leaders, organizers, instigators and accomplices participating in the preparation or execution of a common plan or conspiracy to commit crimes against peace, crimes against humanity and war crimes are responsible for all acts performed by any persons in execution of such a plan. Articles 7 and 8 exclude as legal defences claims that a state has been acting in its own defence or that an individual has been following superior orders. The point is a simple one: if the consequences of the intended actions are themselves illegal, then preparation to inflict such consequences is also illegal. Whatever their disclaimers as to the use of nuclear weapons, the nuclear weapons states are expressly and by implication planning and preparing unlawful actions - the infliction of indiscriminate destruction. The development, deployment and targeting of nuclear weapons have no other rational interpretation.

Several witnesses have dismissed the idea that nuclear weapons will never be used. Accordingly, they also dismiss any argument that what would otherwise be unlawful preparations are not so because the preparations will never in fact ,result in the use of nuclear weapons. On the contrary, they believe the exact opposite - that it is those very preparations which will inevitably lead to use.

Several witnesses also dismiss the alternative argument put forward by the nuclear weapons states based upon the right of self-defence contained in Article 51 of the United Nations Charter. In other words, that they are entitled under the Charter to use or at least to prepare to use nuclear weapons in legitimate self-defence. It is no answer under the Charter, nor under any legal system that we know of, to say that one is merely preparing to act in self- defence where the consequences of such actions are so wholly unreasonable. It is dishonest and perverse to suggest that the unlimited and indiscriminate damage which would result from a nuclear exchange can ever be described as reasonable self-defence. The proposition offends against the entire concept of reason.

The contradictions inherent in the postures of the nuclear weapon states are thrown into clear relief, for example, in the United States' manuals for military instruction (discussed in more detail elsewhere in this document). The manuals assert the lawfulness of using nuclear weapons. On the other hand, they also expressly provide " Conspiracy, direct incitement, and attempts to commit as well as complicity in the commission of crimes against peace, crimes against humanity and war crimes are punishable".

The Nuremberg Charter Articles only mention planning and preparation. If one plans, one has an intention to act under certain circumstances, and planning with nuclear weaponry and warfare in mind is far more than an abstract idea. The war plans are developed with considerable detail; they are also adopted. This involves systems being set up for the use of the weapons and they are actually used in military manoeuvres, which test the plans to ensure they actually work. This is therefore a high level of planning and must be against international law. The possibilities and dangers of accidental use of nuclear weapons also constitute an additional dimension of recklessness in the planning and deployment processes. Such recklessness would be considered unlawful under most legal jurisdictions of which the relevant witnesses were aware.

Professor Griffith stated that it makes no difference that both superpowers advance the same argument for possession, i.e. "I do not personally intend to wage a war" since the stockpile of weapons is still present. Thus it is within the ambit of the Nuremberg Articles' "planning and preparation" and thus against international law.

The intention to use nuclear weapons first was seen as a more serious intent by some witnesses. The Tribunal take the view that it is a more serious breach of the Nuremberg Articles to plan, prepare and deploy the capability for first use of nuclear weapons.

Another key question to consider is whether the resorting to nuclear weapons in the face of a conventional attack would be in itself illegal. Acts done by way of reprisals must not be excessive, are required to bear a reasonable relationship to the degree of violation, otherwise they will be punishable as war crimes.

It is a moot point whether the doctrine of reprisals may not be properly extended to cover nuclear response to large scale conventional attack, but the principles of discrimination, proportionality and so on still apply.

It can also be argued that the development and numerical increase in nuclear weaponry by the nuclear states, combined with no effective negotiations in good faith, are in breach of the 1968 Treaty on the Non-Proliferation of Nuclear Weapons, by failing to honour the undertaking to negotiate in good faith, and by at least indirectly encouraging or inducing some non-nuclear states to acquire a nuclear weapons capability.

Professor Boyle held that the question of the lawfulness of states even to possess nuclear weapons is itself a somewhat speculative and misdirected question, if not outrightly misleading. He claimed that the question may obfuscate the fact that today's acknowledged nuclear weapons states do not simply possess nuclear weapons. Rather, they have actively deployed nuclear weapons in enormous numbers and varieties by attaching them to delivery vehicles that are interconnected with sophisticated command, control communication and intelligence networks. Such nuclear weapons are ready for almost instantaneous launch upon immediate notice. Hence the only meaningful question for him concerns the legality of modern weapons systems as they are currently deployed and programmed for use. He suggested that if the nuclear weapons states had actually kept all their nuclear devices stored in warehouses where they were separated from their respective delivery vehicles, it might be pertinent to answer the question whether or not such mere possession of nuclear weapons was legal under international law. Historically mere possession has not been the case. The nuclear weapons systems maintained by all the world's nuclear weapons states, and especially by the two superpowers, are far beyond this stage of mere possession, and have been at the point of deployment and preparation for immediate use in a thermonuclear war for quite some time. He reminded the Tribunal that under the Nuremberg Principles, such planning, preparation and conspiracy to commit crimes against peace, crimes against humanity, war crimes and genocide, inter alia, constitute international crimes in their own right.

The Tribunal feels that such defensive escalation goes beyond the level of intensity or scope permitted by the rules of target discrimination and proportionality.

The Tribunal concludes that the possession of nuclear weapons and planning of a nuclear war are in breach of Articles 6 and 6(a) of the Nuremberg Charter and the actual use of a nuclear device in all but the most remote location will be in breach of Articles 6 (b) and 6 (c). An individual or organization agreeing to be part of a system which leads to the use of nuclear weapons is also in breach of the relevant Nuremberg Principles.

Following Article 8 people who obey orders may be found guilty. The Nuremberg Judgment affirms the principle that one is obliged to impede illegal action designed towards such heinous crimes, to the extent that one is able. So under such circumstances a moral choice exists whether to follow orders or not, be they civilian or military.

Indeed the likely consequences of nuclear war are admitted in terms by the USA and USSR in the ABM Treaty (and repeated in the Treaty on Limitation of Strategic Offensive Arms, 1979 - unratified) where they admit "..nuclear war would have devastating consequences for all mankind". It is difficult to imagine such a blatant admission accompanied by continuing policies, developments and deployments which are such an affront to the conscience of mankind, and constitute ongoing aggravated Crimes against Humanity. It is entirely within the power of each and every nuclear power to cease such profound unlawfulness forthwith. This admission has considerable legal significance.

The General Principles of customary international law create "universality" of jurisdiction for the prosecution and punishment of those alleged to have committed heinous crimes and found guilty. All government officials and members of military forces who might order or participate in a nuclear attack upon population centres could lawfully be tried by any government of the world community that subsequently obtained control over them for the above-mentioned crimes.

The possession and deployment of nuclear weapons indicates a breach or intention to breach the Nuremberg Charter and all the customary norms of warfare.

There are additional reasons to declare the unlawfulness of possession. Mere possession and deployment under specified circumstances is already capable of being clear violations of the Antarctic Treaty 1959, the Outer Space Treaty 1967, the Nuclear-Weapons Sea-Bed and Ocean Floor Treaty 1971, and the Moon Treaty 1979. These all place restrictions on the possible theatres and regions of any possible nuclear war, and on the deployment of nuclear weapons systems. The failure to have concluded a treaty confirming the unlawfulness of possession can be considered a breach of the Non-Proliferation Treaty 1968, and the failure on the part of some nuclear powers to even start negotiations seriously is a breach of that Treaty. Possession is in clear breach of the Geneva Protocol I 1977.

The requirement to conclude a treaty prohibiting nuclear weapons (and other weapons of mass destruction) is expressed in various United Nations General Assembly Resolutions, the Non-Proliferation Treaty, reconfirmed in the Bacteriological (Biological) and Toxic Weapons Treaty 1971 which states "Determined to act with a view to achieving effective progress towards general and complete disarmament, including the prohibition and elimination of all types of weapons of mass destruction...", the Nuclear Weapons, Sea-Bed and Ocean Floor Treaty which states "..this Treaty constitutes a step towards a treaty on general and complete disarmament...", the ABM Treaty is quoted above, the Treaty on Limitation of Underground Nuclear Weapon Tests 1974 states "Declaring their intention to achieve at the earliest possible date ... nuclear disarmament .

The *Convention on Prohibitions or Restrictions on the Use of Certain Conventional Weapons which may be Deemed to be Excessively Injurious or to have Indiscriminate Effects* states:

> "*Recalling* that every State has the duty, in conformity with the Charter of the United Nations, to refrain in its international relations from the threat or use of force against the sovereignty, territorial integrity or political independence of any State, or in any other manner inconsistent with the purposes of the United Nations.
>
> *Further recalling* the general principle of the protection of the civilian population against the effects of hostilities,
>
> *Basing themselves* on the principle of international law that the right of the parties to an armed conflict to choose methods or means of warfare is not unlimited, and on the principle that prohibits the employment in armed conflicts of weapons, projectiles and material and methods of warfare of a nature to cause superfluous injury or unnecessary suffering,
>
> *Also recalling* that it is prohibited to employ methods or means of warfare which are intended, or may be expected, to cause widespread, long-term and severe damage to the natural environment,
>
> *Confirming their determination* that in cases not covered by this Convention and its annexed Protocols or by other international agreements, the civilian population and the combatants shall at all times remain under the protection and authority of the principles of international law derived from established custom, from the principles of humanity and

from the dictates of public conscience".

Finally, it is instructive to ask the question "could nuclear powers enter into a binding Treaty for the purpose of declaring the possession or use of nuclear weapons to be lawful?". If such a treaty was attempted it would undoubtedly fall foul of Article 53 of the Vienna Convention on the Law of Treaties[4] (see Section 5.1 for the relevant part of this Article).

Hence there is an irresistible conclusion that the possession, deployment and intention to use, of nuclear weapons are profoundly unlawful in existing (and probably future) international law.

---

4 *United Nations Convention on the Law of Treaties,* 1969

[this page is left blank intentionally]

Chapter 5

Public Conscience

This section discusses some of the key issues arising from the evidence presented to the Tribunal on matters of morality and the public conscience. It continues by discussing the roles of mass movements, and some forms of individual protest.

5.1 Morality and Dictates of the Public Conscience

International law is, above all, an attempt to express a set of universal moral values. It was noted in the Introduction that the de Martens clause, which invokes the "laws of humanity" and "the dictates of the public conscience " as determinants of legal principle makes it appropriate to enquire for legal relevance into questions of morality and public conscience as they touch upon war and peace.

The Geneva Gas Protocol 1925 refers to "... the general opinion of the civilised world"; the Vienna Convention on Treaties 1969 refers to " ... a peremptory norm of general international law is a norm accepted and recognized by the international community of States as a whole as a norm from which no derogation is permitted and which can be modified only by a subsequent norm of general international law having the same character"; the Bacteriological (Biological) and Toxic Weapons Treaty 1971 refers to " ... such use would be repugnant to the conscience of mankind and that no effort should be spared to minimise this risk". Therefore additional weight is given to the need for enquiry for legal relevance, into questions of peremptory norms and the conscience of mankind.

It is quite clear that governments and states, as expressed repeatedly and extensively in treaty law as well as customary law, are unable to form lawful policies or act in a moral or normative vacuum, according only to their perceived military or political expediency, with impunity. It is a legal requirement that military policies and activities are consistent with "the general opinion of the civilised world", "the conscience of mankind", and the "laws of humanity" at an absolute minimum.

It was of course completely beyond the scope of a four-day Tribunal to consider the content and meaning of all relevant statements by religious and moral bodies which can be considered as evidence of the dictates of the public conscience by virtue of widespread adherence or acceptance; the Tribunal had to be content with a section of evidence which is minute in terms of the totality of possible evidence. The Tribunal noted that most of the evidence was related to Christian moral interpretations.

One of the witnesses, Dr. Greet, commenced his evidence by quoting a British Council of Churches statement of 24th November 1980; "The doctrine of deterrence based upon the prospects of mutual assured destruction is increasingly offensive to the Christian conscience". He argued that Christian morality provides no justification for the possession and use of nuclear weapons. He presented to the Tribunal, the criteria represented in the Christian concept of a "just war".

For a war to be just, it must:

1. have been undertaken by a lawful authority;
2. have been undertaken for the vindication of an undoubted right that has certainly been infringed;
3. be a last resort, all peaceful means of settlement having failed;
4. offer the possibility of good to be achieved outweighing the evils that war would involve;
5. be waged with the reasonable hope of victory for justice;
6. be waged with the right intention;
7. use methods which are legitimate, i.e. in accordance with man's nature as a rational being, with Christian moral principles and international agreement;
8. many statements of the doctrine also include the provision that military action must not be aimed at non-combatants.

He also regretted that many wars waged by Christians have not been consistent with this doctrine. He proposed that what the Christian believes about the rights and wrongs of particular issues must be determined by sound moral ideology; that is to say by the bringing together of the facts of the situation and the morality that springs from the Christian's faith.

He argued that:

"Christian morality provides no justification for the use of nuclear weapons. But what about the possession of them? It is a basic principle of Christian morality that if it is wrong to do a particular thing, it is also wrong to intend to do it. Those who defend the concept of deterrence may say: 'It is not really our intention to use nuclear weapons; on the contrary we only possess them to ensure they are never used. It is only our intention to use them if they are first used against us'. If the use of nuclear weapons is wrong, it must be wrong in all circumstances and wrong to intend to use them even if attacked"

Monsignor Kent referred the Tribunal to the 2nd Vatican Council of the Roman Catholic Church which declared (*Gaudium et Spes* para 79):

> "As long as the danger of war remains and there is no competent and sufficiently powerful authority at the international level, governments cannot be denied the right to legitimate defense once every means of peaceful settlement has been exhausted". (Vatican, 1965)

The fundamental question is if such a right to defence includes the right to the possession or use of nuclear weapons.

In considering the Christian doctrine of a just war, Monsignor Kent represented to the Tribunal that nuclear weapons must violate several of the conditions, viz;

(i) there must be a serious hope of victory,
(ii) there must also be genuine conviction that the harm done by the war will be in proportion to the good which the war is aimed to achieve and which there is a probability of achieving,
(iii) in war itself the means used should be discriminate.

He concluded that "nuclear deterrence is an unstable and morally flawed position". On a related moral issue he brought to the attention of the Tribunal, the late President Eisenhower's description of the arms race as "theft from the world's poor".

Canon Oestreicher explained to the Tribunal that there are two theologically accepted views within the Christian moral tradition:

- pacifism
- just war

He held that under both views, nuclear weapons are morally unacceptable: "Clearly a pacifist view rules out the use of weapons of all kinds", and, "It is now almost universally accepted as part of Christian orthodoxy that by no sensible stretch of the imagination could the use of nuclear weapons fall within the definitions of a just war". In dealing with the contention that some nuclear weapons could be used in a way no more harmful than some conventional weapons, he stated that although such a contention may be true it should not blind people to the fact that not even all so-called conventional weapons are morally acceptable according to the doctrines of a just war, or, by implication, acceptable under many of the restrictions imposed by the laws of war and peace. At a personal level of responsibility he felt that the most important thing about nuclear defence is that human beings in nuclear research, industry and the armed services must be conditioned to giving their assent to preparation for and if need be waging nuclear war, i.e. conditioning human beings to commit genocide should they be ordered to do so. He drew an analogy with deterring or punishing a criminal by threatening the criminal's wife and children, and planning their deaths. He claimed that although social value systems may be worth defending, nuclear weapons are not effective in preserving any systems which they destroy. Given free choice, there is the point that populations prefer to exercise their own right to life, as evidenced by Canon Oestreicher when he stated to the Tribunal that suicide rates in tyrannies of right and left are not higher than in democracies.

He concluded by stating; "The threat to use nuclear weapons and therefore their existence as well as their use, is fundamentally immoral because it undermines the respect for creation on which the future of life together on this planet depends".

The Rev. Ohkawa described many dehumanising effects of the possession and use of nuclear weapons. The atomic bombing in Japan destroyed all normal human relations such as love, family, friendships, ties to the local community, humanity, and human dignity. In terms of the loss of humanity in the nuclear era, he put the question as:

> "Is it possible for human beings to coexist with nuclear weapons? Can justice, and the policy of nuclear arms exist side by side? I believe that trampling on human character has

been accelerated with the politics that gives top priority to nuclear weapons, that it is a mental assault on human life in advance of a nuclear explosion".

He claimed a loss of human character in the nuclear era; desperation, nothingness, violence, decline in morality, spread of juvenile delinquency, mistrust of fellow humans, national discrimination, repression, famine. He stated that these are the consequences of the unlimited seeking of one's own interests, an unjustifiable policy of strength, and nuclear blackmail. He asked that these be condemned as a serious crime.

In his conclusion, Rev. Ohkawa asked for the establishment of peace with justice, which can only be established when it [justice] is based on the character and dignity of human beings.

The Venerable Sato described his personal regret at his military involvement in the early years of his adulthood. Subsequently he was ordained into the Buddhist Order. He explained to the Tribunal that:

> "Buddhism begins with suffering, we start from the position of suffering, and our task is to remove suffering. The greatest suffering to which we must address ourselves is the killing, the annihilation of mankind which is threatened by nuclear weapons. For the first of the five basic precepts of the Buddha is 'not to kill'. In the wider context of achieving peace, the method is compassion"

5.2 Mass Movements against Nuclear Weapons

Various ways of campaigning were described in evidence. Possible achievements from campaigns and solutions to this global problem of the lawlessness of nuclear states were presented. The nuclear system was compared to a doomsday machine which is out of control. Professor Pentz offered this analogy and felt the only way to prevent a disaster is by effective massive intervention of democracy: Massive Interventions of Democracy (or MID) as a way of wresting the reins of the system away from governments who seem incapable of achieving control.

In Japan for instance, there have been tribunals set up to investigate the questions which have concerned this Tribunal. There have now been over a hundred of these. They are well-organized and attract a good deal of publicity and promotion by reporters from newspapers, TV and radio.

There have also been and are still signature campaigns in Japan and other countries which take the question on to the streets and cities and hopefully make a few more people decide against the possession and use of these weapons.

Monsignor Kent condoned acting to breach minor laws to prevent the breaking of major ones in certain circumstances such as the withholding of a proportion of tax. Such actions are already taking place, (e.g. at Greenham Common). Similar action has also been taken by some U.S. bishops and nuns who entered and occupied a US Airforce base. A prosecution was not however instituted. The purpose of these actions as a measure to prevent the arms race was aptly put by Monsignor Kent: "creating the conditions of the political climate for change and showing them in a quiet, impassionate way that the policies they are adopting put them at risk as much as anybody else".

Professor Boyle, in his assessment of the Reagan administration believed that its only attempts at arms negotiations have been a direct result of the campaigning by the American and European peoples.

5.3 Individual Responsibility and Nuclear Weapons

It is clear from the evidence presented, and the explanations of the Nuremberg Charter shown in Section 4.8 that individuals directly or indirectly participating in the formulation or execution of a common plan or conspiracy to commit crimes against peace, crimes against humanity, and war crimes can be held individually responsible. In addition, individuals have under international law, an affirmative duty to dissociate themselves from any participation or collusion in illegal nuclear policies.

The Nuremberg Tribunal quite clearly addressed that question and recognized throughout the proceedings that an individual has a duty to extricate oneself from a known violation of international law, even at the expense of violating domestic law.

During the Nuremberg hearings, there was the case of a German industrialist whose companies produced equipment used in committing crimes against humanity. The Tribunal determined there was individual responsibility under principles of international law, even though the acts committed did not violate (and in fact were in furtherance of) domestic law. "It is urged that individuals holding no public offices and not representing the state, do not and should not come within the class of persons criminally responsible for a breach of international law. It is asserted that international law is a matter wholly outside the work, interest and knowledge of private individuals. The distinction is unsound. International law, as such, binds every citizen just as does ordinary municipal law... the application of international law to individuals is no novelty"[1]

Professor Boyle took this argument further and proposed, in defence of individuals who lawfully, reasonably, and peacefully challenge their own government's unlawful nuclear policies even if it involves breaches of domestic law, that had the German industrial defendants prayed for peace in a German factory producing death ovens, they would have had a valid international law defence to a criminal trespassing charge, and would have had no fear of liability as war criminals before the Nuremberg Tribunal.

It is also quite clear to the Tribunal that individuals are unable to avail themselves of a defence based upon superior orders.

5.4 Legal Challenges to Nuclear Weapons

Another method of campaigning is to challenge the legal basis of nuclear weapons. As mentioned briefly before, the case of the US bishops and nuns was dropped in the US Courts as it would have set an unhealthy precedent if the jury acquitted them. It would be dangerous to require the judiciary to question national defence policies.

Olivier Russback believed that it is very important to challenge the State in Court as did Jean Hutchinson. The mere challenge creates awareness as it is bound to be reported. Even if the people being sued have immunity, one can appeal and therefore go to the appellate court and thus increase publicity and public awareness.

In Canada an action has been brought with 1.5 million people as plaintiffs against the Canadian Government for an injunction on the flying of a Cruise missile.

An action was started in the US for injuries concerning the possession and use of nuclear weapons. This action was stopped, it being impossible to force governments to stop deployment of Cruise and Pershing II missiles.

Even though one knows the probable outcome, the Tribunal believe that it is important for the wearing down process to be continued since the result of an action itself is not necessarily indicative to the general

1 quoted by Professor Boyle as coming from [*The Flick Case* 6 Trials of the Major War Criminals 1192 (1952)].

public of the correctness or otherwise of the cause.

It can be said that the law must ,relate ultimately to the general moral feeling of ordinary citizens. This said, if the moral feeling of society as a whole is changing, so then must the law. If it does not, the rule of law will not be respected.

When international law and its applicability are examined, awareness increases. Professor Meyrowitz stated that "International law does not operate in a vacuum". There is also a political environment which it reflects and responds to. At the same time there is a political environment which it tries to influence.

This awareness has brought about a growing consensus among legal scholars and in the UN on the question of use. It is this that provides the greater opportunity to translate these esoteric legal conclusions into practical political reality.

Professor Boyle stated that a strategy is needed to try to bring the nuclear powers into line with the principles of law and the only way to do this is to think of the international law on a prospective basis by convincing the military and the government of the inadvisability and dangers of their policies for the whole world in relation to nuclear weapons..

5.5 Mass Movements and The Military

It was felt that although military manuals contain the laws of war and other principles which the military must be governed by, it needs to be pointed out to soldiers that to use nuclear weapons on a city would produce a crime against humanity or a crime against peace and certainly war crime and grave breaches of the Geneva Convention; as well as the fact that what they are doing today, preparation and planning amount to a conspiracy to commit the mentioned crimes as well as genocide.

There is a good foundation from which to start influencing the military. The Bishops' pastoral message to Catholics as well as the examples of people refusing to fire their missiles were discussed earlier. These inconsistencies between nuclear deterrence policies and the laws of war indicate a potential source of leverage which should be exploited

5.6 The United Nations and Nuclear Weapons

Many resolutions come before the General Assembly of the United

Nations on questions related to nuclear weapons, and as a general expression of the opinion of states, a very large majority always vote in favour of resolutions confirming the unlawfulness of nuclear weapons. Predictably the countries normally voting against are either nuclear weapons states or members of alliances with nuclear weapons. By way of example we may quote a summary of one of these Resolutions (SIPRI, 1984):

"15 December 1983:

Reaffirming the declaration that the use of nuclear weapons would be a violation of the Charter of the United Nations and a crime against humanity, contained in its resolutions 1653(XVI) of 24 November 1961, 33/71 B of 14 December 1978, 34/83 G of 11 December 1979, 35/152 D of 12 December 1980 and 36/92 I of 9 December 1981, reiterates its request to the Conference on Disarmament to commence negotiations, as a matter of priority, in order to achieve agreement on an international convention prohibiting the use or threat of use of nuclear weapons under any circumstances, taking as a basis the draft Convention annexed to this Resolution.".

[this page is left blank intentionally]

Chapter 6

Value of International Law

6.1 General Evidence on Value of International Law

It is easy to decry the actions of governments as in breach of international law, but does it really matter? Does international law have any standing in the international community or is it just a series of pious statements, unenforceable and largely ignored?

International law has its roots in historical notions of a binding universal morality. Modern international law is a comparatively recent creation and while it still purports to represent the collective good sense of humanity, it has developed comprehensive and specific legal principles in the last two centuries. In the course of the Nuremberg Judgment in the trial of major war criminals, the International Military Tribunal observed: "the law of war is to be found not only in treaties, but in the customs and practices of states which gradually obtained universal recognition, and from the general principles of justice applied by jurists and practised by military courts. This law is not static, but by continual adaptation follows the needs of a changing world".

That is the theory, but what about the practice? Around 350 years ago Grotius, popularly known as the father of international law, remarked: " . . in our day, as in former times, there is no lack of men who view this branch of the law with contempt as having no reality outside of an empty name. On the lips of men quite generally is the saying..., that in the case of a King or imperial city nothing is unjust which is expedient....".

One can take a modern example of the apparent failure of international law. All of the nuclear powers are parties to the Hague Convention of 1907, which expresses one of the most basic principles of law, namely that "the right of belligerents to adopt means of injuring the enemy is not unlimited". The parties to the Convention undertook not to employ "poison or poisoned weapons", nor "arms projectiles or material calculated to cause unnecessary suffering".

The Tribunal concluded that in the aftermath of a nuclear holocaust if a tribunal similar to Nuremberg was set up, it would indeed find the use of nuclear weapons was contrary to international law. Therefore all Soviet and U.S. (and other nuclear weapons states) government officials who either launched or waged a nuclear war would be guilty of war crimes, crimes against peace and genocide at a minimum. This is cold comfort since the real purpose of international law is not to punish violations after the event but rather to prevent, forestall, or deter war, and nuclear war in particular.

Can international law fulfil its purpose in the nuclear era or as Professor Boyle feared, will government officials in nuclear powers, academics, and military establishments come to view nuclear policy as a matter of the highest National Security interest, with a kind of existence as a metaphysical entity above and beyond the domain of international law?

One witness (referred to as X) stated "Law is not morality, law is something which actually has to be observed. There must be evidence that when laws are broken, people are punished for them, or at least that there is some coherent and impressive form of disapproval of persons who break the laws".

The Tribunal noted that a number of U.N. Resolutions have been passed and yet nothing ,.has changed in military strategic directions since World War II, except breaches of international law in an increasingly pervasive way, with a build up of unlawful weaponry on a massive scale, and the planning and deployment systems to go with them.

Professor Boyle felt that those countries which have nuclear weapons are pursuing a completely lawless and thoroughly reprehensible policy; he alleged they are the law breakers, and it is up to the remainder of the international community to try and induce compliance with the rules of law.

South Africa is an example of a country with policies which the world community finds reprehensible. Other countries are banding together and imposing sanctions; still others are trying to cajole and coerce that country to change and fall in line with the wishes of the international community.

X voiced a low opinion of international law, since in his opinion it rests merely upon consent. In his view, if five states say there are no rules to govern these weapons and if some enter into signing the Geneva Protocols saying that these rules do not apply to the use of nuclear weapons then that is an end to the story.

Professor Griffith disputed this, saying "If the possession of these weapons is illegal the fact that states may come to some sort of accord, does not affect the question of the lawfulness or unlawfulness of possession".

Professor Boyle also disagreed with X on this point with special reference to UN Resolutions and protocols. Professor Boyle's argument ran thus: the military alliances are acting in a manner violative of international law; if they are opposing UN resolutions or refusing to ratify conventions, it is clear that they are opposing such in pursuit of an illegal policy in the first place; "I do not believe their negative votes are entitled to any weight at all". It is not reasonable that five states which are already in serious breach of international law, could make legal what 155 other states deem unacceptable, simply by declaring to be law what the nuclear powers find suits themselves to overcome their own unlawfulness.

An example of such a stance is the UN Resolution 1653 of 1961, which declared that any use of nuclear weapons would be a violation of the UN Charter, contrary to international law and the laws of humanity, and a crime against mankind and civilisation. The U.S., UK, and France all voted against the measure while the USSR supported it.

X also stated that the laws of war were obsolete and have been for a generation. He laid the blame for this at the feet of the UK and US for their conduct in World War II with particular reference to the policy of strategic bombing.

Evidence was presented that strategic bombing made a mockery of the Nuremberg Tribunal, since law must be applied objectively. The ambivalence was shown in that it was not declared a crime to bomb the cities, but was declared a crime not to prevent the lynching of captured pilots and civilians, and it was also a crime to leave the prisoners of your enemy where his colleagues are going to be bombing.

X admitted there had been a change in the years since Korea, of international legal consciousness but still does not feel that there has been a change in the consciousness of Western Societies concerning the inviolability of civilians in warfare. The only way he sees forward would be for governments to ratify the Geneva Protocol which would in effect tie their hands.

In the last six years there has been more debate on the subject than hitherto, as lawyers have been adopting a higher profile and a more positivist attitude towards international law. This stance must now continue its effect upon government and military strategists alike.

6.2 Interpretation of International Law

As pointed out above, interpretation of international law by nuclear states tends to be that at present no rule of international law expressly prohibits the use of nuclear weapons. It is claimed by supporters of nuclear weapons that in the absence of such express prohibition, the use of such weapons against enemy combatants and other military objectives is permitted; that this use is permissible in legitimate self-defence under Article 51 of the UN Charter and it is certainly lawful merely to threaten their use in order to deter an attack.

This interpretation of the law is based on the 'prohibitive theory' which allows any action unless it is expressly prohibited. The other possible interpretation is that of the 'permissive theory' which holds that a State is free to do only what is expressly permitted.

It is hardly a surprise that States choose to follow the prohibitive theory as it concedes an enormous degree of freedom and discretion to governments in their conduct of international relations.

Such an argument presupposes that the anarchic situation prevailing among sovereign states is what the people of the international community intended when they drafted and enacted international law.

The US position for interpreting the law is based upon a case called The Lotus, decided by the Permanent Court of International Justice in 1927 which formulated the prohibitive theory. Professor Boyle pointed out in a well constructed argument that the Lotus Rationale was never intended to have any applicability to the international law of humanitarian conflict operable during warfare. It was intended to be used during peace time.

Professor Boyle continued by saying that any attempt to apply the Lotus Rationale runs up against the de Martens clause. This clause came to the opposite opinion to the Lotus Rationale for the employment of a new weapon, that the burden of proof lies upon the State wishing to use the weapon to justify the use of the new weapon under the existing norms for the international laws of humanitarian conflict. It must also be remembered that the key points of the de Martens Clause have been used repeatedly in treaties, conventions and declarations since 1907 (and since 1927, the date of the Rationale).

One can be drawn to the burning conclusion that if nuclear weapons cannot be used in a manner that does not violate the laws of war, then they cannot be used during a war in legitimate self defence either. So the Lotus Rationale is irrelevant to the issue whether or not the threat or use is legal.

Put another way, semantically the exponents of the "prohibitive theory" explain the lawfulness of nuclear weapons by the mere attachment of the adjective "nuclear" to the noun "weapons ". Many of the properties of nuclear weapons are clearly and repeatedly prohibited in international law. Is it reasonable for an inventor of a new weapon possessing the properties of weapons already clearly and extensively prohibited in international law to evade the law by the mere attachment of an adjective and call the new weapon, say, a widget weapon? Such a proposition is clearly absurd, and may well explain why legal justifications of nuclear weapons are in a distinct minority of opinion and usually commissioned by a nuclear power.

The Hague Conventions, as Professor Arbess stated, are a quite comprehensive code whose overall purpose is to provide restraint and accountability during the conduct of a war. The Tribunal and he find it impossible to believe that the use of dum-dum bullets or one single bayonet against one single military man would be prohibited, while the law would turn a blind eye to the use of the most indiscriminate weapon man has ever conceived. He continued by saying that the restriction of the use of nuclear bombs is implied from the existing international law and there is no more reason to be limited to the grammatical interpretation of international law than there is for domestic law.

Professor Meyrowitz and Professor Griffith were both more concerned with the argument that is often used, that as the laws of war predate nuclear weapons, and therefore fail to mention them, they therefore do not apply. Professor Griffith said that this interpretation "fails to heed the multi-faceted nature of the international law-creating system and is disregarding the fact that legal rules typically are interpreted to encompass matters not specifically mentioned and often not contemplated by their formulators".

Professor Meyrowitz gave a classic example of the adaptability of U.S. law, which dealt with the horse and buggy in its application to new technology, namely the car. He also stressed that there were numerous legal principles throughout the body of law that were formulated in antiquity, adopted by precedent and the common law process over time and articulated as the changes in technology occurred.

Indeed, the whole thrust of moral opinion which also happens to be embedded in numerous treaties executed in recent years, reaffirms case after case the unacceptability of nuclear weapons and other weapons of mass destruction.

The Tribunal is inextricably drawn to the conclusion that international law did apply to the nuclear powers who were cynically interpreting and manipulating international law for their own purposes of continuing to possess, develop and deploy nuclear weapons.

6.3 General Remarks on the Evidence

After considering the evidence placed before this Tribunal, the Tribunal are compelled to come to the conclusion that the possession, deployment and use of nuclear weapons are contrary to all of the relevant principles, norms, customs and treaties in international law.

The Tribunal also conclude that there is no basis under which nuclear powers can arbitrarily exempt themselves from established international law where their nuclear policies are concerned.

The Tribunal also conclude that war preparations are undermining the maintenance of political democracy and constitutional government in the nuclear weapons states, and compromising the sovereign rights for non-nuclear states. The use of nuclear weapons as a part of national policy has failed to prevent the deaths of millions of people as a direct and indirect consequence of war and armed conflict. All the nuclear powers have been involved in armed conflicts during the nuclear age.

Such conclusions places us in considerable difficulty. It has already been pointed out that this Tribunal has been formed to fill a constitutional gap in the present international political system. Humanity as a whole is placed in very great danger precisely because the nuclear states refuse to subject themselves to the established principles of international law, and negotiations held to date do not appear to have been done so in good faith; indeed many of the arguments put by the nuclear powers to justify their possession and use of nuclear weapons display a cynical disregard for the dictates of human conscience, the laws of humanity and the usages established among civilised peoples. The fact that negotiations are proposed and conducted, even if in such bad faith, is prima facie acceptance by the nuclear powers of the inherent unacceptability of nuclear weapons. Further evidence of the inherent unacceptability of nuclear weapons is found in treaties, executed and proposed, of the nuclear age. Humanity at large is completely denied any form of redress; individuals and groups at this point in history have no forum capable of delivering and preserving inalienable human rights as against the lawless nuclear states.

It is imperative that steps be taken at all levels to establish an effective international constitution which is capable of delivering to humanity its rights and render impossible the kind of situations and conducted which led to this Tribunal in the first place.

[this page is left blank intentionally]

Chapter 7

Judgment and Recommendations

7.1 Preamble

Having considered the oral and written evidence presented during hearings and having engaged in some independent inquiry into the legal issues raised, the Tribunal have reached certain Conclusions which are embodied in this Judgment. These conclusions provide the foundation for a series of recommendations that express support for prescribed lines of action and reflect the absence of any enforcement power to assure compliance with international law on these urgent matters of nuclear weapons policy.

The conclusions as to law rest heavily on the main texts of customary and treaty international law: the 1899 and 1907 Hague Conventions on the conduct of warfare; the de Martens clause; the 1949 Geneva Conventions on humanitarian law; the two 1977 Geneva Protocols that extend the coverage of humanitarian law; the Charter of the United Nations; the Nuremberg and Tokyo judgments and the Nuremberg Principles.

The classification of a weapon as either 'nuclear' or 'conventional' should be largely irrelevant to a consideration of the lawfulness of the weapon in international law; unlawfulness will turn upon the effects of the weapon interpreted within the context of established principles of the laws of war and peace, and considerations of public morality, not upon its classification. The need to consider the lawfulness of nuclear weapons per se has arisen through a classification of weapon types into conventional and nuclear, accompanied by a cynical disregard by the nuclear powers for considerations of international law applying to 'nuclear' weapons.

7.2 Judgment of the Tribunal

The London Nuclear Warfare Tribunal was convened in London from the 3rd to the 6th of January, 1985 for the express purpose of conducting An Examination of the Legality of Nuclear Weapons. The members of the Tribunal, having considered the oral and written evidence presented during the four days of hearings, and having engaged in independent inquiry into the legal issues raised,

DECLARE THAT

1. Any reliance on the threat or first use of nuclear weapons is a violation of international law, and constitutes a Crime against Humanity as set forth in the Nuremberg Principle 6(c);
2. Strategic doctrines and official war plans that contemplate first use or first strike with nuclear weapons constitute serious violations of international law, even if postures are only preparatory and contingent, and never are consummated in the form of an actual threat or use of nuclear weapons;
3. The development, production, and deployment of nuclear weapons systems with first–strike characteristics are aggravated instances of unlawful preparations for the sake of national security, and constitute a violation of the Nuremberg prohibition on plans and conspiracies to wage aggressive war;
4. The use of nuclear weapons in a retaliatory mode, after prior armed attack and in accordance with the concept of self–defence in the United Nations Charter, is nevertheless unlawful unless such use is discriminate, proportionate, and without poisonous or cruel effects; since it seems impossible to satisfy such criteria, any use of nuclear weapons, whatever the pretext or justification, is an unlawful and criminal act of war entailing both governmental and individual responsibility;
5. As a consequence of (4), any form of deterrent threat to use nuclear weapons, even if limited to defensive and retaliatory situations, is a continuing violation of the laws of war; at minimum, overcoming deterrence with all deliberate speed is an implicit legal duty for political and military leaders representing governments of nuclear weapons states;
6. Political and military leaders of the nuclear weapons states have also failed to fulfil the legal duty imposed by the preamble of

the Limited Test Ban Treaty (1963) and Article VI of the Non-Proliferation Treaty (1968) to pursue in good faith negotiations seeking general and complete disarmament and an end to all forms of nuclear testing; the continual innovation in weapons systems, seeking maximum military advantage, has brought into being an accelerating arms race with sporadic and mainly propagandistic efforts to achieve progress toward disarmament;

7. Currently proposed extensions of the arms race to outer space, especially in the form of the Strategic Defence Initiative (SDI), constitute separate violations of International Law, and appear incompatible with such existing international treaties as the Outer Space Treaty (1967), Article 1 of the Limited Test Ban Treaty (1963), and the Anti Ballistic Missile Treaty (1972);

8. Planning and preparation for nuclear war also violate the sovereign rights of neutral states to the extent that it causes anxiety about the harmful effects of such warfare and involves the use of weapons of mass destruction whose primary and secondary lethal effects cannot be confined to the territory of belligerent states; such violations of neutral rights are dramatized by the recent experimental indications that extensive nuclear explosions could cause "a nuclear winter", with catastrophic climatic consequences for the northern hemisphere, and possibly beyond.

9. Planning and preparation for nuclear war undermine the development and maintenance of political democracy and constitutional government in the nuclear weapons states.

10. Any statement by any Government to the effect that the 1977 Geneva Protocols were not intended to have any effect on and do not regulate or prohibit the use of nuclear weapons, is ineffective for the purposes of avoiding criminal liability under international law for the possession or use of nuclear weapons by any State, and such statement does not reduce or eliminate individual criminal responsibility in international law for the citizens of such or other states.

On the basis of these conclusions, the Tribunal underscores the following implications.

7.2.1 Implications for Governments

1. Governments are under an urgent obligation to carry out by all available means the requirements of international law as specified above, especially the governments of nuclear weapons states; above all, the United States and the Soviet Union;
2. Governments should, in particular, initiate plans for national security that do not depend on any unlawful threat or use of nuclear weapons;
3. Governments of non-nuclear weapons states have a particular obligation to their citizenry to pursue all lawful and political, means available in international society, including recourse to the International Court of Justice, to secure compliance with international law; governments that opt for a policy of permanent neutrality have special legal standing to take action against plans and preparations for nuclear war.

7.2.2 Implications for Statesmen, Policy-Makers, Strategists, Advisors, Scientists, Engineers, Military Commanders in Nuclear Weapons States and their Allies

1. Violations of laws of war by governments entail criminal responsibility for those individuals who implement such illegal public policy by their activity, even if undertaken in the line of professional duty or pursuant to superior orders;
2. Preparations for nuclear war and threats to use nuclear weapons involve the commission of international crimes, including Crimes Against Humanity in the Nuremberg sense;
3. Preparations to initiate nuclear war by surprise attack or through the deployment of first-strike weapons systems constitute Crimes Against Peace in the Nuremberg sense;
4. Depending upon the overall knowledge and role of an individual, avoidance of criminal taint can be achieved only by withdrawal from all participation, direct and indirect, in criminal and unlawful activity, as well as the discharge of an affirmative duty to secure compliance with international law by all reasonable means.

7.2.3 Implications for Dissenters, Protesters, Resisters, and Ordinary Citizens

1. Symbolic violations of domestic or civil law, if reasonably calculated to encourage compliance with international legal obligations pertaining to nuclear weapons, are examples of lawful civil disobedience, and should accordingly not be treated as punishable by courts or law enforcement officials;
2. Citizens in all stations of life have a right and duty to implement international law even as against their own government and its officials, especially when world peace is in issue as a result of unlawful preparations for general warfare; such reasoning is strengthened in the setting of possible nuclear war as only anticipatory and preventive activities are of value;
3. In the event that official institutions of law on the national and international level fail to secure compliance with international law, then citizens are encouraged to constitute tribunals that operate in a fair and responsible manner to ascertain disputed matters of law and fact.

7.3 Recommendations of the Tribunal

On the basis of this Judgment, the Tribunal believe that a series of Recommendations follow; in many instances, these recommendations are implicit in the Conclusions, but try to take some account of practical concerns, including the reality of vast arsenals of nuclear weapons and patterns of severe mistrust:

1. The main nuclear weapons states should immediately adopt a series of provisional measures to minimise the role of nuclear weapons in national security policy; these provisional measures could include declarations of no first use, a moratorium on testing, freeze on new weapons systems, affirmation of the commitment to avoid the militarization of space, and the disavowal and dismantling of weapons with first-strike characteristics;
2. The initiation of negotiations without preconditions and in good faith to bring national security policy into conformity with international law on matters of nuclear weapons policy as set forth in the Judgment;

3. The initiation of negotiations without preconditions and in good faith on specific steps to achieve the verified destruction of existing stockpiles of nuclear weapons;
4. The immediate effort to obtain a resolution within the General Assembly of the United Nations and in legal and quasi-legal bodies throughout the world to receive with approval the Judgment of this Tribunal, including its Conclusions and Recommendations;
5. The initiation of an effort to obtain an Advisory Opinion of the International Court of Justice on the status of nuclear weapons, strategic doctrines, and war plans;
6. The initiation of an effort to promote an international treaty that embodies the conclusions reached in the Judgment of this Tribunal;
7. The initiation of a massive, global educational program on the subject-matter of nuclear war and on the relevance of international law and the Nuremberg Principles to its avoidance;
8. The initiation of a massive, global effort to persuade lawyers, jurists and their professional associations to pledge their commitment to the implementation of international law and the Nuremberg Principles even in relation to their own government and its leaders;
9. The organization of educational efforts along the lines of the Tribunal's Judgment geared to the specific situation of the various sectors of society, seeking especially to assure that scientists, engineers, doctors, and chaplains will not participate directly or indirectly in preparations for nuclear war;
10. The encouragement within the sectors of various societies of a variety of forms of opposition and acts of resistance to the nuclear arms race and its manifestations, including having recourse to courts and legislatures to challenge the lawfulness of official policies;
11. The promotion of the understanding that acts of resistance reasonably responsive to unlawful policies relating to nuclear weapons should be protected under a new doctrine of "lawful civil disobedience;
12. The acceptance worldwide by professional bodies, of professional codes of conduct that state and emphasise individual and professional responsibility towards humanity when practising any profession or trade.

Chapter 8

World Court Project

8.1 LNWT Recommendation 5

As can be seen from the previous chapter setting out the Judgment and Recommendations of the London Nuclear Warfare Tribunal, the fifth Recommendation is:

> "5. The initiation of an effort to obtain an Advisory Opinion of the International Court of Justice on the status of nuclear weapons, strategic doctrines, and war plans;"

The Recommendation is silent as to who should initiate such an effort but many people took part in activities to seek such an Advisory Opinion from the ICJ. Some people were already involved in such an effort, and others were inspired or influenced by the LNWT Recommendation. That Recommendation provided a very credible aim, and formidable efforts by many people and institutions were focussed on achieving such an aim.

There was no formal link between the LNWT and what emerged as the World Court Project, but there was considerable overlap and influence, including Judges, those who presented evidence, and some who simply attended proceedings of the LNWT. There is discussion of the influences of the LNWT on the WCP, and the effect that the death of the LNWT Tribunal Chairman (Sean MacBride) had on pausing efforts to seek an ICJ Advisory Opinion (Dewes, 1998).

There had been other similar events such as: 'Tribunal Against First Strike and Mass Destructive Weapons', Nuremberg 1983, Petra Kelly and the German Green Party; Falk's trip to New Zealand as a guest of the New Zealand Foundation for Peace Studies; New Zealand canvassing for an ICJ Advisory Opinion was important. Interesting detail about the spread of pre-WCP lobbying and its significance for the ultimate success of WCP is given in Nanda and Krieger (1998).

8.2 The Birth of the World Court Project (WCP)

The World Court Project was launched to UN Missions and the media in Geneva on 14-15 May, 1992. This was part of the International Peace Bureau's 1991-2 Centenary Programme, and co-sponsored by the IPB, the International Association of Lawyers Against Nuclear Arms (IALANA) and the International Physicians for the Prevention of Nuclear War (IPPNW) (IPB, 1992). At that launch meeting were speakers who had been involved in the LNWT, or publication of the first edition of the summary of evidence and Judgment: Richard Falk, Stig Gustavsson, and Bruce Kent.

Of course, prior to the launch event in Geneva, there had been other relevant activities. For example, there was a meeting by IALANA in January 1992 focussed on '...the ICJ project...", with supplementary notes by Nick Grief for the "WCP meeting" in Amsterdam in January 1992. This followed an inaugural meeting of the IALANA General Assembly held in the Hague in September 1989, which "... SPECIFICALLY APPEALED to the Governments of all States members of the United Nations to take immediate steps towards obtaining a resolution by the United Nations Assembly under Article 96 of the United Nations Charter requesting the International Court of Justice to render an advisory opinion on the illegality of the use of nuclear weapons". This initial scope of the 'use of nuclear weapons' (September 1989) was extended to "threat and use" (after a discussion including words such as production, possessions, threat, and use) by a firm majority at the January 1992 meeting. There had also been a World Court referral Network established in 1991.

8.3 Scope of the World Court Project (WCP)

The 'Martens Clause', inserted into the preamble to the Hague Convention II of 1899 and Convention IV of 1907 (set out later in the chapter about Weeramantry's dissenting opinion) puts the laws of humanity and the dictates of the public conscience, firmly into the heart of international humanitarian law.

It is very easy to underestimate the significance of the WCP in terms of the number of organizations affected, and the number of individuals who registered their concerns about the continued possession and possible use of nuclear weapons. While the ICJ was considering the formal request for an Advisory Opinion, *millions* of concerned individuals registered their concerns with the Court. The Court records reveal the logistical difficulty of handling and storing the sheer volume of individual submissions to the Court. The Court had substantial evidence of public concern, and therefore the numbers of organizations and individuals which engaged with the Court's legal process provided the Court with direct material of legal relevance for noting some dictates of the public conscience.

There is no doubt whatsoever, that the matter of the Advisory Opinion before the ICJ inspired the engagement of *millions* of people. This must be one of the largest documented engagements of the public in a legal matter ever recorded, if indeed it does not actually hold the record.

The organizations and individuals engaged with this project came from all over the world.

The number of organizations supporting the WCP in different countries, can be summarized from the lists of those organizations in Dewes (1998), who subtitled her work about the WCP, *'the evolution and impact of an effective citizens' movement'*:

Country	Organizations	Country	Organizations	Country	Organizations
International	30	Greece	1	Panama	1
Afghanistan	1	Guatemala	1	Pakistan	2
Aotearoa/New Zealand	91	Honduras	1	Palestine	2
Argentina	3	Hungary	1	Panama	2
Australia	63	Iceland	1	Philippines	2
Austria	2	India	8	Poland	2
Bangladesh	5	Indonesia	1	Portugal	1
Belarus	1	Iraq	1	Republic of Korea	1
Belgium	6	Ireland	2	Romania	1
Bolivia	2	Israel	1	Russia	3
Brazil	2	Italy	2	Sierra Leone	1
Bulgaria	1	Jamaica	1	Spain	1
Canada	29	Japan	4	Sri Lanka	1
Chile	2	Jordan	1	Sudan	1
Colombia	2	Kazakhstan	1	Sweden	8
Costa Rica	7	Kenya	1	Switzerland	2
Cuba	2	Kuwait	1	Syria	1
Cyprus	7	Latvia	1	Tanzania	2

Country	Organizations	Country	Organizations	Country	Organizations
Czech Republic	2	Lithuania	1	Thailand	1
Denmark	3	Luxembourg	2	Trinidad and Tobago	1
Ecuador	2	Madagascar	2	Turkey	1
Egypt	1	Malaysia	1	Uganda	1
El Salvador	2	Mauritius	1	United Kingdom	15
Estonia	1	Mexico	3	United States	44
Fiji	1	Mongolia	1	Venezuela	1
Finland	5	Nepal	1	Vietnam	1
France	3	Netherlands	43	Zambia	1
Georgian Republic	1	Nicaragua	9	Zimbabwe	3
Germany	5	Nigeria	1		
Ghana	2	Norway	20	TOTAL	442

Having this number of organizations from so many countries under the WCP umbrella is a very impressive achievement — *442 in total*.

In a footnote to Judge Weeramantry's Dissenting Opinion (see later), numbers are provided to indicate at least 3,322,711 individual submissions received by the Court or stored in a warehouse in the Hague because the Court could not physically handle the whole volume.

In addition to collecting submissions by individuals, the WCP and its associated organizations were working behind the scenes to lobby representatives at the UN General Assembly to support a request for the ICJ to give an Advisory Opinion. There was also lobbying to persuade the World Health Organization to make a request to the ICJ for an Advisory Opinion also (as explained shortly, the WHO request proved abortive, but the UN General Assembly request resulted in an Advisory Opinion.

The WCP was launched in 1992, and the ICJ Advisory Opinion delivered in 1996. The time-scale for this project to have succeeded is impressive. However, given the residual equivocation in the Advisory Opinion, the work of an organization such as the WCP is not yet complete, and further work is needed.

Those who are interested in knowing much more detail about the WCP, can obtain that detail from the PhD thesis of Catherine Dewes (Dewes, 1998).

8.4 ICJ Judicial Recognition of WCP

The significance of the World Court Project was recognized explicitly by at least two of the Judges involved in the ICJ Advisory Opinion: Judge Oda mentions the WCP (Oda, 1996; p 113-4) along with two of the WCP associated international organizations. Oddly, he was using that as part of his rationale about why he felt the ICJ should decline to provide an Advisory Opinion!:

> "A statement made by an observer from the International Physicians for the Prevention of Nuclear War at the World Health Assembly in 1993 appears to shed light on what was behind the movement towards the attempt to get the International Court of Justice to render an advisory opinion on the matter in response to a request from the World Health Organization if not from the United Nations General Assembly. The observer stated that "WHO would be right to seek an opinion on the matter from the International Court of Justice".
> An observer from the World Federation of Public Health Associations informed the World Health Assembly that
>
>> "it [itself] had unanimously adopted a resolution on nuclear weapons and public health which, inter alia, urged the World Health Assembly to request an advisory opinion from the International Court of Justice on the legal status of the use of nuclear weapons, so as to remove the cloud of legal doubt under which the nuclear powers continued their involvement with such weapons, as well as to provide the legal basis for the gradual creation of a nuclear-free world".
>
> This matter is referred to in my separate opinion appended to the Court's Opinion in response to the request of the WHO (Legality of the Use by a State of Nuclear Weapons in Armed Conflict, I.C.J. Reports 1996, pp. 88-96).
>
> Another document of interest is an essay in a newsletter of the World Government of World Citizens, a part of which reads as follows:
>
>> "The threat to humanity's existence posed by nuclear weapons has encouraged humans the world over to consider new strategies for influencing their governments. One of these initiatives — the movement to 'illegalize ' nuclear weapons — may increase participation in new governing structures being created to address global problems. The World Court Project is thus taking its place in the forefront of the antinuclear movement.
>> ....
>> To crystallize a united front against nuclear weaponry, several non-governmental organizations (NGOs) . . . have established a World Court Project. These NGOs have successfully lobbied the 'non-aligned' members of the United Nations General Assembly and the U.N.'s World Health Organization (WHO) to establish, according to customary international law, the illegality of nuclear weapons." (World Citizen News, Vol. IX, No. 6, December-January 1996; emphasis added.)

> This gives the impression that the request for an advisory opinion which was made by the General Assembly in 1994 originated in ideas developed by some NGOs."

Another Judge to acknowledge the activities of the World Court Project is Judge Guillaume in his Separate Opinion (Guillaume, 1996; p 65):

> "The opinion requested by the General Assembly of the United Nations (like indeed the one requested by the World Health Assembly) originated in a campaign conducted by an association called International Association of Lawyers Against Nuclear Arms (IALANA), which in conjunction with various other groups launched in 1992 a project entitled "World Court Project" in order to obtain from the Court a proclamation of the illegality of the threat or use of nuclear weapons. These associations worked very intensively to secure the adoption of the resolutions referring the question to the Court and to induce States hostile to nuclear weapons to appear before the Court. Indeed, the Court and the judges received thousands of letters inspired by these groups, appealing both to the Members' conscience and to the public conscience."

Therefore, the influence of the WCP was certainly recognized among the ICJ Judges. It is rather troubling that they seemed to have concerns about the activities of the WCP, but did not make any reference at all to the behind-the-scenes lobbying by the nuclear weapons states!

8.5 Final Comments

It is not necessary to explore the WCP is more detail because it is not of specific *legal* relevance concerning nuclear weapons, even though it is crtically important in terms of demonstrating the potential effectiveness of civil society. Those who would like to know more about the WCP should look at the Dewes dissertation (op. cit.). Another useful source of further information is Chapter 5 "Nongovernmental Organizations (NGOs) and the World Court Project" in the book by Nanda and Krieger (1998). Further information is also available in Grief (1992 and 1993), and Motherson (1992).

Chapter 9

International Court of Justice

9.1 Advisory Opinions from the ICJ

The International Court of Justice (ICJ) is often referred to as the World Court. It is an official organ of the United Nations set up by the United Nations Charter. As such, it is regretfully not available to most people who have some kind of international dispute; individuals and 'collectivities' (companies, associations, and other similar 'legal persons') cannot bring cases before this World Court. The location of the ICJ is the Hague in the Netherlands.

The ICJ deals with only two types of cases: disputes between States; and, requests for advisory opinions from organizations (typically, organs of the UN). Because of these severe restrictions, the effect of the World Court Project must be seen as a formidable achievement - being able to muster enough pressure and support for the World Health Organization and United Nations General Assembly to make formal requests to the ICJ for Advisory Opinions in relation to nuclear weapons.

9.2 Requests for Advisory Opinions about Nuclear Weapons

There were two requests for Advisory Opinions made to the ICJ concerning nuclear weapons. Firstly, the World Health Assembly (WHA) of the World Health Organization (WHO) made a request, then the United Nations General Assembly (UNGA) made a request. The ICJ responses to the requests were delivered on the same day (8th July, 1996). The first request (that by the WHO) must be considered as abortive because the ICJ declined to provide an Advisory Opinion, whereas the UNGA request can be considered successful because the ICJ delivered an Advisory Opinion. That Advisory Opinion, which includes the majority decisions of the ICJ Judges, and the various comments and dissenting opinions of some judges, must be considered to be the best, authoritative, statement concerning the legality of the threat or use of nuclear weapons, made to date.

On 14th May 1993 the WHA of the WHO determined to request an Advisory Opinion from the ICJ:

> 'In view of the health and environmental effects, would the use of nuclear weapons by a State in war or other armed conflict be a breach of its obligations under international law including the WHO Constitution?'

The Request was received by the ICJ and registered on 3rd September 1993.

Following its procedures, the case was considered by the Court, with its decision delivered on 8th July 1996.

Basically, the Court would not give an Advisory Opinion on the question asked, because, by a majority decision of 11-3, the Court considered that it did not have jurisdiction to consider the case:

> "31. Having arrived at the view that the request for an advisory opinion submitted by the WHO does not relate to a question which arises "within the scope of [the] activities" of that Organization in accordance with Article 96, paragraph 2, of the Charter, the Court finds that an essential condition of founding its jurisdiction in the present case is absent and that it cannot, accordingly, give the opinion requested. Consequently, the Court is not called upon to examine the arguments which were laid before it with regard to the exercise of its discretionary power to give an opinion."

That was the end of the WHO request to the ICJ for an Advisory Opinion in relation nuclear weapons.

However, at the end of 1994, the General Assembly of the United Nations decided to ask the International Court of Justice for an advisory opinion:

> 'Is the threat or use of nuclear weapons in any circumstance permitted under international law?'

In the event, the Court decided that it did have jurisdiction to hear the case, and after its deliberations, delivered its Advisory Opinion, also on 8th July 1996 — the same date as it delivered its decision about the WHO request for an Advisory Opinion.

Thus, 8th July 1996 was an historic moment. The world was (and still is) faced with several nation states that not only possess nuclear weapons, but also deploy those weapons with delivery systems and control and command systems, rendering those weapons available for use at very short notice indeed.

Opinion is divided. On the one hand, there are people who consider that nuclear weapons are appropriate devices to deter others from embarking on military activities against their own state. On the other hand, many people consider nuclear weapons to be so horrific, and incapable of being used in any lawful way because of the nature of such weapons.

All states seem to be of the opinion that the world would be a better place if there were no such weapons. Indeed, even the nuclear weapons states have paid frequent lip service to the need to negotiate away such weapons, and have promised in good faith to do so. Nuclear weapons apologists come up with many bizarre and odd reasons why they want the nuclear weapons to be kept, including why they might not even be unlawful under international law. Under the present international world order, with a UN Security Council disabled from effective action by the vetoes of nuclear weapons states, the nearest possibility to a judicial decision, is an Advisory Opinion of the International Court of Justice.

This Advisory Opinion, with the points made by dissenting judges, should be deeply troubling to all who take decisions to possess and deploy nuclear weapons — *whatever their motives, they are profoundly wrong, and contributing to existential breaches of international law including international humanitarian law, putting the whole world at risk.*

The judges at the ICJ are all very eminent jurists with a vast amount of experience to call upon in their deliberations and final conclusions.

For the UNGA Advisory Opinion, there were several unanimous decisions (see 2A, 2C, 2D, 2F in the following pages). The decision to render an Advisory Opinion was not unanimous; one Judge was against — Judge Oda. By far the most contentious decision was 2E with the Judges divided equally, and it was passed only with the benefit of the President's casting vote.

Decision 2E, although given along with the rest of the Advisory Opinion in the following pages, is repeated here to focus the discussion:

> "E. By seven votes to seven, by the President's casting vote,
>
> **It follows from the above-mentioned requirements that the threat or use of nuclear weapons would generally be contrary to the rules of international law applicable in armed conflict, and in particular the principles and rules of humanitarian law;**

> However, in view of the current state of international law, and of the elements of fact at its disposal, the Court cannot conclude definitively whether the threat or use of nuclear weapons would be lawful or unlawful in an extreme circumstance of self-defence, in which the very survival of a State would be at stake;
>
> IN FAVOUR: *President* Bedjaoui; *Judges* Ranjeva, Herczegh, Shi, Fleischhauer, Vereshchetin, Ferrari Bravo;
> AGAINST: *Vice-President* Schwebel; *Judges* Oda, Guillaume, Shahabuddeen, Weeramantry, Koroma, Higgins.

This is an astonishing decision from such an august body as the ICJ. Sadly, it still leaves the door open, even if only by a little bit, to those nuclear weapons owning states who do not wish to see their world order diminished. However, keep in mind that the right to use any weapon is not unlimited. 2E effectively confirms the illegality of nuclear weapons.

There is nothing in customary or international law, any authorization of the threat or use of nuclear weapons (2A - unanimous). There is nothing in customary or international law any comprehensive and universal prohibition of the threat or use of nuclear weapons as such (2B - 11 to 3 majority).

Juxtaposing 2A and 2B highlights one key legal battleground: does anything turn on the presence or absence of a specific kind of weapon? There are many kinds of weapon for which the same observations could be made — there is no explicit authorization or prohibition — therefore any specific case arising from the use of a specific weapon would depend on the specific situation. There are some weapons for which there is specific legal regulation, such as chemical, biological, and small bullets. However, we should not be surprised that the nuclear powers who are in the UN Security Council, holding vetoes over Security Council resolutions, have fought tooth and nail to prevent any explicit prohibition of *nuclear* weapons. As with any other weapon, in a specific case of use, the full corpus of international law would be brought to bear on any decision. Sadly, we have the reality of the use of nuclear weapons on Hiroshima and Nagasaki, but the lawfulness of their use in those specific situations has never been tested, notwithstanding the war crimes trials in Nuremberg and Tokyo. Those trials were very seriously lost opportunities to test the conduct of all the parties in the Second World War — victors' justice — not a balanced look at the conduct of all parties, but an impassioned look at the behaviour of the defeated. What is utterly astonishing about the chronology of those atomic bombings on 6th and 9th August 1945, is that they came *after* the United States had signed the UN Charter on 24th June 1945. The situation is the state equivalent of cognitive dissonance — there is no need to keep any consistency between words and deeds, even if the words are in an international treaty!

UN Charter Article 2 Paragraph 4 states:

> "**Article 2**
> The Organization and its Members, in pursuit of the Purposes stated in Article 1, shall act in accordance with the following Principles
> ...
> 4. All Members shall refrain in their international relations from the threat or use of force against the territorial integrity or political independence of any state, or in any other manner inconsistent with the Purposes of the United Nations.
> ..."

and, UN Charter Article 51 states:

> "51. Nothing in the present Charter shall impair the inherent right of individual or collective self-defence if an armed attack occurs against a Member of the United Nations, until the Security Council has taken measures necessary to maintain international peace and security. Measures taken by Members in the exercise of this right of self-defence shall be immediately reported to the Security Council and shall not in any way affect the authority and responsibility of the Security Council under the present Charter to take at any time such action as it deems necessary in order to maintain or restore international peace and security."

Therefore, the ICJ decision 2C adds nothing new — of course the states are subject to the provisions of the UN Charter. It is difficult to see why the ICJ bothered to include this. However, Judge Weeramantry, in his dissenting opinion (see next chapter) considers that this part of the Advisory Opinion puts to rest any argument, particularly by nuclear weapons states, that their right to use nuclear weapons is unlimited — 2C makes it clear that any possible right to use nuclear weapons is certainly not unlimited.

It is easy to see that 2D — passed unanimously by the judges — is the decision that is by far the strongest decision that renders nuclear weapons to be unlawful. It is listed later, but repeated here to aid the flow of thought:

> "2D. A threat or use of nuclear weapons should also be compatible with the requirements of the international law applicable in armed conflict, particularly those of the principles and rules of international humanitarian law, as well as with specific obligations under treaties and other undertakings which expressly deal with nuclear weapons;"

Thus 2D explicitly applies international humanitarian law to the threat or use of nuclear weapons. As pointed out by several judges, this sets the bar so high for nuclear weapons states, that nuclear weapons would need to be changed so much, that they act effectively as conventional weapons. Indeed, this bar is so high, that it could not be reached in a case involving the weapons used on Hiroshima and Nagasaki.

2F reinforces the need for countries to be negotiating nuclear disarmament in good faith. It is allegations of failures to meet the obligation to negotiate in good faith that lie behind new cases before the ICJ at the time of bringing this book up to date (2015) — see Chapter 11.

9.3 Additional Comments by Judges

As in many judicial systems when a case can be heard by multiple judges, judgments can be unanimous, and Judges may issue their own views or even dissenting opinions.

In the case of this Advisory Opinion, five Judges issued Declarations — President Bedjaoui, Herczegh, Shi, Vereshchetin, and Ferrari Bravo; three Judges issued Separate Opinions — Guillaume, Ranjeva, and Fleischhauer; six Judges issued Dissenting Opinions — Vice-President Schwebel, Oda, Shahabuddeen, Weeramantry, Koroma, and Higgins.

From all those documents additional to the Advisory Opinion, it becomes clear that on the whole, the Judges are not happy about their Advisory Opinion. A great deal of the unhappiness is focussed around 2E (set out above, and in the following pages), but there are other issues.

There is little doubt that on its face, the Advisory Opinion appears to contain inconsistencies and equivocation.

The key issues troubling various Judges appear to be:
- the original question put to the ICJ by the General Assembly includes the expression "in any circumstance" — the gist of the Judges who voted in favour of 2E seems to me to be that the ICJ's remit can only be to state the effects of international law as they are at the moment; hence the answer in a very strict sense must be that there is neither authorization for the use of nuclear weapons *in any circumstance,* not is there prohibition of the use of nuclear weapons *in any circumstance* — but this is not a licence to the nuclear powers — there was insufficient pleading and evidence for the Court to come to an unequivocal decision

— but the overwhelming effect of international humanitarian law is against the legality of nuclear weapons;
- there is potential conflict between a State's absolute right to self-defence, and the absolute applicability of international humanitarian law - what happens if they are in direct conflict with each other in a specific real situation?

9.4 Decision to Give an Advisory Opinion

Only one Judge did not want the Court to give an Advisory Opinion. What were Judge Oda's concerns? He set out his reasons in his Dissenting Opinion (Oda, 1996).

Basically, he was concerned about a lack of precision and reasoning in the request for an Advisory Opinion, and seems to be concerned about possible political lobbying that resulted in the request(s).

Paragraph 3 of his dissenting opinion (Oda, 1996; p 110) starts: "The request was presented to the Court, not so much in order to ascertain its opinion as to seek the endorsement of an alleged legal axiom". It is not clear why there is a problem caused by people who consider it to be axiomatic that the possession and use of nuclear weapons are unlawful under international law. Many legal jurisdictions will refuse to answer hypothetical questions, but one of the foundations of the ICJ is to provide advisory opinions — in many cases, likely to be hypothetical questions. Judge Oda also seems to be concerned about political and lobbying influences behind the Requests for Advisory Opinions. The World Court Project is even mentioned explicitly (Oda, 1996; p 114), along with two of the international bodies associated with the WCP (Oda, 1996; pp 113-4).

Judge Oda's dissenting opinion goes on to present a very helpful history of motions before the UN General Assembly concerning nuclear weapons.

Other Judges hint at the possibility of the Court declining to give its Advisory Opinion. For example see the discussion by Judge Guillaume (Guillaume, 1996; p65).

9.5 Declarations by Judges

President Bedjaoui opens his declaration stating that he is not in favour of declarations and other or dissenting opinions, but that in the light of 2E, he has been moved to do so for this case.

The Court does not have a role to create international law; that responsibility lies on others.

> "8. This very important question of nuclear weapons proved alas to be an area in which the Court had to acknowledge that there is no immediate and clear answer to the question put to it. It is to be hoped that the international community will give the Court credit for having carried out its mission - even if its reply may seem unsatisfactory - and will endeavour as quickly as possible to correct the imperfections of an international law which is ultimately no more than the creation of the States themselves. The Court will at least have had the merit of pointing out these imperfections and calling upon international society to correct them." (Bedjaoui, 1996; p 47).

Those who think this is an apologist view of the law, which leaves the door open to nuclear weapons states to continue to argue they can do what they like because of the lack of express prohibition of *nuclear* weapons in legal provisions, need to read a little further:

> "...There are some who will inevitably interpret operative paragraph 2 E as contemplating the possibility of States using nuclear weapons in exceptional circumstances. For my part, and in the light of the foregoing, I feel obliged in all honesty to construe that paragraph differently, a fact which has enabled me to support the text. My reasons are set out below...11. I cannot sufficiently emphasize that the Court's inability to go beyond this statement of the situation can in no way be interpreted to mean that it is leaving the door ajar to recognition of the legality of the threat or use of nuclear weapons." (Bedjaoui, 1996; p 48)

He goes on to express that nuclear weapons are themselves an existential challenge to international humanitarian law:

> "... *By its very nature the nuclear weapon, a blind weapon, therefore has a destabilizing effect on humanitarian law, the law of discrimination which regulates discernment in the use of weapons. Nuclear weapons, the ultimate evil, destabilize humanitarian law which is the law of the lesser evil. The existence of nuclear weapons is therefore a major challenge to the very existence of humanitarian law,...*" (Bedjaoui, 1996; p 50)

Judge Herczegh does not go so far as a Dissenting Opinion, but he does feel that the Court should have taken a much stronger line with respect to the illegality of nuclear weapons:

> "... In my view, however, in the present state of international law it would have been possible to formulate in the Advisory Opinion a more specific reply to the General Assembly's request, one less burdened with uncertainty and reticence. ..The fundamental principles of international humanitarian law, rightly emphasized in the reasons of the Advisory Opinion, categorically and unequivocally prohibit the use of weapons of mass destruction, including nuclear weapons. International humanitarian

law does not recognize any exceptions to these principles...The relationship between paragraphs 2 C and 2 E of paragraph 105 of the Advisory Opinion is not entirely clear, and their respective content does not seem wholly consistent." (Herczegh, 1996; p 53)

He would also put some of the responsibility back to the UN General Assembly. Now that the UNGA has the benefit of the Advisory Opinion, it should set about strengthening relevant underlying international law:

"...One of the many tasks assigned to the General Assembly - under Article 13 of the Charter of the United Nations - is "the progressive development of international law and its codification"." (Herczegh, 1996; p 54)

Judge Shi's comments are focussed on the idea that nuclear weapons are acceptable because of their deterrent effect. He deals very firmly with that idea:

"...In my view, "nuclear deterrence" is an instrument of policy which certain nuclear-weapon States use in their relations with other States and which is said to prevent the outbreak of a massive armed conflict or war, and to maintain peace and security among nations. Undoubtedly, this practice of certain nuclear-weapon States is within the realm of international politics, not that of law. It has no legal significance from the standpoint of the formation of a customary rule prohibiting the use of nuclear weapons as such. Rather, the policy of nuclear deterrence should be an object of regulation by law, not vice versa." (Shi, 1996; p 55).

As can be seen, he makes the rather obvious point is that it is international law that should be driving the practice of the nuclear weapons states, and not their practice that is driving international law!

Judge Vereshchetin considers himself obliged to explain why he voted in favour of 2E, "which carries the implication of the indecisiveness of the Court and indirectly admits the existence of a "grey area" in the present regulation of the matter". This concern at the incompleteness, or gaps in, current international law, such that the Court could not give a categorical answer in its Advisory Opinion, is shared by other judges. His commentary is focussed on issues arising from a state of *non liquet* (it is not clear), and particularly the role of the ICJ in this case being one of providing an Advisory Opinion rather than trying to resolve an *inter partes* dispute. It is not the responsibility of the Court to 'fill in the gaps' in the present state of international law, that being the responsibility of parties with the competence to create international law. His suggested solution is nuclear disarmament accompanied by a reminder of the existing obligation by States to negotiate 'in good faith' with a view to achieving this goal. (Vereshchetin, 1996; pp 57-59).

Judge Ferrari Bravo introduces material to suggest that nuclear weapons were already illegal before the United nations was created. He is critical of the Advisory Opinion not being clearer: "... in my view that illegality nevertheless already existed and any production of nuclear weapons had, as a consequence, to be justified in the light of that stigma of illegality which could not be effaced. It is, then, to be regretted that such a conclusion is not clear from the reasoning followed by the Court — a reasoning which, on the contrary, is often difficult to read, tortuous and ultimately rather inadequate..." (Ferrari Bravo, 1996; p 61). He is concerned that several conclusions reached by the Court are not included in the operative part, therefore the reader should take account of all the reasoning of the Court, and not just paragraph 105. He alludes to likely problems between Articles 2 and 51 of the UN Charter in the event of actual nuclear exchanges because the functioning of the Security Council is likely to be determined by political issues, rather than legal: "the Security Council cannot function in the face of a major conflict as would probably be the type which is the subject of the present Advisory Opinion". He is clearly of the view that his observations about very early illegality continue:

> "...all the rules produced over the last 50 years, particularly with regard to the humanitarian law of armed conflict, are irreconcilable with the technological development of the construction of nuclear weapons..." (Ferrari Bravo, 1996; p 63).

Thus, in their Declarations, the Judges express a lot of unhappiness with the Court's Advisory Opinion, but put this down to gaps in the present international law. However, it is also clear that notwithstanding their prevarication and equivocation, they doubt that nuclear weapons could in reality be anything other than profoundly unlawful. There is no doubt that the Advisory Opinion, combined with comments in the Declarations (and, as we will see, the Opinions also provide a manifesto for States to get on with their legal obligations to negotiate in good faith and achieve nuclear disarmament, while all the international lawmakers (such as States, and the UN General Assembly) need to get on with the business of filling the current gaps in international law.

9.6 Separate Opinions by Judges

Judge Guillaume also picks up explicitly the earlier work by the World Court Project and IALANA in lobbying the UN General Assembly members to support a request for an ICJ Advisory Opinion. He acknowledges that 'thousands' of letters were received by the Judges and the Court (of course, the Court itself recognizes 'millions'). Notwithstanding his concern on this point, he does concede that none of the States appearing before the Court made any objection on the grounds of such lobbying.

Judge Guillaume raised the issue of the nature and age of some of the earlier origins of customary humanitarian law, but also conceded that no nuclear-weapon state raised this issue. The Advisory Opinion notes the consensus on this.

One theme running through Judge Guillaume's Separate Opinion is identifying situations in which the use of nuclear weapons may well be reasonable (in his view), along with rationale for his view. An example of this is:

> "Customary humanitarian law thus contains only one absolute prohibition: the prohibition of so-called "blind" weapons which are incapable of distinguishing between civilian targets and military targets. But nuclear weapons obviously do not necessarily fall into this category." (Guillaume, 1996; p. 67).

It is difficult to imagine why it is 'obvious' that nuclear weapons do not obviously fall into this category. There was no evidence before the Court of a single incident that would support this (although there were some speculative suggestions).

He does concede that "With regard to nuclear weapons of mass destruction, it is clear however that the damage which they are likely to cause is such that their use could not be envisaged except in extreme cases."

He goes on to discuss deterrence. That discussion led me to believe he is one of the key Judges more in favour of nuclear weapons than other Judges. For example, he says: "... the Court, in my view, ought to have carried its reasoning to its conclusion and explicitly recognized the legality of deterrence for defence of the vital interests of States." (Guillaume, 1996; p 69).

Judge Ranjeva is another Judge troubled by the decision 2E. He voted in favour of it, but much of his Separate Opinion is concerned with construction of the Advisory Opinion, to conclude that the second part of 2E, taken with the other elements of the Advisory Opinion, limits the unilateral exercise of self-defence.

Ultimately, his position is very clear: "The illegality of the threat or use of nuclear weapons will have been affirmed, for the first time, in the international jurisprudence inaugurated by this Advisory Opinion requested by the General Assembly of the United Nations." (Ranjeva, 1996; p 72).

Judge Fleischhauer is also troubled by 2E. His Separate Opinion is focussed primarily on the equality of the rights in international law to be free from violations of international humanitarian law, and the State right of self-defence. Like other Judges, he also requires that "For a recourse to nuclear weapons to be lawful. However, not only would the situation have to be an extreme one, but the conditions on which the lawfulness of the exercise of self-defence generally depends would also always have to be met. These conditions comprise,... that there must be proportionality....", and explaining that the proportionality principle in itself does not rule out nuclear weapons (Fleischhauer, 1996; p. 88). At the same time, he concedes that the humanitarian rules and principles apply to nuclear weapons (*ibid*, p 83).

Those Judges who have accepted that under international law, there may be some very obscure, extreme situation in which the use of nuclear weapons may be lawful, have set the bar extremely high, but those Judges who have examined the situation in greater depth, have also concluded that given the current state of nuclear weapon technology, it is impossible for States to cross that very high bar.

9.7 Dissenting Opinions by Judges

Vice-President Schwebel starts his Dissenting Opinion by drawing out the chasm between the practice of States with respect to the possession and use of nuclear weapons, and the principles of international humanitarian law; the antimony between practice and principle. That is followed by his analysis of practice, the non-proliferation treaty, security Council and general Assembly resolutions, and principle of international humanitarian law. His concern about the Request's "in any circumstances" is brought out:

> "While it is not difficult to conclude that the principles of international humanitarian law - above all, proportionality in the application of force, and discrimination between military and civilian targets - govern the use of nuclear weapons, it does not follow that the application of those

principles to the threat or use of nuclear weapons "in any circumstance" is easy." (Schwebel, 1996; p98).

He then proceeds to discuss very limited situations and extreme cases to show why the application "in any circumstance" is not easy. He has quite a long discussion about Desert Storm and the possible situations if Iraq used chemical or biological weapons of mass destruction. It is difficult to see why the Opinion was delivered as a Dissenting opinion until the end where he talks very briefly about paragraphs 2A, 2B, 2C, 2D, along with 2F being anodyne asseverations[1] of the obvious. He obviously feel that 2F should not have been included as it is not responsive to the Request for an Opinion, but it is odd that he related this primarily to Article VI of the non-proliferation treaty (*ibid*, p 107).

The Dissenting Opinion of Judge Oda has already been discussed above, as the only Judge who disagreed with the decision of the Court to accede to giving an Advisory opinion.

Judge Shahabuddeen is also troubled by the possible interpretation of equivocation in 2E and asserts that the Court should have answered the General assembly's question — one way or another. His obvious preference was for the Court to have ruled that nuclear weapons are unlawful in all circumstances. Throughout his Dissenting Opinion, he expresses the grave endangerment of mankind, civilization (and other species), and that any system of law must consider such endangerment to be unlawful.

> "The question raises the difficult issue as to whether, in the special circumstances of the use of nuclear weapons, it is possible to reconcile the imperative need of a State to defend itself with the no less imperative need to ensure that, in doing so, it does not imperil the survival of the human species. If a reconciliation is not possible, which side should give way?" (Shahabuddeen, 1996; p 153).

On the whole, he agrees with the first paragraph of 2E, but his problem is with its second paragraph. The nuclear States and others who consider that nuclear weapons such as 'tactical', battlefield, or 'clean' may be lawful are reminded that the non-proliferation treaty made no distinction between 'types' of nuclear weapons. Those who advocate a policy of 'deterrence' are unable to demonstrate how the effects of nuclear weapons would stop at the borders of warring states, let alone guarantee that effects are proportionate, discriminating, and without damage to future generations.

---

1 Solemn or emphatic declarations that sooth wounded or excited feelings?

As far as commentators who assert that the Court's Advisory Opinion, particularly the second part of 2E indicates a *non liquet*, then:

> "If international law has nothing to say on the subject of the use of nuclear weapons, this necessarily means that international law does not include a rule authorizing such use. Absent such authorization, States do not have a right to use nuclear weapons." (*ibid*, p 168).

He has a discussion of the "Lotus" case, as that is used by those in favour of a right to use nuclear weapons, but "Whichever way the issue in "Lotus" was determined, the Court's determination could be accommodated within the framework of an international society consisting of "Co-existing independent communities". Not so as regards the issue whether there is a right to use nuclear weapons." The effects of pre-existing [pre-existing before the nuclear age] law are clear:

> "the Martens Clause provided its own self-sufficient and conclusive authority for the proposition that there were already in existence principles of international law under which considerations of humanity could themselves exert legal force to govern military conduct in cases in which no relevant rule was provided by conventional law. Accordingly, it was not necessary to locate elsewhere the independent existence of such principles of international law; the source of the principles lay in the Clause itself." (*ibid*, p 186).

and from Nuremberg:

> "the rules of international law must be followed even if it results in the loss of a battle or even a war. Expediency or necessity cannot warrant their violation." (*ibid*, p 197)

The core of his concerns can be seen as "...It would, at any rate, seem curious that a World Court should consider itself compelled by the law to reach the conclusion that a State has the legal right, even in limited circumstances, to put the planet to death...", and,

> "To recall what was said at the beginning of this opinion, the great unsettled issue on which the future of the world depends is how to reconcile the imperative need of a State to defend itself with the no less imperative need to ensure that, in doing so, it does not imperil the survival of the human species. Humanitarian law, it is said, must be read as being subject to an exception which allows a State to use nuclear weapons in self defence when its survival is at stake, that is to Say, even if such use would otherwise breach that law, and this for the reason that no system of law obliges those subject to it to commit suicide. That is the argument which underlies the second part of subparagraph E of paragraph 2 of the operative paragraph of the Court's Advisory Opinion." (*ibid*, p 204).

The Dissenting Opinion of Judge Weeramantry is so clear in its view that nuclear weapons cannot be lawful in any circumstances, and with legal argument to explain that position more extensively than the Court's Advisory Opinion itself, that it has been reproduced in full in this book — and can be found in the next chapter.

Judge Koroma is another Judge troubled by 2E. His Dissenting Opinion gives his reasoning following some clear unequivocal observations:

> "This finding ... is not only unsustainable on the basis of existing international law, but, as I shall demonstrate later, is totally at variance with the weight and abundance of material presented to the Court... It is my considered opinion based on the existing law and the available evidence that the use of nuclear weapons in any circumstance would be unlawful under international law."

This is quite a damning Dissenting Opinion. Reasoning follows these early observations.

Judge Higgins is yet another Judge troubled by 2E. She places some of her reasoning on the need for a balancing between necessity and humanity with some comments about the law of suffering applying to combatants, and civilian casualties should not be 'excessive'. Her fundamental difficulty leading to her dissenting opinion is:

> "The first four of these findings [2A, 2B, 2C, 2D] are in a sense stepping stones to the heart of the matter, which is to be found in paragraph 2 E... the Court effectively pronounces a *non liquet* on the key issue on the grounds of uncertainty in the present state of the law, and of facts. 1 find this approach inconsistent." (Higgins, 1996; p 361).

It would have been interesting to see her articulation of an alternative.

9.8 Voting

The voting for the substantive parts of the Court's decisions can be summarized as:

Judge	1	2A	2B	2C	2D	2E	2F
President Bedjaoui	F	F	F	F	F	F	F
Judge Ferrari Bravo	F	F	F	F	F	F	F
Judge Fleischhauer	F	F	F	F	F	F	F
Judge Guillaume	F	F	F	F	F	A	F

Judge	1	2A	2B	2C	2D	2E	2F
Judge Herczegh	F	F	F	F	F	F	F
Judge Higgins	F	F	F	F	F	A	F
Judge Koroma	F	F	A	F	F	A	F
Judge Oda	A	F	F	F	F	A	F
Judge Ranjeva	F	F	F	F	F	F	F
Vice-President Schwebel	F	F	F	F	F	A	F
Judge Shahabuddeen	F	F	A	F	F	A	F
Judge Shi	F	F	F	F	F	F	F
Judge Vereshchetin	F	F	F	F	F	F	F
Judge Weeramantry	F	F	A	F	F	A	F

F = FOR A = AGAINST

Details of the wording of various sections can be found at the end of this chapter.

9.9 Commentary on the Advisory Opinion

The following pages reproduce that Advisory Opinion. Very regrettably, that Advisory Opinion does contain equivocations that mean the initial question is not yet fully resolved by the ICJ.

Reading the various additional statements and dissenting opinions of the judges, it becomes clear that some of the judges are acutely aware of the fundamental inadequacies of the Advisory Opinion. Although not completely expressed in terms of unanimous decisions, most are unanimous, but clearly there is an equal split over 2E. It is very unsatisfactory that this was accepted merely by the casting vote of the President, in accordance with the ICJ Statute, Article 55.

2E is absolutely critical to this Advisory Opinion. There is far more legal argument in the Dissenting Opinions than there is in the Advisory Opinion itself. In one sense, the ICJ has failed to do its job by being unable to come up with a wording for 2E that could attract a unanimous vote, or at least a substantial majority vote. Under Article 60 there is no appeal, but maybe the General Assembly should ask the Court to construe 2E.

The following pages reproduce that Advisory Opinion. However, given the equivocations, and suggestions of non liquet, the most comprehensive statement of the law may well be that of Judge Weeramantry, so his Dissenting Opinion is included in the next chapter. It is a good indication of likely judgments in the event of any nuclear weapon use.

The decision to include only one of the Dissenting Opinions was taken primarily for practical reasons and space limitations for this book. All the Declarations, Separate Opinions, and Dissenting Opinions present important perspectives and the interested reader is advised very strongly to read ALL the material associated with this Advisory Opinion. Serious thought is being given to producing a complementary volume to this book, to make all these materials available easily. For the full text of the Advisory Opinions and all the Judges' associated documents, see International Court of Justice (1998).

9.10 Other Commentaries

This book has several very specific purposes related to presenting the key steps from the London Nuclear Warfare Tribunal, through the efforts of the World Court Project, via the International Court of Justice, to current activities that are important parts of the story of trying to achieve nuclear disarmament.

This book is not a broader commentary on the legal issues related to nuclear weapons. The International Court of Justice material sets out the range of relevant issues extremely well. With the Advisory Opinion, Dissenting Opinion and ICJ Application, there is a wealth of information about all relevant issues.

There have been some interesting compilations of more academic debates about relevant legal issues, and the interested reader would benefit from reading them. For example, you could look at the book edited by de Chazournes and Sands (1999), or, Nystuen, Casey-Maslen, and, Bersagel (2014).

9.10 Preamble and Advisory Opinion - Full Text

The following 34 pages set out the full text of the Preamble and the full Advisory Opinion in relation to the Request from the United Nations General Assembly. It has been rendered into an efficient form for this book. Anyone who needs to make specific use of this is advised to obtain an official copy from the International Court of Justice (ICJ, 1996b) so full reference can be made if necesssary to the original pagination in the original Judgment.

INTERNATIONAL COURT OF JUSTICE
General List No. 95

8 July 1996

LEGALITY OF THE THREAT OR USE OF NUCLEAR WEAPONS

Jurisdiction of the Court to give the advisory opinion requested — Article 65, paragraph 1, of the Statute — Body authorized to request an opinion — Article 96, paragraphs 1 and 2, of the Charter — Activities of the General Assembly — "Legal question" — Political aspects of the question posed — Motives said to have inspired the request and political implications that the opinion might have.

Discretion of the Court as to whether or not it will give an opinion — Article 65, paragraph 1, of the Statute — Compelling reasons — Vague and abstract question — Purposes for which the opinion is sought — Possible effects of the opinion on current negotiations — Duty of the Court not to legislate.

Formulation of the question posed — English and French texts — Clear objective — Burden of proof.

Applicable law — International Covenant on Civil and Political Rights — Arbitrary deprivation of life — Convention on the Prevention and Punishment of the Crime of Genocide — Intent against a group as such — Existing norms relating to the safeguarding and protection of the environment — Environmental considerations as an element to be taken into account in the implementation of the law applicable in armed conflict — Application of most directly relevant law: law of the Charter and law applicable in armed conflict.

Unique characteristics of nuclear weapons.

Provisions of the Charter relating to the threat or use of force -Article 2, paragraph 4 — The Charter neither expressly prohibits, nor permits, the use of any specific weapon — Article 51 — Conditions of necessity and proportionality

- The notions of "threat" and "use" of force stand together — Possession of nuclear weapons, deterrence and threat.

Specific rules regulating the lawfulness or unlawfulness of the recourse to nuclear weapons as such — Absence of specific prescription authorizing the threat or use of nuclear weapons — Unlawfulness per se: treaty law — Instruments prohibiting the use of poisoned weapons — Instruments expressly prohibiting the use of certain weapons of mass destruction — Treaties concluded in order to limit the acquisition, manufacture and possession of nuclear weapons, the deployment and testing of nuclear weapons — Treaty of Tlatelolco — Treaty of Rarotonga — Declarations made by nuclear-weapon States on the occasion of the extension of the Non-Proliferation Treaty — Absence of comprehensive and universal conventional prohibition of the use or the threat of use of nuclear weapons as such — Unlawfulness per se: customary law — Consistent practice of non-utilization of nuclear weapons — Policy of deterrence — General Assembly resolutions affirming the illegality of nuclear weapons — Continuing tensions between the nascent opinio juris and the still strong adherence to the practice of deterrence.

Principles and rules of international humanitarian law — Prohibition of methods and means of warfare precluding any distinction between civilian and military targets or resulting in unnecessary suffering to combatants — Martens Clause — Principle of neutrality — Applicability of these principles and rules to nuclear weapons — Conclusions.

Right of a State to survival and right to resort to self-defence — Policy of deterrence — Reservations to undertakings given by certain nuclear-weapon States not to resort to such weapons.

Current state of international law and elements of fact available to the Court — Use of nuclear weapons in an extreme circumstance of self-defence in which the very survival of a State is at stake.

Article VI of the Non-Proliferation Treaty — Obligation to negotiate in good faith and to achieve nuclear disarmament in all its aspects.

ADVISORY OPINION

Present: *President* BEDJAOUI; *Vice-President* SCHWEBEL; *Judges* ODA, GUILLAUME, SHAHABUDDEEN, WEERAMANTRY, RANJEVA, HERCZEGH, SHI, FLEISCHHAUER, KOROMA, VERESHCHETIN, FERRARI BRAVO, HIGGINS; *Registrar* VALENCIA-OSPINA.

On the legality of the threat or use of nuclear weapons,
THE COURT, composed as above, *gives the following Advisory Opinion*:

1. The question upon which the advisory opinion of the Court has been requested is set forth in resolution 49/75 K adopted by the General Assembly of the United Nations (hereinafter called the "General Assembly") on 15 December 1994. By a letter dated 19 December 1994, received in the Registry by facsimile on 20 December 1994 and filed in the original on 6 January 1995, the Secretary-General of the United Nations officially communicated to the Registrar the decision taken by the General Assembly to submit the question to the Court for an advisory opinion. Resolution 49/75 K, the English text of which was enclosed with the letter, reads as follows:

   "*The General Assembly,*
   Conscious that the continuing existence and development of nuclear weapons pose serious risks to humanity,
   Mindful that States have an obligation under the Charter of the United Nations to refrain from the threat or use of force against the territorial integrity or political independence of any State,
   Recalling its resolutions 1653 (XVI) of 24 November 1961, 33171 B of 14 December 1978, 34/83 G of 11 December 1979, 35/152 D of 12 December 1980, 36/92 I of 9 December 1981, 45/59 B of 4 December 1990 and 46/37 D of 6 December 1991, in which it declared that the use of nuclear weapons would be a violation of the Charter and a crime against humanity,
   Welcoming the progress made on the prohibition and elimination of weapons of mass destruction, including the Convention on the Prohibition of the Development, Production and Stockpiling of Bacteriological (Biological) and Toxin Weapons and on Their Destruction[2] and the Convention on the Prohibition of the Development, Production, Stockpiling and Use of Chemical Weapons and on Their Destruction[3],
   Convinced that the complete elimination of nuclear weapons is the only guarantee against the threat of nuclear war,
   Noting the concerns expressed in the Fourth Review Conference of the Parties to the Treaty on the Non-Proliferation of Nuclear Weapons that insufficient progress had been made towards the complete elimination of nuclear weapons at the earliest possible time,
   Recalling that, convinced of the need to strengthen the rule of law in international relations, it has declared the period 1990-1999 the United Nations Decade of International Law[4],
   Noting that Article 96, paragraph 1, of the Charter empowers the General Assembly to request the International Court of Justice to give an advisory opinion on any legal question,
   Recalling the recommendation of the Secretary-General, made in his

---
[2] Resolution 2826 (XXVI), annex.
[3] See *Official Records of the General Assembly, Forty-seventh Session, Supplement No. 27* (A/47/27), appendix I
[4] Resolution 44/23.

report entitled 'An Agenda for Peace'[5], that United Nations organs that are authorized to take advantage of the advisory competence of the International Court of Justice turn to the Court more frequently for such opinions,

Welcoming resolution 46/40 of 14 May 1993 of the Assembly of the World Health Organization, in which the organization requested the International Court of Justice to give an advisory opinion on whether the use of nuclear weapons by a State in war or other armed conflict would be a breach of its obligations under international law, including the Constitution of the World Health Organization,

Decides, pursuant to Article 96, paragraph I, of the Charter of the United Nations, to request the International Court of Justice urgently to render its advisory opinion on the following question: 'Is the threat or use of nuclear weapons in any circumstance permitted under international law?"

2. Pursuant to Article 65, paragraph 2, of the Statute, the Secretary-General of the United Nations communicated to the Court a dossier of documents likely to throw light upon the question.

3. By letters dated 21 December 1994, the Registrar, pursuant to Article 66, paragraph 1, of the Statute, gave notice of the request for an advisory opinion to all States entitled to appear before the Court.

4. By an Order dated 1 February 1995 the Court decided that the States entitled to appear before it and the United Nations were likely to be able to furnish information on the question, in accordance with Article 66, paragraph 2, of the Statute. By the same Order, the Court fixed, respectively, 20 June 1995 as the time-limit within which written statements might be submitted to it on the question, and 20 September 1995 as the time-limit within which States and organizations having presented written statements might submit written comments on the other written statements in accordance with Article 66, paragraph 4, of the Statute. In the aforesaid Order, it was stated in particular that the General Assembly had requested that the advisory opinion of the Court be rendered "urgently"; reference was also made to the procedural time-limits already fixed for the request for an advisory opinion previously submitted to the Court by the World Health Organization on the question of the *Legality of the Use by a State of Nuclear Weapons in Armed Conflict*.

On 8 February 1995, the Registrar addressed to the States entitled to appear before the Court and to the United Nations the special and direct communication provided for in Article 66, paragraph 2, of the Statute.

5. Written statements were filed by the following States: Bosnia and Herzegovina, Burundi, Democratic People's Republic of Korea, Ecuador, Egypt, Finland, France, Germany, India, Ireland, Islamic Republic of Iran, Italy, Japan, Lesotho, Malaysia, Marshall Islands, Mexico, Nauru, Netherlands, New Zealand, Qatar, Russian Federation, Samoa, San Marino, Solomon Islands, Sweden, United Kingdom of Great Britain and Northern Ireland, and United States of America. In addition, written comments on those written statements were submitted by the following States: Egypt, Nauru and Solomon Islands. Upon receipt of those statements and comments, the Registrar communicated the text to all States having taken part in the written proceedings.

6. The Court decided to hold public sittings, opening on 30 October 1995, at which oral statements might be submitted to the Court by any State or organization

---

[5] A/47/277-S/24111.

117

which had been considered likely to be able to furnish information on the question before the Court. By letters dated 23 June 1995, the Registrar requested the States entitled to appear before the Court and the United Nations to inform him whether they intended to take part in the oral proceedings; it was indicated, in those letters, that the Court had decided to hear, during the same public sittings, oral statements relating to the request for an advisory opinion from the General Assembly as well as oral statements concerning the above-mentioned request for an advisory opinion laid before the Court by the World Health Organization, on the understanding that the United Nations would be entitled to speak only in regard to the request submitted by the General Assembly, and it was further specified therein that the participants in the oral proceedings which had not taken part in the written proceedings would receive the text of the statements and comments produced in the course of the latter.

7. By a letter dated 20 October 1995, the Republic of Nauru requested the Court's permission to withdraw the written comments submitted on its behalf in a document entitled "Response to submissions of other States". The Court granted the request and, by letters dated 30 October 1995, the Deputy-Registrar notified the States to which the document had been communicated, specifying that the document consequently did not form part of the record before the Court.

8. Pursuant to Article 106 of the Rules of Court, the Court decided to make the written statements and comments submitted to the Court accessible to the public, with effect from the opening of the oral proceedings.

9. In the course of public sittings held from 30 October 1995 to 15 November 1995, the Court heard oral statements in the following order by:

for the Commonwealth of Australia	Mr. Gavan Griffith, Q.C., Solicitor-General of Australia, Counsel, The Honourable Gareth Evans, Q.C., Senator, Minister for Foreign Affairs, Counsel ;
for the Arab Republic of Egypt	Mr. George Abi-Saab, Professor of International Law, Graduate Institute of International Studies, Geneva, Member of the Institute of International Law
for the French Republic	Mr. Marc Perrin de Brichambaut, Director of Legal Affairs, Ministry of Foreign Affairs, Mr. Alain Pellet, Professor of International Law, University of Paris X and Institute of Political Studies, Paris
for the Federal Republic of Germany	Mr. Hartmut Hillgenberg, Director-General of Legal Affairs, Ministry of Foreign Affairs
for Indonesia	H.E. Mr. Johannes Berchmans Soedarmanto Kadarisman, Ambassador of Indonesia to the Netherlands
for Mexico	H.E. Mr. Sergio Gonzalez Galvez, Ambassador, Under-Secretary of Foreign Relations
for the Islamic Republic of Iran	H.E. Mr. Mohammad J. Zarif, Deputy Minister, Legal and International Affairs, Ministry of Foreign Affairs

for Italy	Mr. Umberto Leanza, Professor of International Law at the Faculty of Law at the University of Rome "Tor Vergata", Head of the Diplomatic Legal Service at the Ministry of Foreign Affairs
for Japan	H.E. Mr. Takekazu Kawamura, Ambassador, Director General for Arms Control and Scientific Affairs, Ministry of Foreign Affairs, Mr. Takashi Hiraoka, Mayor of Hiroshima, Mr. Iccho Itoh, Mayor of Nagasaki
for Malaysia	H.E. Mr. Tan Sri Razali Ismail, Ambassador, Permanent Representative of Malaysia to the United Nations, Dato' Mohtar Abdullah, Attorney-General
for New Zealand	The Honourable Paul East, Q.C., Attorney-General of New Zealand, Mr. Allan Bracegirdle, Deputy Director of Legal Division of the New Zealand Ministry for Foreign Affairs and Trade
for the Philippines	H.E. Mr. Rodolfo S. Sanchez, Ambassador of the Philippines to the Netherlands, Professor Merlin N. Magallona, Dean, College of Law, University of the Philippines
for Qatar	H.E. Mr. Najeeb ibn Mohammed Al-Nauimi, Minister of Justice
for the Russian Federation	Mr. A. G. Khodakov, Director, Legal Department, Ministry of Foreign Affairs
for San Marino	Mrs. Federica Bigi, Embassy Counsellor, Official in Charge of Political Directorate, Department of Foreign Affairs
for Samoa	H.E. Mr. Neroni Slade, Ambassador and Permanent Representative of Samoa to the United Nations, Miss Laurence Boisson de Chazournes, Assistant Professor, Graduate Institute of International Studies, Geneva, Mr. Roger S. Clark, Distinguished Professor of Law, Rutgers University School of Law, Camden, New Jersey
for the Marshall Islands	The Honourable Theodore G. Kronmiller, Legal Counsel, Embassy of the Marshall Islands to the United States of America, Mrs. Lijon Eknilang, Council Member, Rongelap Atoll Local Government

for Solomon Islands	The Honourable Victor Ngele, Minister of Police and National Security, Mr. Jean Salmon, Professor of Law, Universite libre de Bruxelles, Mr. Eric David, Professor of Law, Universite libre de Bruxelles, Mr. Philippe Sands, Lecturer in Law, School of Oriental and African Studies, London University, and Legal Director, Foundation for International Environmental Law and Development, Mr. James Crawford, Whewell Professor of International Law, University of Cambridge
for Costa Rica	Mr. Carlos Vargas-Pizarro, Legal Counsel and Special Envoy of the Government of Costa Rica
for the United Kingdom of Great Britain and Northern Ireland	The Rt. Honourable Sir Nicholas Lyell, Q.C., M.P., Her Majesty's Attorney-General
for the United States of America	Mr. Conrad K. Harper, Legal Adviser, United States Department of State, Mr. Michael J. Matheson, Principal Deputy Legal Adviser, United States Department of State, Mr. John H. McNeill, Senior Deputy General Counsel, United States Department of Defense
for Zimbabwe	Mr. Jonathan Wutawunashe, Charge d'affaires a.i., Embassy of the Republic of Zimbabwe in the Netherlands

Questions were put by Members of the Court to particular participants in the oral proceedings, who replied in writing, as requested, within the prescribed time-limits; the Court having decided that the other participants could also reply to those questions on the same terms, several of them did so. Other questions put by Members of the Court were addressed, more generally, to any participant in the oral proceedings; several of them replied in writing, as requested, within the prescribed time-limits.

* * *

10. The Court must first consider whether it has the jurisdiction to give a reply to the request of the General Assembly for an advisory opinion and whether, should the answer be in the affirmative, there is any reason it should decline to exercise any such jurisdiction.
    The Court draws its competence in respect of advisory opinions from Article 65, paragraph 1, of its Statute. Under this Article, the Court

    "may give an advisory opinion on any legal question at the request of whatever body may be authorized by or in accordance with the Charter of the United Nations to make such a request".

11. For the Court to be competent to give an advisory opinion, it is thus necessary at the outset for the body requesting the opinion to be "authorized by or in accordance with the Charter of the United Nations to make such a request". The Charter

provides in Article 96, paragraph 1, that: "The General Assembly or the Security Council may request the International Court of Justice to give an advisory opinion on any legal question."

Some States which oppose the giving of an opinion by the Court argued that the General Assembly and Security Council are not entitled to ask for opinions on matters totally unrelated to their work. They suggested that, as in the case of organs and agencies acting under Article 96, paragraph 2, of the Charter, and notwithstanding the difference in wording between that provision and paragraph 1 of the same Article, the General Assembly and Security Council may ask for an advisory opinion on a legal question only within the scope of their activities.

In the view of the Court, it matters little whether this interpretation of Article 96, paragraph 1, is or is not correct; in the present case, the General Assembly has competence in any event to seise the Court. Indeed, Article 10 of the Charter has conferred upon the General Assembly a competence relating to "any questions or any matters" within the scope of the Charter. Article 11 has specifically provided it with a competence to "consider the general principles ... in the maintenance of international peace and security, including the principles governing disarmament and the regulation of armaments". Lastly, according to Article 13, the General Assembly "shall initiate studies and make recommendations for the purpose of ... encouraging the progressive development of international law and its codification".

12. The question put to the Court has a relevance to many aspects of the activities and concerns of the General Assembly including those relating to the threat or use of force in international relations, the disarmament process, and the progressive development of international law. The General Assembly has a long-standing interest in these matters and in their relation to nuclear weapons. This interest has been manifested in the annual First Committee debates, and the Assembly resolutions on nuclear weapons; in the holding of three special sessions on disarmament (1978, 1982 and 1988) by the General Assembly, and the annual meetings of the Disarmament Commission since 1978; and also in the commissioning of studies on the effects of the use of nuclear weapons. In this context, it does not matter that important recent and current activities relating to nuclear disarmament are being pursued in other fora.

Finally, Article 96, paragraph 1, of the Charter cannot be read as limiting the ability of the Assembly to request an opinion only in those circumstances in which it can take binding decisions. The fact that the Assembly's activities in the above-mentioned field have led it only to the making of recommendations thus has no bearing on the issue of whether it had the competence to put to the Court the question of which it is seised.

13. The Court must furthermore satisfy itself that the advisory opinion requested does indeed relate to a "legal question" within the meaning of its Statute and the United Nations Charter.

The Court has already had occasion to indicate that questions

"framed in terms of law and rais[ing] problems of international law .... are by their very nature susceptible of a reply based on law ... [and] appear ... to be questions of a legal character" (*Western Sahara, Advisory Opinion, I.C.J. Reports 1975*, p 18, para. 15).

The question put to the Court by the General Assembly is indeed a legal one, since the Court is asked to rule on the compatibility of the threat or use of nuclear weapons with the relevant principles and rules of international law. To do this, the Court must identify the existing principles and rules, interpret them and apply them to the threat or use of nuclear weapons, thus offering a reply to the question posed based on law.

The fact that this question also has political aspects, as, in the nature of things, is the case with so many questions which arise in international life, does not suffice to deprive it of its character as a "legal question" and to "deprive the Court of a competence expressly conferred on it by its Statute" (*Application for Review of Judgement No. 158 of the United Nations Administrative Tribunal, Advisory Opinion, I.C.J. Reports 1973*, p. 172, para. 14). Whatever its political aspects, the Court cannot refuse to admit the legal character of a question which invites it to discharge an essentially judicial task, namely, an assessment of the legality of the possible conduct of States with regard to the obligations imposed upon them by international law (cf. *Conditions of Admission of a State to Membership in the United Nations (Article 4 of Charter), Advisory Opinion, 1948, I.C.J. Reports 1947-1948*, pp. 61-62 ; *Competence of the General Assembly for the Admission of a State to the United Nations, Advisory Opinion, I.C.J.. Reports 1950*, pp. 6-7; *Certain Expenses of the United Nations (Article 17, paragraph 2, of the Charter), Advisory Opinion, I. CJ. Reports 1962*, p. 155).

Furthermore, as the Court said in the Opinion it gave in 1980 concerning the *Interpretation of the Agreement of 25 March 1951 between the WHO and Egypt* :

"Indeed, in situations in which political considerations are prominent it may be particularly necessary for an international organization to obtain an advisory opinion from the Court as to the legal principles applicable with respect to the matter under debate ..." (*I.C.J. Reports 1980*, p. 87, para. 33.)

The Court moreover considers that the political nature of the motives which may be said to have inspired the request and the political implications that the opinion given might have are of no relevance in the establishment of its jurisdiction to give such an opinion.

*

14. Article 65, paragraph 1, of the Statute provides: "The Court *may* give an advisory opinion ..." (Emphasis added.) This is more than an enabling provision. As the Court has repeatedly emphasized, the Statute leaves a discretion as to whether or not it will give an advisory opinion that has been requested of it, once it has established its competence to do so. In this context, the Court has previously noted as follows:

"The Court's Opinion is given not to the States, but to the organ which is entitled to request it; the reply of the Court, itself an 'organ of the United Nations', represents its participation in the activities of the Organization, and, in principle, should not be refused." (*Interpretation of Peace Treaties with Bulgaria, Hungary and Romania, First Phase, Advisory Opinion, I.C.J. Reports 1950, p. 71 ; see also Reservations to the Convention on the Prevention and Punishment of the Crime of Genocide, Advisory Opinion, I.C.J. Reports 1951, p. 19; Judgments of the Administrative Tribunal of the !LO upon Complaints Made against Unesco, Advisory Opinion, I.C.J. Reports 1956, p. 86; Certain Expenses of the United Nations (Article 17,para graph 2, of the Charter), Advisory Opinion, I.C.J. Reports 1962, p. 155; and Applicability of Article VI, Section 22, of the Convention on the Privileges and Immunities of the United Nations, Advisory Opinion, I.C.J. Reports 1989*, p. 189.)

The Court has constantly been mindful of its responsibilities as "the principal judicial organ of the United Nations" (Charter, Art. 92). When considering each request, it is mindful that it should not, in principle, refuse to give an advisory opinion. In accordance with the consistent jurisprudence of the Court, only "compelling reasons" could lead it to such a refusal (*Judgments of the Administrative Tribunal of the ILO upon Complaints Made against Unesco, Advisory Opinion, I.C.J. Reports 1956, p. 86; Certain Expenses of the United Nations (Article 17, paragraph 2, of the Charter), Advisory Opinion, I.C.J. Reports 1962, p. 155; Legal Consequences for States of the Continued Presence of South Africa in Namibia (South West Africa) notwithstanding Security Council Resolution 276 (1970), Advisory Opinion, I.C.J. Reports 1971, p. 27; Application for Review of Judgement No. 158 of the United Nations Administrative Tribunal, Advisory Opinion, I.C.J. Reports 1973, p. 183; Western Sahara, Advisory Opinion, I.C.J. Reports 1975, p. 21; and Applicability of Article VI, Section 22, of the Convention on the Privileges and Immunities of the United Nations, Advisory Opinion, I. C.J. Reports 1989*, p. 191). There has been no refusal, based on the discretionary power of the Court, to act upon a request for advisory opinion in the history of the present Court; in the case concerning the *Legality of the Use by a State of Nuclear Weapons in Armed Conflict*, the refusal to give the World Health Organization the advisory opinion requested by it was justified by the Court's lack of jurisdiction in that case. The Permanent Court of International Justice took the view on only one occasion that it could not reply to a question put to it, having regard to the very particular circumstances of the case, among which were that the question directly concerned an already existing dispute, one of the States parties to which was neither a party to the Statute of the Permanent Court nor a Member of the League of Nations, objected to the proceedings, and refused to take part in any way (*Status of Eastern Carelia, P.C.I.J.., Series B, No. 5*).

15. Most of the reasons adduced in these proceedings in order to persuade the Court that in the exercise of its discretionary power it should decline to render the opinion requested by General Assembly resolution 49/75 K were summarized in the following statement made by one State in the written proceedings:

    "The question presented is vague and abstract, addressing complex issues which are the subject of consideration among interested States and within other bodies of the United Nations which have an express mandate to address these matters. An opinion by the Court in regard to the question presented would provide no practical assistance to the General Assembly in carrying out its functions under the Charter. Such an opinion has the potential of undermining progress already made or being made on this sensitive subject and, therefore, is contrary to the interests of the United Nations Organization." (United States of America, Written Statement, pp. 1-2; cf. pp. 3-7, II. See also United Kingdom, Written Statement, pp. 9-20, paras. 2.23-2.45; France, Written Statement, pp. 13-20, paras. 5-9; Finland, Written Statement, pp. 1-2; Netherlands, Written Statement, pp. 3-4, paras. 6-13; Germany, Written Statement, pp. 3-6, para. 2 (b).)

    In contending that the question put to the Court is vague and abstract, some States appeared to mean by this that there exists no specific dispute on the subject-matter of the question. In order to respond to this argument, it is necessary to distinguish between requirements governing contentious procedure and those applicable to advisory opinions. The purpose of the advisory function is not to settle — at least directly — disputes between States, but to offer legal advice to the organs and institutions requesting the opinion (cf. *Interpretation of Peace Treaties with Bulgaria, Hungary and Romania, First Phase, Advisory Opinion, I.C.J. Reports 1950*, p. 71). The fact that the question put to the Court does not relate to a specific dispute should consequently not lead the Court to decline to give the opinion requested.

    Moreover, it is the clear position of the Court that to contend that it should not deal with a question couched in abstract terms is "a mere affirmation devoid of any justification", and that "the Court may give an advisory opinion on any legal question, abstract or otherwise" (*Conditions of Admission of a State to Membership in the United Nations (Article 4 of Charter), Advisory Opinion, 1948, I.C.J. Reports 1947-1948, p. 61* ; see also *Effect of Awards of Compensation Made by the United Nations Administrative Tribunal, Advisory Opinion, I.C.J. Reports 1954, p. 51;* and *Legal Consequences for States of the Continued Presence of South Africa in Namibia (South West Africa) notwithstanding Security Council Resolution 276 (1970), Advisory Opinion, I.C.J. Reports 1971*, p. 27, para. 40).

Certain States have however expressed the fear that the abstract nature of the question might lead the Court to make hypothetical or speculative declarations outside the scope of its judicial function. The Court does not consider that, in giving an advisory opinion in the present case, it would necessarily have to write "scenarios", to study various types of nuclear weapons and to evaluate highly complex and controversial technological, strategic and scientific information. The Court will simply address the issues arising in all their aspects by applying the legal rules relevant to the situation.

16. Certain States have observed that the General Assembly has not explained to the Court for what precise purposes it seeks the advisory opinion. Nevertheless, it is not for the Court itself to purport to decide whether or not an advisory opinion is needed by the Assembly for the performance of its functions. The General Assembly has the right to decide for itself on the usefulness of an opinion in the light of its own needs.

Equally, once the Assembly has asked, by adopting a resolution, for an advisory opinion on a legal question, the Court, in determining whether there are any compelling reasons for it to refuse to give such an opinion, will not have regard to the origins or to the political history of the request, or to the distribution of votes in respect of the adopted resolution.

17. It has also been submitted that a reply from the Court in this case might adversely affect disarmament negotiations and would, therefore, be contrary to the interest of the United Nations. The Court is aware that, no matter what might be its conclusions in any opinion it might give, they would have relevance for the continuing debate on the matter in the General Assembly and would present an additional element in the negotiations on the matter. Beyond that, the effect of the opinion is a matter of appreciation. The Court has heard contrary positions advanced and there are no evident criteria by which it can prefer one assessment to another. That being so, the Court cannot regard this factor as a compelling reason to decline to exercise its jurisdiction.

18. Finally, it has been contended by some States that in answering the question posed, the Court would be going beyond its judicial role and would be taking upon itself a law-making capacity. It is clear that the Court cannot legislate, and, in the circumstances of the present case, it is not called upon to do so. Rather its task is to engage in its normal judicial function of ascertaining the existence or otherwise of legal principles and rules applicable to the threat or use of nuclear weapons. The contention that the giving of an answer to the question posed would require the Court to legislate is based on a supposition that the present *corpus juris* is devoid of relevant rules in this matter. The Court could not accede to this argument; it states the existing law and does not legislate. This is so even if, in stating and applying the law, the Court necessarily has to specify its scope and sometimes note its general trend.

19. In view of what is stated above, the Court concludes that it has the authority to deliver an opinion on the question posed by the General Assembly, and that there exist no "compelling reasons" which would lead the Court to exercise its discretion not to do so.

An entirely different question is whether the Court, under the constraints placed upon it as a judicial organ, will be able to give a complete answer to the question asked of it. However, that is a different matter from a refusal to answer at all.

* * *

20. The Court must next address certain matters arising in relation to the formulation of the question put to it by the General Assembly. The English text asks: "Is the threat or use of nuclear weapons in any circumstance permitted under international law?" The French text of the question reads as follows: "Est-il permis en droit international de recourir a la menace ou a l'emploi d'armes nuclaires en toute circonstance?" It was suggested that the Court was being asked by the General Assembly whether it was permitted to have recourse to nuclear weapons in every circumstance, and it was contended that such a question would inevitably invite a simple negative answer.

The Court finds it unnecessary to pronounce on the possible divergences between the English and French texts of the question posed. Its real objective is clear: to determine the legality or illegality of the threat or use of nuclear weapons.

21. The use of the word "permitted" in the question put by the General Assembly was criticized before the Court by certain States on the ground that this implied that the threat or the use of nuclear weapons would only be permissible if authorization could be found in a treaty provision or in customary international law. Such a starting point, those States submitted, was incompatible with the very basis of international law, which rests upon the principles of sovereignty and consent; accordingly, and contrary to what was implied by use of the word "permitted", States are free to threaten or use nuclear weapons unless it can be shown that they are bound not to do so by reference to a prohibition in either treaty law or customary international law. Support for this contention was found in dicta of the Permanent Court of International Justice in the "*Lotus*" case that "restrictions upon the independence of States cannot... be presumed" and that international law leaves to States "a wide measure of discretion which is only limited in certain cases by prohibitive rules" (*P.C.I.J., Series A, No. 10*, pp. 18 and 19). Reliance was also placed on the dictum of the present Court in the case concerning *Military and Paramilitary Activities in and against Nicaragua (Nicaragua v. United States of America)* that:

> "in international law there are no rules, other than such rules as may be accepted by the State concerned, by treaty or otherwise, whereby the level of armaments of a sovereign State can be limited" (*I.C.J. Reports 1986*, p. 135, para. 269).

For other States, the invocation of these dicta in the "Lotus" case was inapposite; their status in contemporary international law and applicability in the very different circumstances of the present case were challenged. It was also contended that the above-mentioned dictum of the present Court was directed to the *possession* of armaments and was irrelevant to the threat or use of nuclear weapons.

Finally, it was suggested that, were the Court to answer the question put by the Assembly, the word "permitted" should be replaced by "prohibited".

22. The Court notes that the nuclear-weapon States appearing before it either accepted, or did not dispute, that their independence to act was indeed restricted by the principles and rules of international law, more particularly humanitarian law (see below, paragraph 86), as did the other States which took part in the proceedings.

Hence, the argument concerning the legal conclusions to be drawn from the use of the word "permitted", and the questions of burden of proof to which it was said to give rise, are without particular significance for the disposition of the issues before the Court.

* *

23. In seeking to answer the question put to it by the General Assembly, the Court must decide, after consideration of the great corpus of international law norms available to it, what might be the relevant applicable law.

*

24. Some of the proponents of the illegality of the use of nuclear weapons have argued that such use would violate the right to life as guaranteed in Article 6 of the International Covenant on Civil and Political Rights, as well as in certain regional instruments for the protection of human rights. Article 6, paragraph 1, of the International Covenant provides as follows: "Every human being has the inherent right to life. This right shall be protected by law. No one shall be arbitrarily deprived of his life."

In reply, others contended that the International Covenant on Civil and Political Rights made no mention of war or weapons, and it had never been envisaged that the legality of nuclear weapons was regulated by that instrument. It was suggested that the Covenant was directed to the protection of human rights in peacetime, but that questions relating to unlawful loss of life in hostilities were governed by the law applicable in armed conflict.

25. The Court observes that the protection of the International Covenant of Civil and Political Rights does not cease in times of war, except by operation of Article 4 of the Covenant whereby certain provisions may be derogated from in a time of national emergency. Respect for the right to life is not, however, such a provision. In principle, the right not arbitrarily to be deprived of one's life applies also in hostilities. The test of what is an arbitrary deprivation of life, however, then falls to be determined by the applicable *lex specialis*, namely, the law applicable in armed conflict which is designed to regulate the conduct of hostilities. Thus whether a particular loss of life, through the use of a certain weapon in warfare, is to be considered an arbitrary deprivation of life contrary to Article 6 of the Covenant, can only be decided by reference to the law applicable in armed conflict and not deduced from the terms of the Covenant itself.

26. Some States also contended that the prohibition against genocide, contained in the Convention of 9 December 1948 on the Prevention and Punishment of the Crime of Genocide, is a relevant rule of customary international law which the Court must apply. The Court recalls that in Article II of the Convention genocide is defined as

> "any of the following acts committed with intent to destroy, in whole or in part, a national, ethnical, racial or religious group, as such :
> (a) Killing members of the group;
> (b) Causing serious bodily or mental harm to members of the group;
> (c) Deliberately inflicting on the group conditions of life calculated to bring about its physical destruction in whole or in part;
> (d) Imposing measures intended to prevent births within the group;
> (e) Forcibly transferring children of the group to another group."

It was maintained before the Court that the number of deaths occasioned by the use of nuclear weapons would be enormous; that the victims could, in certain cases, include persons of a particular national, ethnic, racial or religious group; and that the intention to destroy such groups could be inferred from the fact that the user of the nuclear weapon would have omitted to take account of the well-known effects of the use of such weapons.

The Court would point out in that regard that the prohibition of genocide would be pertinent in this case if the recourse to nuclear weapons did indeed entail the element of intent, towards a group as such, required by the provision quoted above. In the view of the Court, it would only be possible to arrive at such a conclusion after having taken due account of the circumstances specific to each case.

*

27. In both their written and oral statements, some States furthermore argued that any use of nuclear weapons would be unlawful by reference to existing norms relating to the safeguarding and protection of the environment, in view of their essential importance.

Specific references were made to various existing international treaties and instruments. These included Additional Protocol I of 1977 to the Geneva Conventions of 1949, Article 35, paragraph 3, of which prohibits the employment of "methods or means of warfare which are intended, or may be expected, to cause widespread, long-term and severe damage to the natural environment"; and the Convention of 18 May 1977 on the Prohibition of Military or Any Other Hostile Use of Environmental Modification Techniques, which prohibits the use of weapons which have "widespread, long-lasting or severe effects" on the environment (Art. 1). Also cited were Principle 21 of the Stockholm Declaration of 1972 and Principle 2 of the Rio Declaration of 1992 which express the common conviction of the States concerned that they have a duty

> "to ensure that activities within their jurisdiction or control do not cause damage to the environment of other States or of areas beyond the limits of national jurisdiction".

These instruments and other provisions relating to the protection and safeguarding of the environment were said to apply at all times, in war as well as in peace, and it was contended that they would be violated by the use of nuclear weapons whose consequences would be widespread and would have transboundary effects.

28. Other States questioned the binding legal quality of these precepts of environmental law; or, in the context of the Convention on the Prohibition of Military or Any Other Hostile Use of Environmental Modification Techniques, denied that it was concerned at all with the use of nuclear weapons in hostilities; or, in the case of Additional Protocol I, denied that they were generally bound by its terms, or recalled that they had reserved their position in respect of Article 35, paragraph 3, thereof.

It was also argued by some States that the principal purpose of environmental treaties and norms was the protection of the environment in time of peace. It was said that those treaties made no mention of nuclear weapons. It was also pointed out that warfare in general, and nuclear warfare in particular, were not mentioned in their texts and that it would be destabilizing to the rule of law and to confidence in international negotiations if those treaties were now interpreted in such a way as to prohibit the use of nuclear weapons.

29. The Court recognizes that the environment is under daily threat and that the use of nuclear weapons could constitute a catastrophe for the environment. The Court also recognizes that the environment is not an abstraction but represents the living space, the quality of life and the very health of human beings,

including generations unborn. The existence of the general obligation of States to ensure that activities within their jurisdiction and control respect the environment of other States or of areas beyond national control is now part of the corpus of international law relating to the environment.

30. However, the Court is of the view that the issue is not whether the treaties relating to the protection of the environment are or are not applicable during an armed conflict, but rather whether the obligations stemming from these treaties were intended to be obligations of total restraint during military conflict.

The Court does not consider that the treaties in question could have intended to deprive a State of the exercise of its right of self-defence under international law because of its obligations to protect the environment. Nonetheless, States must take environmental considerations into account when assessing what is necessary and proportionate in the pursuit of legitimate military objectives. Respect for the environment is one of the elements that go to assessing whether an action is in conformity with the principles of necessity and proportionality.

This approach is supported, indeed, by the terms of Principle 24 of the Rio Declaration, which provides that:

"Warfare is inherently destructive of sustainable development. States shall therefore respect international law providing protection for the environment in times of armed conflict and cooperate in its further development, as necessary."

31. The Court notes furthermore that Articles 35, paragraph 3, and 55 of Additional Protocol I provide additional protection for the environment. Taken together, these provisions embody a general obligation to protect the natural environment against widespread, long-term and severe environmental damage; the prohibition of methods and means of warfare which are intended, or may be expected, to cause such damage; and the prohibition of attacks against the natural environment by way of reprisals.

These are powerful constraints for all the States having subscribed to these provisions.

32. General Assembly resolution 47/37 of 25 November 1992 on the "Protection of the Environment in Times of Armed Conflict" is also of interest in this context. It affirms the general view according to which environmental considerations constitute one of the elements to be taken into account in the implementation of the principles of the law applicable in armed conflict: it states that "destruction of the environment, not justified by military necessity and carried out wantonly, is clearly contrary to existing international law". Addressing the reality that certain instruments are not yet binding on all States, the General Assembly in this resolution "*[a]ppeals* to all States that have not yet done so to consider becoming parties to the relevant international conventions".

In its recent Order in the *Request for an Examination of the Situation in Accordance with Paragraph 63 of the Court's Judgment of 20 December 1974 in the* Nuclear Tests (New Zealand v. France) *Case*, the Court stated that its conclusion was "without prejudice to the obligations of States to respect and protect the natural environment" (*Order of 22 September 1995, I.C.J. Reports 1995*, p. 306, para. 64). Although that statement was made in the context of nuclear testing, it naturally also applies to the actual use of nuclear weapons in armed conflict.

33. The Court thus finds that while the existing international law relating to the protection and safeguarding of the environment does not specifically prohibit the use of nuclear weapons, it indicates important environmental factors that are properly to be taken into account in the context of the implementation of the

principles and rules of the law applicable in armed conflict.

*

34. In the light of the foregoing the Court concludes that the most directly relevant applicable law governing the question of which it was seised, is that relating to the use of force enshrined in the United Nations Charter and the law applicable in armed conflict which regulates the conduct of hostilities, together with any specific treaties on nuclear weapons that the Court might determine to be relevant.

* *

35. In applying this law to the present case, the Court cannot however fail to take into account certain unique characteristics of nuclear weapons.

The Court has noted the definitions of nuclear weapons contained in various treaties and accords. It also notes that nuclear weapons are explosive devices whose energy results from the fusion or fission of the atom. By its very nature, that process, in nuclear weapons as they exist today, releases not only immense quantities of heat and energy, but also powerful and prolonged radiation. According to the material before the Court, the first two causes of damage are vastly more powerful than the damage caused by other weapons, while the phenomenon of radiation is said to be peculiar to nuclear weapons. These characteristics render the nuclear weapon potentially catastrophic. The destructive power of nuclear weapons cannot be contained in either space or time. They have the potential to destroy all civilization and the entire ecosystem of the planet.

The radiation released by a nuclear explosion would affect health, agriculture, natural resources and demography over a very wide area.

Further, the use of nuclear weapons would be a serious danger to future generations. Ionizing radiation has the potential to damage the future environment, food and marine ecosystem, and to cause genetic defects and illness in future generations.

36. In consequence, in order correctly to apply to the present case the Charter law on the use of force and the law applicable in armed conflict, in particular humanitarian law, it is imperative for the Court to take account of the unique characteristics of nuclear weapons, and in particular their destructive capacity, their capacity to cause untold human suffering, and their ability to cause damage to generations to come.

* * *

37. The Court will now address the question of the legality or illegality of recourse to nuclear weapons in the light of the provisions of the Charter relating to the threat or use of force.

38. The Charter contains several provisions relating to the threat and use of force. In Article 2, paragraph 4, the threat or use of force against the territorial integrity or political independence of another State or in any other manner inconsistent with the purposes of the United Nations is prohibited. That paragraph provides:

> "All Members shall refrain in their international relations from the threat or use of force against the territorial integrity or political independence of any State, or in any other manner inconsistent with the Purposes of the United Nations."

This prohibition of the use of force is to be considered in the light of other relevant provisions of the Charter. In Article 51, the Charter recognizes the inherent right of individual or collective self-defence if an armed attack occurs. A further lawful use of force is envisaged in Article 42, whereby the Security Council may take military enforcement measures in conformity with Chapter VII of the Charter.

39. These provisions do not refer to specific weapons. They apply to any use of force, regardless of the weapons employed. The Charter neither expressly prohibits, nor permits, the use of any specific weapon, including nuclear weapons. A weapon that is already unlawful *per se*, whether by treaty or custom, does not become lawful by reason of its being used for a legitimate purpose under the Charter.

40. The entitlement to resort to self-defence under Article 51 is subject to certain constraints. Some of these constraints are inherent in the very concept of self-defence. Other requirements are specified in Article 51.

41. The submission of the exercise of the right of self-defence to the conditions of necessity and proportionality is a rule of customary international law. As the Court stated in the case concerning *Military and Paramilitary Activities in and against Nicaragua (Nicaragua v. United States of America)* : there is a "specific rule whereby self-defence would warrant only measures which are proportional to the armed attack and necessary to respond to it, a rule well established in customary international law" *I.C.J. Reports 1986*, p. 94, para. 176). This dual condition applies equally to Article 51 of the Charter, whatever the means of force employed.

42. The proportionality principle may thus not in itself exclude the use of nuclear weapons in self-defence in all circumstances. But at the same time, a use of force that is proportionate under the law of self-defence, must, in order to be lawful, also meet the requirements of the law applicable in armed conflict which comprise in particular the principles and rules of humanitarian law.

43. Certain States have in their written and oral pleadings suggested that in the case of nuclear weapons, the condition of proportionality must be evaluated in the light of still further factors. They contend that the very nature of nuclear weapons, and the high probability of an escalation of nuclear exchanges, mean that there is an extremely strong risk of devastation. The risk factor is said to negate the possibility of the condition of proportionality being complied with. The Court does not find it necessary to embark upon the quantification of such risks; nor does it need to enquire into the question whether tactical nuclear weapons exist which are sufficiently precise to limit those risks: it suffices for the Court to note that the very nature of all nuclear weapons and the profound risks associated therewith are further considerations to be borne in mind by States believing they can exercise a nuclear response in self-defence in accordance with the requirements of proportionality.

44. Beyond the conditions of necessity and proportionality, Article 51 specifically requires that measures taken by States in the exercise of the right of self-defence shall be immediately reported to the Security Council; this article further provides that these measures shall not in any way affect the authority and responsibility of the Security Council under the Charter to take at any time such action as it deems necessary in order to maintain or restore international peace and security. These requirements of Article 51 apply whatever the means of force used in self-defence.

45. The Court notes that the Security Council adopted on 11 April 1995, in the context of the extension of the Treaty on the Non-Proliferation of Nuclear Weapons, resolution 984 (1995) by the terms of which, on the one hand, it

"*[t]akes note* with appreciation of the statements made by each of the nuclear-weapon States (S/1995/261, S/1995/262, S/1995/263, S/1995/264, S/1995/265), in which they give security assurances against the use of nuclear weapons to non-nuclear-weapon States that are Parties to the Treaty on the Non-Proliferation of Nuclear Weapons",

and, on the other hand, it

"*[w]elcomes* the intention expressed by certain States that they will provide or support immediate assistance, in accordance with the Charter, to any non-nuclear-weapon State Party to the Treaty on the Non-Proliferation of Nuclear Weapons that is a victim of an act of, or an object of a threat of, aggression in which nuclear weapons are used".

46. Certain States asserted that the use of nuclear weapons in the conduct of reprisals would be lawful. The Court does not have to examine, in this context, the question of armed reprisals in time of peace, which are considered to be unlawful. Nor does it have to pronounce on the question of belligerent reprisals save to observe that in any case any right of recourse to such reprisals would, like self-defence, be governed *inter alia* by the principle of proportionality.

47. In order to lessen or eliminate the risk of unlawful attack, States sometimes signal that they possess certain weapons to use in self-defence against any State violating their territorial integrity or political independence. Whether a signalled intention to use force if certain events occur is or is not a "threat" within Article 2, paragraph 4, of the Charter depends upon various factors. If the envisaged use of force is itself unlawful, the stated readiness to use it would be a threat prohibited under Article 2, paragraph 4. Thus it would be illegal for a State to threaten force to secure territory from another State, or to cause it to follow or not follow certain political or economic paths. The notions of "threat" and "use" of force under Article 2, paragraph 4, of the Charter stand together in the sense that if the use of force itself in a given case is illegal — for whatever reason — the threat to use such force will likewise be illegal. In short, if it is to be lawful, the declared readiness of a State to use force must be a use of force that is in conformity with the Charter. For the rest, no State — whether or not it defended the policy of deterrence — suggested to the Court that it would be lawful to threaten to use force if the use of force contemplated would be illegal.

48. Some States put forward the argument that possession of nuclear weapons is itself an unlawful threat to use force. Possession of nuclear weapons may indeed justify an inference of preparedness to use them. In order to be effective, the policy of deterrence, by which those States possessing or under the umbrella of nuclear weapons seek to discourage military aggression by demonstrating that it will serve no purpose, necessitates that the intention to use nuclear weapons be credible. Whether this is a "threat" contrary to Article 2, paragraph 4, depends upon whether the particular use of force envisaged would be directed against the territorial integrity or political independence of a State, or against the Purposes of the United Nations or whether, in the event that it were intended as a means of defence, it would necessarily violate the principles of necessity and proportionality. In any of these circumstances the use of force, and the threat to use it, would be unlawful under the law of the Charter.

49. Moreover, the Security Council may take enforcement measures under Chapter VII of the Charter. From the statements presented to it the Court does not consider it necessary to address questions which might, in a given case, arise from the application of Chapter VII.

50. The terms of the question put to the Court by the General Assembly in resolution 49/75 K could in principle also cover a threat or use of nuclear weapons by a State within its own boundaries. However, this particular aspect has not been dealt with by any of the States which addressed the Court orally or in writing in these proceedings. The Court finds that it is not called upon to deal with an internal use of nuclear weapons.

* * *

51. Having dealt with the Charter provisions relating to the threat or use of force, the Court will now turn to the law applicable in situations of armed conflict. It will first address the question whether there are specific rules in international law regulating the legality or illegality of recourse to nuclear weapons *per se* ; it will then examine the question put to it in the light of the law applicable in armed conflict proper, i.e. the principles and rules of humanitarian law applicable in armed conflict, and the law of neutrality.

* *

52. The Court notes by way of introduction that international customary and treaty law does not contain any specific prescription authorizing the threat or use of nuclear weapons or any other weapon in general or in certain circumstances, in particular those of the exercise of legitimate self defence. Nor, however, is there any principle or rule of international law which would make the legality of the threat or use of nuclear weapons or of any other weapons dependent on a specific authorization. State practice shows that the illegality of the use of certain weapons as such does not result from an absence of authorization but, on the contrary, is formulated in terms of prohibition.

*

53. The Court must therefore now examine whether there is any prohibition of recourse to nuclear weapons as such; it will first ascertain whether there is a conventional prescription to this effect.

54. In this regard, the argument has been advanced that nuclear weapons should be treated in the same way as poisoned weapons. In that case, they would be prohibited under:

   (a) the Second Hague Declaration of 29 July 1899, which prohibits "the use of projectiles the object of which is the diffusion of asphyxiating or deleterious gases";
   (b) Article 23 (a) of the Regulations respecting the laws and customs of war on land annexed to the Hague Convention IV of 18 October 1907, whereby "it is especially forbidden : . . . to employ poison or poisoned weapons"; and
   (c) the Geneva Protocol of 17 June 1925 which prohibits "the use in war of asphyxiating, poisonous or other gases, and of all analogous liquids, materials or devices".

55. The Court will observe that the Regulations annexed to the Hague Convention IV do not define what is to be understood by "poison or poisoned weapons" and that different interpretations exist on the issue. Nor does the 1925 Protocol specify the meaning to be given to the term "analogous materials or devices". The terms have been understood, in the practice of States, in their ordinary sense as covering

weapons whose prime, or even exclusive, effect is to poison or asphyxiate. This practice is clear, and the parties to those instruments have not treated them as referring to nuclear weapons.

56. In view of this, it does not seem to the Court that the use of nuclear weapons can be regarded as specifically prohibited on the basis of the above-mentioned provisions of the Second Hague Declaration of 1899, the Regulations annexed to the Hague Convention IV of 1907 or the 1925 Protocol (see paragraph 54 above).

57. The pattern until now has been for weapons of mass destruction to be declared illegal by specific instruments. The most recent such instruments are the Convention of 10 April 1972 on the Prohibition of the Development, Production and Stockpiling of Bacteriological (Biological) and Toxin Weapons and on Their Destruction — which prohibits the possession of bacteriological and toxic weapons and reinforces the prohibition of their use — and the Convention of 13 January 1993 on the Prohibition of the Development, Production, Stockpiling and Use of Chemical Weapons and on Their Destruction — which prohibits all use of chemical weapons and requires the destruction of existing stocks. Each of these instruments has been negotiated and adopted in its own context and for its own reasons. The Court does not find any specific prohibition of recourse to nuclear weapons in treaties expressly prohibiting the use of certain weapons of mass destruction.

58. In the last two decades, a great many negotiations have been conducted regarding nuclear weapons; they have not resulted in a treaty of general prohibition of the same kind as for bacteriological and chemical weapons. However, a number of specific treaties have been concluded in order to limit:

   (a) the acquisition, manufacture and possession of nuclear weapons (Peace Treaties of 10 February 1947; State Treaty for the Re-establishment of an Independent and Democratic Austria of 15 May 1955; Treaty of Tlatelolco of 14 February 1967 for the Prohibition of Nuclear Weapons in Latin America, and its Additional Protocols; Treaty of 1 July 1968 on the Non-Proliferation of Nuclear Weapons; Treaty of Rarotonga of 6 August 1985 on the Nuclear Weapon-Free Zone of the South Pacific, and its Protocols; Treaty of 12 September 1990 on the Final Settlement with respect to Germany) ;
   (b)) the deployment of nuclear weapons (Antarctic Treaty of 1 December 1959; Treaty of 27 January 1967 on Principles Governing the Activities of States in the Exploration and Use of Outer Space, including the Moon and Other Celestial Bodies; Treaty of Tlatelolco of 14 February 1967 for the Prohibition of Nuclear Weapons in Latin America, and its Additional Protocols; Treaty of 11 February 1971 on the Prohibition of the Emplacement of Nuclear Weapons and Other Weapons of Mass Destruction on the Sea-Bed and the Ocean Floor and in the Subsoil Thereof ; Treaty of Rarotonga of 6 August 1985 on the Nuclear-Weapon-Free Zone of the South Pacific, and its Protocols); and
   (c)) the testing of nuclear weapons (Antarctic Treaty of 1 December 1959; Treaty of 5 August 1963 Banning Nuclear Weapon Tests in the Atmosphere, in Outer Space and under Water ; Treaty of 27 January 1967 on Principles Governing the Activities of States in the Exploration and Use of Outer Space, including the Moon and Other Celestial Bodies; Treaty of Tlatelolco of 14 February 1967 for the Prohibition of Nuclear Weapons in Latin America, and its Additional

Protocols; Treaty of Rarotonga of 6 August 1985 on the Nuclear-Weapon-Free Zone of the South Pacific, and its Protocols).

59. Recourse to nuclear weapons is directly addressed by two of these Conventions and also in connection with the indefinite extension of the Treaty on the Non-Proliferation of Nuclear Weapons of 1968:

(a) the Treaty of Tlatelolco of 14 February 1967 for the Prohibition of Nuclear Weapons in Latin America prohibits, in Article 1, the use of nuclear weapons by the Contracting Parties. It further includes an Additional Protocol II open to nuclear-weapon States outside the region, Article 3 of which provides:
"The Governments represented by the undersigned Plenipotentiaries also undertake not to use or threaten to use nuclear weapons against the Contracting Parties of the Treaty for the Prohibition of Nuclear Weapons in Latin America."

The Protocol was signed and ratified by the five nuclear-weapon States. Its ratification was accompanied by a variety of declarations. The United Kingdom Government, for example, stated that "in the event of any act of aggression by a Contracting Party to the Treaty in which that Party was supported by a nuclear-weapon State", the United Kingdom Government would "be free to reconsider the extent to which they could be regarded as committed by the provisions of Additional Protocol II". The United States made a similar statement. The French Government, for its part, stated that it "interprets the undertaking made in article 3 of the Protocol as being without prejudice to the full exercise of the right of self-defence confirmed by Article 51 of the Charter". China reaffirmed its commitment not to be the first to make use of nuclear weapons. The Soviet Union reserved "the right to review" the obligations imposed upon it by Additional Protocol II, particularly in the event of an attack by a State party either "in support of a nuclear-weapon State or jointly with that State". None of these statements drew comment or objection from the parties to the Treaty of Tlatelolco.

(b) the Treaty of Rarotonga of 6 August 1985 establishes a South Pacific Nuclear Free Zone in which the Parties undertake not to manufacture, acquire or possess any nuclear explosive device (Art. 3). Unlike the Treaty of Tlatelolco, the Treaty of Rarotonga does not expressly prohibit the use of such weapons. But such a prohibition is for the States parties the necessary consequence of the prohibitions stipulated by the Treaty. The Treaty has a number of protocols. Protocol 2, open to the five nuclear-weapon States, specifies in its Article 1 that:

"Each Party undertakes not to use or threaten to use any nuclear explosive device against:
(a)) Parties to the Treaty; or
(b)) any territory within the South Pacific Nuclear Free Zone for which a State that has become a Party to Protocol 1 is internationally responsible."

China and Russia are parties to that Protocol. In signing it, China and the Soviet Union each made a declaration by which they reserved the "right to reconsider" their obligations under the said Protocol; the Soviet Union also referred to certain circumstances in which it would consider itself released from those obligations. France, the United

Kingdom and the United States, for their part, signed Protocol 2 on 25 March 1996, but have not yet ratified it. On that occasion, France declared, on the one hand, that no provision in that Protocol "shall impair the full exercise of the inherent right of self defence provided for in Article 51 of the ... Charter" and, on the other hand, that "the commitment set out in Article 1 of [that] Protocol amounts to the negative security assurances given by France to non-nuclear-weapon States which are parties to the Treaty on Non-Proliferation", and that "these assurances shall not apply to States which are not parties" to that Treaty. For its part, the United Kingdom made a declaration setting out the precise circumstances in which it "will not be bound by [its] undertaking under Article 1 of the Protocol.

(c) as to the Treaty on the Non-Proliferation of Nuclear Weapons, at the time of its signing in 1968 the United States, the United Kingdom and the USSR gave various security assurances to the non nuclear-weapon States that were parties to the Treaty. In resolution 255 (1968) the Security Council took note with satisfaction of the intention expressed by those three States to

> "provide or support immediate assistance, in accordance with the Charter, to any non-nuclear-weapon State Party to the Treaty on the Non-Proliferation ... that is a victim of an act of, or an object of a threat of, aggression in which nuclear weapons are used".

On the occasion of the extension of the Treaty in 1995, the five nuclear-weapon States gave their non-nuclear-weapon partners, by means of separate unilateral statements on 5 and 6 April 1995, positive and negative security assurances against the use of such weapons. All the five nuclear-weapon States first undertook not to use nuclear weapons against non-nuclear-weapon States that were parties to the Treaty on the Non-Proliferation of Nuclear Weapons. However, these States, apart from China, made an exception in the case of an invasion or any other attack against them, their territories, armed forces or allies, or on a State towards which they had a security commitment, carried out or sustained by a non nuclear-weapon State party to the Non-Proliferation Treaty in association or alliance with a nuclear-weapon State. Each of the nuclear-weapon States further undertook, as a permanent member of the Security Council, in the event of an attack with the use of nuclear weapons, or threat of such attack, against a non-nuclear weapon State, to refer the matter to the Security Council without delay and to act within it in order that it might take immediate measures with a view to supplying, pursuant to the Charter, the necessary assistance to the victim State (the commitments assumed comprising minor variations in wording). The Security Council, in unanimously adopting resolution 984 (1995) of 11 April 1995, cited above, took note of those statements with appreciation. It also recognized

> "that the nuclear-weapon State permanent members of the Security Council will bring the matter immediately to the attention of the Council and seek Council action to provide, in accordance with the Charter, the necessary assistance to the State victim";

and welcomed the fact that

"the intention expressed by certain States that they will provide or support immediate assistance, in accordance with the Charter, to any non-nuclear-weapon State Party to the Treaty on the Non Proliferation of Nuclear Weapons that is a victim of an act of, or an object of a threat of, aggression in which nuclear weapons are used".

60. Those States that believe that recourse to nuclear weapons is illegal stress that the conventions that include various rules providing for the limitation or elimination of nuclear weapons in certain areas (such as the Antarctic Treaty of 1959 which prohibits the deployment of nuclear weapons in the Antarctic, or the Treaty of Tlatelolco of 1967 which creates a nuclear-weapon-free zone in Latin America) or the conventions that apply certain measures of control and limitation to the existence of nuclear weapons (such as the 1963 Partial Test-Ban Treaty or the Treaty on the Non-Proliferation of Nuclear Weapons) all set limits to the use of nuclear weapons. In their view, these treaties bear witness, in their own way, to the emergence of a rule of complete legal prohibition of all uses of nuclear weapons.

61. Those States who defend the position that recourse to nuclear weapons is legal in certain circumstances see a logical contradiction in reaching such a conclusion. According to them, those Treaties, such as the Treaty on the Non-Proliferation of Nuclear Weapons, as well as Security Council resolutions 255 (1968) and 984 (1995) which take note of the security assurances given by the nuclear-weapon States to the non nuclear-weapon States in relation to any nuclear aggression against the latter, cannot be understood as prohibiting the use of nuclear weapons, and such a claim is contrary to the very text of those instruments. For those who support the legality in certain circumstances of recourse to nuclear weapons, there is no absolute prohibition against the use of such weapons. The very logic and construction of the Treaty on the Non-Proliferation of Nuclear Weapons, they assert, confirm this. This Treaty, whereby, they contend, the possession of nuclear weapons by the five nuclear-weapon States has been accepted, cannot be seen as a treaty banning their use by those States; to accept the fact that those States possess nuclear weapons is tantamount to recognizing that such weapons may be used in certain circumstances. Nor, they contend, could the security assurances given by the nuclear-weapon States in 1968, and more recently in connection with the Review and Extension Conference of the Parties to the Treaty on the Non-Proliferation of Nuclear Weapons in 1995, have been conceived without its being supposed that there were circumstances in which nuclear weapons could be used in a lawful manner. For those who defend the legality of the use, in certain circumstances, of nuclear weapons, the acceptance of those instruments by the different non-nuclear-weapon States confirms and reinforces the evident logic upon which those instruments are based.

62. The Court notes that the treaties dealing exclusively with acquisition, manufacture, possession, deployment and testing of nuclear weapons, without specifically addressing their threat or use, certainly point to an increasing concern in the international community with these weapons; the Court concludes from this that these treaties could therefore be seen as foreshadowing a future general prohibition of the use of such weapons, but they do not constitute such a prohibition by themselves. As to the treaties of Tlatelolco and Rarotonga and their Protocols, and also the declarations made in connection with the indefinite extension of the Treaty on the Non-Proliferation of Nuclear Weapons, it emerges from these instruments that:

(a) a number of States have undertaken not to use nuclear weapons in specific zones (Latin America; the South Pacific) or against certain other States (non-nuclear-weapon States which are parties to the Treaty on the Non-Proliferation of Nuclear Weapons);

(b)) nevertheless, even within this framework, the nuclear-weapon States have reserved the right to use nuclear weapons in certain circumstances; and

(c)) these reservations met with no objection from the parties to the Tlatelolco or Rarotonga Treaties or from the Security Council.

63. These two treaties, the security assurances given in 1995 by the nuclear-weapon States and the fact that the Security Council took note of them with satisfaction, testify to a growing awareness of the need to liberate the community of States and the international public from the dangers resulting from the existence of nuclear weapons. The Court moreover notes the signing, even more recently, on 15 December 1995, at Bangkok, of a Treaty on the Southeast Asia Nuclear-Weapon-Free Zone, and on 11 April 1996, at Cairo, of a treaty on the creation of a nuclear weapons-free zone in Africa. It does not, however, view these elements as amounting to a comprehensive and universal conventional prohibition on the use, or the threat of use, of those weapons as such.

*

64. The Court will now turn to an examination of customary international law to determine whether a prohibition of the threat or use of nuclear weapons as such flows from that source of law. As the Court has stated, the substance of that law must be "looked for primarily in the actual practice and opinio Juris of States" (*Continental Shelf (Libyan Arab Jamahiriya/Malta), Judgment, I.C.J. Reports 1985*, p. 29, para. 27).

65. States which hold the view that the use of nuclear weapons is illegal have endeavoured to demonstrate the existence of a customary rule prohibiting this use. They refer to a consistent practice of non-utilization of nuclear weapons by States since 1945 and they would see in that practice the expression of an *opinio juris* on the part of those who possess such weapons.

66. Some other States, which assert the legality of the threat and use of nuclear weapons in certain circumstances, invoked the doctrine and practice of deterrence in support of their argument. They recall that they have always, in concert with certain other States, reserved the right to use those weapons in the exercise of the right to self-defence against an armed attack threatening their vital security interests. In their view, if nuclear weapons have not been used since 1945, it is not on account of an existing or nascent custom but merely because circumstances that might justify their use have fortunately not arisen.

67. The Court does not intend to pronounce here upon the practice known as the "policy of deterrence". It notes that it is a fact that a number of States adhered to that practice during the greater part of the Cold War and continue to adhere to it. Furthermore, the members of the international community are profoundly divided on the matter of whether non-recourse to nuclear weapons over the past 50 years constitutes the expression of an *opinio juris*. Under these circumstances the Court does not consider itself able to find that there is such an *opinio juris*.

68. According to certain States, the important series of General Assembly resolutions, beginning with resolution 1653 (XVI) of 24 November 1961, that deal with nuclear weapons and that affirm, with consistent regularity, the illegality of nuclear weapons, signify the existence of a rule of international customary law which prohibits recourse to those weapons. According to other States, however,

the resolutions in question have no binding character on their own account and are not declaratory of any customary rule of prohibition of nuclear weapons; some of these States have also pointed out that this series of resolutions not only did not meet with the approval of all of the nuclear-weapon States but of many other States as well.

69. States which consider that the use of nuclear weapons is illegal indicated that those resolutions did not claim to create any new rules, but were confined to a confirmation of customary law relating to the prohibition of means or methods of warfare which, by their use, overstepped the bounds of what is permissible in the conduct of hostilities. In their view, the resolutions in question did no more than apply to nuclear weapons the existing rules of international law applicable in armed conflict; they were no more than the "envelope" or *instrumentum* containing certain pre-existing customary rules of international law. For those States it is accordingly of little importance that the *instrumentum* should have occasioned negative votes, which cannot have the effect of obliterating those customary rules which have been confirmed by treaty law.

70. The Court notes that General Assembly resolutions, even if they are not binding, may sometimes have normative value. They can, in certain circumstances, provide evidence important for establishing the existence of a rule or the emergence of an *opinio juris*. To establish whether this is true of a given General Assembly resolution, it is necessary to look at its content and the conditions of its adoption ; it is also necessary to see whether an opinio Juris exists as to its normative character. Or a series of resolutions may show the gradual evolution of the *opinio juris* required for the establishment of a new rule.

71. Examined in their totality, the General Assembly resolutions put before the Court declare that the use of nuclear weapons would be "a direct violation of the Charter of the United Nations"; and in certain formulations that such use "should be prohibited". The focus of these resolutions has sometimes shifted to diverse related matters; however, several of the resolutions under consideration in the present case have been adopted with substantial numbers of negative votes and abstentions; thus, although those resolutions are a clear sign of deep concern regarding the problem of nuclear weapons, they still fall short of establishing the existence of an *opinio juris* on the illegality of the use of such weapons.

72. The Court further notes that the first of the resolutions of the General Assembly expressly proclaiming the illegality of the use of nuclear weapons, resolution 1653 (XVI) of 24 November 1961 (mentioned in subsequent resolutions), after referring to certain international declarations and binding agreements, from the Declaration of St. Petersburg of 1868 to the Geneva Protocol of 1925, proceeded to qualify the legal nature of nuclear weapons, determine their effects, and apply general rules of customary international law to nuclear weapons in particular. That application by the General Assembly of general rules of customary law to the particular case of nuclear weapons indicates that, in its view, there was no specific rule of customary law which prohibited the use of nuclear weapons; if such a rule had existed, the General Assembly could simply have referred to it and would not have needed to undertake such an exercise of legal qualification.

73. Having said this, the Court points out that the adoption each year by the General Assembly, by a large majority, of resolutions recalling the content of resolution 1653 (XVI), and requesting the member States to conclude a convention prohibiting the use of nuclear weapons in any circumstance, reveals the desire of a very large section of the international community to take, by a specific and express prohibition of the use of nuclear weapons, a significant step forward along the

road to complete nuclear disarmament. The emergence, as *lex lata*, of a customary rule specifically prohibiting the use of nuclear weapons as such is hampered by the continuing tensions between the nascent opinio Juris on the one hand, and the still strong adherence to the practice of deterrence on the other.

* *

74. The Court not having found a conventional rule of general scope, nor a customary rule specifically proscribing the threat or use of nuclear weapons per se, it will now deal with the question whether recourse to nuclear weapons must be considered as illegal in the light of the principles and rules of international humanitarian law applicable in armed conflict and of the law of neutrality.

75. A large number of customary rules have been developed by the practice of States and are an integral part of the international law relevant to the question posed. The "laws and customs of war" — as they were traditionally called — were the subject of efforts at codification undertaken in The Hague (including the Conventions of 1899 and 1907), and were based partly upon the St. Petersburg Declaration of 1868 as well as the results of the Brussels Conference of 1874. This "Hague Law" and, more particularly, the Regulations Respecting the Laws and Customs of War on Land, fixed the rights and duties of belligerents in their conduct of operations and limited the choice of methods and means of injuring the enemy in an international armed conflict. One should add to this the "Geneva Law" (the Conventions of 1864, 1906, 1929 and 1949), which protects the victims of war and aims to provide safeguards for disabled armed forces personnel and persons not taking part in the hostilities. These two branches of the law applicable in armed conflict have become so closely interrelated that they are considered to have gradually formed one single complex system, known today as international humanitarian law. The provisions of the Additional Protocols of 1977 give expression and attest to the unity and complexity of that law.

76. Since the turn of the century, the appearance of new means of combat has — without calling into question the longstanding principles and rules of international law — rendered necessary some specific prohibitions of the use of certain weapons, such as explosive projectiles under 400 grammes, dum-dum bullets and asphyxiating gases. Chemical and bacteriological weapons were then prohibited by the 1925 Geneva Protocol. More recently, the use of weapons producing "non-detectable fragments", of other types of "mines, booby traps and other devices", and of "incendiary weapons", was either prohibited or limited, depending on the case, by the Convention of 10 October 1980 on Prohibitions or Restrictions on the Use of Certain Conventional Weapons Which May Be Deemed to Be Excessively Injurious or to Have Indiscriminate Effects. The provisions of the Convention on "mines, booby traps and other devices" have just been amended, on 3 May 1996, and now regulate in greater detail, for example, the use of anti-personnel land mines.

77. All this shows that the conduct of military operations is governed by a body of legal prescriptions. This is so because "the right of belligerents to adopt means of injuring the enemy is not unlimited" as stated in Article 22 of the 1907 Hague Regulations relating to the laws and customs of war on land. The St. Petersburg Declaration had already condemned the use of weapons "which uselessly aggravate the suffering of disabled men or make their death inevitable". The aforementioned Regulations relating to the laws and customs of war on land, annexed to the Hague Convention IV of 1907, prohibit the use of "arms, projectiles, or material calculated to cause unnecessary suffering" (Art. 23).

78. The cardinal principles contained in the texts constituting the fabric of humanitarian law are the following. The first is aimed at the protection of the civilian population and civilian objects and establishes the distinction between combatants and non-combatants; States must never make civilians the object of attack and must consequently never use weapons that are incapable of distinguishing between civilian and military targets. According to the second principle, it is prohibited to cause unnecessary suffering to combatants: it is accordingly prohibited to use weapons causing them such harm or uselessly aggravating their suffering. In application of that second principle, States do not have unlimited freedom of choice of means in the weapons they use.

The Court would likewise refer, in relation to these principles, to the Martens Clause, which was first included in the Hague Convention II with Respect to the Laws and Customs of War on Land of 1899 and which has proved to be an effective means of addressing the rapid evolution of military technology. A modern version of that clause is to be found in Article 1, paragraph 2, of Additional Protocol I of 1977, which reads as follows:

> "In cases not covered by this Protocol or by other international agreements, civilians and combatants remain under the protection and authority of the principles of international law derived from established custom, from the principles of humanity and from the dictates of public conscience."

In conformity with the aforementioned principles, humanitarian law, at a very early stage, prohibited certain types of weapons either because of their indiscriminate effect on combatants and civilians or because of the unnecessary suffering caused to combatants, that is to say, a harm greater than that unavoidable to achieve legitimate military objectives. If an envisaged use of weapons would not meet the requirements of humanitarian law, a threat to engage in such use would also be contrary to that law.

79. It is undoubtedly because a great many rules of humanitarian law applicable in armed conflict are so fundamental to the respect of the human person and "elementary considerations of humanity" as the Court put it in its Judgment of 9 April 1949 in the *Corfu Channel case (I.C.J. Reports 1949*, p. 22), that the Hague and Geneva Conventions have enjoyed a broad accession. Further these fundamental rules are to be observed by all States whether or not they have ratified the conventions that contain them, because they constitute intransgressible principles of international customary law.

80. The Nuremberg International Military Tribunal had already found in 1945 that the humanitarian rules included in the Regulations annexed to the Hague Convention IV of 1907 "were recognized by all civilized nations and were regarded as being declaratory of the laws and customs of war" (*Trial of the Major War Criminals, 14 November 1945-1 October 1946*, Nuremberg, 1947, Vol. 1, p. 254).

81. The Report of the Secretary-General pursuant to paragraph 2 of Security Council resolution 808 (1993), with which he introduced the Statute of the International Tribunal for the Prosecution of Persons Responsible for Serious Violations of International Humanitarian Law Committed in the Territory of the Former Yugoslavia since 1991, and which was unanimously approved by the Security Council (resolution 827 (1993)), stated:

> "In the view of the Secretary-General, the application of the principle *nullum crimen sine lege* requires that the international tribunal should apply rules of international humanitarian law which are beyond any doubt part of customary law . . .

The part of conventional international humanitarian law which has beyond doubt become part of international customary law is the law applicable in armed conflict as embodied in : the Geneva Conventions of 12 August 1949 for the Protection of War Victims; the Hague Convention (IV) Respecting the Laws and Customs of War on Land and the Regulations annexed thereto of 18 October 1907; the Convention on the Prevention and Punishment of the Crime of Genocide of 9 December 1948; and the Charter of the International Military Tribunal of 8 August 1945."

82. The extensive codification of humanitarian law and the extent of the accession to the resultant treaties, as well as the fact that the denunciation clauses that existed in the codification instruments have never been used, have provided the international community with a corpus of treaty rules the great majority of which had already become customary and which reflected the most universally recognized humanitarian principles. These rules indicate the normal conduct and behaviour expected of States.

83. It has been maintained in these proceedings that these principles and rules of humanitarian law are part of *jus cogens* as defined in Article 53 of the Vienna Convention on the Law of Treaties of 23 May 1969. The question whether a norm is part of the *jus cogens* relates to the legal character of the norm. The request addressed to the Court by the General Assembly raises the question of the applicability of the principles and rules of humanitarian law in cases of recourse to nuclear weapons and the consequences of that applicability for the legality of recourse to these weapons. But it does not raise the question of the character of the humanitarian law which would apply to the use of nuclear weapons. There is, therefore, no need for the Court to pronounce on this matter.

84. Nor is there any need for the Court to elaborate on the question of the applicability of Additional Protocol I of 1977 to nuclear weapons. It need only observe that while, at the Diplomatic Conference of 1974-1977, there was no substantive debate on the nuclear issue and no specific solution concerning this question was put forward, Additional Protocol I in no way replaced the general customary rules applicable to all means and methods of combat including nuclear weapons. In particular, the Court recalls that all States are bound by those rules in Additional Protocol I which, when adopted, were merely the expression of the pre-existing customary law, such as the Martens Clause, reaffirmed in the first article of Additional Protocol I. The fact that certain types of weapons were not specifically dealt with by the 1974-1977 Conference does not permit the drawing of any legal conclusions relating to the substantive issues which the use of such weapons would raise.

85. Turning now to the applicability of the principles and rules of humanitarian law to a possible threat or use of nuclear weapons, the Court notes that doubts in this respect have sometimes been voiced on the ground that these principles and rules had evolved prior to the invention of nuclear weapons and that the Conferences of Geneva of 1949 and 1974-1977 which respectively adopted the four Geneva Conventions of 1949 and the two Additional Protocols thereto did not deal with nuclear weapons specifically. Such views, however, are only held by a small minority. In the view of the vast majority of States as well as writers there can be no doubt as to the applicability of humanitarian law to nuclear weapons.

86. The Court shares that view. Indeed, nuclear weapons were invented after most of the principles and rules of humanitarian law applicable in armed conflict had already come into existence; the Conferences of 1949 and 1974-1977 left these

weapons aside, and there is a qualitative as well as quantitative difference between nuclear weapons and all conventional arms. However, it cannot be concluded from this that the established principles and rules of humanitarian law applicable in armed conflict did not apply to nuclear weapons. Such a conclusion would be incompatible with the intrinsically humanitarian character of the legal principles in question which permeates the entire law of armed conflict and applies to all forms of warfare and to all kinds of weapons, those of the past, those of the present and those of the future. In this respect it seems significant that the thesis that the rules of humanitarian law do not apply to the new weaponry, because of the newness of the latter, has not been advocated in the present proceedings. On the contrary, the newness of nuclear weapons has been expressly rejected as an argument against the application to them of international humanitarian law:

> "In general, international humanitarian law bears on the threat or use of nuclear weapons as it does of other weapons.
> International humanitarian law has evolved to meet contemporary circumstances, and is not limited in its application to weaponry of an earlier time. The fundamental principles of this law endure: to mitigate and circumscribe the cruelty of war for humanitarian reasons." (New Zealand, Written Statement, p. 15, paras. 63-64.)

None of the statements made before the Court in any way advocated a freedom to use nuclear weapons without regard to humanitarian constraints. Quite the reverse; it has been explicitly stated,

> "Restrictions set by the rules applicable to armed conflicts in respect of means and methods of warfare definitely also extend to nuclear weapons" (Russian Federation, CR 95/29, p. 52);

and

> "So far as the customary law of war is concerned, the United Kingdom has always accepted that the use of nuclear weapons is subject to the general principles of the *jus in bello*" (United Kingdom, CR 95/34, p. 45);

> "The United States has long shared the view that the law of armed conflict governs the use of nuclear weapons — just as it governs the use of conventional weapons" (United States of America, CR 95/34, p. 85).

87. Finally, the Court points to the Martens Clause, whose continuing existence and applicability is not to be doubted, as an affirmation that the principles and rules of humanitarian law apply to nuclear weapons.

*

88. The Court will now turn to the principle of neutrality which was raised by several States. In the context of the advisory proceedings brought before the Court by the WHO concerning the *Legality of the Use by a State of Nuclear Weapons in Armed Conflict*, the position was put as follows by one State:

> "The principle of neutrality, in its classic sense, was aimed at preventing the incursion of belligerent forces into neutral territory, or attacks on the persons or ships of neutrals. Thus: 'the territory of neutral powers is inviolable' (Article 1 of the Hague Convention (V) Respecting the Rights and Duties of Neutral Powers and Persons in Case of War on Land, concluded on 18 October 1907); 'belligerents are bound to respect the

sovereign rights of neutral powers . . .' (Article 1 to the Hague Convention (XIII) Respecting the Rights and Duties of Neutral Powers in Naval War, concluded on 18 October 1907), 'neutral states have equal interest in having their rights respected by belligerents . . .' (Preamble to Convention on Maritime Neutrality, concluded on 20 February 1928). It is clear, however, that the principle of neutrality applies with equal force to transborder incursions of armed forces and to the transborder damage caused to a neutral State by the use of a weapon in a belligerent State." (Nauru, Written Statement (I), p. 35, IV E.)

The principle so circumscribed is presented as an established part of the customary international law.

89. The Court finds that as in the case of the principles of humanitarian law applicable in armed conflict, international law leaves no doubt that the principle of neutrality, whatever its content, which is of a fundamental character similar to that of the humanitarian principles and rules, is applicable (subject to the relevant provisions of the United Nations Charter), to all international armed conflict, whatever type of weapons might be used.

*

90. Although the applicability of the principles and rules of humanitarian law and of the principle of neutrality to nuclear weapons is hardly disputed, the conclusions to be drawn from this applicability are, on the other hand, controversial.

91. According to one point of view, the fact that recourse to nuclear weapons is subject to and regulated by the law of armed conflict does not necessarily mean that such recourse is as such prohibited. As one State put it to the Court:

"Assuming that a State's use of nuclear weapons meets the requirements of self-defence, it must then be considered whether it conforms to the fundamental principles of the law of armed conflict regulating the conduct of hostilities" (United Kingdom, Written Statement, p. 40, para. 3.44);

"the legality of the use of nuclear weapons must therefore be assessed in the light of the applicable principles of international law regarding the use of force and the conduct of hostilities, as is the case with other methods and means of warfare" (ibid., p. 75, para. 4.2 (3));

and

"The reality . . . is that nuclear weapons might be used in a wide variety of circumstances with very different results in terms of likely civilian casualties. In some cases, such as the use of a low yield nuclear weapon against warships on the High Seas or troops in sparsely populated areas, it is possible to envisage a nuclear attack which caused comparatively few civilian casualties. It is by no means the case that every use of nuclear weapons against a military objective would inevitably cause very great collateral civilian casualties." (Ibid., p. 53, para. 3.70; see also United States of America, CR 95/34, pp. 89-90.)

92. Another view holds that recourse to nuclear weapons could never be compatible with the principles and rules of humanitarian law and is therefore prohibited. In the event of their use, nuclear weapons would in all circumstances be unable to draw any distinction between the civilian population and combatants, or between civilian objects and military objectives, and their effects, largely uncontrollable,

could not be restricted, either in time or in space, to lawful military targets. Such weapons would kill and destroy in a necessarily indiscriminate manner, on account of the blast, heat and radiation occasioned by the nuclear explosion and the effects induced; and the number of casualties which would ensue would be enormous. The use of nuclear weapons would therefore be prohibited in any circumstance, notwithstanding the absence of any explicit conventional prohibition. That view lay at the basis of the assertions by certain States before the Court that nuclear weapons are by their nature illegal under customary international law, by virtue of the fundamental principle of humanity.

93. A similar view has been expressed with respect to the effects of the principle of neutrality. Like the principles and rules of humanitarian law, that principle has therefore been considered by some to rule out the use of a weapon the effects of which simply cannot be contained within the territories of the contending States.

94. The Court would observe that none of the States advocating the legality of the use of nuclear weapons under certain circumstances, including the "clean" use of smaller, low yield, tactical nuclear weapons, has indicated what, supposing such limited use were feasible, would be the precise circumstances justifying such use; nor whether such limited use would not tend to escalate into the all-out use of high yield nuclear weapons. This being so, the Court does not consider that it has a sufficient basis for a determination on the validity of this view.

95. Nor can the Court make a determination on the validity of the view that the recourse to nuclear weapons would be illegal in any circumstance owing to their inherent and total incompatibility with the law applicable in armed conflict. Certainly, as the Court has already indicated, the principles and rules of law applicable in armed conflict — at the heart of which is the overriding consideration of humanity — make the conduct of armed hostilities subject to a number of strict requirements. Thus, methods and means of warfare, which would preclude any distinction between civilian and military targets, or which would result in unnecessary suffering to combatants, are prohibited. In view of the unique characteristics of nuclear weapons, to which the Court has referred above, the use of such weapons in fact seems scarcely reconcilable with respect for such requirements. Nevertheless, the Court considers that it does not have sufficient elements to enable it to conclude with certainty that the use of nuclear weapons would necessarily be at variance with the principles and rules of law applicable in armed conflict in any circumstance.

96. Furthermore, the Court cannot lose sight of the fundamental right of every State to survival, and thus its right to resort to self-defence, in accordance with Article 51 of the Charter, when its survival is at stake.

    Nor can it ignore the practice referred to as "policy of deterrence", to which an appreciable section of the international community adhered for many years. The Court also notes the reservations which certain nuclear weapon States have appended to the undertakings they have given, notably under the Protocols to the Treaties of Tlatelolco and Rarotonga, and also under the declarations made by them in connection with the extension of the Treaty on the Non-Proliferation of Nuclear Weapons, not to resort to such weapons.

97. Accordingly, in view of the present state of international law viewed as a whole, as examined above by the Court, and of the elements of fact at its disposal, the Court is led to observe that it cannot reach a definitive conclusion as to the legality or illegality of the use of nuclear weapons by a State in an extreme circumstance of self-defence, in which its very survival would be at stake.

***

98. Given the eminently difficult issues that arise in applying the law on the use of force and above all the law applicable in armed conflict to nuclear weapons, the Court considers that it now needs to examine one further aspect of the question before it, seen in a broader context.

    In the long run, international law, and with it the stability of the international order which it is intended to govern, are bound to suffer from the continuing difference of views with regard to the legal status of weapons as deadly as nuclear weapons. It is consequently important to put an end to this state of affairs: the long-promised complete nuclear disarmament appears to be the most appropriate means of achieving that result.

99. In these circumstances, the Court appreciates the full importance of the recognition by Article VI of the Treaty on the Non-Proliferation of Nuclear Weapons of an obligation to negotiate in good faith a nuclear disarmament. This provision is worded as follows:

    "Each of the Parties to the Treaty undertakes to pursue negotiations in good faith on effective measures relating to cessation of the nuclear arms race at an early date and to nuclear disarmament, and on a treaty on general and complete disarmament under strict and effective international control."

    The legal import of that obligation goes beyond that of a mere obligation of conduct ; the obligation involved here is an obligation to achieve a precise result — nuclear disarmament in all its aspects — by adopting a particular course of conduct, namely, the pursuit of negotiations on the matter in good faith.

100. This twofold obligation to pursue and to conclude negotiations formally concerns the 182 States parties to the Treaty on the Non Proliferation of Nuclear Weapons, or, in other words, the vast majority of the international community.

     Virtually the whole of this community appears moreover to have been involved when resolutions of the United Nations General Assembly concerning nuclear disarmament have repeatedly been unanimously adopted. Indeed, any realistic search for general and complete disarmament, especially nuclear disarmament, necessitates the co-operation of all States.

101. Even the very first General Assembly resolution, unanimously adopted on 24 January 1946 at the London session, set up a commission whose terms of reference included making specific proposals for, among other things, "the elimination from national armaments of atomic weapons and of all other major weapons adaptable to mass destruction". In a large number of subsequent resolutions, the General Assembly has reaffirmed the need for nuclear disarmament. Thus, in resolution 808 A (IX) of 4 November 1954, which was likewise unanimously adopted, it concluded

    "that a further effort should be made to reach agreement on comprehensive and co-ordinated proposals to be embodied in a draft international disarmament convention providing for: . . . (b) The total prohibition of the use and manufacture of nuclear weapons and weapons of mass destruction of every type, together with the conversion of existing stocks of nuclear weapons for peaceful pur poses."

    The same conviction has been expressed outside the United Nations context in various instruments.

102. The obligation expressed in Article VI of the Treaty on the Non Proliferation of Nuclear Weapons includes its fulfilment in accordance with the basic principle of good faith. This basic principle is set forth in Article 2, paragraph 2, of the Charter. It was reflected in the Declaration on Friendly Relations between States (resolution 2625 (XXV) of 24 October 1970) and in the Final Act of the Helsinki Conference of 1 August 1975. It is also embodied in Article 26 of the Vienna Convention on the Law of Treaties of 23 May 1969, according to which "[e]very treaty in force is binding upon the parties to it and must be performed by them in good faith".
Nor has the Court omitted to draw attention to it, as follows:

> "One of the basic principles governing the creation and performance of legal obligations, whatever their source, is the principle of good faith. Trust and confidence are inherent in international co-operation, in particular in an age when this co-operation in many fields is becoming increasingly essential." (*Nuclear Tests (Australia v. France), Judgment, I.C.J. Reports 1974*, p. 268, para. 46.)

103. In its resolution 984 (1995) dated 11 April 1995, the Security Council took care to reaffirm "the need for all States Parties to the Treaty on the Non-Proliferation of Nuclear Weapons to comply fully with all their obligations" and urged

> "all States, as provided for in Article VI of the Treaty on the Non-Proliferation of Nuclear Weapons, to pursue negotiations in good faith on effective measures relating to nuclear disarmament and on a treaty on general and complete disarmament under strict and effective international control which remains a universal goal".

The importance of fulfilling the obligation expressed in Article VI of the Treaty on the Non-Proliferation of Nuclear Weapons was also reaffirmed in the final document of the Review and Extension Conference of the parties to the Treaty on the Non-Proliferation of Nuclear Weapons, held from 17 April to 12 May 1995.
In the view of the Court, it remains without any doubt an objective of vital importance to the whole of the international community today.

* * *

104. At the end of the present Opinion, the Court emphasizes that its reply to the question put to it by the General Assembly rests on the totality of the legal grounds set forth by the Court above (paragraphs 20 to 103), each of which is to be read in the light of the others. Some of these grounds are not such as to form the object of formal conclusions in the final paragraph of the Opinion ; they nevertheless retain, in the view of the Court, all their importance.

* * *

[Paragraph 105 on the next page]

105. For these reasons,

THE COURT,

(1) By thirteen votes to one,

Decides to comply with the request for an advisory opinion;

IN FAVOUR: *President* Bedjaoui; *Vice-President* Schwebel; *Judges* Guillaume, Shahabuddeen, Weeramantry, Ranjeva, Herczegh, Shi, Fleischhauer, Koroma, Vereshchetin, Ferrari Bravo, Higgins;
AGAINST: *Judge* Oda;

(2) *Replies* in the following manner to the question put by the General Assembly:

A. Unanimously,

There is in neither customary nor conventional international law any specific authorization of the threat or use of nuclear weapons;

B. By eleven votes to three,

There is in neither customary nor conventional international law any comprehensive and universal prohibition of the threat or use of nuclear weapons as such;

IN FAVOUR : *President* Bedjaoui; *Vice-President* Schwebel ; *Judges* Oda, Guillaume, Ranjeva, Herczegh, Shi, Fleischhauer, Vereshchetin, Ferrari Bravo, Higgins;
AGAINST : *Judges* Shahabuddeen, Weeramantry, Koroma;

C. Unanimously,

A threat or use of force by means of nuclear weapons that is contrary to Article 2, paragraph 4, of the United Nations Charter and that fails to meet all the requirements of Article 51, is unlawful;

D. Unanimously,

A threat or use of nuclear weapons should also be compatible with the requirements of the international law applicable in armed conflict, particularly those of the principles and rules of international humanitarian law, as well as with specific obligations under treaties and other undertakings which expressly deal with nuclear weapons;

E. By seven votes to seven, by the President's casting vote,

It follows from the above-mentioned requirements that the threat or use of nuclear weapons would generally be contrary to the rules of international law applicable in armed conflict, and in particular the principles and rules of humanitarian law;
However, in view of the current state of international law, and of the elements of fact at its disposal, the Court cannot conclude definitively whether the threat or use of nuclear weapons would be lawful or unlawful in an extreme circumstance of self-defence, in which the very survival of a State would be at stake;

IN FAVOUR : *President* Bedjaoui; *Judges* Ranjeva, Herczegh, Shi, Fleischhauer, Vereshchetin, Ferrari Bravo;
AGAINST : *Vice-President* Schwebel; *Judges* Oda, Guillaume, Shahabuddeen, Weeramantry, Koroma, Higgins;

F. Unanimously,

There exists an obligation to pursue in good faith and bring to a conclusion negotiations leading to nuclear disarmament in all its aspects under strict and effective international control.

Done in English and in French, the English text being authoritative, at the Peace Palace, The Hague, this eighth day of July, one thousand nine hundred and ninety-six, in two copies, one of which will be placed in the archives of the Court and the other transmitted to the Secretary-General of the United Nations.

(Signed) Mohammed BEDJAOUI,
President.
(Signed) Eduardo VALENCIA-OSPINA,
Registrar.

President BEDJAOUI, Judges HERCZEGH, Sm, VERESHCHETIN and FERRARI BRAVO append declarations to the Advisory Opinion of the Court.

Judges GUILLAUME, RANJEVA AND FLEISCHHAUER append separate opinions to the Advisory Opinion of the Court.

Vice-President SCHWEBEL, Judges ODA, SHAHABUDDEEN, WEERAMANTRY, KOROMA and HIGGINS append dissenting opinions to the Advisory Opinion of the Court.

(Initialled) M.B.
(Initialled) E.V.O.

[this page is left blank intentionally]

Chapter 10

Dissenting Opinion of Judge Weeramantry

Table of Contents (see the book table of contents for page numbers)

Preliminary Observations on the Opinion of the Court
    (a) Reasons for dissent
    (b) The positive aspects of the Court's Opinion
    (c) Particular comments on the final paragraph

        (i) Paragraph 2 B -(11 votes to 3)
        (ii) Paragraph 2 E -(7 votes to 7. Casting vote in favour by the President)
        (iii) Paragraph 2 A - (Unanimous)
        (iv) Paragraph 2 C -(Unanimous)
        (v) Paragraph 2 D -(Unanimous)
        (vi) Paragraph 2 F -(Unanimous)
        (vii) Paragraph 1 - (13 votes to 1)

I. INTRODUCTION

    1. Fundamental importance of issue before the Court
    2. Submissions to the Court
    3. Some preliminary observations on the United Nations Charter
    4. The law relevant to nuclear weapons
    5. Introductory observations on humanitarian law
    6. Linkage between humanitarian law and the realities of war
    7. The limit situation created by nuclear weapons
    8. Possession and use
    9. Differing attitudes of States supporting legality
    10. The importance of a clarification of the law

II. NATURE AND EFFECTS OF NUCLEAR WEAPONS

    1. The nature of the nuclear weapon
    2. Euphemisms concealing the realities of nuclear war
    3. The effects of the nuclear weapon

        (a) Damage to the environment and the ecosystem
        (b) Damage to future generations
        (c) Damage to civilian populations
        (d) The nuclear winter
        (e) Loss of life
        (f) Medical effects of radiation
        (g) Heat and blast
        (h) Congenital deformities

(i) Transnational damage
(j) Potential to destroy all civilization
   (i) Social institutions
   (ii) Economic structures
   (iii) Cultural treasures
(k) The electromagnetic pulse
(l) Damage to nuclear reactors
(m) Damage to food productivity
(n) Multiple nuclear explosions resulting from self-defence
(o) "The shadow of the mushroom cloud"

4. The uniqueness of nuclear weapons
5. The differences in scientific knowledge between the present time and 1945
6. Do Hiroshima and Nagasaki show that nuclear war is survivable?
7. A perspective from the past

III. HUMANITARIAN LAW

1. "Elementary considerations of humanity"
2. Multicultural background to the humanitarian laws of war
3. Outline of humanitarian law
4. Acceptance by States of the Martens Clause
5. "The dictates of public conscience"
6. Impact of the United Nations Charter and human rights on "considerations of humanity" and "dictates of public conscience"
7. The argument that "collateral damage" is unintended
8. Illegality exists independently of specific prohibitions
9. The "*Lotus*" decision
10. Specific rules of the humanitarian law of war

   (a) The prohibition against causing unnecessary suffering
   (b) The principle of proportionality
   (c) The principle of discrimination
   (d) Respect for non-belligerent States
   (e) The prohibition against genocide
   (/) The prohibition against environmental damage
   (g) Human rights law

11. Juristic opinion
12. The 1925 Geneva Gas Protocol

   (i) Is radiation poisonous?
   (ii) Does radiation involve contact of the body with "materials"?

13. Article 23 (a) of the Hague Regulations

IV. SELF-DEFENCE

1. Unnecessary suffering
2. Proportionality/error
3. Discrimination
4. Non-belligerent States
5. Genocide
6. Environmental damage
7. Human rights

V. SOME GENERAL CONSIDERATIONS

1. Two philosophical perspectives
2. The aims of war
3. The concept of a "threat of force" under the United Nations Charter
4. Equality in the texture of the laws of war
5. The logical contradiction of a dual regime in the laws of war
6. Nuclear decision-making

VI. THE ATTITUDE OF THE INTERNATIONAL COMMUNITY TOWARDS NUCLEAR WEAPONS

1. The universality of the ultimate goal of complete elimination
2. Overwhelming majorities in support of total abolition
3. World public opinion
4. Current prohibitions
5. Partial bans
6. Who are the States most specially concerned?
7. Have States, by participating in regional treaties, recognized nuclear weapons as lawful?

VII. SOME SPECIAL ASPECTS

1. The Non-Proliferation Treaty
2. Deterrence

    (i) Meaning of deterrence
    (ii) Deterrence — from what?
    (iii) The degrees of deterrence
    (iv) Minimum deterrence
    (v) The problem of credibility
    (vi) Deterrence distinguished from possession
    (vii) The legal problem of intention
    (viii) The temptation to use the weapons maintained for deterrence
    (ix) Deterrence and sovereign equality
    (x) Conflict with the St. Petersburg principle

3. Reprisals
4. Internal wars
5. The doctrine of necessity
6. Limited or tactical or battlefield nuclear weapons

VIII. SOME ARGUMENTS AGAINST THE GRANT OF AN ADVISORY OPINION

1. The Advisory Opinion would be devoid of practical effects
2. Nuclear weapons have preserved world peace

IX. CONCLUSION

1. The task before the Court
2. The alternatives before humanity

APPENDIX (demonstrating danger to neutral States) Comparison of the effects of bombs.

Preliminary Observations on the Opinion of the Court

(a) Reasons for Dissent

My considered opinion is that the use or threat of use of nuclear weapons is illegal *in any circumstances whatsoever*. It violates the fundamental principles of international law, and represents the very negation of the humanitarian concerns which underlie the structure of humanitarian law. It offends conventional law and, in particular, the Geneva Gas Protocol of 1925, and Article 23 (a) of the Hague Regulations of 1907. It contradicts the fundamental principle of the dignity and worth of the human person on which all law depends. It endangers the human environment in a manner which threatens the entirety of life on the planet.

I regret that the Court has not held directly and categorically that the use or threat of use of the weapon is unlawful *in all circumstances without exception*. The Court should have so stated in a vigorous and forth right manner which would have settled this legal question now and for ever.

Instead, the Court has moved in the direction of illegality with some far-reaching pronouncements that strongly point in that direction, while making other pronouncements that are both less than clear and clearly wrong.

I have therefore been obliged to title this a dissenting opinion, although there are some parts of the Court's Opinion with which I agree, and which may still afford a substantial basis for a conclusion of illegality. Those aspects of the Court's Opinion are discussed below. They do take the law far on the road towards total prohibition. In this sense, the Court's Opinion contains positive pronouncements of significant value.

There are two of the six operative sections of the second part of the Opinion with which I profoundly disagree. I believe those two paragraphs state the law wrongly and incompletely, and I have felt compelled to vote against them.

However, I have voted in favour of paragraph 1 of the *dispositif*, and in favour of four out of the six items in paragraph 2.

(b) The Positive Aspects of the Court's Opinion

This Opinion represents the first decision of this Court, and indeed of any international tribunal, that clearly formulates limitations on nuclear weapons in terms of the United Nations Charter. It is the first such decision which expressly addresses the contradiction between nuclear weapons and the laws of armed conflict and international humanitarian law. It is the first such decision which expresses the view that the use of nuclear weapons is hemmed in and limited by a variety of treaty obligations.

In the environmental field, it is the first Opinion which expressly embodies, in the context of nuclear weapons, a principle of "prohibition of methods and means of warfare which are intended, or may be expected, to cause" widespread, long-term and severe environmental damage, and "the prohibition of attacks against the natural environment by way of reprisals" (para. 31).

In the field of nuclear disarmament, it also reminds all nations of their obligation to bring these negotiations to their conclusion in all their aspects, thereby ending the continuance of this threat to the integrity of international law.

Once these propositions are established, one needs only to examine the effects of the use of nuclear weapons to conclude that there is no possibility whatsoever of a use or threat of use that does not offend these principles. This Opinion examines at some length the numerous unique qualities of the nuclear weapon which stand in flagrant contradiction of the basic values underlying the United Nations Charter, international law, and international humanitarian law. In the light of that information, it becomes demonstrably impossible for the weapon to comply with the basic postulates laid down by the Court, thus rendering them illegal in terms of the unanimous finding of the Court.

In particular, I would mention the requirement, in Article 2 (4) of the Charter, of compliance with the Purposes of the United Nations. Those Purposes involve respect for human rights, and the dignity and worth of the human person. They also involve friendly relations among nations, and good neighbourliness (see Article 1 (Purposes and Principles) read with the Preamble). The linkage of legality with compliance with these principles has now been judicially established. Weapons of warfare which can kill a million or a billion human beings (according to the estimates placed before the Court) show scant regard for the dignity and worth of the human person, or for the principle of good neighbourliness. They stand condemned upon the principles laid down by the Court.

Even though I do not agree with the entirety of the Court's Opinion, strong indicators of illegality necessarily flow from the unanimous parts of that Opinion. Further details of the total incompatibility of the weapons with the principles laid down by the Court appear in the body of this Opinion.

It may be that further clarification will be possible in the future.

I proceed now to make some comments on the individual paragraphs of part 2 of the *dispositif*. I shall deal first with the two paragraphs with which I disagree.

(c) Particular Comments on the Final Paragraph

(i) Paragraph 2B — (11 votes to 3)

Regarding paragraph 2 B, I am of the view that there are comprehensive and universal limitations imposed by treaty upon the use of nuclear weapons. Environmental treaties and, in particular, the Geneva Gas Protocol and Article 23 (a) of the Hague Regulations, are among these. These are dealt with in my opinion. I do not think it is correct to say that there are no conventional prohibitions upon the use of the weapon.

(ii) Paragraph 2E — (7 votes to 7. Casting vote in favour by the President)

I am in fundamental disagreement with both sentences contained within this paragraph.

I strongly oppose the presence of the word "generally" in the first sentence. The word is too uncertain in content for use in an Advisory Opinion, and I cannot assent to a proposition which, even by remotest implication, leaves open any possibility that the use of nuclear weapons would not be contrary to law in any circumstances whatsoever. I regret the presence of this word in a sentence which otherwise states the law correctly. It would also appear that the word "generally" introduces an element of internal contradiction into the Court's Opinion, for in paragraphs 2C and 2D of the Court's Opinion, the Court concludes that nuclear weapons must be consistent with the United Nations Charter, the principles of international law, and the principles of humanitarian law, and, such consistency being impossible, the weapon becomes illegal.

The word "generally" admits of many meanings, ranging through various gradations, from "as a general rule; commonly", to "universally; with respect to all or nearly all"[1] Even with the latter meaning, the word opens a window of permissibility, however narrow, which does not truly reflect the law. There should be no niche in the legal principle, within which a nation may seek refuge, constituting itself the sole

---

1 *The Shorter Oxford English Dictionary*, 3rd ed., 1987, Vol. I, p. 840. (OED, 1987)

judge in its own cause on so important a matter.

The main purpose of this opinion is to show that, not generally but always, the threat or use of nuclear weapons would be contrary to the rules of international law and, in particular, to the principles and rules of humanitarian law. Paragraph 2E should have been in those terms, and the Opinion need have stated no more.

The second paragraph of 2E states that the current state of international law is such that the Court cannot conclude definitely whether the threat or use of the weapon would or would not be lawful in extreme circumstances of self-defence. It seems self-evident to me that once nuclear weapons are resorted to, the laws of war (the *jus in bello*) take over, and that there are many principles of the laws of war, as recounted in this opinion, which totally forbid the use of such a weapon. The existing law is sufficiently clear on this matter to have enabled the Court to make a definite pronouncement without leaving this vital question, as though sufficient principles are not already in existence to determine it. All the more should this uncertainty have been eliminated in view of the Court's very definite findings as set out earlier.

(iii) Paragraph 2A — (Unanimous)

Speaking for myself, I would have viewed this unquestionable proposition as a preliminary recital, rather than as part of the *dispositif*.

(iv) Paragraph 2C — (Unanimous)

The positive features of this paragraph have already been noted. The Court, in this paragraph, has unanimously endorsed Charter-based pre-conditions to the legality of nuclear weapons, which are diametrically opposed to the results of the use of the weapon. I thus read paragraph 2C of the *dispositif* as rendering the use of the nuclear weapon illegal without regard to the circumstances in which the weapon is used -whether in aggression or in self-defence, whether internationally or internally, whether by individual decision or in concert with other nations. A unanimous endorsement of this principle by all the judges of this Court takes the principle of illegality of use of nuclear weapons a long way forward from the stage when there was no prior judicial consideration of legality of nuclear weapons by any international tribunal.

Those contending that the use of nuclear weapons was within the law argued strongly that what is not expressly prohibited to a State is permitted. On this basis, the use of the nuclear weapon was said to be a matter on which the State's freedom was not limited. I see the limitations laid down in paragraph 2C as laying that argument to rest.

(v) Paragraph 2D — (Unanimous)

This paragraph, also unanimously endorsed by the Court, lays down the further limitation of compatibility with the requirements of international law applicable in armed conflict, and particularly with the rules of international humanitarian law and specific treaty obligations.

There is a large array of prohibitions laid down here.

My opinion will show what these rules and principles are, and how it is impossible, in the light of the nature and effects of nuclear weapons, for these to be satisfied.

If the weapon is demonstrably contrary to these principles, it is unlawful in accordance with this paragraph of the Court's Opinion.

(vi) Paragraph 2F — (Unanimous)

This paragraph is strictly outside the terms of reference of the question. Yet, in the overall context of the nuclear weapons problem, it is a useful reminder of State obligations, and I have accordingly voted in favour of it.

The ensuing opinion sets out my views on the question before the Court. Since the question posed to the Court relates only to use and threat of use, this opinion does not deal with the legality of other important aspects of nuclear weapons, such as possession, vertical or horizontal proliferation, assembling or testing.

I should also add that I have some reservations in regard to some of the reasoning in the body of the Court's Opinion. Those reservations will appear in the course of this opinion. In particular, while agreeing with the Court in the reasoning by which it rejects the various objections raised to admissibility and jurisdiction, I would register my disagreement with the statement in paragraph 14 of the Opinion that the refusal to give the World Health Organization the advisory opinion requested by it was justified by the Court's lack of jurisdiction in that case. My disagreement with that proposition is the subject of my dissenting opinion in that case.

I am of the view that in dealing with the question of reprisals (para. 46), the Court should have affirmatively pronounced on the question of the unlawfulness of belligerent reprisals. I do not agree also with its treatment of the question of intent towards a group as such in relation to genocide, and with its treatment of nuclear deterrence. These aspects are considered in this opinion.

(vii) Paragraph 1 — (13 votes to 1)

One other matter needs to be mentioned before I commence the substantive part of this dissenting opinion. I have voted in favour of the first finding of the Court, recorded in item 1 of the *dispositif*, which follows from the Court's rejection of the various objections to admissibility and jurisdiction which were taken by the States arguing in favour of the legality of nuclear weapons. I strongly support the views expressed by the Court in the course of its reasoning on these matters, but I have some further thoughts upon these objections, which I have set out in my dissenting opinion in relation to the WHO request, where also similar objections were taken. There is no need to repeat those observations in this opinion, in view of the Court's conclusions. However, what I have stated on these matters in that dissenting opinion should be read as supplementary to this opinion as well.

* * *

I. Introduction

1. Fundamental Importance of Issue before the Court

I now begin the substantive part of this opinion.

This case has from its commencement been the subject of a wave of global interest unparalleled in the annals of this Court. Thirty-five States have filed written statements before the Court and 24 have made oral submissions. A multitude of organizations, including several NGOs, have also sent communications to the Court and submitted materials to it; and nearly two million signatures have been actually received by the Court from various organizations and individuals from around 25 countries. In addition, there have been other shipments of signatures so voluminous that the Court could not physically receive them and they have been lodged in various other depositories. If these are also taken into account, the total number of signatures has been estimated by the Court's archivist at over three million[2]. The overall number

---

2 In a memorandum responding to an enquiry regarding the number of signatures received, the archivist

of signatures, all of which could not be deposited in the Court, is well in excess of this figure. The largest number of signatures has been received from Japan, the only nation that has suffered a nuclear attack[3]. Though these organizations and individuals have not made formal submissions to the Court, they evidence a groundswell of global public opinion which is not without legal relevance, as indicated later in this opinion.

The notion that nuclear weapons are inherently illegal, and that a knowledge of such illegality is of great practical value in obtaining a nuclear-free world, is not new. Albert Schweitzer referred to it, in a letter to Pablo Casals, as early as 1958 in terms of:

> "the most elementary and most obvious argument: namely, that international law prohibits weapons with an unlimitable effect, which cause unlimited damage to people outside the battle zone. This is the case with atomic and nuclear weapons . . . The argument that these weapons are contrary to international law contains everything that we can reproach them with. It has the advantage of being a *legal argument* . . . No government can deny that these weapons violate international law . . . and international law cannot be swept aside!"[4]

Though lay opinion has thus long expressed itself on the need for attention to the legal aspects, the matter has not thus far been the subject of any authoritative judicial pronouncement by an international tribunal. It was considered by the courts in Japan in the *Shimoda* case[5] but, until the two current requests for advisory opinions from this Court, there has been no international judicial consideration of the question. The responsibility placed upon the Court is thus of an extraordinarily onerous nature, and its pronouncements must carry extraordinary significance.

This matter has been strenuously argued before the Court from opposing points of view. The Court has had the advantage of being addressed by a number of the most distinguished practitioners in the field of international law. In their submissions before the Court, they have referred to the historic nature of this request by the General Assembly and the request of the World Health Organization, which has been heard along with it. In the words of one of them, these requests:

> "will constitute milestones in the history of the Court, if not in history *per se*. It is probable that these requests concern the most important legal issue which has ever been submitted to the Court." (Salmon, Solomon Islands, CR 95/32, p. 38.)

In the words of another, "It is not every day that the opportunity of pleading for the survival of humanity in such an august forum is offered." (David, Solomon Islands, CR 95/32, p. 49 .)

It is thus the gravest of possible issues which confronts the Court in this Advisory Opinion. It requires the Court to scrutinize every available source of international law, quarrying deep, if necessary, into its very bedrock. Seams of untold strength and richness lie therein, waiting to be quarried. Do these sources contain principles mightier than might alone, wherewith to govern the mightiest weapon of destruction yet devised?

It needs no emphasis that the function of the Court is to state the law as it now is, and not as it is envisaged in the future. Is the use or threat of use of nuclear weapons

---

observes that : "To be precise in this matter is to count the stars in the sky."

3 The sponsors of a Declaration of Public Conscience from Japan have stated, in a communication to the Registrar, that they have stored in a warehouse in The Hague, 1,757,757 signatures, which the Court had no space to accommodate, in addition to the 1,564,954 actually deposited with the Court. Another source, based in Europe, has reckoned the declarations it has received, in connection with the current applications to the Court, at 3,691,899, of which 3,338,408 have been received from Japan.

4 *Albert Schweitzer, Letters 1905-1965*, H. W. Baher (ed.), J. Neugroschel (trans.), 1992, p. 280, letter to Pablo Casals dated 3 October 1958; emphasis added. (Baher, 1992).

5 *Shimoda v. The Japanese State, The Japanese Annual of International Law*, 1964, pp. 212-252.

illegal under presently existing principles of law, rather than under aspirational expectations of what the law should be? The Court's concern in answering this request for an opinion is with *lex lata* not with *lex ferenda*.

At the most basic level, three alternative possibilities could offer themselves to the Court as it reaches its decision amidst the clash of opposing arguments. If indeed the principles of international law decree that the use of the nuclear weapon is legal, it must so pronounce. The anti-nuclear forces in the world are immensely influential, but that circumstance does not swerve the Court from its duty of pronouncing the use of the weapons legal if that indeed be the law. A second alternative conclusion is that the law gives no definite indication one way or the other. If so, that neutral fact needs to be declared, and a new stimulus may then emerge for the development of the law. Thirdly, if legal rules or principles dictate that the nuclear weapon is illegal, the Court will so pronounce, undeterred again by the immense forces ranged on the side of the legality of the weapon. As stated at the very commencement, this last represents my considered view. The forces ranged against the view of illegality are truly colossal. However, collisions with the colossal have not deterred the law on its upward course towards the concept of the rule of law. It has not flinched from the task of imposing constraints upon physical power when legal principle so demands. It has been by a determined stand against forces that seemed colossal or irresistible that the rule of law has been won. Once the Court determines what the law is, and ploughs its furrow in that direction, it cannot pause to look over its shoulder at the immense global forces ranged on either side of the debate.

2. Submissions to the Court

Apart from submissions relating to the competence of the General Assembly to request this opinion, a large number of submissions on the substantive law have been made on both sides by the numerous States who have appeared before the Court or tendered written submissions.

Though there is necessarily an element of overlap among some of these submissions, they constitute in their totality a vast mass of material, probing the laws of war to their conceptual foundations. Extensive factual material has also been placed before the Court in regard to the many ways in which the nuclear weapon stands alone, even among weapons of mass destruction, for its unique potential of damaging humanity and its environment for generations to come.

On the other hand, those opposing the submission of illegality have argued that, despite a large number of treaties dealing with nuclear weapons, no single clause in any treaty declares nuclear weapons to be illegal in specific terms. They submit that, on the contrary, the various treaties on nuclear weapons entered into by the international community, including the Nuclear Non-Proliferation Treaty (NPT) in particular, carry a clear implication of the current legality of nuclear weapons in so far as concerns the nuclear powers. Their position is that the principle of the illegality of the use or threat of use of nuclear weapons still lies in the future, although considerable progress has been made along the road leading to that result. It is *lex ferenda* in their submission, and not yet of the status of *lex lata*. Much to be desired, but not yet achieved, it is a principle waiting to be born.

This opinion cannot possibly do justice to all of the formal submissions made to the Court, but will attempt to deal with some of the more important among them.

3. Some Preliminary Observations on the United Nations Charter

It was only a few weeks before the world was plunged into the age of the atom that the United Nations Charter was signed. The subscribing nations adopted this document at San Francisco on 26 June 1945. The bomb was dropped on Hiroshima on 6 August 1945. Only 40 days intervened between the two events, each so pregnant with meaning for the human future. The United Nations Charter opened a new vista of hope. The bomb opened new vistas of destruction.

Accustomed as it was to the destructiveness of traditional war, the world was shaken and awe-struck at the power of the nuclear bomb — a small bomb by modern standards. The horrors of war, such as were known to those who drafted the Charter, were thus only the comparatively milder horrors of World War II, as they had been experienced thus far. Yet these horrors, seared into the conscience of humanity by the most devastating conflict thus far in human history, were sufficient to galvanize the world community into action, for, in the words of the United Nations Charter, they had "brought untold sorrow to mankind". The potential to bring untold sorrow to mankind was within weeks to be multiplied several-fold by the bomb. Did that document, drafted in total unawareness of this escalation in the weaponry of war, have anything to say of relevance to the nuclear age which lay round the corner?

There are six keynote concepts in the opening words of the Charter which have intense relevance to the matter before the Court.

The Charter's very first words are "We, the peoples of the United Nations" — thereby showing that all that ensues is the will of the peoples of the world. Their collective will and desire is the very source of the United Nations Charter and that truth should never be permitted to recede from view. In the matter before the Court, the peoples of the world have a vital interest, and global public opinion has an important influence on the development of the principles of public international law. As will be observed later in this opinion, the law applicable depends heavily upon "the principles of humanity" and "the dictates of public conscience", in relation to the means and methods of warfare that are permissible.

The Charter's next words refer to the determination of those peoples to save succeeding generations from the scourge of war. The only war they knew was war with non-nuclear weapons. That resolve would presumably have been steeled even further had the destructiveness and the inter-generational effects of nuclear war been known.

The Charter immediately follows those two key concepts with a third — the dignity and worth of the human person. This is recognized as the cardinal unit of value in the global society of the future. A means was about to reveal itself of snuffing it out by the million with the use of a single nuclear weapon.

The fourth observation in the Charter, succeeding hard on the heels of the first three, is the equal rights of nations large and small. This is an ideal which is heavily eroded by the concept of nuclear power.

The next observation refers to the maintenance of obligations arising from treaties and *"other sources of international law"* (emphasis added). The argument against the legality of nuclear weapons rests principally not upon treaties, but upon such "other sources of international law" (mainly humanitarian law), whose principles are universally accepted.

The sixth relevant observation in the preamble to the Charter is its object of promoting social progress and better standards of life in larger freedom. Far from moving towards this Charter ideal, the weapon we are considering is one which has the potential to send humanity back to the stone age if it survives at all.

It is indeed as though, with remarkable prescience, the founding fathers had picked out the principal areas of relevance to human progress and welfare which could be shattered by the appearance only six weeks away of a weapon which for ever would alter the contours of war — a weapon which was to be described by one of its creators, in the words of ancient oriental wisdom, as a "shatterer of worlds"[6].

The Court is now faced with the duty of rendering an opinion in regard to the legality of this weapon. The six cardinal considerations set out at the very commencement of the Charter need to be kept in constant view, for each of them offers guidelines not to be lightly ignored.

---

6 Robert Oppenheimer, quoting *The Bhagvadgita*. See Peter Goodchild, *Robert Oppenheimer: Shatterer of Worlds,* 1980. (Goodchild, 1980).

4. *The Law Relevant to Nuclear Weapons*

As Oscar Schachter observes, the law relevant to nuclear weapons is "much more comprehensive than one might infer from the discussions of nuclear strategists and political scientists" [7], and the range of applicable law could be considered in the following five categories:

1. The international law applicable generally to armed conflicts — the *jus in bello*, sometimes referred to as the "humanitarian law of war".
2. The *jus ad bellum* — the law governing the right of States to go to war. This law is expressed in the United Nations Charter and related customary law.
3. The *lex specialis* — the international legal obligations that relate specifically to nuclear arms and weapons of mass destruction.
4. The whole corpus of international law that governs State obligations and rights generally, which may affect nuclear weapons policy in particular circumstances.
5. National law, constitutional and statutory, that may apply to decisions on nuclear weapons by national authorities.

All of these will be touched upon in the ensuing opinion, but the main focus of attention will be on the first category mentioned above.

This examination will also show that each one of the sources of international law, as set out in Article 38 (I) of the Court's Statute, supports the conclusion that the use of nuclear weapons in any circumstances is illegal.

5. *Introductory Observations on Humanitarian Law*

It is in the department of humanitarian law that the most specific and relevant rules relating to this problem can be found.

Humanitarian law and custom have a very ancient lineage. They reach back thousands of years. They were worked out in many civilizations — Chinese, Indian, Greek, Roman, Japanese, Islamic, modern European, among others. Through the ages many religious and philosophical ideas have been poured into the mould in which modern humanitarian law has been formed. They represented the effort of the human conscience to mitigate in some measure the brutalities and dreadful sufferings of war. In the language of a notable declaration in this regard (the St. Petersburg Declaration of 1868), international humanitarian law is designed to "conciliate the necessities of war with the laws of humanity". In recent times, with the increasing slaughter and devastation made possible by modern weaponry, the dictates of conscience have prompted ever more comprehensive formulations.

It is today a substantial body of law, consisting of general principles flexible enough to accommodate unprecedented developments in weaponry, and firm enough to command the allegiance of all members of the community of nations. This body of general principles exists in addition to over 600 special provisions in the Geneva Conventions and their Additional Protocols, apart from numerous other conventions on special matters such as chemical and bacteriological weapons. It is thus an important body of law in its own right, and this case in a sense puts it to the test.

Humanitarian law is ever in continuous development. It has a vitality of its own. As observed by the 1945 Nuremberg Tribunal, which dealt with undefined "crimes against humanity" and other crimes, "[the law of war] is not static, but by continual adaptation follows the needs of a changing world" [8]. Humanitarian law grows as the sufferings of war keep escalating. With the nuclear weapon, those sufferings reach

---
7 Proceedings of the Canadian Conference on Nuclear Weapons and the Law, published as *Lawyers and the Nuclear Debate*, Maxwell Cohen and Margaret Gouin (eds.), 1988, p. 29. (Cohen and Gouin, 1988)
8 *Trial of the Major War Criminals before the International Military Tribunal*, 1948, Vol. 22, p. 464.

a limit situation, beyond which all else is academic. Humanitarian law, as a living discipline, must respond sensitively, appropriately and meaningfully.

By their very nature, problems in humanitarian law are not abstract, intellectual enquiries which can be pursued in ivory-tower detachment from the sad realities which are their stuff and substance. Not being mere exercises in logic and black-letter law, they cannot be logically or intellectually disentangled from their terrible context. Distasteful though it be to contemplate the brutalities surrounding these legal questions, the legal questions can only be squarely addressed when those brutalities are brought into vivid focus.

The brutalities tend often to be hidden behind a veil of generalities and platitudes — such as that all war is brutal or that nuclear weapons are the most devastating weapons of mass destruction yet devised. It is necessary to examine more closely what this means in all its stark reality. A close and unvarnished picture is required of the actual human sufferings involved, and of the multifarious threats to the human condition posed by these weapons. Then only can humanitarian law respond appropriately. Indeed, it is by turning the spotlight on the agonies of the battlefield that modern humanitarian law began. This opinion will therefore examine the factual effects of nuclear weapons in that degree of minimum detail which is necessary to attract to these considerations the matching principles of humanitarian law.

6. *Linkage between Humanitarian Law and the Realities of War*

The nineteenth century tended to view war emotionally, as a glorious enterprise, and practically, as a natural extension of diplomacy. Legitimized by some philosophers, respected by nearly all statesmen, and glorified by many a poet and artist, its brutalities tended to be concealed behind screens of legitimacy, respectability and honour.

Henri Dunant's Memory of Solferino, written after a visit to the battlefield of Solferino in 1859, dragged the brutalities of war into public view in a manner which shook contemporary civilization out of its complacency and triggered off the development of modern humanitarian law. That spirit of realism needs to be constantly rekindled if the law is not to stray too far from its subject matter, and thus become sterile.

Dunant's historic account touched the conscience of his age to the extent that a legal response seemed imperative. Here is his description of the raw realities of war as practised in his time:

> "Here is a hand-to-hand struggle in all its horror and frightfulness: Austrians and Allies trampling each other under foot, killing one another on piles of bleeding corpses, felling their enemies with their rifle butts, crushing skulls, ripping bellies open with sabre and bayonet. No quarter is given. It is a sheer butchery...
>
> A little further on, it is the same picture, only made the more ghastly by the approach of a squadron of cavalry, which gallops by, crushing dead and dying beneath its horses' hoofs. One poor man has his jaw carried away; another his head shattered; a third, who could have been saved, has his chest beaten in.
>
> Here comes the artillery, following the cavalry and going at full gallop. The guns crash over the dead and wounded, strewn pell-mell on the ground. Brains spurt under the wheels, limbs are broken and torn, bodies mutilated past recognition — the soil is literally puddled with blood, and the plain littered with human remains."

His description of the aftermath is no less powerful:

> "The stillness of the night was broken by groans, by stifled sighs of

anguish and suffering. Heart-rending voices kept calling for help. Who could ever describe the agonies of that fearful night?

When the sun came up on the twenty-fifth, it disclosed the most dreadful sights imaginable. Bodies of men and horses covered the battlefield: corpses were strewn over roads, ditches, ravines, thickets and fields: the approaches of Solferino were literally thick with dead."

Such were the realities of war, to which humanitarian law was the response of the legal conscience of the time. The nuclear weapon has increased the savagery a thousandfold since Dunant wrote his famous words. The conscience of our time has accordingly responded in appropriate measure, as amply demonstrated by the global protests, the General Assembly resolutions, and the universal desire to eliminate nuclear weapons altogether. It does not sit back in a spirit of scholarly detachment, drawing its conclusions from refined exercises in legal logic.

Just as it is through close contact with the raw facts of artillery and cavalry warfare that modern humanitarian law emerged, it is through a consideration of the raw facts of nuclear war that an appropriate legal response can emerge.

While we have moved from the cruelties of cavalry and artillery to the exponentially greater cruelties of the atom, we now enjoy a dual advantage, not present in Dunant's time — the established discipline of humanitarian law and ample documentation of the human suffering involved. Realities infinitely more awful than those which confronted Dunant's age of simpler warfare cannot fail to touch the legal conscience of our age.

Here is an eyewitness description from the first use of the weapon in the nuclear age — one of hundreds of such scenes which no doubt occurred simultaneously, and many of which have been recorded in contemporary documentation. The victims were not combatants, as was the case at Solferino:

"It was a horrible sight. Hundreds of injured people who were trying to escape to the hills passed our house. The sight of them was almost unbearable. Their faces and hands were burnt and swollen; and great sheets of skin had peeled away from their tissues to hang down like rags on a scarecrow. They moved like a line of ants. All through the night they went past our house, but this morning they had stopped. I found them lying on both sides of the road, so thick that it was impossible to pass without stepping on them.

And they had no faces! Their eyes, noses and mouths had been burned away, and it looked like their ears had been melted off. It was hard to tell front from back. One soldier, whose features had been destroyed and was left with his white teeth sticking out, asked me for some water but I didn't have any. (I clasped my hands and prayed for him. He didn't say anything more.) His plea for water must have been his last words." [9].

Multiply this a thousand-fold or even a million-fold and we have a picture of just one of the many possible effects of nuclear war.

Massive documentation details the sufferings caused by nuclear weapons — from the immediate charring and mutilation for miles from the site of the explosion, to the lingering after-effects — the cancers and the leukaemias which imperil human health, the genetic mutations which threaten human integrity, the environmental devastation which endangers the human habitat, the disruption of all organization, which undermines human society.

The Hiroshima and Nagasaki experience were two isolated incidents three days apart. They tell us very little of the effects of multiple explosions that would almost

---

9 *Hiroshima Diary: The Journal of a Japanese Physician August 6-September 30, 1945*, by Michihiko Hachiya, M.D., translated and edited by Warner Wells, M.D., University of North Carolina Press, 1955, pp. 14-15.(Hachiya, 1955).

inevitably follow in quick succession in the event of a nuclear war today (see Section II.6 below). Moreover, 50 years of development have intervened, with bombs being available now which carry 70 or even 700 times the explosive power of the Hiroshima and Nagasaki bombs. The devastation of Hiroshima and Nagasaki could be magnified several-fold by just one bomb today, let alone a succession of bombs.

7. *The Limit Situation Created by Nuclear Weapons*

Apart from human suffering, nuclear weapons, as observed earlier, take us into a limit situation. They have the potential to destroy all civilization — all that thousands of years of effort in all cultures have produced. It is true "the dreary story of sickened survivors lapsing into stone-age brutality is not an assignment that any sensitive person undertakes willingly", but it is necessary to "contemplate the likely outcome of mankind's present course clear-sightedly"[10]. Since nuclear weapons can destroy all life on the planet, they imperil all that humanity has ever stood for, and humanity itself.

An analogy may here be drawn between the law relating to the environment and the law relating to war.

At one time it was thought that the atmosphere, the seas and the land surface of the planet were vast enough to absorb any degree of pollution and yet rehabilitate themselves. The law was consequently very lax in its attitude towards pollution. However, with the realization that a limit situation would soon be reached, beyond which the environment could absorb no further pollution without danger of collapse, the law found itself compelled to reorientate its attitude towards the environment.

With the law of war, it is no different. Until the advent of nuclear war, it was thought that however massive the scale of a war, humanity could survive and reorder its affairs. With the nuclear weapon, a limit situation was reached, in that the grim prospect opened out that humanity may well fail to survive the next nuclear war, or that all civilization may be destroyed. That limit situation has compelled the law of war to reorientate its attitudes and face this new reality.

8. *Possession and Use*

Although it is the use of nuclear weapons, and not possession, that is the subject of this reference, many arguments have been addressed to the Court which deal with possession and which therefore are not pertinent to the issues before the Court.

For example, the Court was referred, in support of the position that nuclear weapons are a matter within the sovereign authority of each State, to the following passage in *Military and Paramilitary Activities in and against Nicaragua (Nicaragua v. United States of America)*:

> "'in international law there are no rules, other than such rules as may be accepted by the State concerned, by treaty or otherwise, whereby the *level of armaments* of a sovereign State can be limited' (*I.C.J. Reports 1986*, p. 135)" (CR 95/23, p. 79, France; emphasis added).

This passage clearly relates to possession, not use.

Much was made also of the Nuclear Non-Proliferation Treaty, as permitting nuclear weapons to the nuclear weapons States. Here again such permission, if any, as may be inferred from that treaty relates to *possession* and not *use*, for nowhere does the NPT contemplate or deal with the use or threat of use of nuclear weapons. On questions of use or threat of use, the NPT is irrelevant.

---

10 "The Medical and Ecological Effects of Nuclear War", by Don G. Bates, Professor of the History of Medicine, McGill University, in *McGill Law Journal*, 1983, Vol. 28, p. 717.

9. Differing Attitudes of States Supporting Legality

There are some significant differences between the positions adopted by States supporting the legality of the use of nuclear weapons. Indeed, in relation to some very basic matters, there are divergent approaches among the nuclear States themselves.

Thus the French position is that

> "This criterion of proportionality does not itself rule out in principle the utilization, whether in response or as a matter of first use, of any particular weapon whatsoever, including a nuclear weapon, *provided that such use is intended to withstand an attack and appears to be the most appropriate means of doing so.*" (French Written Statement, p. 29, emphasis added.)

According to this view, the factors referred to could, in a given case, even outweigh the principle of proportionality. It suggests that the governing criterion determining the permissibility of the weapon is whether it is the most appropriate means of withstanding the attack. The United States position is that:

> "Whether an attack with nuclear weapons would be disproportionate depends entirely on the circumstances, including the nature of the enemy threat, the importance of destroying the objective, the character, size and likely effects of the device, and the magnitude of the risk to civilians." (United States Written Statement, p. 23.)

The United States position thus carefully takes into account such circumstances as the character, size and effects of the device and the magnitude of risk to civilians.

The position of the Russian Federation is that the "Martens Clause" (see Section III.4) is not working at all and that today the Martens Clause may formally be considered inapplicable (Written Statement, p. 13).

The United Kingdom, on the other hand, while accepting the applicability of the Martens Clause, submits that the clause does not on its own establish the illegality of nuclear weapons (United Kingdom Written Statement, p. 48, para. 3.58). The United Kingdom argues that the terms of the Martens Clause make it necessary to point to a rule of customary law outlawing the use of nuclear weapons.

These different perceptions of the scope, and indeed of the very basis of the claim of legality on the part of the nuclear powers themselves, call for careful examination in the context of the question addressed to the Court.

10. The Importance of a Clarification of the Law

The importance of a clarification of the law upon the legality of nuclear weapons cannot be overemphasized.

On 6 June 1899, Mr. Martens (presiding over the Second Subcommission of the Second Commission of the Hague Conference), after whom the Martens Clause has been named (which will be referred to at some length in this opinion), made the following observations in reply to the contention that it was preferable to leave the laws of war in a vague state. He said:

> "But is this opinion quite just? Is this uncertainty advantageous to the weak? Do the weak become stronger because the *duties* of the strong are not determined? Do the strong become weaker because their *rights* are specifically defined and consequently limited? I do not think so. I am fully convinced that it is particularly in the interest of the weak that these rights and duties be defined ....
>
> Twice, in 1874 and 1899, two great international Conferences have

gathered together the most competent and eminent men of the civilized world on the subject. They have not succeeded in determining the laws and customs of war. They have separated, leaving utter vagueness for all these questions....

To leave uncertainty hovering over these questions would necessarily be to allow the interests of force to triumph over those of humanity ..."[11].

It is in this quest for clarity that the General Assembly has asked the Court to render an opinion on the use of nuclear weapons. The nations who control these weapons have opposed this application, and so have some others. It is in the interests of all nations that this matter be clarified which, for one reason or another, has not been specifically addressed for the past 50 years. It has remained unresolved and has hung over the future of humanity, like a great question mark, raising even issues so profound as the future of human life upon the planet.

The law needs to be clearly stated in the light of State rights and obligations under the new world dispensation brought about by the United Nations Charter which, for the first time in human history, outlawed war by the consensus of the community of nations. Fifty years have passed since that epoch-making document which yet lay in the distant future when Martens spoke. Those 50 years have been years of inaction, in so far as concerns the clarification of this most important of legal issues ever to face the global community.

II. Nature and Effects of Nuclear Weapons

1. *The Nature of the Nuclear Weapon*

The matter before the Court involves the application of humanitarian law to questions of fact, not the construction of humanitarian law as an abstract body of knowledge.

The Court is enquiring into the question whether the use of nuclear weapons produces factual consequences of such an inhumane nature as to clash with the basic principles of humanitarian law. Both in regard to this Advisory Opinion and in regard to that sought by the World Health Organization, a vast mass of factual material has been placed before the Court as an aid to its appreciation of the many ways in which the effects of nuclear weapons attract the application of various principles of humanitarian law. It is necessary to examine these specific facts, at least in outline, for they illustrate, more than any generalities can, the unique features of the nuclear weapon.

Moreover, the contention that nuclear war is in some way containable renders essential a detailed consideration of the unique and irreversible nature of the effects of nuclear weapons.

2. *Euphemisms Concealing the Realities of Nuclear War*

It would be a paradox if international law, a system intended to promote world peace and order, should have a place within it for an entity that can cause total destruction of the world system, the millennia of civilization which have produced it, and humanity itself. A factor which powerfully conceals that contradiction, even to the extent of keeping humanitarian law at bay, is the use of euphemistic language — the disembodied language of military operations and the polite language of diplomacy. They conceal the horror of nuclear war, diverting attention to intellectual concepts such as self-defence, reprisals, and proportionate damage which can have little relevance to a situation of total destruction.

---

11 J. B. Scott, "The Conference of 1899", *The Proceedings of the Hague Peace Conferences*, 1920, pp. 506-507; emphasis added

Horrendous damage to civilians and neutrals is described as collateral damage, because it was not directly intended; incineration of cities becomes "considerable thermal damage". One speaks of "acceptable levels of casualties", even if megadeaths are involved. Maintaining the balance of terror is described as "nuclear preparedness"; assured destruction as "deterrence", total devastation of the environment as "environmental damage". Clinically detached from their human context, such expressions bypass the world of human suffering, out of which humanitarian law has sprung.

As observed at the commencement of this opinion, humanitarian law needs to be brought into juxtaposition with the raw realities of war if it is to respond adequately. Such language is a hindrance to this process[12].

Both ancient philosophy and modern linguistics have clearly identified the problem of the obscuring of great issues through language which conceals their key content. Confucius, when asked how he thought order and morality could be created in the State, answered, "By correcting names." By this he meant calling each thing by its correct name[13].

Modern semantics has likewise exposed the confusion caused by words of euphemism, which conceal the true meanings of concepts[14]. The language of nuclear war, rich in these euphemisms, tends to sidetrack the real issues of extermination by the million, incineration of the populations of cities, genetic deformities, inducement of cancers, destruction of the food chain, and the imperilling of civilization. The mass extinction of human lives is treated with the detachment of entries in a ledger which can somehow be reconciled. If humanitarian law is to address its tasks with clarity, it needs to strip away these verbal dressings and come to grips with its real subject-matter. Bland and disembodied language should not be permitted to conceal the basic contradictions between the nuclear weapon and the fundamentals of international law.

3. *The Effects of the Nuclear Weapon*

Before 1945 "the highest explosive effect of bombs was produced by TNT devices of about 20 tons"[15]. The nuclear weapons exploded in Hiroshima and Nagasaki were more or less of the explosive power of 15 and 12 kilotons respectively, that is, 15,000 and 12,000 tons of TNT (trinitrotoluene) respectively. Many of the weapons existing today and in process of being tested represent several multiples of the explosive power of these bombs. Bombs in the megaton (equivalent to a million tons of TNT) and multiple megaton range are in the world's nuclear arsenals, some being even in excess of 20 megatons (equivalent to 20 million tons of TNT). A one-megaton bomb, representing the explosive power of a million tons of TNT, would be around 70 times the explosive power of the bombs used on Japan, and a 20-megaton bomb well over a thousand times that explosive power.

Since the mind is numbed by such abstract figures and cannot comprehend them, they have been graphically concretized in various ways. One of them is to picture the quantity of TNT represented by a single one-megaton bomb, in terms of its transport by rail. It has been estimated that this would require a train 200 miles long[16]. When one is carrying death and destruction to an enemy in war through the use of a single one megaton bomb, it assists the comprehension of this phenomenon to think in terms of a 200-mile train loaded with TNT being driven into enemy territory, to be exploded there. It cannot be said that international law would consider this legal. Nor

---

12 This aspect is addressed in a volume of contemporary philosophical explorations of the problem of war, *The Critique of War*, Robert Ginsberg (ed.), 1969. See, in particular, Chap. 6, "War and the Crisis of Language", by Thomas Merton. (Ginsberg, 1969).
13 Cited in Robert S. Hartman, "The Revolution against War", in *The Critique of War*, (ibid. p. 324).
14 They serve to build these figments of hell into the system of power politics, and to dim the minds of the nuclear citizens." (*Ibid.*, p. 325.).
15 N. Singh and E. McWhinney, *Nuclear Weapons and Contemporary International Law*, 1989, p. 29.
16 Bates, op. cit., p. 719. (Bates, 1983).

does it make any difference if the train is not 200 miles long, but 100 miles, 50 miles, 10 miles, or only 1 mile. Nor, again, could it matter if the train is 1,000 miles long, as would be the case with a 5-megaton bomb, or 4,000 miles long, as would be the case with a 20-megaton bomb.

Such is the power of the weapon upon which the Court is deliberating — power which dwarfs all historical precedents, even if they are considered cumulatively. A 5-megaton weapon would represent more explosive power than all of the bombs used in World War II and a 20-megaton bomb "more than all of the explosives used in all of the wars in the history of mankind"[17].

The weapons used at Hiroshima and Nagasaki are "small" weapons compared with those available today and, as observed earlier, a one megaton bomb would represent around 70 Hiroshimas and a 15-megaton bomb around 1,000 Hiroshimas. Yet the unprecedented magnitude of its destructive power is only one of the unique features of the bomb. It is unique in its uncontainability in both space and time. It is unique as a source of peril to the human future. It is unique as a source of continuing danger to human health, even long after its use. Its infringement of humanitarian law goes beyond its being a weapon of mass destruction[18]; to reasons which penetrate far deeper into the core of humanitarian law.

Atomic weapons have certain special characteristics distinguishing them from conventional weapons, which were summarized by the United States Atomic Energy Commission in terms that:

> "it differs from other bombs in three important respects: *first*, the amount of energy released by an atomic bomb is a thousand or more times as great as that produced by the most powerful TNT bombs; *secondly*, the explosion of the bomb is accompanied by highly penetrating and deleterious invisible rays, in addition to intense heat and light; and, *thirdly*, the substances which remain after the explosion are radio-active, emitting radiations capable of producing harmful consequences in living organisms"[19].

The following more detailed analysis is based on materials presented to the Court, which have not been contradicted at the hearings, even by the States contending that the use of nuclear weapons is not illegal. They constitute the essential factual foundation on which the legal arguments rest, and without which the legal argument is in danger of being reduced to mere academic disputation.

(a) Damage to the environment and the ecosystem[20].

The extent of damage to the environment, which no other weapon is capable of causing, has been summarized in 1987 by the World Commission on the Environment and Development in the following terms:

> "The likely consequences of nuclear war make other threats to the environment pale into insignificance. Nuclear weapons represent a qualitatively new step in the development of warfare. One thermonuclear bomb can have an explosive power greater than all the explosives used in wars since the invention of gunpowder. In addition to the destructive effects of blast and heat, immensely magnified by these weapons, they introduce a new lethal agent — ionising radiation — that extends lethal

---

17 Bates, op. cit., p. 719.
18 The Final Document of the First Special Session of the United Nations General Assembly devoted to Disarmament (1978) unanimously categorized nuclear weapons as weapons of mass destruction, a conclusion which was adopted by consensus (CR 95125, p. 17).
19 *Effects of Atomic Weapons*, prepared by the United States Atomic Energy Commission in co-operation the Department of Defense, 1950, cited in Singh and McWhinney, *op. cit.*, p. 30. (and see Glasstone and Dolan, 1977 - and Glasstone et al., 1950 - and later versions)
20 On environmental law, see further Section III. JO (f) below.

effects over both space and time."[21].

Nuclear weapons have the potential to destroy the entire ecosystem of the planet. Those already in the world's arsenals have the potential of destroying life on the planet several times over.

Another special feature of the nuclear weapon, referred to at the hearings, is the damage caused by ionizing radiation to coniferous forests, crops, the food chain, livestock and the marine ecosystem.

(b) Damage to future generations

The effects upon the ecosystem extend, for practical purposes, beyond the limits of all foreseeable historical time. The half-life of one of the by products of a nuclear explosion — plutonium 239 — is over 20,000 years. With a major nuclear exchange it would require several of these "half life" periods before the residuary radioactivity becomes minimal. Half-life is "the period in which the rate of radioactive emission by a pure sample falls by a factor of two. Among known radioactive isotopes, half-lives range from about 10^{-7} seconds to 10^{16} years"[22].

The following table[23] gives the half-lives of the principal radioactive elements that result from a nuclear test:

Nucleid	Half-life
Cesium 137	30.2 years
Strontium 90	28.6 years
Plutonium 239	24, 100 years
Plutonium 240	6,570 years
Plutonium 241	14.4 years
Americium 241	432 years

Theoretically, this could run to tens of thousands of years. At any level of discourse, it would be safe to pronounce that no one generation is entitled, for whatever purpose, to inflict such damage on succeeding generations.

This Court, as the principal judicial organ of the United Nations, empowered to state and apply international law with an authority matched by no other tribunal must, in its jurisprudence, pay due recognition to the rights of future generations. If there is any tribunal that can recognize and protect their interests under the law, it is this Court.

It is to be noted in this context that the rights of future generations have passed the stage when they were merely an embryonic right struggling for recognition. They have woven themselves into international law through major treaties, through juristic opinion and through general principles of law recognized by civilized nations.

Among treaties may be mentioned, the 1979 London Ocean Dumping Convention, the 1973 Convention on International Trade in Endangered Species, and the 1972 Convention Concerning the Protection of the World Cultural and Natural Heritage. All of these expressly incorporate the principle of protecting the natural environment for future generations, and elevate the concept to the level of binding State obligation.

Juristic opinion is now abundant, with several major treatises appearing upon the

---

21 World Commission on Environment and Development ("the Brundtland Commission"), *Our Common Future*, 1987, p. 295, cited in CR 95122, p. 55 (see Bruntland, 1987).
22 *Encyclopaedia Britannica Micropaedia*, 1992 ed., Vol. 9, p. 893.
23 Source: *Radioecology*, Holm ed., 1995, World Scientific Publishing Co..

subject and with such concepts as intergenerational equity and the common heritage of mankind being academically well established[24]. Moreover, there is a growing awareness of the ways in which a multiplicity of traditional legal systems across the globe protect the environment for future generations. To these must be added a series of major international declarations commencing with the 1972 Stockholm Declaration on the Human Environment.

When incontrovertible scientific evidence speaks of pollution of the environment on a scale that spans hundreds of generations, this Court would fail in its trust if it did not take serious note of the ways in which the distant future is protected by present law. The ideals of the United Nations Charter do not limit themselves to the present, for they look forward to the promotion of social progress and better standards of life, and they fix their vision, not only on the present, but on "succeeding generations". This one factor of impairment of the environment over such a seemingly infinite time span would by itself be sufficient to call into operation the protective principles of international law which the Court, as the pre-eminent authority empowered to state them, must necessarily apply.

(c) Damage to civilian populations

This needs no elaboration, for nuclear weapons surpass all other weapons of mass destruction in this respect. In the words of a well-known study of the development of international law:

> "A characteristic of the weapons of mass destruction — the ABC weapons — is that their destructive effect cannot be limited in space and time to military objectives. Consequently their use would imply the extinction of unforeseeable and indeterminable masses of the civilian population. This means also that their actual employment would be — even in the absence of explicit treaty provisions — contrary to international law, but it is also true that the problem of the weapons of mass destruction has grown out of the sphere of humanitarian law taken in the narrow sense and has become one of the fundamental issues of the peaceful coexistence of States with different social systems."[25].

(d) The nuclear winter

One of the possible after-effects of an exchange of nuclear weapons is the nuclear winter, a condition caused by the accumulation of hundreds of millions of tons of soot in the atmosphere, in consequence of fires in cities, in forests and the countryside, caused by nuclear weapons. The smoke cloud and the debris from multiple explosions blots out sunlight, resulting in crop failures throughout the world and global starvation. Starting with the paper by Turco, Toon, Ackerman, Pollack and Sagan (known as the TTAPS study after the names of its authors) on "Nuclear Winter: Global Consequences of Multiple Nuclear Explosions"[26], an enormous volume of detailed scientific work has been done on the effect of the dust and smoke clouds generated in nuclear war. The TTAPS study showed that smoke clouds in one hemisphere could within weeks move into the other hemisphere[27]. TTAPS and other studies show that

---

24 For further references, see Edith Brown Weiss, *In Fairness to Future Generations: International Law, Common Patrimony and Intergenerational Equity,* 1989.
25 Geza Herczegh, *Development of International Humanitarian Law,* 1984, p. 93. "ABC weapons" refer to atomic, biological and chemical weapons.
26 *Science,* 23 December 1983, Vol. 222, p. 1283..
27 The movement of a cloud of dust particles from one hemisphere to another, with the resultant effects resembling those of a nuclear winter, are not futuristic scenarios unrelated to past experience. In 1815, the eruption of the Indonesian volcano, Tambora, injected dust and smoke into the atmosphere on a scale so great as to result in worldwide crop failure and darkness in 1816. The *Scientific American,* March 1984, p. 58, reproduced a poem, "Darkness", written by Lord Byron, thought to have been

a small temperature drop of a few degrees during the ripening season, caused by the nuclear winter, can result in extensive crop failure even on a hemispherical scale. Such consequences are therefore ominous for non-combatant countries also.

> "There is now a consensus that the climatic effects of a nuclear winter and the resulting lack of food aggravated by the destroyed infrastructure could have a greater overall impact on the global population than the immediate effects of the nuclear explosions. The evidence is growing that in a post-war nuclear world Homo Sapiens will not have an ecological niche to which he could flee. It is apparent that life everywhere on this planet would be threatened."[28].

(e) Loss of life

The WHO estimate of the number of dead in the event of the use of a single bomb, a limited war and a total war varies from one million to one billion, with, in addition, a similar number of injured in each case.

Deaths resulting from the only two uses of nuclear weapons in war — Hiroshima and Nagasaki — were 140,000 and 74,000 respectively, according to the representative of Japan, out of total populations of 350,000 and 240,000 respectively. Had these same bombs been exploded in cities with densely packed populations of millions, such as Tokyo, New York, Paris, London or Moscow, the loss of life would have been incalculably more.

An interesting statistic given to the Court by the Mayor of Nagasaki is that the bombing of Dresden by 773 British aircraft followed by a shower of 650,000 incendiary bombs by 450 American aircraft caused 135,000 deaths — a similar result to a single nuclear bomb on Hiroshima — a "small" bomb by today's standards.

(f) Medical effects of radiation

Nuclear weapons produce instantaneous radiation, in addition to which there is also radioactive fallout.

> "It is well established that residual nuclear radiation is a feature of the fission or Atomic bomb as much as the thermo-nuclear weapon known as the 'fusion bomb' or H-bomb."[29].

Over and above the immediate effects just set out, there are longer term effects

---

inspired by this year without a summer. At a hearing of the United States Senate on the effects of nuclear war, in December 1983, the Russian physicist, Kapitza, drew attention to this poem, in the context of the effects of nuclear war, referring to it as one well known to Russians through its translation by the novelist Ivan Turgenev. Here are some extracts, capturing with poetic vision the human despair and the environmental desolation of the post nuclear scene:

> "A fearful hope was all the world contain'd ; Forests were set on fire — but hour by hour They fell and faded — and the crackling trunks Extinguish'd with a crash — and all was black. The brows of men by the despairing light
> Wore an unearthly aspect, as by fits
> The flashes fell upon them; some lay down And hid their eyes and wept ; ...
>
> ... The world was void,
> The populous and the powerful was a lump, Seasonless, herbless, treeless, manless, lifeless — A lump of death — a chaos of hard clay.
> The rivers, lakes, and ocean all stood still, And nothing stirr'd within their silent depths; Ships sailorless lay rotting on the sea ...".

28 Wilfrid Bach, "Climatic Consequences of Nuclear War", in Proceedings of the Sixth World Congress of the International Physicians for the Prevention of Nuclear War (IPPNW), Cologne, 1986, published as *Maintain Life on Earth!*, 1987, p. 154.

29 Singh and McWhinney, *op. cit.*, p. 123.

caused by ionizing radiation acting on human beings and on the environment. Such ionization causes cell damage and the changes that occur may destroy the cell or diminish its capacity to function[30].

After a nuclear attack the victim population suffers from heat, blast and radiation, and separate studies of the effects of radiation are complicated by injuries from blast and heat. Chernobyl has however given an opportunity for study of the effects of radiation alone, for:

> "Chernobyl represents the largest experience in recorded time of the effects of whole body radiation on human subjects, uncomplicated by blast and/ or burn."[31].

Apart from the long-term effects such as keloids and cancers, these effects include in the short-term anorexia, diarrhoea, cessation of production of new blood cells, haemorrhage, bone marrow damage, damage to the central nervous system, convulsions, vascular damage, and cardiovascular collapse[32].

Chernobyl, involving radiation damage alone, in a comparatively lightly populated area, strained the medical resources of a powerful nation and necessitated the pouring in of medical personnel, supplies and equipment from across the Soviet Union - 5,000 trucks, 800 buses, 240 ambulances, helicopters and special trains[33]. Yet the Chernobyl explosion was thought to be approximately that of a half-kiloton bomb[34] — about one twenty-fifth of the comparatively "small" Hiroshima bomb, which was only one seventieth the size of a one-megaton bomb. As observed already, the nuclear arsenals contain multi-megaton bombs today.

The effects of radiation are not only agonizing, but are spread out over an entire lifetime. Deaths after a long life of suffering have occurred in Hiroshima and Nagasaki, decades after the nuclear weapon hit those cities. The Mayor of Hiroshima has given the Court some glimpses of the lingering agonies of the survivors — all of which is amply documented in a vast literature that has grown up around the subject. Indonesia made reference to Antonio Cassese's *Violence and Law in the Modern Age* (1988), which draws attention to the fact that "the quality of human suffering ... does not emerge from the figures and statistics only ... but from the account of survivors". These records of harrowing suffering are numerous and well known[35].

Reference should also be made to the many documents received by the Registry in this regard, including materials from the *International Symposium: Fifty Years since the Atomic Bombing of Hiroshima and Nagasaki*. It is not possible in this opinion even to attempt the briefest summary of the details of these sufferings.

The death toll from lingering death by radiation is still adding to the numbers. Over 320,000 people who survived but were affected by radiation suffer from various malignant tumours caused by radiation, including leukaemia, thyroid cancer, breast cancer, lung cancer, gastric cancer, cataracts and a variety of other after-effects more than half a century later, according to statistics given to the Court by the representative of Japan. With nuclear weapons presently in the world's arsenals of several multiples of the power of those explosions, the scale of damage expands exponentially.

As stated by WHO (CR 95/22, pp. 23-24), overexposure to radiation suppresses the body's immune systems and increases victims' vulnerability to infection and

---

30 Herbert Abrams, "Chernobyl and the Short-Term Medical Effects of Nuclear War", in Proceedings of the IPPNW Congress, *op. cit.*, p. 122..
31 *Ibid.*, p. 120.
32 *Ibid.*, pp. 122-125.
33 *Ibid.*, p. 121.
34 *Ibid.*, p. 127.
35 Among the internationally known contemporary accounts are John Hersey, *Hiroshima* (to which *The New Yorker* devoted its whole issue of 31 August 1946, and which has since appeared as a Penguin Classic, 1946); *Hiroshima Diary: The Journal of a Japanese Physician* August 6-September 30, 1945, by Michihiko Hachiya, M.D., University of North Carolina Press, 1955; and *The Day Man Lost Hiroshima, 6 August 1945*, Kodansha, 1972. They are all part of a voluminous documentation.

cancers.

Apart from an increase in genetic effects and the disfiguring keloid tumours already referred to, radiation injuries have also given rise to psychological traumas which continue to be noted among the survivors of Hiroshima and Nagasaki. Radiation injuries result from direct exposure, from radiation emitted from the ground, from buildings charged with radioactivity, and from radioactive fallout back to the ground several months later from soot or dust which had been whirled up into the stratosphere by the force of the explosion[36].

In addition to these factors, there is an immense volume of specific material relating to the medical effects of nuclear war. A fuller account of this medical material appears in my dissenting opinion on the WHO request (*I.C.J. Reports* 1996, pp. 115-127). That medical material should also be considered as incorporated in this account of the unique effects of the nuclear weapon.

(g) Heat and blast

Nuclear weapons cause damage in three ways — through heat, blast and radiation. As stated by the WHO representative, while the first two differ quantitatively from those resulting from the explosion of conventional bombs, the third is peculiar to nuclear weapons. In addition to instantaneous radiation, there is also radioactive fallout.

The distinctiveness of the nuclear weapon can also be seen from statistics of the magnitude of the heat and blast it produces. The representative of Japan drew our attention to estimates that the bomb blasts in Hiroshima and Nagasaki produced temperatures of several million degrees centigrade and pressures of several hundred thousand atmospheres. In the bright fireball of the nuclear explosion, the temperature and pressure are said indeed to be the same as those at the centre of the sun[37]. Whirlwinds and firestorms were created approximately 30 minutes after the explosion. From these causes 70,147 houses in Hiroshima and 18,400 in Nagasaki were destroyed. The blastwind set up by the initial shockwave had a speed of nearly 1,000 miles per hour, according to figures given to the Court by the Mayor of Hiroshima. The blast

> "turns people and debris into projectiles that hurl into stationary objects and into each other. Multiple fractures, puncture wounds and the smashing of skulls, limbs and internal organs makes the list of possible injuries endless."[38]

(h) Congenital deformities

The intergenerational effects of nuclear weapons mark them out from other classes of weapons. As the delegation of the Solomon Islands put it, the adverse effects of the bomb are

> "virtually permanent — reaching into the distant future of the human race — if it will have a future, which a nuclear conflict would put in doubt" (CR 95/32, p. 36).

Apart from damage to the environment which successive generations will inherit far into the future, radiation also causes genetic damage and will result in a crop of deformed and defective offspring, as proved in Hiroshima and Nagasaki (where

---

36 Over the effects of radiation, see, generally, *Nuclear Radiation in Warfare*, 1981, by Professor Joseph Rotblat, the Nobel Laureate.
37 Bates, op. cit., p. 722. Cf. the reference in The Bhagvadgita, "brighter than a thousand suns", which was widely used by nuclear scientists -as in Robert Jungk, *Brighter than a Thousand Suns: A Personal History of the Atomic Scientist*, Penguin, 1982, and Oppenheimer's famous quote from the same source.
38 Ibid., p. 723.

those who were in the vicinity of the explosion — the *Hibakusha* — have complained for years of social discrimination against them on this account), and in the Marshall Islands and elsewhere in the Pacific. According to the Mayor of Nagasaki :

> "the descendants of the atomic bomb survivors will have to be monitored for several generations to clarify the genetic impact, which means that the descendants will be forced to live in anxiety for generations to come" (CR 95127 , p. 43).

The Mayor of Hiroshima told the Court that children "exposed in their mothers' womb were often born with microcephalia, a syndrome involving mental retardation and incomplete growth" (*ibid.*, p. 29). In the Mayor's words:

> "For these children, no hope remains of becoming normal individuals. Nothing can be done for them medically. The atomic bomb stamped its indelible mark on the lives of these utterly innocent unborn babies." (*ibid.*, p. 30.)

In Japan the social problem of *Hibakusha* covers not only persons with hideous keloid growths, but also deformed children and those exposed to the nuclear explosions, who are thought to have defective genes which transmit deformities to their children. This is a considerable human rights problem, appearing long after the bomb and destined to span the generations.

Mrs. Lijon Eknilang, from the Marshall Islands, told the Court of genetic abnormalities never before seen on that island until the atmospheric testing of nuclear weapons. She gave the Court a moving description of the various birth abnormalities seen on that island after the exposure of its population to radiation. She said that Marshallese women

> "give birth, not to children as we like to think of them, but to things we could only describe as 'octopuses', 'apples', 'turtles', and other things in our experience. We do not have Marshallese words for these kinds of babies because they were never born before the radiation came.
>
> Women on Rongelap, Likiep, Ailuk and other atolls in the Marshall Islands have given birth to these 'monster babies' . . . . One woman on Likiep gave birth to a child with two heads. . . . There is a young girl on Ailuk today with no knees, three toes on each foot and a missing arm . . .
>
> The most common birth defects on Rongelap and nearby islands have been 'jellyfish' babies. These babies are born with no bones in their bodies and with transparent skin. We can see their brains and hearts beating . . . . Many women die from abnormal pregnancies and those who survive give birth to what looks like purple grapes which we quickly hide away and bury. . . .
>
> My purpose for travelling such a great distance to appear before the Court today, is to plead with you to do what you can not to allow the suffering that we Marshallese have experienced to be repeated in any other community in the world." (CR 95/32, pp. 30- 31.)

From another country which has had experience of deformed births, Vanuatu, there was a similar moving reference before the World Health Assembly, when that body was debating a reference to this Court on nuclear weapons. The Vanuatu delegate spoke of the birth, after nine months, of "a substance that breathes but does not have a face, legs or arms"[39].

---

39 Record of the 13th Plenary Meeting, Forty-Sixth World Health Assembly, 14 May 1993, doc. A46/VR/13, p. 11, furnished to the Court by WHO.

(i) Transnational damage

Once a nuclear explosion takes place, the fallout from even a single local detonation cannot be confined within national boundaries[40]. According to WHO studies, it would extend hundreds of kilometres downwind and the gamma ray exposure from the fallout could reach the human body, even outside national boundaries, through radioactivity deposited in the ground, through inhalation from the air, through consumption of contaminated food, and through inhalation of suspended radioactivity. The diagram appended to this opinion, extracted from the WHO Study, comparing the areas affected by conventional bombs and nuclear weapons, demonstrates this convincingly. Such is the danger to which neutral populations would be exposed.

All nations, including those carrying out underground tests, are in agreement that extremely elaborate protections are necessary in the case of underground nuclear explosions in order to prevent contamination of the environment. Such precautions are manifestly quite impossible in the case of the use of nuclear weapons in war — when they will necessarily be exploded in the atmosphere or on the ground. The explosion of nuclear weapons in the atmosphere creates such acknowledgedly deleterious effects that it has already been banned by the Partial Nuclear Test Ban Treaty, and considerable progress has already been made towards a Total Test Ban Treaty. If the nuclear powers now accept that explosions below ground, in the carefully controlled conditions of a test, are so deleterious to health and the environment that they should be banned, this ill accords with the position that above ground explosions in uncontrolled conditions are acceptable.

The transboundary effects of radiation are illustrated by the nuclear meltdown in Chernobyl which had devastating effects over a vast area, as the by-products of that nuclear reaction could not be contained. Human health, agricultural and dairy produce and the demography of thousands of square miles were affected in a manner never known before. On 30 November 1995, the United Nation's Under-Secretary-General for Humanitarian Affairs announced that thyroid cancers, many of them being diagnosed in children, are 285 times more prevalent in Belarus than before the accident, that about 375,000 people in Belarus, Russia and Ukraine remain displaced and often homeless — equivalent to numbers displaced in Rwanda by the fighting there — and that about 9 million people have been affected in some way[41]. Ten years after Chernobyl, the tragedy still reverberates over large areas of territory, not merely in Russia alone, but also in other countries such as Sweden. Such results, stemming from a mere accident rather than a deliberate attempt to cause damage by nuclear weapons, followed without the heat or the blast injuries attendant on a nuclear weapon. They represented radiation damage alone — only one of the three lethal aspects of nuclear weapons. They stemmed from an event considerably smaller in size than the explosions of Hiroshima and Nagasaki.

(j) Potential to destroy all civilization

Nuclear war has the potential to destroy all civilization. Such a result could be achieved through the use of a minute fraction of the weapons already in existence in the arsenals of the nuclear powers.

As Former Secretary of State, Dr. Henry Kissinger, once observed, in relation to strategic assurances in Europe:

> "The European allies should not keep asking us to multiply strategic assurances that we cannot possibly mean, or if we do mean, we should not want to execute because if we execute, *we risk the destruction of civilization*."[42]

---

40 See diagram appended from *Effects of Nuclear War on Health and Health Services*, World Health Organization, 2nd ed., 1987, p. 16.
41 *New York Times Service*, reported in *International Herald Tribune*, 30 November 1995.
42 Henry A. Kissinger, "NATO Defense and the Soviet Threat", Survival, November December 1979, p.

So, also, Robert McNamara, United States Secretary of Defense from 1961 to 1968, has written:

> "Is it realistic to expect that a nuclear war could be limited to the detonation of tens or even hundreds of nuclear weapons, even though each side would have tens of thousands of weapons remaining available for use? The answer is clearly no."[43]

Stocks of weapons may be on the decline, but one scarcely needs to think in terms of thousands or even hundreds of weapons. Tens of weapons are enough to wreak all the destructions that have been outlined at the commencement of this opinion.

Such is the risk attendant on the use of nuclear weapons — a risk which no single nation is entitled to take, whatever the dangers to itself. An individual's right to defend his own interests is a right he enjoys against his opponents. In exercising that right, he cannot be considered entitled to destroy the village in which he lives.

(i) Social institutions

All the institutions of ordered society — judiciaries, legislatures, police, medical services, education, transport, communications, postal and telephone services, and newspapers — would disappear together in the immediate aftermath of a nuclear attack. The country's command centres and higher echelons of administrative services would be paralysed. There would be "social chaos on a scale unprecedented in human history"[44].

(ii) *Economic structures*

Economically, society would need to regress even beyond that of the Middle Ages to the levels of man's most primitive past. One of the best known studies examining this scenario summarizes the situation in this way:

> "The task ... would be not to restore the old economy but to invent a new one, on a far more primitive level. ... The economy of the Middle Ages, for example, was far less productive than our own, but it was exceedingly complex, and it would not be within the capacity of people in our time suddenly to establish a medieval economic system in the ruins of their twentieth-century one. ... Sitting among the debris of the Space Age, they would find that the pieces of a shattered modern economy around them - here an automobile, there a washing machine - were mismatched to their elemental needs. ... [T]hey would not be worrying about rebuilding the automobile industry or the electronics industry: they would be worrying about how to find nonradioactive berries in the woods, or how to tell which trees had edible bark."[45]

(iii) Cultural treasures

Another casualty to be mentioned in this regard is the destruction of the cultural treasures representing the progress of civilization through the ages. The importance of the protection of this aspect of civilization was recognized by the Hague Convention of 14 May 1954, for the protection of cultural property in the case of armed conflict, which decreed that cultural property is entitled to special protection. Historical

---

266 (address in Brussels), cited by Robert S. McNamara in "The Military Role of Nuclear Weapons: Perceptions and Misperceptions", *Foreign Affairs*, 1983- 1984, No. 62, Vol. 1, p. 59; emphasis added.
43 Robert S. McNamara, op. cit., p. 71.
44 Bates, op. cit., p. 726.
45 Jonathan Schell, *The Fate of the Earth*, 1982, pp. 69-70, cited in Bates, *op. cit.* p. 727.

monuments, works of art or places of worship which constitute the cultural or spiritual heritage of peoples must not be the objects of any acts of hostility.

Additional Protocol II provides that cultural property and places of worship which constitute the cultural and spiritual heritage of peoples must not be attacked. Such attacks are grave breaches of humanitarian law under the Conventions and the Protocol. The protection of culture in wartime is considered so important by the world community that UNESCO has devised a special Programme for the Protection of Culture in Wartime. Whenever any cultural monuments were destroyed, there has been a public outcry and an accusation that the laws of war had been violated.

Yet it is manifest that the nuclear bomb is no respecter of such cultural treasures[46]. It will incinerate and flatten every object within its radius of destruction, cultural monument or otherwise.

Despite the blitz on many great cities during World War II, many a cultural monument in those cities stood through the war. That will not be the case after nuclear war.

That this is a feature of considerable importance in all countries can be illustrated from the statistics in regard to one. The number of listed monuments in the Federal Republic of Germany alone, in 1986, was around 1 million, of which Cologne alone had around 9,000 listed buildings[47]. A nuclear attack on a city such as Cologne would thus deprive Germany, in particular, and the world community in general, of a considerable segment of their cultural inheritance, for a single bomb would easily dispose of all 9,000 monuments, leaving none standing — a result which no wartime bombing in World War II could achieve.

Together with all other structures, they will be part of the desert of radioactive rubble left in the aftermath of the nuclear bomb. If the preservation of humanity's cultural inheritance is of any value to civilization, it is important to note that it will be an inevitable casualty of the nuclear weapon.

(k) The electromagnetic pulse

Another feature distinctive to nuclear weapons is the electromagnetic pulse. The literature indicates that this has the effect of displacing electrons out of air molecules in the upper atmosphere and these electrons are then displaced by the earth's magnetic field. As they spin down and around the lines of magnetic force, they transmit a very sudden and intensive burst of energy — the electromagnetic pulse — which throws all electronic devices out of action. As these systems go haywire, all communication lines are cut, health services (among other essential services) disrupted and organized modern life collapses. Even the command and control systems geared for responses to nuclear attack can be thrown out of gear, thus creating a fresh danger of unintended release of nuclear weapons.

A standard scientific dictionary, *Dictionnaire encyclopedique d'electronique*, describes the effects of the electromagnetic pulse in the following terms:

> "Electromagnetic pulse, nuclear pulse; strong pulse of electro-magnetic energy radiated by a nuclear explosion in the atmosphere; caused by collisions between the gamma rays emitted during the first nanoseconds of the explosion and the electrons in the molecules in the atmosphere; the electromagnetic pulse produced by a nuclear explosion of an average force at around 400 km altitude can instantly put out of service the greater part of semiconductor electronic equipment in a large country, such as the United States, as well as a large part of its energy distribution networks, without other effects being felt on the ground, with military consequences

---

46 On State responsibility to protect the cultural heritage, see Article 5 of the World Heritage Convention, 1972 (The Convention for the Protection of the World Cultural and Natural Heritage).
47 See Hiltrud Kier, "UNESCO Programme for the Protection of Culture in Wartime", in Documents of the Sixth World Congress of IPPNW, op. cit., p. 199.

easy to imagine."[48]

An important aspect of the electromagnetic pulse is that it travels at immense speeds, so that the disruption of communication systems caused by the radioactive contamination immediately can spread beyond national boundaries and disrupt communication lines and essential services in neutral countries as well. Having regard to the dominance of electronic communication in the functioning of modern society at every level, this would be an unwarranted interference with such neutral States.

Another important effect of the electromagnetic pulse is the damage to electrical power and control systems from nuclear weapons — indeed electromagnetic pulse could lead to a core melt accident in the event of nuclear power facilities being in the affected area[49].

(l) Damage to nuclear reactors

The enormous area of devastation and the enormous heat released would endanger all nuclear power stations within the area, releasing dangerous levels of radioactivity apart from that released by the bomb itself. Europe alone has over 200 atomic power stations dotted across the continent, some of them close to populated areas. In addition, there are 150 devices for uranium enrichment[50]. A damaged nuclear reactor could give rise to:

> "lethal doses of radiation to exposed persons 150 miles downwind and would produce significant levels of radioactive contamination of the environment more than 600 miles away"[51].

The nuclear weapon used upon any country in which the world's current total of 450 nuclear reactors is situated could leave in its wake a series of Chernobyls.

The effects of such radiation could include anorexia, cessation of production of new blood cells, diarrhoea, haemorrhage, damage to the bone marrow, convulsions, vascular damage and cardiovascular collapse[52].

(m) Damage to food productivity

Unlike other weapons, whose direct impact is the most devastating part of the damage they cause, nuclear weapons can cause far greater damage by their delayed after-effects than by their direct effects. The detailed technical study, Environmental Consequences of Nuclear War, while referring to some uncertainties regarding the indirect effects of nuclear war, states:

> "What can be said with assurance, however, is that the Earth's human population has a much greater vulnerability to the indirect effects of nuclear war, especially mediated through impacts on food productivity and food availability, than to the direct effects of nuclear war itself."[53]

The nuclear winter, should it occur in consequence of multiple nuclear exchanges, could disrupt all global food supplies.

After the United States tests in the Pacific in 1954, fish caught in various parts

---

48 Michel Fleutry, *Dictionnaire encyclopedique d'electronique* (anglais-franr:ais), 1995, p. 250. [Translation by the Registry.]
49 Gordon Thompson, "Nuclear Power and the Threat of Nuclear War", in Documents of the Sixth World Congress of IPPNW, *op. cit.*, p. 240.
50 William E. Butler (ed.), Control over Compliance with International Law, 1991, p. 24.
51 Bates, *op. cit.*, p. 720.
52 See Herbert Abrams, *op. cit.*, pp. 122-125.
53 SCOPE publication 28, released at the Royal Society, London, on 6 January 1986, Vol. I, p. 481.

of the Pacific, as long as eight months after the explosions, were contaminated and unfit for human consumption, while crops in various parts of Japan were affected by radioactive rain. These were among the findings of an international Commission of medical specialists appointed by the Japanese Association of Doctors against A- and H-bombs[54]. Further:

> "The use of nuclear weapons contaminates water and food, as well as the soil and the plants that may grow on it. This is not only in the area covered by immediate nuclear radiation, but also a much larger unpredictable zone which is affected by the radio-active fall out."[55]

(n) Multiple nuclear explosions resulting from self-defence

If the weapon is used in self-defence after an initial nuclear attack, the ecosystem, which had already sustained the impact of the first nuclear attack, would have to absorb on top of this the effect of the retaliatory attack, which may or may not consist of a single weapon, for the stricken nation will be so ravaged that it will not be able to make fine evaluations of the exact amount of retaliatory force required. In such event, the tendency to release as strong a retaliation as is available must enter into any realistic evaluation of the situation. The ecosystem would in that event be placed under the pressure of multiple nuclear explosions, which it would not be able to absorb without permanent and irreversible damage. Capital cities with densely packed populations could be targeted. The fabric of civilization could be destroyed.

It is said of some of the most ruthless conquerors of the past that, after they dealt with a rebellious town, they ensured that it was razed to the ground with no sound or sign of life left in it — not even the bark of a dog or the purr of a kitten. If any student of international law were asked whether such conduct was contrary to the laws of war, the answer would surely be "Of course!" There would indeed be some surprise that the question even needed to be asked. In this age of higher development, the nuclear weapon goes much further, leaving behind it nothing but a total devastation, wrapped in eerie silence.

(o) "The shadow of the mushroom cloud"

As pointed out in the Australian submissions (CR 95122, p. 49), the entire post-war generation lies under a cloud of fear — sometimes described as the "shadow of the mushroom cloud", which pervades all thoughts about the human future. This fear, which has hung like a blanket of doom over the thoughts of children in particular, is an evil in itself and will last so long as nuclear weapons remain. The younger generation needs to grow up in a climate of hope, not one of despair that at some point in their life, there is a possibility of their life being snuffed out in an instant, or their health destroyed, along with all they cherish, in a war to which their nation may not even be a party.

* * *

This body of information shows that, even among weapons of mass destruction, many of which are already banned under international law, the nuclear weapon stands alone, unmatched for its potential to damage all that humanity has built over the centuries and all that humanity relies upon for its continued existence.

I close this section by citing the statement placed before the Court by Professor Joseph Rotblat, a member of the British team on the Manhattan Project in Los Alamos, a Rapporteur for the 1983 WHO investigation into the Effects of Nuclear

---

54 As referred to in Singh and McWhinney, op. cit., p. 124.
55 Ibid., p. 122.

War on Health and Health Services, and a Nobel Laureate. Professor Rotblat was a member of one of the delegations, but was prevented by ill health from attending the Court.

Here is a passage from his statement to the Court:

> "I have read the written pleadings prepared by the United Kingdom and the United States. Their view of the legality of the use of nuclear weapons is premised on three assumptions: (a) that they would not necessarily cause unnecessary suffering; (b) that they would not necessarily have indiscriminate effects on civilians; (c) that they would not necessarily have effects on territories of third States. It is my professional opinion — set out above and in the WHO reports referred to — that on any reasonable set of assumptions their argument is unsustainable on all three points." (CR 95/32, Annex, p. 2.)

4. *The Uniqueness of Nuclear Weapons*

After this factual review, legal argument becomes almost superfluous, for it can scarcely be contended that any legal system can contain within itself a principle which permits the entire society which it serves to be thus decimated and destroyed — along with the natural environment which has sustained it from time immemorial[56]. The dangers are so compelling that a range of legal principles surges through to meet them.

It suffices at the present stage of this opinion to outline the reasons for considering the nuclear weapon unique, even among weapons of mass destruction. Nuclear weapons

(1) cause death and destruction ;
(2) induce cancers, leukaemia, keloids and related afflictions;
(3) cause gastro-intestinal, cardiovascular and related afflictions;
(4) continue for decades after their use to induce the health-related problems mentioned above;
(5) damage the environmental rights of future generations;
(6) cause congenital deformities, mental retardation and genetic damage;
(7) carry the potential to cause a nuclear winter;
(8) contaminate and destroy the food chain ;
(9) imperil the ecosystem;
(10) produce lethal levels of heat and blast ;
(11) produce radiation and radioactive fallout;
(12) produce a disruptive electromagnetic pulse;
(13) produce social disintegration ;
(14) imperil all civilization ;
(15) threaten human survival;
(16) wreak cultural devastation ;
(17) span a time range of thousands of years;
(18) threaten all life on the planet ;
(19) irreversibly damage the rights of future generations;
(20) exterminate civilian populations;
(21) damage neighbouring States;
(22) produce psychological stress and fear syndromes

as no other weapons do.

---

56 See further, on this aspect, Section V.1 below.

Any one of these would cause concern serious enough to place these weapons in a category of their own, attracting with special intensity the principles of humanitarian law. In combination they make the case for their application irrefutable. This list is by no means complete. However, to quote the words of a recent study:

> "Once it becomes clear that all hope for twentieth century man is lost if a nuclear war is started, it hardly adds any meaningful knowledge to learn of additional effects." [57]

The words of the General Assembly, in its "Declaration on the Prevention of Nuclear Catastrophe" (1981), aptly summarize the entirety of the foregoing facts:

> "all the horrors of past wars and other calamities that have befallen people would pale in comparison with what is inherent in the use of nuclear weapons, capable of destroying civilization on earth"[58]

Here then is the background to the consideration of the legal question with which the Court is faced. Apart from this background of hard and sordid fact, the legal question cannot be meaningfully addressed. Juxtapose against these consequences — so massively destructive of all the principles of humanity — the accepted principles of humanitarian law, and the result can scarcely be in doubt. As the ensuing discussion will point out, humanitarian principles are grotesquely violated by the consequences of nuclear weapons. This discussion will show that these effects of the nuclear weapon and the humanitarian principles of the laws of war are a contradiction in terms.

5. *The Differences in Scientific Knowledge between the Present Time and 1945*

On 17 July 1945, United States Secretary of War, Stimson, informed Prime Minister Churchill of the successful detonation of the experimental nuclear bomb in the New Mexican desert, with the cryptic message "Babies satisfactorily born."[59]. A universe of knowledge has grown up regarding the effects of the bomb since that fateful day when the advent of this unknown weapon could, even cryptically, be so described.

True, much knowledge regarding the power of the bomb was available then, but the volume of knowledge now available on the effects of nuclear weapons is exponentially greater. In addition to numerous military studies, there have been detailed studies by WHO and other concerned organizations such as International Physicians for the Prevention of Nuclear War (IPPNW); the TTAPS studies on the nuclear winter; the studies of the Scientific Committee on Problems of the Environment (SCOPE); the International Council of Scientific Unions (ICSU); the United Nations Institute of Disarmament Research (UNIDIR); and literally hundreds of others. Much of this material has been placed before the Court or deposited in the library by WHO and various States that have appeared before the Court in this matter.

Questions of knowledge, morality and legality in the use of nuclear weapons, considered in the context of 1995, are thus vastly different from those questions considered in the context of 1945, and need a totally fresh approach in the light of this immense quantity of information. This additional information has a deep impact upon the question of the legality now before the Court.

Action with full knowledge of the consequences of one's act is totally different in law from the same action taken in ignorance of its consequences. Any nation using the nuclear weapon today cannot be heard to say that it does not know its

---

57 Bates, *op. cit.*, p. 721.
58 Resolution 36/100 of 9 December 1981.
59 Winston Churchill, *The Second World War*, Vol. 6, "Triumph and Tragedy", 1953, p. 63.

consequences. It is only in the context of this knowledge that the question of legality of the use of nuclear weapons can be considered in 1996.

6. *Do Hiroshima and Nagasaki Show that Nuclear War Is Survivable?*

Over and above all these specific aspects of the rules of humanitarian law, and in a sense welding them together in one overall consideration, is the question of survivability of the target population — indeed, of the human race. Survivability is the limit situation of each individual danger underlying each particular principle of humanitarian law. The extreme situation that is reached if each danger is pressed to the limit of its potential is the situation of non-survivability. We reach that situation with nuclear war. In the fact that nuclear war could spell the end of the human race and of all civilization, all these principles thus coalesce.

A fact that obscures perception of the danger that nuclear war may well be unsurvivable is the experience of Hiroshima and Nagasaki. The fact that nuclear weapons were used in Japan and that that nation emerged from the war resilient and resurgent may lull the observer into a sense of false security that nuclear war is indeed survivable. International law itself has registered this complacency, for there is what may be described as an underlying subliminal assumption that nuclear war has been proved to be survivable.

It is necessary therefore to examine briefly some clear differences between that elementary scenario of a nuclear attack half a century ago and the likely characteristics of a nuclear war today. The following differences may be noted:

1. The bombs used in Hiroshima and Nagasaki were of not more than 15 kilotons explosive power. The bombs available for a future nuclear war will be many multiples of this explosive power.
2. Hiroshima and Nagasaki ended the war. The limit of that nuclear war was the use of two "small" nuclear weapons. The next nuclear war, should it come, cannot be assumed to be so restricted, for multiple exchanges must be visualized.
3. The target country in Hiroshima and Nagasaki was not a nuclear power. Nor were there any other nuclear powers to come to its assistance. A future nuclear war, if it occurs, will be in a world bristling with nuclear weapons which exist, not for display, but for a purpose. The possibility of even a minute fraction of those weapons being called into service is therefore an ever present danger to be reckoned with in a future nuclear war.
4. Hiroshima and Nagasaki, important though they were, were not the nerve centres of Japanese government and administration. Major cities and capitals of the warring States are likely to be targeted in a future nuclear war.
5. Major environmental consequences such as the nuclear winter which could result from a multiple exchange of nuclear weapons - could not result from the "small" bombs used in Hiroshima and Nagasaki.

Hiroshima and Nagasaki thus do not prove the survivability of nuclear war. They are, rather, a forewarning on a minuscule scale of the dangers to be expected in a future nuclear war. They remove any doubt that might have existed, had the question of the legality of nuclear weapons been argued on the basis of scientific data alone, without a practical demonstration of their effect on human populations.

Every one of the evils which the rules of humanitarian law are designed to prevent thus comes together in the questions of survival attendant on the future use of nuclear weapons in war.

7. *A Perspective from the Past*

This section of the present opinion has surveyed in the broadest outline the effects of the bomb in the light of the known results of its use and in the light of scientific information available today. The non-conformity of the bomb with the norms of humanitarian law and, indeed, with the basic principles of international law seems upon this evidence to be self-evident, as more fully discussed later in this opinion.

It adds a sense of perspective to this discussion to note that even before the evidence of actual use, and even before the wealth of scientific material now available, a percipient observer was able, while the invention of the nuclear bomb still lay far in the distance, to detect the antithesis between the nuclear bomb and every form of social order — which would of course include international law. H. G. Wells, in *The World Set Free*, visualized the creation of the bomb on the basis of information already known in 1913 resulting from the work of Einstein and others on the correlation of matter and energy. Projecting his mind into the future with remarkable prescience, he wrote in 1913:

> "The atomic bombs had dwarfed the international issues to complete insignificance . . . we speculated upon the possibility of stopping the use of these frightful explosives before the world was utterly destroyed. For to us it seemed quite plain these bombs, and the still greater power of destruction of which they were the pre-cursors, might quite easily shatter every relationship and institution of mankind."[60]

The power that would be unleashed by the atom was known theoretically in 1913. That theoretical knowledge was enough, even without practical confirmation, to foresee that the bomb could shatter every human relationship and institution. International law is one of the most delicate of those relationships and institutions.

It seems remarkable that the permissibility of the weapon under international law is still the subject of serious discussion, considering that the power of the bomb was awesomely demonstrated 40 years after its consequences were thus seen as "quite plain", and that the world has had a further 50 years of time for reflection after that event.

III. Humanitarian Law

It could indeed be said that the principal question before the Court is whether the nuclear weapon can in any way be reconciled with the basic principles of humanitarian law.

The governance of nuclear weapons by the principles of humanitarian law has not been in doubt at any stage of these proceedings, and has now been endorsed by the unanimous opinion of the Court (para. 105 (2) D). Indeed, most of the States contending that the use of nuclear weapons is lawful have acknowledged that their use is subject to international humanitarian law.

Thus the Russian Federation has stated:

> "Naturally, all that has been said above does not mean that the use of nuclear weapons is not limited at all. Even if the use of nuclear weapons is in principle justifiable — in individual or collective self-defence — that use shall be made within the framework of limitations imposed by humanitarian law with respect to means and methods of conducting military activities. It is important to note that with respect to nuclear weapons those limitations are limitations under customary rather than treaty law." (Written Statement, p. 18.)

---

60 H. G. Wells, *The First Men in the Moon and The World Set Free*, Literary Press, London, undated reprint of 1913 ed., p. 237. See, also, the reference to Wells in R. J. Lifton and Richard Falk, *Indefensible Weapons*, 1982, p. 59.

The United States states:

> "The United States has long taken the position that various principles of the international law of armed conflict would apply to the use of nuclear weapons as well as to other means and methods of warfare. This in no way means, however, that the use of nuclear weapons is precluded by the law of war. As the following will demonstrate, the issue of the legality depends on the precise circumstances involved in any particular use of a nuclear weapon." (Written Statement, p. 21.)

So, also, the United Kingdom:

> "It follows that the law of armed conflict by which the legality of any given use of nuclear weapons falls to be judged includes all the provisions of customary international law (including those which have been codified in Additional Protocol I) and, where appropriate, of conventional law but excludes those provisions of Protocol I which introduced new rules into the law." (Written Statement, p. 46, para. 3.55.)

The subordination of nuclear weapons to the rules of humanitarian law has thus been universally recognized, and now stands judicially confirmed as an incontrovertible principle of international law.

It remains then to juxtapose the leading principles of humanitarian law against the known results of nuclear weapons, as already outlined. When the principles and the facts are lined up alongside each other, the total incompatibility of the principles with the facts leads inescapably to but one conclusion — that nuclear weapons are inconsistent with humanitarian law. Since they are unquestionably governed by humanitarian law, they are unquestionably illegal.

Among the prohibitions of international humanitarian law relevant to this case are the prohibitions against weapons which cause superfluous injury, weapons which do not differentiate between combatants and civilians, and weapons which do not respect the rights of neutral States.

A more detailed consideration follows.

1. *"Elementary Considerations of Humanity"*

This phrase gives expression to a core concept of humanitarian law. Is the conduct of a State in any given situation contrary to the elementary considerations of humanity? One need go no further than to formulate this phrase, and then recount the known results of the bomb as outlined above. The resulting contrast between light and darkness is so dramatic as to occasion a measure of surprise that their total incompatibility has even been in doubt. One wonders whether, in the light of common sense, it can be doubted that to exterminate vast numbers of the enemy population, to poison their atmosphere, to induce in them cancers, keloids and leukaemias, to cause congenital defects and mental retardation in large numbers of unborn children, to devastate their territory and render their food supply unfit for human consumption — whether acts such as these can conceivably be compatible with "elementary considerations of humanity". Unless one can in all conscience answer such questions in the affirmative, the argument is at an end as to whether nuclear weapons violate humanitarian law, and therefore violate international law.

President Woodrow Wilson, in an address delivered to a joint session of Congress on 2 April 1917, gave elegant expression to this concept when he observed:

> "By painful stage after stage has that law been built up, with meager enough results, indeed, . . . but always with a clear view, at least, of what the heart

and conscience of mankind demanded."[61]

In relation to nuclear weapons, there can be no doubt as to "what the heart and conscience of mankind" demand. As was observed by another American President, President Reagan, "I pray for the day when nuclear weapons will no longer exist anywhere on earth"[62]. That sentiment, shared by citizens across the world — as set out elsewhere in this opinion — provides the background to modern humanitarian law, which has progressed from the time when President Wilson described its results as "meager ... indeed".

The ensuing portions of this opinion are devoted to an examination of the present state of development of the principles of humanitarian law.

2. Multicultural Background to the Humanitarian Laws of War

It greatly strengthens the concept of humanitarian laws of war to note that this is not a recent invention, nor the product of any one culture. The concept is of ancient origin, with a lineage stretching back at least three millennia. As already observed, it is deep-rooted in many cultures — Hindu, Buddhist, Chinese, Christian, Islamic and traditional African. These cultures have all given expression to a variety of limitations on the extent to which any means can be used for the purposes of fighting one's enemy. The problem under consideration is a universal problem, and this Court is a universal Court, whose composition is required by its Statute to reflect the world's principal cultural traditions[63]. The multicultural traditions that exist on this important matter cannot be ignored in the Court's consideration of this question, for to do so would be to deprive its conclusions of that plenitude of universal authority which is available to give it added strength — the strength resulting from the depth of the tradition's historical roots and the width of its geographical spread[64].

Of special relevance in connection with nuclear weapons is the ancient South Asian tradition regarding the prohibition on the use of hyper-destructive weapons. This is referred to in the two celebrated Indian epics, the *Ramayana* and the *Mahabharatha*, which are known and regularly re-enacted through the length and breadth of South and South-East Asia, as part of the living cultural tradition of the region. The references in these two epics are as specific as can be on this principle, and they relate to a historical period around three thousand years ago.

The *Ramayana*[65] tells the epic story of a war between Rama, prince of Ayodhya in India, and Ravana, ruler of Sri Lanka. In the course of this epic struggle, described in this classic in the minutest detail, a weapon of war became available to Rama's half-brother, Lakshmana, which could "destroy the entire race of the enemy, including those who could not bear arms".

Rama advised Lakshmana that the weapon could not be used in the war

> "because such destruction en masse was forbidden by the ancient laws of war, even though Ravana was fighting an unjust war with an unrighteous objective"[66].

---

[61] Address of the President of the United States at a Joint Session of the Two Houses of Congress, 2 April 1917, reprinted in *American Journal of International Law*, 1917, Vol. 11, Supp., p. 144. The President was speaking in the context of the indiscriminate German submarine attacks on shipping which he described as "a warfare against mankind"

[62] Speech of 16 June 1983, referred to by Robert S. McNamara, op. cit., p. 60.

[63] I note in this context the sad demise of our deeply respected Latin American colleague, Judge Andres Aguilar-Mawdsley, six days before the hearings of the case commenced, thus reducing the Court to fourteen, and depriving its composition of a Latin American component.

[64] As observed in a contemporary study of the development of international humanitarian law, there is evidence "of efforts made by every people in every age to reduce the devastation of war" (Herczegh, *op. cit.*, p. 14).

[65] *The Ramayana*, Romesh Chunder Dutt (trans.).

[66] See Nagendra Singh, "The Distinguishable Characteristics of the Concept of the Law as It Developed in Ancient India", in *Liber Amicorum for the Right Honourable Lord Wilberforce*, 1987, p. 93.

These laws of war which Rama followed were themselves ancient in his time. The laws of Manu forbade stratagems of deceit, all attacks on unarmed adversaries and non-combatants, irrespective of whether the war being fought was a just war or not[67]. The Greek historian Megasthenes[68] makes reference to the practice in India that warring armies left farmers tilling the land unmolested, even though the battle raged close to them. He likewise records that the land of the enemy was not destroyed with fire nor his trees cut down[69].

The *Mahabharatha* relates the story of an epic struggle between the Kauravas and the Pandavas. It refers likewise to the principle forbidding hyperdestructive weapons when it records that:

> "Arjuna, observing the laws of war, refrained from using the '*pasupathastra*', a hyper-destructive weapon, because when the fight was restricted to ordinary conventional weapons, the use of extra ordinary or unconventional types was not even moral, let alone in conformity with religion or the recognized laws of warfare."[70]

Weapons causing unnecessary suffering were also banned by the Laws of Manu as, for example, arrows with hooked spikes which, after entering the body would be difficult to take out, or arrows with heated or poisoned tips[71].

The environmental wisdom of ancient Judaic tradition is also reflected in the following passage from Deuteronomy (20: 19):

> "When you are trying to capture a city, do not cut down its fruit trees, even though the siege lasts a long time. Eat the fruit but do not destroy the trees. *The trees are not your enemies.*" (Emphasis added.)

Recent studies of warfare among African peoples likewise reveal the existence of humanitarian traditions during armed conflicts, with moderation and clemency shown to enemies[72]. For example, in some cases of traditional African warfare, there were rules forbidding the use of particular weapons and certain areas had highly developed systems of etiquette, conventions, and rules, both before hostilities commenced, during hostilities, and after the cessation of hostilities — including a system of compensation[73].

In the Christian tradition, the Second Lateran Council of 1139 offers an interesting illustration of the prohibition of weapons which were too cruel to be used in warfare — the crossbow and the siege machine, which were condemned as "deadly and odious to God"[74]. Nussbaum, in citing this provision, observes that, it "certainly appears curious in the era of the atomic bomb". There was a very early recognition here of the dangers that new techniques were introducing into the field of battle. Likewise, in other fields of the law of war, there were endeavours to bring it within some forms of control as, for example, by the proclamation of "Truces of God" — days during

---

The relevant passage of *The Ramayana* is *Yuddha Kanda (Sloka)*, VIII.39.
67 *Manusmrti*, vii, 91, 92.
68 c.350 BC - c.290 BC — ancient Greek historian and diplomat sent on embassies by Seleucus I to Chandragupta Maurya, who wrote the most complete account of India then known to the Greek world.
69 Megasthenes, *Fragments*, cited in N. Singh, *Juristic Concepts of Ancient Indian Polity*, 1980, pp. 162-163.
70 *Mahabharatha, Udyog Parva*, 194.12, cited in Nagendra Singh, "The Distinguishable Characteristics of the Concept of Law as It Developed in Ancient India", op. cit., p. 93.
71 *Manusmrti*, VII.90, cited in N. Singh, *India and International Law*, 1973, p. 72.
72 See Y. Diallo, *Traditions africaines et droit humanitaire*, 1978, p. 16; E. Bello, *African Customary Humanitarian Law*, ICRC, 1980, both referred to in Herczegh, *op. cit.*, p. 14.
73 Bello, *op. cit.*, pp. 20-21.
74 Resolutions of the Second Lateran Council, Canon XXIX, cited by Nussbaum, *A Concise History of the Law of Nations*, 1947, p. 25.

which feuds were not permitted which were expanded in some church jurisdictions to periods from sunset on Wednesday to sunrise on Monday[75].

Gratian's *Decretum* in the twelfth century was one of the first Christian works dealing with these principles, and the ban imposed by the Second Lateran Council was an indication of the growing interest in the subject. However, in Christian philosophy, while early writers such as St. Augustine examined the concept of the just war (*jus ad bellum*) in great detail, the *jus in bello* was not the subject of detailed study for some centuries.

Vitoria gathered together various traditions upon the subject, including traditions of knightly warfare from the age of chivalry; Aquinas worked out a well-developed doctrine relating to the protection of non combatants; and other writers fed the growing stream of thought upon the subject.

In the Islamic tradition, the laws of war forbade the use of poisoned arrows or the application of poison on weapons such as swords or spears[76]. Unnecessarily cruel ways of killing and mutilation were expressly forbidden. Non-combatants, women and children, monks and places of worship were expressly protected. Crops and livestock were not to be destroyed[77] by anyone holding authority over territory. Prisoners were to be treated mercifully in accordance with such Qur'anic passages as "Feed for the love of Allah, the indigent, the orphan and the captive."[78]. So well developed was Islamic law in regard to conduct during hostilities that it ordained not merely that prisoners were to be well treated, but that if they made a last will during captivity, the will was to be transmitted to the enemy through some appropriate channel[79].

The Buddhist tradition went further still, for it was totally pacifist, and would not countenance the taking of life, the infliction of pain, the taking of captives or the appropriation of another's property or territory in any circumstances whatsoever. Since it outlaws war altogether, it could under no circumstances lend its sanction to weapons of destruction — least of all to a weapon such as the nuclear bomb.

> "According to Buddhism there is nothing that can be called a 'just war' -which is only a false term coined and put into circulation to justify and excuse hatred, cruelty, violence and massacre. Who decides what is just and unjust? The mighty and the victorious are 'just', and the weak and the defeated are 'unjust'. Our war is always 'just' and your war is always 'unjust'. Buddhism does not accept this position."[80]

In rendering an advisory opinion on a matter of humanitarian law concerning the permissibility of the use of force to a degree capable of destroying all of humanity, it would be a grave omission indeed to neglect the humanitarian perspectives available from this major segment of the world's cultural traditions[81].

Examples of the adoption of humanitarian principles in more recent history are numerous. For example, in the Crimean War in 1855, the use of sulphur was proposed at the Siege of Sebastopol, but would not be permitted by the British Government, just as during the American Civil War the use of chlorine in artillery shells by the Union forces was proposed in 1862, but rejected by the Government[82].

---

75 *Ibid.*, p. 26.
76 See N. Singh, *India and International Law, op. cit.*, p. 216.
77 *Qur'an*, II.205.
78 *Ibid.*, LXXVII.8; emphasis added.
79 S. R. Hassan, *The Reconstruction of Legal Thought in Islam*, 1974, p. 177. See, generally, Majid Khadduri, *War and Peace in the Law of Islam*, 1955. For a brief summary of the Islamic law relating to war, see C. G. Weeramantry, *Islamic Jurisprudence: Some International Perspectives*, 1988, pp. 134-138.
80 Walpola Rahula, *What the Buddha Taught*, 1959, p. 84.
81 On Buddhism and international law, see, generally, K. N. Jayetilleke, "The Principles of International Law in Buddhist Doctrine", *Recueil des cours de l'Academie de droit international de La Haye*, Vol. 120 (1967-I), pp. 441-567.
82 See L. S. Wolfe, "Chemical and Biological Warfare: Effects and Consequences", *McGill Law Journal*, 1983, Vol. 28, p. 735. See, also, "Chemical Warfare" in *Encyclopaedia Britannica*, 1959, Vol. 5, pp. 353-358.

It is against such a varied cultural background that these questions must be considered and not merely as though they are a new sentiment invented in the nineteenth century and so slenderly rooted in universal tradition that they may be lightly overridden.

Grotius' concern with the cruelties of war is reflected in his lament that:

> "when arms were once taken up, all reverence for divine and human law was thrown away, just as if men were thenceforth authorized to commit all crimes without restraint"[83].

The foundations laid by Grotius were broad-based and emphasized the absolute binding nature of the restrictions on conduct in war. In building that foundation, Grotius drew upon the collective experience of humanity in a vast range of civilizations and cultures.

Grotius' encyclopedic study of literature, from which he drew his principles, did not of course cover the vast mass of Hindu, Buddhist and Islamic literature having a bearing on these matters, and he did not have the benefit of this considerable supplementary source, demonstrating the universality and the extreme antiquity of the branch of law we call the *jus in bello*.

3. Outline of Humanitarian Law

Humanitarian principles have long been part of the basic stock of concepts embedded in the corpus of international law. Modern international law is the inheritor of a more than hundred-year heritage of active humanitarian concern with the sufferings of war. This concern has aimed at placing checks upon the tendency, so often prevalent in war, to break every precept of human compassion. It has succeeded in doing so in several specific areas, but animating and underlying all those specific instances are general principles of prevention of human suffering that goes beyond the purposes and needs of war.

The credit goes to the United States of America for one of the earliest initiatives in reducing humanitarian law to written form for the guidance of its armies. During the War of Secession, President Lincoln directed Professor Lieber to prepare instructions for the armies of General Grant — regulations which Mr. Martens, the delegate of Czar Nicholas II, referred to at the 1899 Peace Conference as having resulted in great benefit, not only to the United States troops but also to those of the Southern Confederacy. Paying tribute to this initiative, Martens described it as an example, of which the Brussels Conference of 1874 convoked by Emperor Alexander II, was "the logical and natural development". This conference in turn led to the Peace Conference of 1899, and in its turn to the Hague Conventions which assume so much importance in this case[84].

The St. Petersburg Declaration of 1868 provided that "the only legitimate object which States should endeavour to accomplish during war is to weaken the military forces of the enemy" — and many subsequent declarations have adopted and reinforced this principle[85]. It gives expression to a very ancient rule of war accepted by many civilizations[86].

The Martens Clause, deriving its name from Mr. Martens, was, by unanimous vote, inserted into the preamble to the Hague Convention II of 1899, and Convention IV of 1907, with respect to the Laws and Customs of War on Land. It provided that:

---

83 Grotius, *Prolegomena*, para. 28, trans. Whewell.
84 For Martens's speech, see *The Proceedings of the Hague Peace Conferences, op. cit.*, pp. 505-506.
85 The Hague Regulations of 1899 and 1907, Art. 25; the Hague Convention (IX) of 1907, Art. 1 ; League of Nations Assembly resolution of 30 September 1928 ; United Nations General Assembly resolutions 2444 (XXIII) of 19 December 1968 and 2675 (XXV) of 9 December 1970; Additional Protocol I to the 1949 Geneva Conventions, Arts. 48 and 51.
86 See Section V.2. below on "The Aims of War".

"Until a more complete code of the laws of war has been issued, the High Contracting Parties deem it expedient to declare that, *in cases not included in the Regulations adopted by them*, the inhabitants and the belligerents remain under the protection and the rule of the principles of the law of nations, as they result from the usages established among civilized peoples, from the laws of humanity, and the dictates of the public conscience." (Emphasis added.)

Although the Martens Clause was devised to cope with disagreements among the parties to the Hague Peace Conferences regarding the status of resistance movements in occupied territory, it is today considered applicable to the whole of humanitarian law[87]. It appears in one form or another in several major treaties on humanitarian law[88]. The Martens Clause clearly indicates that, behind such specific rules as had already been formulated, there lay a body of general principles sufficient to be applied to such situations as had not already been dealt with by a specific rule[89].

To be read in association with this is Article 22 of the 1907 Hague Regulations which provides that, "The right of belligerents to adopt means of injuring the enemy is not unlimited."

These were indications also that international law, far from being insensitive to such far-reaching issues of human welfare, has long recognized the pre-eminent importance of considerations of humanity in fashioning its attitudes and responses to situations involving their violation, however they may occur. These declarations were made, it is to be noted, at a time when the development of modern weaponry was fast accelerating under the impact of technology. It was visualized that more sophisticated and deadly weaponry was on the drawing boards of military establishments throughout the world and would continue to be so for the foreseeable future. These principles were thus meant to apply to weapons existing then as well as to weapons to be created in the future, weapons already known and weapons as yet unvisualized. They were general principles meant to be applied to new weapons as well as old.

The parties to the Geneva Conventions of 1949 expressly recognized the Martens Clause as a living part of international law — a proposition which no international jurist could seriously deny.

As McDougal and Feliciano have observed:

"To accept as lawful the deliberate terrorization of the enemy community by the infliction of large-scale destruction comes too close to rendering pointless all legal limitations on the exercise of violence."[90]

International law has long distinguished between conventional weapons and those which are unnecessarily cruel. It has also shown a continuing interest in this problem. For example, the Convention on Prohibitions or Restrictions on the Use of Certain Conventional Weapons Which May be Deemed to be Excessively Injurious or to Have Indiscriminate Effects, 1980, dealt in three separate Protocols with such weapons as those which injure by fragments, which in the human body escape detection (Protocol I); Mines, Booby Traps and Other Devices (Protocol II); and

---

87 See D. Fleck (ed.), *The Handbook of Humanitarian Law in Armed Conflicts*, 1995, p. 29.
88 First Geneva Convention 1949, Art. 63, para. 4; Second Geneva Convention, Art. 62, para. 4; Third Geneva Convention, Art. 142, para. 4; Fourth Geneva Convention, Art. 158, para. 4; Inhumane Weapons Convention, 1980, Preamble, para. 5.
89 At the last meeting of the Fourth Commission of the Peace Conference, on 26 September 1907, Mr. Martens summarized its achievements in terms that,

"If from the days of antiquity to our own time people have been repeating the Roman adage '*Inter arma silent leges*', we have loudly proclaimed, '*Inter arma vivant leges*'. This is the greatest triumph of law and justice over brute force and the necessities of war." (J. B. Scott, "The Conference of 1907", *The Proceedings of the Hague Peace Conferences*, 1921, Vol. III, p. 914.)
90 M. S. McDougal and F. P. Feliciano, *Law and Minimum World Public Order : The Legal Regulation of International Coercion*, 1961, p. 657.

Incendiary Weapons (Protocol III).

If international law had principles within it strong enough in 1899 to recognize the extraordinary cruelty of the "dum dum" or exploding bullet as going beyond the purposes of war[91], and projectiles diffusing asphyxiating or deleterious gases as also being extraordinarily cruel[92], it would cause some bewilderment to the objective observer to learn that in 1996 it is so weak in principles that, with over a century of humanitarian law behind it, it is still unable to fashion a response to the cruelties of nuclear weapons as going beyond the purposes of war. At the least, it would seem passing strange that the expansion within the body of a single soldier of a single bullet is an excessive cruelty which international law has been unable to tolerate since 1899, and that the incineration in one second of a hundred thousand civilians is not. This astonishment would be compounded when that weapon has the capability, through multiple use, of endangering the entire human species and all civilization with it.

Every branch of knowledge benefits from a process of occasionally stepping back from itself and scrutinizing itself objectively for anomalies and absurdities. If a glaring anomaly or absurdity becomes apparent and remains unquestioned, that discipline is in danger of being seen as floundering in the midst of its own technicalities. International law is happily not in this position, but if the conclusion that nuclear weapons are illegal is wrong, it would indeed be.

As will appear from the ensuing discussion, international law is not so lacking in resources as to be unable to meet this unprecedented challenge. Humanitarian law is not a monument to uselessness in the face of the nuclear danger. It contains a plethora of principles wide enough, deep enough and powerful enough to handle this problem.

Humanitarian law has of course received recognition from the jurisprudence of this Court (for example, *Corfu Channel, I.C.J. Reports 1949*, p. 22; *Border and Transborder Armed Actions (Nicaragua v. Honduras), I.C.J. Reports 1988*, p. 114), but this Court has not so far had occasion to examine it in any depth. This case offers it the opportunity *par excellence* for so doing.

4. Acceptance by States of the Martens Clause

The Martens Clause has commanded general international acceptance. It has been incorporated into a series of treaties, as mentioned elsewhere in this opinion, has been applied by international judicial tribunals, has been incorporated into military manuals[93], and has been generally accepted in international legal literature as indeed encapsulating in its short phraseology the entire philosophy of the law of war.

At the Krupp Trial (1948), it was described as:

> "a general clause, making the usages established among civilised nations, the laws of humanity and the dictates of the public conscience into the legal yardstick to be applied if and when the specific provisions of the Convention and the Regulations annexed to it do not cover specific cases occurring in warfare, or concomitant to warfare"[94].

The Clause has been described by Lord Wright as furnishing the keynote to the Hague Regulations which particularize a great many war crimes,

> "leaving the remainder to the governing effect of that sovereign clause which does really in a few words state the whole animating and motivating principle of the law of war, and indeed of all law, because the object of all law is to secure as far as possible in the mutual relations of the human

---

91 International Declaration Respecting Expanding Bullets, signed at The Hague, 29 July 1899.
92 International Declaration Respecting Asphyxiating Gases, signed at The Hague, 29 July 1899.
93 See Section III. I 0 (a) below.
94 *Law Reports of Trials of War Criminals,* Vol. 10, p. 133.

beings concerned the rule of law and of justice and of humanity"[95].

The Martens Clause has thus become an established and integral part of the corpus of current customary international law. International law has long passed the stage when it could be debated whether such principles had crystallized into customary international law. No State would today repudiate any one of these principles.

A generally accepted test of recognition of rules of customary international law is that the rule should be "so widely and generally accepted, that it can hardly be supposed that any civilized State would repudiate it"[96]. While no State today would repudiate any one of these principles, what seems to be in dispute is the application of those principles to the specific case of nuclear weapons which, for some unarticulated reason, seem to be placed above and beyond the rules applicable to other weapons. If humanitarian law regulates the lesser weapons for fear that they may cause the excessive harm which those principles seek to prevent, it must *a fortiori* regulate the greater. The attempt to place nuclear weapons beyond the reach of these principles lacks the support not only of the considerations of humanity, but also of the considerations of logic.

These considerations are also pertinent to the argument that customary law cannot be created over the objection of the nuclear weapon States (United States Written Statement, p. 9)[97]. The general principles of customary law applicable to the matter commanded the allegiance of the nuclear-weapon States long before nuclear weapons were invented. It is on those general principles that the illegality of nuclear weapons rests.

It seems clear that if the principles are accepted and remain undisputed, the applicability of those principles to the specific case of nuclear weapons cannot reasonably be in doubt.

5. *"The Dictates of Public Conscience"*

This phraseology, stemming from the Martens Clause, lies at the heart of humanitarian law. The Martens Clause and many subsequent formulations of humanitarian principles recognize the need that strongly held public sentiments in relation to humanitarian conduct be reflected in the law.

The phrase is, of course, sufficiently general to pose difficulties in certain cases in determining whether a particular sentiment is shared widely enough to come within this formulation.

However, in regard to the use or threat of use of nuclear weapons, there is no such uncertainty, for on this issue the conscience of the global community has spoken, and spoken often, in the most unmistakable terms. Resolutions of the General Assembly over the years are not the only evidence of this. Vast numbers of the general public in practically every country, organized professional bodies of a multinational character[98], and many other groupings across the world have proclaimed time and again their conviction that the public conscience dictates the non-use of nuclear weapons. Across the world, presidents and prime ministers, priests and prelates, workers and students, and women and children have continued to express themselves strongly against the bomb and its dangers. Indeed, this conviction underlies the conduct of the entire world community of nations when, for example, in the NPT, it accepts that all nuclear weapons must eventually be got rid of. The recent Non-Proliferation Review Conference of 1995 reconfirmed this objective. The work currently in progress towards a total test ban treaty reconfirms this again.

---
95 Foreword by Lord Wright to the last volume of the *Law Reports of Trials of War Criminals*, Vol. 15, p. xiii. See, further, the discussion of the Martens Clause in Singh and McWhinney, *op. cit.*, pp. 46 et seq., referring, inter alia, to the two passages cited above.
96 *West Rand Central Gold Mining Co., Ltd. v. R* (1905), 2 KB, p. 407.
97 On this aspect, see further Section VI.6 below.
98 See, on these organizations, Section VI.3 below.

Reference is made in the next section (Section VI.6) to the heightening of public sensitivity towards humanitarian issues, resulting from the vast strides made by human rights law ever since the United Nations Charter in 1945.

General Assembly resolutions on the matter are numerous[99]. To cite just one of them, resolution 1653 (XVI) of 1961 declared that :

> "The use of nuclear and thermo-nuclear weapons is contrary to the spirit, letter and aims of the United Nations and, as such, a direct violation of the Charter of the United Nations"

and asserted, with more specific reference to international law, that such use was "contrary to the rules of international law and to the laws of humanity". In addition, the "threat" to use nuclear weapons, and not merely their actual use, has been referred to by the General Assembly as prohibited[100].

Nuclear weapons have been outlawed by treaty in numerous areas of planetary space — the sea-bed, Antarctica, Latin America and the Caribbean, the Pacific, and Africa, not to speak of outer space. Such universal activity and commitment would be altogether inconsistent with a global acceptance of the compatibility of these weapons with the general principles of humanity. They point rather to a universal realization that there is in them an element which deeply disturbs the public conscience of this age.

As has been well observed in this regard:

> "in this burgeoning human rights era especially, respecting an issue that involves potentially the fate of human civilization itself, it is not only appropriate but mandated that the legal expectations of all members of human society, official and non-official, be duly taken into account"[101].

It is a truism that there is no such thing as a unanimous opinion held by the entire world community on any principle, however lofty. Yet it would be hard to find a proposition so widely and universally accepted as that nuclear weapons should not be used. The various expressions of opinion on this matter "are expressive of a far-flung community consensus that nuclear weapons and warfare do not escape the judgment of the humanitarian rules of armed conflict"[102].

The incompatibility between "the dictates of public conscience" and the weapon appears starkly, if one formulates the issues in the form of questions that may be addressed to the public conscience of the world, as typified by the average citizen in any country.

Here are a few questions, from an extensive list that could be compiled:

> Is it lawful for the purposes of war to induce cancers, keloid growths or

---

99 Resolution 1653 (XVI) of 24 November 1961 ("Declaration on the Prohibition of the Use of Nuclear and Thermo-nuclear Weapons") ; resolution 2936 (XXVII) of 29 November 1972 ("Non-Use of Force in International Relations and Permanent Prohibition of the Use of Nuclear Weapons"); resolution 33171 B of 14 December 1978 ("Non-Use of Nuclear Weapons and Prevention of Nuclear War"); resolution 34/83 G of 11 December 1979 ("Non-Use of Nuclear Weapons and Prevention of Nuclear War") ; resolution 36192 I of 9 December 1981 ("Non-Use of Nuclear Weapons and Prevention of Nuclear War"); resolution 44/117 C of 15 December 1989 ("Convention on the Prohibition of the Use of Nuclear Weapons"); resolution 45/59 B of 4 December 1990 ("Convention on the Prohibition of the Use of Nuclear Weapons"); resolution 46/37 D of 6 December 1991 ("Convention on the Prohibition of the Use of Nuclear Weapons"). See, also, e.g., resolution 36/100 of 9 December 1981 ("Declaration on the Prevention of Nuclear Catastrophe"), para. 1 "States and statesmen that resort first to the use of nuclear weapons will be committing the gravest crime against humanity".
100 Resolution 2936 (XXVII) of 29 November 1972 ("Non-Use of Force in International Relations and Permanent Prohibition of the Use of Nuclear Weapons"), preambular paragraph 10.
101 Burns H. Weston, "Nuclear Weapons and International Law: Prolegomenon to General Illegality", *New York Law School Journal of International and Comparative Law*, 1982-1983, Vol. 4, p. 252, and authorities therein cited.
102 *Ibid.*, p. 242.

leukaemias in large numbers of the enemy population ?

Is it lawful for the purposes of war to inflict congenital deformities and mental retardation on unborn children of the enemy population ?

Is it lawful for the purposes of war to poison the food supplies of the enemy population?

Is it lawful for the purposes of war to inflict any of the above types of damage on the population of countries that have nothing to do with the quarrel leading to the nuclear war ?

Many more such questions could be asked.

If it is conceivable that any of these questions can be answered in the affirmative by the public conscience of the world, there may be a case for the legality of nuclear weapons. If it is not, the case against nuclear weapons seems unanswerable.

6. *Impact of the United Nations Charter and Human Rights on "Considerations of Humanity" and "Dictates of Public Conscience*[103]

The enormous developments in the field of human rights in the post war years, commencing with the Universal Declaration of Human Rights in 1948, must necessarily make their impact on assessments of such concepts as "considerations of humanity" and "dictates of public conscience". This development in human rights concepts, both in their formulation and in their universal acceptance, is more substantial than the developments in this field for centuries before. The public conscience of the global community has thus been greatly strengthened and sensitized to "considerations of humanity" and "dictates of public conscience". Since the vast structure of internationally accepted human rights norms and standards has become part of common global consciousness today in a manner unknown before World War II, its principles tend to be invoked immediately and automatically whenever a question arises of humanitarian standards.

This progressive development must shape contemporary conceptions of humanity and humanitarian standards, thus elevating the level of basic expectation well above what it was when the Martens Clause was formulated.

In assessing the magnitude of this change, it is helpful to recall that the first movement towards modern humanitarian law was achieved in a century (the nineteenth century) which is often described as the "Clausewitzean century" for the reason that, in that century, war was widely regarded as a natural means for the resolution of disputes, and a natural extension of diplomacy. Global sentiment has moved an infinite distance from that stance, for today the United Nations Charter outlaws all resort to force by States (Art. 2 (4)), except in the case of self-defence (Art. 51). The Court's Opinion highlights the importance of these articles, with farreaching implications which this opinion has addressed at the every outset (see "Preliminary Observations"). There is a firm commitment in Article 2 (3) that all members shall settle their international disputes by peaceful means, in such manner that international peace and security, and justice, are not endangered. This totally altered stance regarding the normalcy and legitimacy of war has undoubtedly heightened the "dictates of public conscience" in our time.

Charter provisions bearing on human rights, such as Articles 1, 55, 62 and 76, coupled with the Universal Declaration of 1948, the twin Covenants on Civil and Political Rights and Economic, Social and Cultural Rights of 1966, and the numerous specific conventions formulating human rights standards, such as the Convention against Torture — all of these, now part of the public conscience of the global community, make the violation of humanitarian standards a far more developed and definite concept than in the days when the Martens Clause emerged. Indeed, so well are human rights norms and standards ingrained today in global consciousness, that

---

103 See, also, Section III.10 (g) below.

they flood through into every corner of humanitarian law.

Submissions on these lines were made to the Court (for example, by Australia, CR 95122, p. 25) in presentations which drew attention further to the fact that the General Assembly has noted the linkage between human rights and nuclear weapons when it condemned nuclear war "as a violation of the foremost human right — the right to life"[104]

Parallel to the developments in human rights, there has been another vast area of development — environmental law, which has likewise heightened the sensitivity of the public conscience to environmentally related matters which affect human rights. As observed by the International Law Commission in its consideration of State responsibility, conduct gravely endangering the preservation of the human environment violates principles "which are now so deeply rooted in the conscience of mankind that they have become particularly essential rules of general international law"[105].

7. *The Argument that "Collateral Damage" Is Unintended*

It is not to the point that such results are not directly intended, but are "by-products" or "collateral damage" caused by nuclear weapons. Such results are known to be the necessary consequences of the use of the weapon. The author of the act causing these consequences cannot in any coherent legal system avoid legal responsibility for causing them, any less than a man careering in a motor vehicle at 150 kilometres per hour through a crowded market street can avoid responsibility for the resulting deaths on the ground that he did not intend to kill the particular persons who died.

The plethora of literature on the consequences of the nuclear weapon is so much part of common universal knowledge today that no disclaimer of such knowledge would be credible.

8. *Illegality Exists Independently of Specific Prohibitions*

Much of the argument of States opposing illegality was based on the proposition that what is not expressly prohibited to a State is permitted. Some practical illustrations would be of assistance in testing this proposition:

(a) If tomorrow a ray were invented which would immediately incinerate all living things within a radius of 100 miles, does one need to wait for an international treaty specifically banning it to declare that it offends the basic principles of the *jus in bello* and cannot therefore be legitimately used in war? It would seem rather ridiculous to have to await the convening of an international conference, the drafting of a treaty, and all the delays associated with the process of ratification, before the law can treat such a weapon as illegal.

(b) The fallacy of the argument that what is not expressly prohibited is permitted appears further from an illustration used earlier in this opinion. The argument advanced would presuppose that, immediately prior to the treaties outlawing bacteriological weapons, it was legal to use warheads packed with the most deadly germs wherewith to cause lethal epidemics among the enemy population. This conclusion strains credibility and is tenable only if one totally discounts the pre-existing principles of humanitarian law.

---

104 General Assembly resolution 38/75 of 15 December 1983 ("Condemnation of Nuclear War"), operative paragraph I.
105 Report of the International Law Commission on the work of its twenty-eighth session, *Yearbook of the International Law Commission*, 1976, Vol. II, Part II, p. 109, para. 33.

The fact that no treaty or declaration expressly condemns the weapon as illegal does not meet the point that illegality is based upon principles of customary international law which run far deeper than any particular weapon or any particular declaration. Every weapon proscribed by international law for its cruelty or brutality does not need to be specified any more than every implement of torture needs to be specified in a general prohibition against torture. It is the *principle* that is the subject of customary international law. The *particular* weapon or implement of torture becomes relevant only as an application of undisputed *principles* — principles which have been more than once described as being such that no civilized nation would deny them.

It will always be the case that weapons technologists will from time to time invent weapons based on new applications of technology, which are different from any weapons known before. One does not need to wait until some treaty specifically condemns that weapon before declaring that its use is contrary to the principles of international law.

If, as is indisputably the case, the Martens Clause represents a universally accepted principle of international law, it means that beyond the domain of express prohibitions there lies the domain of the general principles of humanitarian law. It follows that "If an act of war is not expressly prohibited by international agreements or customary law, this does not necessarily mean that it is actually permissible."[106]

It is self-evident that no system of law can depend for its operation or development on specific prohibitions *ipsissimis verbis*. Any developed system of law has, in addition to its specific commands and prohibitions, an array of general principles which from time to time are applied to specific items of conduct or events which have not been the subject of an express ruling before. The general principle is then applied to the specific situation and out of that particular application a rule of greater specificity emerges.

A legal system based on the theory that what is not expressly prohibited is permitted would be a primitive system indeed, and international law has progressed far beyond this stage. Even if domestic systems could function on that basis, — which indeed is doubtful — international law, born of generations of philosophical thinking, cannot. Modern legal philosophy in many jurisdictions has exposed the untenability of this view in regard to domestic systems and, a fortiori, the same applies to international law. As a well-known text on jurisprudence observes:

> "The rules of every legal order have an enveloping blanket of principles and doctrines as the earth is surrounded by air, and these not only influence the operation of rules but sometimes condition their very existence."[107]

More to the point than the question whether any treaty speaks of the illegality of nuclear weapons is whether any single provision of any treaty or declaration speaks of the legality of nuclear weapons. The fact is that, though there is a profusion of international documents dealing with many aspects of nuclear weapons, not one of these contains the shred of a suggestion that the use or threat of use of nuclear weapons is legal. By way of contrast, the number of international declarations which expressly pronounce against the legality or the use of nuclear weapons is legion. These are referred to elsewhere in this opinion.

The general principles provide both nourishment for the development of the law and an anchorage to the mores of the community. If they are to be discarded in the manner contended for, international law would be cast adrift from its conceptual moorings. "The general principles of law recognized by civilized nations" remains law, even though indiscriminate mass slaughter *through the nuclear weapon*, irreversible damage to future generations *through the nuclear weapon*, environmental devastation *through the nuclear weapon*, and irreparable damage to neutral States *through the nuclear weapon* are not expressly prohibited in international treaties. If the italicized words are

---

106 D. Fleck, *op. cit.*, p. 28, basing this principle on the Martens Clause.
107 Dias, *Jurisprudence*, 4th ed., 1976, p. 287.

deleted from the previous sentence, no one could deny that the acts mentioned therein are prohibited by international law. It seems specious to argue that the principle of prohibition is defeated by the absence of particularization of the weapon.

The doctrine that the sovereign is free to do whatever statute does not expressly prohibit is a long-exploded doctrine. Such extreme positivism in legal doctrine has led humanity to some of its worst excesses. History has demonstrated that power, unrestrained by principle, becomes power abused. Black-letter formulations have their value, but by no stretch of the imagination can they represent the totality of the law.

With specific reference to the laws of war, it would also set at nought the words of the Martens Clause, whose express terms are that, "Until a more complete code of the laws of war has been issued, the High Contracting Parties ... declare that, *in cases not included in the Regulations adopted by them* ..." (emphasis added), the humanitarian principles it sets out would apply.

Thus, by express agreement, if that indeed were necessary, the wide range of principles of humanitarian law contained within customary international law would be applicable to govern this matter, for which no specific provision has yet been made by treaty.

9. *The "Lotus" Decision*

Much of the argument based on the absence of specific illegality was anchored to the "*Lotus*" decision. In that case, the Permanent Court addressed its enquiry to the question:

"whether or not under international law there is a principle which would have prohibited Turkey, in the circumstances of the case before the Court, from prosecuting Lieutenant Demons" (*P.C.I.J., Series A, No. 10*, p. 21).

In the absence of such a principle or of a specific rule to which it had expressly consented, it was held that the authority of a State could not be limited.

Indeed, even within the terms of the "*Lotus*" case, these principles become applicable, for, in relation to the laws of war, there is the express acceptance by the nuclear powers that the humanitarian principles of the laws of war should apply. Apart from the nuclear powers, some other powers who have opposed a finding of illegality before this Court (or not adopted a clear-cut position in regard to the present request), were also parties to the Hague Convention, for example, Germany, Netherlands, Italy and Japan.

The "*Lotus*" case was decided in the context of a collision on the high seas, in time of peace, between the *Lotus*, flying the French flag and a vessel flying the Turkish flag. Eight Turkish sailors and passengers died and the French officer responsible was sought to be tried for manslaughter in the Turkish courts. This was a situation far removed from that to which the humanitarian laws of war apply. Such humanitarian law was already a well-established concept at the time of the "*Lotus*" decision, but was not relevant to it. It would have been furthest from the mind of the Court deciding that case that its dictum, given in such entirely different circumstances, would be used in an attempt to negative all that the humanitarian laws of war had built up until that time — for the interpretation now sought to be given to the "*Lotus*" case is nothing less than that it overrides even such well-entrenched principles as the Martens Clause, which expressly provides that its humanitarian principles would apply "in cases not included in the Regulations adopted by them".

Moreover, at that time, international law was generally treated in two separate categories — the laws of peace and the laws of war — a distinction well recognized in the structure of the legal texts of that time. The principle the "*Lotus*" court was enunciating was formulated entirely within the context of the laws of peace.

It is implicit in "*Lotus*" that the sovereignty of other States should be respected.

One of the characteristics of nuclear weapons is that they violate the sovereignty of other countries who have in no way consented to the intrusion upon their fundamental sovereign rights, which is implicit in the use of the nuclear weapon. It would be an interpretation totally out of context that the *"Lotus"* decision formulated a theory, equally applicable in peace and war, to the effect that a State could do whatever it pleased so long as it had not bound itself to the contrary. Such an interpretation of "Lotus" would cast a baneful spell on the progressive development of international law.

It is to be noted also that just four years earlier, the Permanent Court, in dealing with the question of State sovereignty, had observed in *Nationality Decrees Issued in Tunis and Morocco* that the sovereignty of States would be proportionately diminished and restricted as international law developed (*Advisory Opinion, 1923, P.C.I.J., Series B, No. 4*, pp. 121- 125, 127, 130). In the half century that has elapsed since the *"Lotus"* case, it is quite evident that international law — and the law relating to humanitarian conduct in war — have developed considerably, imposing additional restrictions on State sovereignty over and above those that existed at the time of the *"Lotus"* case. This Court's own jurisprudence in the *Corfu Channel* case sees customary international law as imposing a duty on all States so to conduct their affairs as not to injure others, even though there was no prohibition *ipsissimis verbis* of the particular act which constituted a violation of the complaining nation's rights. This Court cannot in 1996 construe *"Lotus"* so narrowly as to take the law backward in time even beyond the Martens Clause.

10. Specific Rules of the Humanitarian Law of War

There are several interlacing principles which together constitute the fabric of international humanitarian law. Humanitarian law reveals not a paucity, but rather an abundance of rules which both individually and cumulatively render the use or threat of use of nuclear weapons illegal.

The rules of the humanitarian law of war have clearly acquired the status of *jus cogens*, for they are fundamental rules of a humanitarian character, from which no derogation is possible without negating the basic considerations of humanity which they are intended to protect. In the words of Roberto Ago, the rules of *jus cogens* include:

> "the fundamental rules concerning the safeguarding of peace, and notably those which forbid recourse to force or threat of force; *fundamental rules of a humanitarian nature* (prohibition of genocide, slavery and racial discrimination, *protection of essential rights of the human person in time of peace and war*); the rules prohibiting any infringement of the independence and sovereign equality of States; the rules which ensure to all members of the international community the enjoyment of certain common resources (high seas, outer space, etc.)"[108]

The question under consideration is not whether there is a prohibition in peremptory terms of nuclear weapons specifically so mentioned, but whether there are basic principles of a *jus cogens* nature which are violated by nuclear weapons. If there are such principles which are of a jus cogens nature, then it would follow that the weapon itself would be prohibited under the *jus cogens* concept.

As noted at the commencement of Part III, most of the States which support the view that the use of nuclear weapons is lawful acknowledge that international humanitarian law applies to their use, and that such use must conform to its principles.

---

[108] *Recueil des cours de l'Academie de droit international de La Haye*, Vol. 134 (1971), p. 324, footnote 37; emphasis added. See, also, the detailed study of various peremptory norms in the international law of armed conflict, in Lauri Hannikainen, *Peremptory Norms (Jus Cogens) in International Law*, 1988, pp. 596-715, where the author finds that many of the principles of the humanitarian law of war are *jus cogens*.

Among the more important of the relevant principles of international law are:

(a) the prohibition against causing unnecessary suffering;
(b) the principle of proportionality;
(c) the principle of discrimination between combatants and non-combatants;
(d) the obligation to respect the territorial sovereignty of non-belligerent States;
(e) the prohibition against genocide and crimes against humanity;
(f) the prohibition against causing lasting and severe damage to the environment;
(g) human rights law.

(a) The prohibition against causing unnecessary suffering

The Martens Clause, to which reference has already been made, gave classic formulation to this principle in modern law, when it spelt out the impermissibility of weapons incompatible with "the laws of humanity and the dictates of public conscience".

The prohibition against cruel and unnecessary suffering, long a part of the general principles of humanitarian law, has been embodied in such a large number of codes, declarations, and treaties as to constitute a firm and substantial body of law, each document applying the general principles to a specific situation or situations[109]. They illustrate the existence of overarching general principles transcending the specific instances dealt with.

The principle against unnecessary suffering has moreover been incorporated into standard military manuals. Thus the British Manual of Military Law, issued by the War Office in 1916, and used in World War I, reads:

"IV. The Means of Carrying on War

39. The first principle of war is that the enemy's powers of resistance must be weakened and destroyed. The means that may be employed to inflict injury on him are not however unlimited [footnote cites Hague Rules 22, 'Belligerents have not an unlimited right as to the choice of means of injuring the enemy']. They are in practice definitely restricted by international conventions and declarations, and also by the customary rules of warfare. And, moreover, there are the dictates of morality, civilization and chivalry, which ought to be obeyed.
   . . . .
42. It is expressly forbidden to employ arms, projectiles or material calculated to cause unnecessary suffering [Hague Rules 23 (e)]. Under this heading might be included such weapons as lances with a barbed head, irregularly shaped bullets, projectiles filled with broken glass and the like; also the scoring of the surface of bullets, the filing off the end of their hard case, and smearing on them any substance likely to inflame or wound. The prohibition is not, however, intended to apply to the use of explosives contained in mines, aerial torpedoes, or hand-grenades." (Pp. 242-243.)

Such was the Manual the British forces used in World War I, long before the principles of humanitarian warfare were as well entrenched as they now are[110].

As early as 1862, Franz Lieber accepted the position that even military necessity is subject to the law and usages of war, and this was incorporated in the instructions

---

109 Examples are the Lieber Code of 1863 (adopted by the United States for the Government of Armies in the Field); the Declaration of St. Petersburg of 1868; the Hague Conventions of 1899 and 1907; the Protocol for the Prohibition of the Use in War of Asphyxiating, Poisonous or Other Gases, and of Bacteriological Methods of Warfare of 1925; the Hague Rules of Air Warfare of 1923; the Nuremberg Charter of 1945; and the four Geneva Conventions of 1949.
110 On the importance of validity of military manuals, see Singh and McWhinney, *op. cit.*, pp. 52-53.

for the army[111]. Modern United States War Department Field Manuals are in strict conformity with the Hague Regulations and expressly subject military necessity to "the customary and conventional laws of war"[112].

The facts set out in Part II of this opinion are more than sufficient to establish that the nuclear weapon causes unnecessary suffering going far beyond the purposes of war.

An argument that has been advanced in regard to the principle regarding "unnecessary suffering" is that, under Article 23 (e) of the 1907 Hague Regulations, it is forbidden, "To employ arms, projectiles, or material *calculated* to cause unnecessary suffering" (emphasis added). The nuclear weapon, it is said, is not *calculated* to cause suffering, but suffering is rather a part of the "incidental side effects" of nuclear weapons explosions. This argument is met by the well-known legal principle that the doer of an act must be taken to have intended its natural and foreseeable consequences (see Section 111.7 above). It is, moreover, a literal interpretation which does not take into account the spirit and underlying rationale of the provision — a method of interpretation particularly inappropriate to the construction of a humanitarian instrument. It may also be said that nuclear weapons are indeed deployed "in part with a view to utilising the destructive effects of radiation and fall-out"[113]

(b) The principle of proportionality

See discussion in Part IV below,.

(c) The principle of discrimination

The principle of discrimination originated in the concern that weapons of war should not be used indiscriminately against military targets and civilians alike. Non-combatants needed the protection of the laws of war. However, the nuclear weapon is such that non-discrimination is built into its very nature. A weapon that can flatten a city and achieve by itself the destruction caused by thousands of individual bombs is not a weapon that discriminates. The radiation it releases over immense areas does not discriminate between combatant and non-combatant, or indeed between combatant and neutral States.

Article 48 of the Additional Protocol I to the Geneva Conventions of 1949 repeats as a "Basic Rule" the well-accepted rule of humanitarian law:

> "In order to ensure respect for and protection of the civilian population and civilian objects, the Parties to the conflict shall *at all times* distinguish between the civilian population and combatants and between civilian objects and military objectives and accordingly shall direct their operations only against military objectives." (Emphasis added.)

The rule of discrimination between civilian populations and military personnel is, like some of the other rules of *jus in bello*, of ancient vintage and shared by many cultures. We have referred already to the ancient Indian practice that Indian peasants would pursue their work in the fields, in the face of invading armies, confident of the protection afforded them by the tradition that war was a matter for the combatants[114] This scenario, idyllic though it may seem, and so out of tune with the brutalities of war, is a useful reminder that basic humanitarian principles such as discrimination do not aim at fresh standards unknown before.

The protection of the civilian population in times of armed conflict has for long

---

111 General Orders 100, *Instructions for the Government of the Armies of the United States in the Field*, s. 14.
112 Singh and McWhinney, *op. cit.*, p. 59.
113 Ian Brownlie, "Some Legal Aspects of the Use of Nuclear Weapons", *International and Comparative Law Quarterly*, 1965, Vol. 14, p. 445.
114 Nagendra Singh, *op. cit.*, footnote 69 above.

been a well-established rule of international humanitarian law. Additional Protocol I to the Geneva Conventions (1949) provides by Article 51 (5)(b) that the "indiscriminate attacks" which it prohibits include:

> "an attack which may be expected to cause incidental loss of civilian life, injury to civilians, damage to civilian objects, or a combination thereof, which would be excessive in relation to the concrete and direct military advantage anticipated".

So, also, Article 57 (2) (b) prohibits attacks when :

> "the attack may be expected to cause incidental loss of civilian life, injury to civilians, damage to civilian objects, or a combination thereof, which would be excessive in relation to the concrete and direct military advantage anticipated".

The many facets of this rule were addressed in the resolution of the International Law Institute, passed at its Edinburgh Conference in 1969[115] which referred to them as prohibited by existing law as at that date. The acts described as prohibited by existing law included the following:

> "all attacks for whatsoever motive or by whatsoever means for the annihilation of any group, region or urban centre with no possible distinction between armed forces and civilian populations or between military objectives and non-military objects"[116];

> "any action whatsoever designed to terrorize the civilian population"[117];

> "the use of all weapons which, by their nature, affect indiscriminately both military objectives and non-military objects, or both armed forces and civilian populations. In particular, it prohibits the use of weapons the destructive effect of which is so great that it cannot be limited to specific military objectives or is otherwise uncontrollable ..., as well as of 'blind' weapons."[118]

(d) Respect for non-belligerent States

When nuclear weapons are used their natural and foreseeable consequence of irreparable damage to non-belligerent third parties is a necessary consideration to be taken into reckoning in deciding the permissibility of the weapon. It is not merely a single non-belligerent State that might be irretrievably damaged, but the entire global community of States. The uncontainability of radiation extends it globally. The enormous area of damage caused by nuclear weapons, as compared with the most powerful conventional weapons, appears from the diagram appended to this opinion, which is taken from WHO studies. When wind currents scatter these effects further, it is well established by the TTAPS and other studies that explosions in one hemisphere can spread their deleterious effects even to the other hemisphere. No portion of the globe — and therefore no country — could be free of these effects.

The argument of lack of intention has been addressed in this context as well. In terms of this argument, an action directed at an enemy State is not intended to cause damage to a third party, and if such damage in fact ensues, it is not culpable. This

---

115 On the eminent juristic support for this proposition, see Section III.I! below.
116 *Annuaire de l'Institut de droit international,* 1969, No. 53, Vol. II, p. 377, para. 8 ; Iran, CR 95/26, p. 47, footnote 45.
117 *Annuaire de l'Institut de droit international,* 1969, No. 53, Vol. II, p. 377, para. 6.
118 *Ibid.,* para. 7.

199

argument has already been dealt with in an earlier section of this opinion, when it was pointed out that such an argument is untenable (see Section III.7). The launching of a nuclear weapon is a deliberate act. Damage to neutrals is a natural, foreseeable and, indeed, inevitable consequence. International law cannot contain a rule of non-responsibility which is so opposed to the basic principles of universal jurisprudence.

(e) The prohibition against genocide[119]

The Court's treatment of the relevance of genocide to the nuclear weapon is, in my view, inadequate (paragraph 26 of the Opinion).

Nuclear weapons used in response to a nuclear attack, especially in the event of an all-out nuclear response, would be likely to cause genocide by triggering off an all-out nuclear exchange, as visualized in Section IV below. Even a single "small" nuclear weapon, such as those used in Japan, could be instruments of genocide, judging from the number of deaths they are known to have caused. If cities are targeted, a single bomb could cause a death toll exceeding a million. If the retaliatory weapons are more numerous, on WHO's estimates of the effects of nuclear war, even a billion people, both of the attacking State and of others, could be killed. This is plainly genocide and, whatever the circumstances, cannot be within the law.

When a nuclear weapon is used, those using it must know that it will have the effect of causing deaths on a scale so massive as to wipe out entire populations. Genocide, as defined in the Genocide Convention (Art. II), means any act committed with intent to destroy, in whole or in part, a national, ethnical, racial or religious group, as such. Acts included in the definition are killing members of the group, causing serious bodily or mental harm to members of the group, and deliberately inflicting on the group conditions of life calculated to bring about its physical destruction in whole or in part.

In discussions on the definition of genocide in the Genocide Convention, much play is made upon the words "as such". The argument offered is that there must be an intention to target a particular national, ethnical, racial or religious group qua such group, and not incidentally to some other act. However, having regard to the ability of nuclear weapons to wipe out blocks of population ranging from hundreds of thousands to millions, there can be no doubt that the weapon targets, in whole or in part, the national group of the State at which it is directed.

Nuremberg held that the extermination of the civilian population in whole or in part is a crime against humanity. This is precisely what a nuclear weapon achieves.

(f) The prohibition against environmental damage

The environment, the common habitat of all Member States of the United Nations, cannot be damaged by any one or more members to the detriment of all others. Reference has already been made, in the context of dictates of public conscience (Section III.6 above), to the fact that the principles of environmental protection have become "so deeply rooted in the conscience of mankind that they have become particularly essential rules of general international law"[120]. The International Law Commission has indeed classified massive pollution of the atmosphere or of the seas as an international crime[121]. These aspects have been referred to earlier.

Environmental law incorporates a number of principles which are violated by nuclear weapons. The principle of intergenerational equity and the common heritage principle have already been discussed. Other principles of environmental law, which this request enables the Court to recognize and use in reaching its conclusions, are the precautionary principle, the principle of trusteeship of earth resources, the

---
119 See, further, Section III.10 (g) below on human rights law.
120 Report of the International Law Commission on the work of its twenty-eighth session, *Yearbook of the International Law Commission*, 1976, Vol. II, Part II, p. 109, para. 33.
121 Draft Article 19 (3) (d) on "State Responsibility" of the International Law Commission, *ibid.*, p. 96.

principle that the burden of proving safety lies upon the author of the act complained of, and the "polluter pays principle", placing on the author of environmental damage the burden of making adequate reparation to those affected[122]. There have been juristic efforts in recent times to formulate what have been described as "principles of ecological security" — a process of norm creation and codification of environmental law which has developed under the stress of the need to protect human civilization from the threat of self-destruction.

One writer[123] in listing eleven such principles, includes among them the "Prohibition of Ecological Aggression", deriving this principle *inter alia* from such documents as the 1977 Convention on the Prohibition of Military or Any Other Hostile Use of Environmental Modification Techniques which entered into force on 5 October 1978 (1108 UNTS, p. 151), and the United Nations General Assembly resolution "Historical responsibility of States for the preservation of nature for present and future generations" (General Assembly resolution 35/8 of 30 October 1980).

The same writer points out that,

> "Under Soviet [now Russian] legal doctrine, the deliberate and hostile modification of the environment — ecocide — is unlawful and considered an international crime." [124]

Another writer, drawing attention to the need for a co-ordinated, collective response to the global environmental crisis and the difficulty of envisioning such a response, observes:

> "But circumstances are forcing just such a response; if we cannot embrace the preservation of the earth as our new organizing principle, the very survival of our civilization will be in doubt."[125]

Here, forcefully stated, is the driving force behind today's environmental law — the "new organizing principle" of preservation of the earth, without which all civilization is in jeopardy.

A means already at work for achieving such a co-ordinated collective response is international environmental law, and it is not to be wondered at that these basic principles ensuring the survival of civilization, and indeed of the human species, are already an integral part of that law.

The same matter is put in another perspective in an outstanding study, already referred to:

> "The self-extinction of our species is not an act that anyone describes as sane or sensible; nevertheless, it is an act that, without quite admitting it to ourselves, we plan in certain circumstances to commit. Being impossible as a fully intentional act, unless the perpetrator has lost his mind, it can come about only through a kind of inadvertence as a 'side effect' of some action that we do intend, such as the defense of our nation, or the defense of liberty, or the defense of socialism, or the defense of whatever else we happen to believe in. To that extent, our failure to acknowledge the magnitude and significance of the peril is a necessary condition for doing the deed. We can do it only if we don't quite know what we're doing. If we did acknowledge

---

[122] See the references to these principles in my dissenting opinion in *Request for an Examination of the Situation in Accordance with Paragraph 63 of the Court's Judgment of 20 December 1974 in the Nuclear Tests (New Zealand v. France) Case, I. C. J. Reports 1995*, pp. 339-347.

[123] A. Timoshenko, "Ecological Security: Global Change Paradigm", *Columbia Journal of International Environmental Law and Policy*, 1990, Vol. 1, p. 127.

[124] Timoshenko, *op. cit.*

[125] A. Gore, *Earth in the Balance: Ecology and the Human Spirit*, 1992, p. 295, cited in Guruswamy, Palmer and Weston, *International Environmental Law and World Order*, 1994, p. 264.

the full dimensions of the peril, admitting clearly and without reservation that any use of nuclear arms is likely to touch off a holocaust in which the continuance of all human life would be put at risk, extinction would at that moment become not only 'unthinkable' but also undoable."[126]

These principles of environmental law thus do not depend for their validity on treaty provisions. They are part of customary international law. They are part of the *sine qua non* for human survival.

Practical recognitions of the principle that they are an integral part of customary international law are not difficult to find in the international arena. Thus, for example, the Security Council, in resolution 687 of 1991, referred to Iraq's liability "under international law . . . for environmental damage" resulting from the unlawful invasion of Kuwait. This was not a liability arising under treaty, for Iraq was not a party to either the 1977 ENMOD Convention, nor the 1977 Protocols, nor any other specific treaty dealing expressly with the matter. Iraq's liability to which the Security Council referred in such unequivocal terms was clearly a liability arising under customary international law[127].

Nor are these principles confined to either peace or war, but cover both situations, for they proceed from general duties, applicable alike in peace and war[128].

The basic principle in this regard is spelt out by Article 35 (3) of the 1977 Additional Protocol I to the Geneva Convention in terms prohibiting

> "methods or means of warfare which are intended, or may be expected, to cause widespread, long-term and severe damage to the natural environment".

Article 55 prohibits

> "the use of methods or means of warfare which are intended or may be expected to cause such damage to the natural environment and thereby to prejudice the health or survival of the population".

The question is not whether nuclear weapons were or were not intended to be covered by these formulations. It is sufficient to read them as stating undisputed principles of customary international law. To consider that these general principles are not explicit enough to cover nuclear weapons, or that nuclear weapons were designedly left unmentioned and are therefore not covered, or even that there was a clear understanding that these provisions were not intended to cover nuclear weapons, is to emphasize the incongruity of prohibiting lesser weapons of environmental damage, while leaving intact the infinitely greater agency of causing the very damage which it was the rationale of the treaty to prevent.

If there are general duties arising under customary international law, it clearly matters not that the various environmental agreements do not specifically refer to damage by nuclear weapons. The same principles apply whether we deal with belching furnaces, leaking reactors or explosive weapons. The mere circumstance that coal furnaces or reactors are not specifically mentioned in environmental treaties cannot lead to the conclusion that they are exempt from the incontrovertible and well-established standards and principles laid down therein.

Another approach to the applicability of environmental law to the matter before the Court is through the principle of good neighbourliness, which is both impliedly and expressly written into the United Nations Charter. This principle is one of the

---

126 Jonathan Schell, *The Fate of the Earth*, 1982, p. 186.
127 A submission to this effect was made by the Solomon Islands in the hearings before the Court (CR 95132, Sands, p. 71).
128 See, for example, the phraseology of Principle 21 of the Stockholm Declaration and Principle 2 of the Rio Declaration, referring to the duties of States to prevent damage to the environment of other States.

bases of modern international law, which has seen the demise of the principle that sovereign States could pursue their own interests in splendid isolation from each other. A world order in which every sovereign State depends on the same global environment generates a mutual interdependence which can only be implemented by co-operation and good neighbourliness.

The United Nations Charter spells this out as "the general principle of good-neighbourliness, due account being taken of the interests and well being of the rest of the world, in social, economic, and commercial matters" (Art. 74). A course of action that can destroy the global environment will take to its destruction not only the environment, but the social, economic and commercial interests that cannot exist apart from that environment. The Charter's express recognition of such a general duty of good neighbourliness makes this an essential part of international law.

This Court, from the very commencement of its jurisprudence, has supported this principle by spelling out the duty of every State not to "allow knowingly its territory to be used for acts contrary to the rights of other States" (*Corfu Channel, I.C.J. Reports 1949*, p. 22).

The question of State responsibility in regard to the environment is dealt with more specifically in my dissenting opinion on the WHO request (*I.C.J. Reports 1996*, pp. 139-143), and that discussion must be regarded as supplementary to the discussion of environmental considerations in this opinion. As therein pointed out, damage to the environment caused by nuclear weapons is a breach of State obligation, and this adds another dimension to the illegality of the use or threat of use of nuclear weapons.

(g) Human rights law[129]

This opinion has dealt in Section III.3 with the ways in which the development of human rights in the post-war years has made an impact on "considerations of humanity" and "dictates of public conscience".

Concentrating attention more specifically on the rights spelt out in the Universal Declaration of Human Rights, it is possible to identify the right to dignity (Preamble and Art. 1), the right to life, the right to bodily security (Art. 3), the right to medical care (Art. 25 (1)), the right to marriage and procreation (Art. 16 (1)), the protection of motherhood and childhood (Art. 25 (2)), and the right to cultural life (Art. 27 (1)), as basic human rights which are endangered by nuclear weapons.

It is part of established human rights law doctrine that certain rights are non-derogable in any circumstances. The right to life is one of them. It is one of the rights which constitute the irreducible core of human rights.

The preamble to the Declaration speaks of recognition of the inherent dignity of all members of the human family as the foundation of freedom, justice and peace in the world. Article 1 follows this up with the specific averment that "All human beings are born free and equal in dignity and rights." Article 6 states that everyone has the right to recognition everywhere as a person before the law. The International Covenant on Civil and Political Rights made this right more explicit and imposed on States the affirmative obligation of protecting it by law. Article 6 (1) states, "Every human being has the inherent right to life. This right shall be protected by law." States parties to the Covenant expressly assumed the responsibility to implement the provisions of the Covenant.

The European Convention for the Protection of Human Rights and Fundamental Freedoms (1950, Art. 2) and the American Convention of Human Rights (1969, Art. 4) likewise confirm the right to life. It is one of the non-derogable rights and an integral part of the irreducible core of human rights.

It has been argued that the right to life is not an absolute right and that the taking of life in armed hostilities is a necessary exception to this principle. However, when a weapon has the potential to kill between one million and one

---

[129] See, also, Section III.6 below.

billion people, as WHO has told the Court, human life becomes reduced to a level of worthlessness that totally belies human dignity as understood in any culture. Such a deliberate action by any State is, in any circumstances whatsoever, incompatible with a recognition by it of that respect for basic human dignity on which world peace depends, and respect for which is assumed on the part of all Member States of the United Nations.

This is not merely a provision of the Universal Declaration on Human Rights and other human rights instruments, but is fundamental Charter law as enshrined in the very preamble to the United Nations Charter, for one of the ends to which the United Nations is dedicated is "to reaffirm faith in fundamental human rights, in the *dignity and worth* of the human person" (emphasis added). No weapon ever invented in the long history of man's inhumanity to man has so negatived the dignity and worth of the human person as has the nuclear bomb.

Reference should also be made to the General Comment of the United Nations Human Rights Committee entitled "The Right to Life and Nuclear Weapons"[130] which endorsed the view of the General Assembly that the right to life is especially pertinent to nuclear weapons[131]. Stating that nuclear weapons are among the greatest threats to life and the right to life, it carried its view of the conflict between nuclear weapons and international law so far as to propose that their use should be recognized as crimes against humanity.

All of these human rights follow from one central right — a right described by Rene Cassin as "the right of human beings to exist" (CR 95/ 32, p. 64, including footnote 20). This is the foundation of the elaborate structure of human rights that has been painstakingly built by the world community in the post-war years.

Any endorsement of the legality of the use, in any circumstances whatsoever, of a weapon which can snuff out life by the million would tear out the foundations beneath this elaborate structure which represents one of the greatest juristic achievements of this century. That structure, built upon one of the noblest and most essential concepts known to the law, cannot theoretically be maintained if international law allows this right to any State. It could well be written off the books.

11. Juristic Opinion

It would be correct to say that the bulk of juristic opinion is of the view that nuclear weapons offend existing principles of humanitarian law. Juristic opinion is an important source of international law and there is no room in this opinion for a citation of all the authorities. It will suffice, for present purposes, to refer to a resolution already noted in an earlier part of this discussion — the resolution adopted by the Institute of International Law in 1969, at its Edinburgh Session, at a time when juristic writing on nuclear arms had not reached its present level of intensity and was in fact quite scarce.

The finding of the Institute, already cited (see Section III.10 (b) above), that *existing* international law prohibits, in particular, the use of weapons whose destructive effect "is so great that it cannot be limited to specific military objectives or is otherwise uncontrollable . . ., as well as of 'blind' weapons"[132], was adopted by 60 votes, with one against and two abstentions. Those voting in favour included Charles De Visscher, Lord McNair, Roberto Ago, Suzanne Bastid, Erik Castren, Sir Gerald Fitzmaurice, Wilfred Jenks, Sir Robert Jennings, Charles Rousseau, Grigory Tunkin, Sir Humphrey Waldock, Jose Maria Ruda, Oscar Schachter and Kotaro Tanaka, to select a few from an illustrious list of the most eminent international lawyers of the time.

---

130 Gen. C 14/23, reproduced in M. Nowak, *United Nations Covenant on Civil and Political Rights*, 1983, p. 861.
131 General Assembly resolution 38175, "Condemnation of Nuclear War", first operative paragraph.
132 *Annuaire de l'Institut de droit international,* 1969, No. 53, Vol. II, p. 377, para. 7.

12. *The 1925 Geneva Gas Protocol*

Quite independently of the various general principles that have been invoked in the discussion thus far, there is a conventional basis on which it has been argued that nuclear weapons are illegal. It is for this reason that I have voted against paragraph 2 B of the *dispositif* which holds that there is not, in conventional international law, a comprehensive and universal prohibition of the threat or use of nuclear weapons as such. I refer, in particular, to the Protocol for the Prohibition of the Use in War of Asphyxiating, Poisonous or Other Gases and of Bacteriological Methods of Warfare, 17 June 1925 (commonly referred to as the Geneva Gas Protocol). It is so comprehensive in its prohibition that, in my view, it clearly covers nuclear weapons, which thus become the subject of conventional prohibition. There is considerable scholarly opinion favouring this view[133] Moreover, if radiation is a poison, it is caught up also by the prohibition on poison weapons contained in Article 23 (a) of the Hague Regulations. The rule against poisonous weapons has indeed been described as "The most time-honoured special prohibition on the subject of weapons and instruments of war."[134] It is a rule recognized from the remotest historical periods and in a wide spread of cultures.

The Geneva Gas Protocol was drafted in very wide terms. It prohibits "the use in war of asphyxiating, *poisonous*, or other gases and of all analogous liquids, materials or devices" (emphasis added).

If this Protocol is to be applicable to nuclear weapons, it must be shown:

(1) that radiation is *poisonous*; and
(2) that it involves the contact of *materials* with the human body.

If both these questions are answered in the affirmative, the damage to the human body caused by radiation would be covered by the terms of the Protocol.

(i) Is radiation poisonous?

Poison is generally defined as a substance which, of its own force, damages health on contact with or absorption by the body[135]. The discussion of the effects of radiation in Section 11.3 (f) above can leave one in no doubt that the effects of radiation are that it destroys life or damages the functions of the organs and tissues.

Schwarzenberger points out that if introduced into the body in sufficiently large doses, radiation produces symptoms indistinguishable from poisoning[136].

---

133 See Burns H. Weston, *op. cit.*, p. 241; E. Castren, *The Present Law of War and Neutrality*, 1954, p. 207; G. Schwarzenberger, *The Legality of Nuclear Weapons*, 1958, pp. 37-38 ; N. Singh, *Nuclear Weapons and International Law*, 1959, pp. 162-166; Falk, Meyrowitz and Sanderson, "Nuclear Weapons and International Law", *Indian Journal of International Law*, 1980, Vol. 20, p. 563; Julius Stone, *Legal Controls of International Conflict*, 1954, p. 556; Spaight, *Air Power and War Rights*, 3rd ed., 1947, pp. 275-276; H. Lauterpacht (ed.), in *Oppenheim's International Law*, Vol. 2, 7th ed., 1952, p. 348.

134 Singh and McWhinney, *op. cit.*, p. 120.

135 The *McGraw-Hill Dictionary of Scientific and Technical Terms* defines poison as "A substance that in relatively small doses has an action that either destroys life or impairs seriously the functions of organs and tissues" (2nd ed., 1978, p. 1237).
The definition of poison in the *Oxford English Dictionary* is that poison is:
"Any substance which, when introduced to or absorbed by a living organism, destroys life or injures health, irrespective of mechanical means or direct thermal changes. Particularly applied to a substance capable of destroying life by rapid action, and when taken in a small quantity. Fig. phr. to hate like poison.
But the more scientific use is recognized in the phrase slow poison, indicating the accumulative effect of a deleterious drug or agent taken for a length of time." (Vol. XII, p. 2, 1989 ed.)

136 *The Legality of Nuclear Weapons*, 1958, p. 35. He remarks very severely that they "inflict death or serious damage to health in, as Gentili would have put it, a manner more befitting demons than civilised human beings". The reference is to Gentili's observation that, though war is struggle between men, the use of such means as poison makes it "a struggle of demons" (*De Jure Belli Libri Tres* (1612), Book II, Chap. VI, p. 161, trans. J. C. Rolfe).

Once it is established that radioactive radiation is a poison, it is also covered by the prohibition on poison weapons contained in the Hague Regulations already referred to. It poisons, indeed in a more insidious way than poison gas, for its effects include the transmission of genetic disorders for generations.

The NATO countries have themselves accepted that poisoning is an effect of nuclear weapons, for Annex II to the Protocol on Arms Control of the Paris Agreements of 23 October 1954, on the accession of the Republic of Germany to the North Atlantic Treaty, defines a nuclear weapon as any weapon:

> "designed to contain or utilise, nuclear fuel or radioactive isotopes and which, by explosion or other uncontrolled nuclear transformation . . . is capable of mass destruction, mass injury or *mass poisoning*" (emphasis added).

(ii) Does radiation involve contact of the body with "materials"?

The definitions of poison speak of it in terms of its being a "substance". The Geneva Gas Protocol speaks of "materials" which are poisonous. It is necessary therefore to know whether radiation is a "substance" or a "material", or merely a ray such as a light ray, which, when it impinges on any object, does not necessarily bring a substance or material in contact with that object. If it is the former, it would satisfy the requirements of the Geneva Gas Protocol.

The definition of "radioactive" in the *Shorter Oxford Dictionary* is as follows: "Capable (as radium) of emitting spontaneously rays consisting of *material particles* travelling at high velocities."[137]

Scientific discussions[138] draw a distinction between the spectrum of electromagnetic radiations that have zero mass when (theoretically) at rest, such as radio waves, microwaves, infrared rays, visible light, ultra violet rays, x-rays, and gamma rays, and the type of radiation that includes such particles as electrons, protons and neutrons which have mass. When such forms of particulate matter travel at high velocities, they are regarded as radiation.

The ionizing radiation caused by nuclear weapons is of the latter kind. It consists *inter alia* of a stream of particles[139] coming into contact with the human body and causing damage to tissues. In other words, it is a material substance that causes damage to the body and cannot fall outside the prohibition of poisonous weapons laid down by the Geneva Gas Protocol.

The question whether radiation is a "material" seems thus beyond doubt. In the words of Schwarzenberger:

> "the words 'all analogous liquids, materials or devices' are so comprehensively phrased as to include any weapons of an analogous character, irrespective of whether they were known or in use at the time of the signature of the Protocol. If the radiation and fall-out effects of nuclear weapons can be likened to poison, all the more can they be likened to poison gas . . ."[140]

There has been some discussion in the literature of the question whether the material transmitted should be in gaseous form as the provision in question deals with materials "analogous" to gases. It is to be noted in the first place that the wording of the provision itself takes the poisons out of the category of *gases* because it speaks also of analogous *liquids, materials*, and even devices. However, even in terms of *gases*, it is clear that the distinction between solids, liquids and gases has never been strictly

---

137 3rd ed., 1987, Vol. II, p. 1738 ; emphasis added.
138 See *Encyclopaedia Britannica Macropaedia*, Vol. 26, pp. 471 *et seq.* on "Radiation".
139 The definitions of radiation in the *McGraw-Hill Dictionary of Physics and Mathematics* (1978, p. 800) is "a stream of particles, . . . or high energy photons, or a mixture of these".
140 *Op. cit.*, p. 38.

applied in military terminology to the words "gas". As Singh and McWhinney point out, in strict scientific language, mustard gas is really a liquid and chlorine is really a gas, but in military terminology both are categorized as gas[141].

The case that nuclear weapons are covered by the Geneva Gas Protocol seems therefore to be irrefutable. Further, if indeed radioactive radiation constitutes a poison, the prohibition against it would be declaratory of a universal customary law prohibition which would apply in any event whether a State is party or not to the Geneva Protocol of 1925[142].

Yet another indication, available in terms of the Geneva Gas Protocol, is that the word "devices" would presumably cover a nuclear bomb, irrespective of the question whether radiation falls within the description of "analogous materials".

Nuclear weapons, being unknown at the time of the documents under consideration, could not be more specifically described, but are covered by the description and intent of the Protocol and the Hague Regulations.

It has been submitted by the United States that:

> "This prohibition was not intended to apply, and has not been applied, to weapons that are designed to kill or injure by other means, even though they may create asphyxiating or poisonous by products." (Written Statement, p. 25.)

If, in fact, radiation is a major by-product of a nuclear weapon — as indeed it is — it is not clear on what jurisprudential principle an exemption can thus be claimed from the natural and foreseeable effects of the use of the weapon. Such "by-products" are sometimes described as collateral damage but, collateral or otherwise, they are a major consequence of the bomb and cannot in law be taken to be unintended, well known as they are.

Besides, such an argument involves the legally unacceptable contention that if an act involves both legal and illegal consequences, the former justify or excuse the latter.

13. *Article 23 (a) of the Hague Regulations*

The foregoing discussion demonstrates that radiation is a poison. Using the same line of reasoning, it follows that there is also a clear contravention of Article 23 (a) of the Hague Regulations which frames its prohibition in unequivocal terms[143]. No extended discussion is called for in this context, and it is well accepted that the categorical prohibition against poisoning therein contained is one of the oldest and most widely recognized laws of war. Since "the universally accepted practice of civilised nations has regarded poison as banned", the prohibition contained in Article 23 (a) has been considered as binding even on States not parties to this conventional provision.

> "Thus, apart from purely conventional law, the customary position based on the general principles of law would also bar the use in warfare of poisonous substances as not only barbarous, inhuman and uncivilised, but also treacherous."[144]

IV. Self-Defence

Self-defence raises probably the most serious problems in this case. The second

---

141 *Op. cit.*, p. 126.
142 See, to this effect, Schwarzenberger, *op. cit.*, pp. 37-38, in relation to chemical and bacteriological weapons.
143 See Singh and McWhinney, *op. cit.*, pp. 127 and 121.
144 *Ibid.*, p. 121.

sentence in paragraph 2 E of the *dispositif* states that, in the current state of international law and of the elements of fact at its disposal, the Court cannot conclude definitively whether the threat or use of nuclear weapons would be lawful or unlawful in an extreme circumstance of self-defence, in which the very survival of a State would be at stake. I have voted against this clause as I am of the view that the threat or use of nuclear weapons would not be lawful in any circumstances whatsoever, as it offends the fundamental principles of the *jus in bello*. This conclusion is clear and follows inexorably from well-established principles of international law.

If a nation is attacked, it is clearly entitled under the United Nations Charter to the right of self-defence. Once a nation thus enters into the domain of the *jus in bello*, the principles of humanitarian law apply to the conduct of self-defence, just as they apply to the conduct of any other aspect of military operations. We must hence examine what principles of the *jus in bello* apply to the use of nuclear weapons in self-defence.

The first point to be noted is that the use of *force* in self-defence (which is an undoubted right) is one thing and the use of *nuclear weapons* in self-defence is another. The permission granted by international law for the first does not embrace the second, which is subject to other governing principles as well.

All of the seven principles of humanitarian law discussed in this opinion apply to the use of nuclear weapons in self-defence, just as they apply to their use in any aspect of war. Principles relating to unnecessary suffering, proportionality, discrimination, non-belligerent States, genocide, environmental damage and human rights would all be violated, no less in self-defence than in an open act of aggression. The *jus in bello* covers all use of force, whatever the reasons for resort to force. There can be no exceptions, without violating the essence of its principles.

The State subjected to the first attack could be expected to respond in kind. After the devastation caused by a first attack, especially if it be a nuclear attack, there will be a tendency to respond with any nuclear fire-power that is available.

Robert McNamara, in dealing with the response to initial strikes, states:

> "But under such circumstances, leaders on both sides would be under unimaginable pressure to avenge their losses and secure the interests being challenged. And each would fear that the opponent might launch a larger attack at any moment. Moreover, they would both be operating with only partial information because of the disruption to communications caused by the chaos on the battlefield (to say nothing of possible strikes against communication facilities). Under such conditions, it is highly likely that rather than surrender, each side would launch a larger attack, hoping that this step would bring the action to a halt by causing the opponent to capitulate."[145]

With such a response, the clock would accelerate towards global catastrophe, for a counter-response would be invited and, indeed, could be automatically triggered off.

It is necessary to reiterate here the undoubted right of the State that is attacked to use all the weaponry available to it for the purpose of repulsing the aggressor. Yet this principle holds only *so long as such weapons do not violate the fundamental rules of warfare embodied in those rules.* Within these constraints, and for the purpose of repulsing the enemy, the full military power of the State that is attacked can be unleashed upon the aggressor. While this is incontrovertible, one has yet to hear an argument in any forum, or a contention in any academic literature, that a nation attacked, for example, with chemical or biological weapons is entitled to use chemical or biological weapons in self-defence, or to annihilate the aggressor's population. It is strange that the most devastating of all the weapons of mass destruction can be conceived of as offering a singular exception to this most obvious conclusion following from the bedrock principles of humanitarian law.

---

145 McNamara, *op. cit.*, pp. 71-72.

That said, a short examination follows of the various principles of humanitarian law which could be violated by self-defence.

1. Unnecessary Suffering

The harrowing suffering caused by nuclear weapons, as outlined earlier in this opinion, is not confined to the aggressive use of such weapons. The lingering sufferings caused by radiation do not lose their intensity merely because the weapon is used in self-defence.

2. Proportionality/Error

The principle of proportionality may on first impressions appear to be satisfied by a nuclear response to a nuclear attack. Yet, viewed more carefully, this principle is violated in many ways. As France observed :

> "The assessment of the necessity and proportionality of a response to attack depends on the nature of the attack, its scope, the danger it poses and the adjustment of the measures of response to the desired defensive purpose." (CR 95/23, pp. 82-83.)

For these very reasons, precise assessment of the nature of the appropriate and proportionate response by a nation stricken by a nuclear attack becomes impossible[146]. If one speaks in terms of a nuclear response to a nuclear attack, that nuclear response will tend, as already noted, to be an all-out nuclear response which opens up all the scenarios of global armageddon which are so vividly depicted in the literature relating to an all-out nuclear exchange.

Moreover, one is here speaking in terms of measurement — measurement of the intensity of the attack and the proportionality of the response. But one can measure only the measurable. With nuclear war, the quality of measurability ceases. Total devastation admits of no scales of measurement. We are in territory where the principle of proportionality becomes devoid of meaning.

It is relevant also, in the context of nuclear weapons, not to lose sight of the possibility of human error. However carefully planned, a nuclear response to a nuclear attack cannot, in the confusion of the moment, be finely graded so as to assess the strength of the weapons of attack, and to respond in like measure. Even in the comparatively tranquil and leisured atmosphere of peace, error is possible, even to the extent of unleashing an unintentional nuclear attack. This has emerged from studies of unintentional nuclear war[147]. The response, under the stress of nuclear attack, would be far more prone to accident.

According to the *Bulletin of the Atomic Scientists*:

> "Top decision-makers as well as their subordinate information suppliers rely on computers and other equipment which have become even more complex and therefore more vulnerable to malfunction. Machine failures or human failures or a combination of the two could, had they not been discovered within minutes, have caused unintended nuclear war in a number of reported cases."[148]

The result would be all-out nuclear war.

Here again there is confirmation from statesmen, who have had much experience

---

[146] On this, see further Section II.3 (n) above and Section VII.6 below.
[147] For example, *Risks of Unintentional Nuclear War*, United Nations Institute of Disarmament Research (UNIDIR), 1982.. Frei (1982).
[148] June 1982, Vol. 38, p. 68.

in matters of foreign and military policy, that all-out nuclear war is likely to ensue. Robert McNamara observes:

> "It is inconceivable to me, as it has been to others who have studied the matter, that 'limited' nuclear wars would remain limited — any decision to use nuclear weapons would imply a high probability of the same cataclysmic consequences as a total nuclear exchange."[149]

Former Secretary of State, Dr. Kissinger, has also written to the same effect:

> "Limited war is not simply a matter of appropriate military forces and doctrines. It also places heavy demands on the discipline and subtlety of the political leadership and on the confidence of the society in it. For limited war is psychologically a much more complex problem than all-out war. . . . An all-out war will in all likelihood be decided so rapidly — if it is possible to speak of decision in such a war — and the suffering it entails will be so vast as to obscure disputes over the nuances of policy."[150]

He proceeds to observe:

> "Limited nuclear war is not only impossible, according to this line of reasoning, but also undesirable. For one thing, it would cause devastation in the combat zone approaching that of thermonuclear war in severity. We would, therefore, be destroying the very people we were seeking to protect."[151]

It is thus no fanciful speculation that the use of nuclear weapons in self-defence would result in a cataclysmic nuclear exchange. That is a risk which humanitarian law would consider to be totally unacceptable. It is a risk which no legal system can sanction.

3. Discrimination

As already observed earlier in this opinion, nuclear weapons violate the principle of discrimination between armed forces and civilians. True, other weapons also do, but the intensity of heat and blast, not to speak of radiation, are factors which place the nuclear weapon in a class apart from the others. When one speaks of weapons that count their victims by hundreds of thousands, if not millions, principles of discrimination cease to have any legal relevance.

4. Non-belligerent States

One of the principal objections to the use of nuclear weapons in self-defence occurs under this head.

Self-defence is a matter of purely internal jurisdiction only if such defence can be undertaken without clearly causing damage to the rights of non-belligerent States. The moment a strategy of self-defence implies damage to a non-belligerent third party, such a matter ceases to be one of purely internal jurisdiction. It may be that the act of self-defence inadvertently and unintentionally causes damage to a third State. Such a situation is understandable and sometimes does occur, but that is not the case here.

---

149 *Op. cit.*, p. 72.
150 Henry Kissinger, *Nuclear Weapons and Foreign Policy*, 1957, p. 167.
151 *Ibid.*, p. 175.

5. Genocide

The topic of genocide has already been covered[152]. Self-defence, which will, as shown in the discussion on proportionality, result in all probability in all-out nuclear war, is even more likely to cause genocide than the act of launching an initial strike. If the killing of human beings, in numbers ranging from a million to a billion, does not fall within the definition of genocide, one may well ask what will.

No nation can be seen as entitled to risk the destruction of civilization for its own national benefit.

6. Environmental Damage

Similar considerations exist here, as in regard to genocide. The wide-spread contamination of the environment may even lead to a nuclear winter and to the destruction of the ecosystem. These results will ensue equally, whether the nuclear weapons causing them are used in aggression or in self-defence.

International law relating to the environment, in so far as it concerns nuclear weapons, is dealt with at greater length in my dissenting opinion on the World Health Organization request (*I.C.J. Reports 1996*, pp. 139-143), and the discussion in that opinion should be considered as supplementary to the above discussion.

7. Human Rights

All the items of danger to human rights as recounted earlier in this opinion would be equally operative whether the weapons are used in aggression or in self-defence.

* * *

The humanitarian principles discussed above have long passed the stage of being merely philosophical aspirations. They are the living law and represent the high watermark of legal achievement in the difficult task of imposing some restraints on the brutalities of unbridled war. They provide the ground-rules for military action today and have been forged by the community of nations under the impact of the sufferings of untold millions in two global cataclysms and many smaller wars. As with all legal principles, they govern without distinction all nations great and small.

It seems difficult, with any due regard to the consistency that must underlie any credible legal system, to contemplate that all these hard-won principles should bend aside in their course and pass the nuclear weapon by, leaving that unparalleled agency of destruction free to achieve on a magnified scale the very evils which these principles were designed to prevent.

* * *

Three other aspects of the argument before the Court call for brief mention in the context of self-defence.

The United Kingdom relied (Written Statement, para. 3.40) on a view expressed by Judge Ago in his addendum to the Eighth Report on State Responsibility, to the effect that:

> "The action needed to halt and repulse the attack may well have to assume dimensions disproportionate to those of the attack suffered. What matters in this respect is the result to be achieved by the 'defensive' action, and not

---

152 See Section III.10 *(e)* above.

the forms, substance and strength of the action itself."[153]

Ago is here stressing that the defensive action must always be related to its purpose, that of halting and repelling the attack. As he observes, in the same paragraph:

"The requirement of the *proportionality* of the action taken in self-defence ... concerns the relationship between that action and its purpose, namely ... that of halting and repelling the attack."

That purpose is to halt and repulse the attack, not to exterminate the aggressor, or to commit genocide of its population. His reference to forms, substance and strength is expressly set out by him, within the context of this purpose, and cannot be read as setting at nought all the other requirements of humanitarian law such as those relating to damage to neutral States, unnecessary suffering, or the principle of discrimination. The statement of so eminent a jurist cannot be read in the sense of neutralizing the classic and irreducible requirements of the *jus in bello*— requirements which, moreover, had received massive endorsement from the Institute of International Law over which he was later to preside with such distinction. The Edinburgh Session of 1969 adopted by a majority of 60 to 1, with 2 abstentions, the resolution[154] prohibiting weapons affecting indiscriminately both military and non-military objects, both armed forces and civilian populations, and weapons designed to terrorize the civilian population. Ago himself was a member of that majority.

The second submission calling for attention is the suggestion that Security Council resolution 984 (1995) (United Kingdom Written Statement, para. 3.42 and Annex D) in some way endorses the view that the use of nuclear weapons, in response to an armed attack, should not be regarded as necessarily unlawful.

A careful perusal of the resolution shows that it reassures the non nuclear-weapon States that the Security Council and the nuclear-weapon States will act immediately in the event that such States are victims of nuclear aggression. It *avoids any mention whatsoever* of the measures to be adopted to protect the victim. Had such been the intention, and had such use of nuclear weapons been legal, this was the occasion *par excellence* for the Security Council to have said so.

For the sake of completeness, it should here be pointed out that, even if the Security Council had expressly endorsed the use of such weapons, it is this Court which is the ultimate authority on questions of legality, and that such an observation, even if made, would not prevent the Court from making its independent pronouncement on this matter.

The third factor calling for mention is that much of the argument of those opposing illegality seems to blur the distinction between the *jus ad bellum* and the *jus in bello*. Whatever be the merits or otherwise of resorting to the use of force (the province of the *jus ad bellum*), when once the domain of force is entered, the governing law in that domain is the *jus in bello*. The humanitarian laws of war take over and govern all who participate, assailant and victim alike. The argument before the Court has proceeded as though, once the self-defence exception to the prohibition of the use of force comes into operation, the applicability of the *jus in bello* falls away. This supposition is juristically wrong and logically untenable. The reality is, of course, that while the *jus ad bellum* only opens the door to the use of force (in self-defence or by the Security Council), whoever enters that door must function subject to the *jus in bello*. The contention that the legality of the use of force justifies a breach of humanitarian law is thus a total *non-sequitur*.

* * *

Upon a review therefore, no exception can be made to the illegality of the use of

---

153 *Yearbook of the International Law Commission*, 1980, Vol. II, Part I, p. 69, para. 121.
154 Already noted in Section III.I I above.

nuclear weapons merely because the weapons are used in self-defence.

Collective self-defence, where another country has been attacked, raises the same issues as are discussed above.

Anticipatory self-defence — the pre-emptive strike before the enemy has actually attacked — cannot legally be effected by a nuclear strike, for a first strike with nuclear weapons would axiomatically be prohibited by the basic principles already referred to. In the context of non-nuclear weaponry, all the sophistication of modern technology and the precise targeting systems now developed would presumably be available for this purpose.

V. Some General Considerations

1. Two Philosophical Perspectives

This opinion has set out a multitude of reasons for the conclusion that the resort to nuclear weapons for any purpose entails the risk of the destruction of human society, if not of humanity itself. It has also pointed out that any rule permitting such use is inconsistent with international law itself.

Two philosophical insights will be referred to in this section — one based on rationality, and the other on fairness.

In relation to the first, all the postulates of law presuppose that they contribute to and function within the premise of the continued existence of the community served by that law. Without the assumption of that continued existence, no rule of law and no legal system can have any claim to validity, however attractive the juristic reasoning on which it is based. That taint of invalidity affects not merely the particular rule. The legal system, which accommodates that rule, itself collapses upon its foundations, for legal systems are postulated upon the continued existence of society. Being part of society, they must themselves collapse with the greater entity of which they are a part. This assumption, lying at the very heart of the concept of law, often recedes from view in the midst of the nuclear discussion.

Without delving in any depth into philosophical discussions of the nature of law, it will suffice for present purposes to refer briefly to two tests proposed by two pre-eminent thinkers about justice of the present era — H. L. A. Hart and John Rawls.

Hart, a leading jurist of the positivistic school, has, in a celebrated exposition of the minimum content of natural law, formulated this principle pithily in the following sentence:

> "We are committed to it as something presupposed by the terms of the discussion; for our concern is with social arrangements for continued existence, not with those *of a suicide club*."[155]

His reasoning is that:

> "there are certain rules of conduct which any social organization must contain if it is to be viable. Such rules do in fact constitute a common element in the law and conventional morality of all societies which have progressed to the point where these are distinguished as different forms of social control."[156]

International law is surely such a social form of control devised and accepted by the constituent members of that international society — the nation States.

---

155 H. L. A. Hart, *The Concept of Law*, 1961, p. 188 ; emphasis added.
156 *Ibid.*

Hart goes on to note that :

> "Such universally recognized principles of conduct which have a basis in elementary truths concerning human beings, their natural environment, and aims, may be considered the *minimum content* of Natural Law, in contrast with the more grandiose and more challengeable constructions which have often been proffered under that name."[157]

Here is a recognized minimum accepted by positivistic jurisprudence which questions some of the more literal assumptions of other schools. We are down to the common denominator to which all legal systems must conform.

To approach the matter from another standpoint, the members of the international community have for the past three centuries been engaged in the task of formulating a set of rules and principles for the conduct of that society — the rules and principles we call international law. In so doing, they must ask themselves whether there is a place in that set of rules for a rule under which it would be legal, for whatever reason, to eliminate members of that community or, indeed, the entire community itself. Can the international community, which is governed by that rule, be considered to have given its acceptance to that rule, whatever be the approach of that community — positivist, natural law, or any other? Is the community of nations, to use Hart's expression a "suicide club"?

This aspect has likewise been stressed by perceptive jurists from the non-nuclear countries who are alive to the possibilities facing their countries in conflicts between other States in which, though they are not parties, they can be at the receiving end of the resulting nuclear devastation. Can international law, which purports to be a legal system for the entire global community, accommodate any principles which make possible the destruction of their communities?

> "No legal system can confer on any of its members the right to annihilate the community which engenders it and whose activities it seeks to regulate. In other words, there cannot be a *legal* rule, which *permits* the threat or use of nuclear weapons. In sum, nuclear weapons are an unprecedented event which calls for rethinking the self-understanding of traditional international law. Such rethinking would reveal that the question is not whether one interpretation of existing laws of war prohibits the threat or use of nuclear weapons and another permits it. Rather, the issue is whether the debate can take place at all in the world of law. The question is in fact one which cannot be legitimately addressed by law at all since it cannot tolerate an interpretation which negates its very essence. The end of law is a rational order of things, with survival as its core, whereas nuclear weapons eliminate all hopes of realizing it. In this sense, nuclear weapons are unlawful by definition."[158]

The aspect stressed by Hart that the proper end of human activity is survival is reflected also in the words of Nagendra Singh, a former President of this Court, who stated, in his pioneering study of nuclear weapons, that:

> "It would indeed be arrogant for any single nation to argue that to save humanity from bondage it was thought necessary to destroy humanity itself . . . No nation acting on its own has a right to destroy its kind, or even to destroy thousands of miles of land and its inhabitants in the vain hope that a crippled and suffering humanity — a certain result of nuclear warfare — was a more laudable objective than the loss of human dignity

---
157 Ibid., p. 189; emphasis added.
158 B. S. Chimni, "Nuclear Weapons and International Law: Some Reflections", in *International Law in Transition: Essays in Memory of Judge Nagendra Singh*, 1992, p. 142; emphasis added. (Pathak and Dhokalia 1992).

— an uncertain result which may or may not follow from the non-use of nuclear weapons."[159]

Nagendra Singh expressed the view, in the same work, that "resort to such weapons is not only incompatible with the laws of war, but irreconcilable with international law itself"[160].

Another philosophical approach to the matter is along the lines of the "veil of ignorance" posited by John Rawls in his celebrated study of justice as fairness[161].

If one is to devise a legal system under which one is prepared to live, this exposition posits as a test of fairness of that system that its members would be prepared to accept it if the decision had to be taken behind a veil of ignorance as to the future place of each constituent member within that legal system.

A nation considering its allegiance to such a system of international law, and not knowing whether it would fall within the group of nuclear nations or not, could scarcely be expected to subscribe to it if it contained a rule by which legality would be accorded to the use of a weapon by others which could annihilate it. Even less would it consent if it is denied even the right to possess such a weapon and, least of all if it could be annihilated or irreparably damaged in the quarrels of others to which it is not in any way a party.

One would indeed be in a desirable position in the event that it was one's lot to become a member of the nuclear group but, if there was a chance of being cast into the non-nuclear group, would one accept such a legal system behind a veil of ignorance as to one's position? Would it make any difference if the members of the nuclear group gave an assurance, which no one could police, that they would use the weapon only in extreme emergencies? The answers to such questions cannot be in doubt. By this test of fairness and legitimacy, such a legal system would surely fail.

Such philosophical insights are of cardinal value in deciding upon the question whether the illegality of use would constitute a minimum component of a system of international law based on rationality or fairness. By either test, widely accepted in the literature of modern jurisprudence, the rule of international law applicable to nuclear weapons would be that their use would be impermissible.

Fundamental considerations such as these tend to be overlooked in discussions relating to the legality of nuclear weapons. On matter so intrinsic to the validity of the entire system of international law, such perspectives cannot be ignored.

2. *The Aims of War*

War is never an end in itself. It is only a means to an end. This was recognized in the St. Petersburg Declaration of 1868, already noted (in Section III.3 on humanitarian law), which stipulated that the weakening of the military forces of the enemy was the only legitimate object of war. Consistently with this principle, humanitarian law has worked out the rule, already referred to, that "The right of belligerents to adopt means of injuring the enemy is not unlimited" (Article 22 of the Hague Rules, 1907).

All study of the laws of war becomes meaningless unless it is anchored to the ends of war, for thus alone can the limitations of war be seen in their proper context. This necessitates a brief excursus into the philosophy of the aims of war. Literature upon the subject has existed for upwards of twenty centuries.

Reference has already been made, in the context of hyperdestructive weapons, to the classical Indian tradition reflected in India's greatest epics, the *Ramayana* and the *Mahabharatha*. The reason behind the prohibition was that the weapon went beyond the purposes of war.

This was precisely what Aristotle taught when, in Book VII of *Politics*, he wrote

---
159 Nagendra Singh, *Nuclear Weapons and International Law*, 1959, pp. 242-243.
160 *Ibid.*, p. 17..
161 John Rawls, *A Theory of Justice*, 1972.

that, "War must be looked upon simply as a means to peace."[162] It will be remembered that Aristotle was drawing a distinction between actions that are no more than necessary or useful, and actions which are good in themselves. Peace was good in itself, and war only a means to this end. Without the desired end, namely peace, war would therefore be meaningless and useless. Applying this to the nuclear scenario, a war which destroys the other party is totally lacking in meaning and utility, and hence totally lacks justification. Aristotle's view of war was that it is a temporary interruption of normalcy, with a new equilibrium resulting from it when that war inevitably comes to an end.

The philosophy of the balance of power which dominated European diplomacy since the Peace of Utrecht in 1713 presupposed not the elimination of one's adversary, but the achievement of a workable balance of power in which the vanquished had a distinct place. Even the extreme philosophy that war is a continuation of the processes of diplomacy, which Clausewitz espoused, presupposed the continuing existence, as a viable unit, of the vanquished nation.

The United Nations Charter itself is framed on the basic principle that the use of force is outlawed (except for the strictly limited exception of self-defence), and that the purpose of the Charter is to free humanity from the scourge of war. Peace between the parties is the outcome the Charter envisages and not the total devastation of any party to the conflict.

Nuclear weapons render these philosophies unworkable. The nuclear exchanges of the future, should they ever take place, will occur in a world in which there is no monopoly of nuclear weapons. A nuclear war will not end with the use of a nuclear weapon by a single power, as happened in the case of Japan. There will inevitably be a nuclear exchange, especially in a world in which nuclear weapons are triggered for instant and automatic reprisal in the event of a nuclear attack.

Such a war is not one in which a nation, as we know it, can survive as a viable entity. The spirit that walks the nuclear wasteland will be a spirit of total despair, haunting victors (if there are any) and vanquished alike. We have a case here of methodology of warfare which goes beyond the purposes of war.

3. *The Concept of a "Threat of Force" under the United Nations Charter*

The question asked by the General Assembly relates to the use of force and the threat of force. Theoretically, the use of force, even with the simplest weapon, is unlawful under the United Nations Charter. There is no purpose therefore in examining whether the use of force with a nuclear weapon is contrary to international law. When even the use of a single rifle is banned, it makes little sense to enquire whether a nuclear weapon is banned.

The question of a threat of force, within the meaning of the Charter, needs some attention. To determine this question, an examination of the concept of threat of force in the Charter becomes necessary.

Article 2 (4) of the United Nations Charter outlaws threats against the territorial integrity or political independence of any State. As reaffirmed in the Declaration on Principles of International Law Concerning Friendly Relations 1970:

> "Such a threat or use of force constitutes a violation of international law and the Charter of the United Nations and shall never be employed as a means of settling international issues." (General Assembly resolution 2625 (XXV).)

Other documents confirming the international community's understanding that threats are outside the pale of international law include the 1965 Declaration on the Inadmissibility of Intervention in the Domestic Affairs of States and the Protection

---

162 Aristotle, *Politics*, trans. John Warrington, Heron Books, 1934, p. 212.

of Their Independence and Sovereignty (General Assembly resolution 2131 (XX)), and the 1987 Declaration on the Enhancement of the Principle of Non-Use of Force (General Assembly resolution 42/22, para. 2).

It is to be observed that the United Nations Charter draws no distinction between the use of force and the threat of force. Both equally lie outside the pale of action within the law.

Numerous international documents confirm the prohibition on the threat of force without qualification. Among these are the 1949 Declaration on Essentials of Peace (General Assembly resolution 290 (IV)); the 1970 Declaration on the Strengthening of International Security (General Assembly resolution 2734 (XXV)); and the 1988 Declaration on the Prevention and Removal of Disputes and Situations Which May Threaten International Peace and Security and on the Role of the United Nations in This Field (General Assembly resolution 43/51). The Helsinki Final Act (1975) requires participating States to refrain from the threat or use of force. The Pact of Bogota (the American Treaty on Pacific Settlement) is even more specific, requiring the contracting parties to "refrain from the threat or the use of force, or from any other means of coercion for the settlement of their controversies ...".

The principle of non-use of threats is thus as firmly grounded as the principle of non-use of force and, in its many formulations, it has not been made subject to any exceptions. If therefore deterrence is a form of threat, it must come within the prohibitions of the use of threats.

A more detailed discussion follows in Section VII.2 of the concept of deterrence.

4. Equality in the Texture of the Laws of War

There are some structural inequalities built into the current international legal system, but the substance of international law — its corpus of norms and principles — applies equally to all. Such equality of all those who are subject to a legal system is central to its integrity and legitimacy. So it is with the body of principles constituting the corpus of international law. Least of all can there be one law for the powerful and another law for the rest. No domestic system would accept such a principle, nor can any international system which is premised on a concept of equality.

In the celebrated words of the United States Chief Justice John Marshall in 1825,

> "No principle of general law is more universally acknowledged than the perfect equality of nations. Russia and Geneva have equal rights."[163]

As with all sections of the international legal system, the concept of equality is built into the texture of the laws of war.

Another anomaly is that if, under customary international law, the use of the weapon is legal, this is inconsistent with the denial, to 180 of the 185 Members of the United Nations, of even the right to *possession* of this weapon. Customary international law cannot operate so unequally, especially if, as is contended by the nuclear powers, the use of the weapon is essential to their self-defence. Self-defence is one of the most treasured rights of States and is recognized by Article 51 of the United Nations Charter as the inherent right of every Member State of the United Nations. It is a wholly unacceptable proposition that this right is granted in different degrees to different Members of the United Nations family of nations.

De facto inequalities ·always exist and will continue to exist so long as the world community is made up of sovereign States, which are necessarily unequal in size, strength, wealth and influence. But a great conceptual leap is involved in translating *de facto* inequality into inequality *de jure*. It is precisely such a leap that is made by those arguing, for example, that when the Protocols to the Geneva Conventions did

---

163 *The Antelope* case, [1825] 10 *Wheaton*, p. 122. Cf. Vattel, "A dwarf is as much a man as a giant is; a small republic is no less a sovereign state than the most powerful Kingdom." (*Droit des gens*, Fenwick trans. in *Classics of International Law*, S. 18.)

not pronounce on the prohibition of the use of nuclear weapons, there was an implicit recognition of the legality of their use by the nuclear powers. Such silence meant an agreement not to deal with the question, not a consent to legality of use. The "understandings" stipulated by the United States and the United Kingdom that the rules established or newly introduced by the 1977 Additional Protocol to the four 1949 Geneva Conventions would not regulate or prohibit the use of nuclear weapons do not undermine the basic principles which antedated these formal agreements and received expression in them. They rest upon no conceptual or juristic reason that can make inroads upon those principles. It is conceptually impossible to treat the silence of these treaty provisions as overruling or overriding these principles.

Similar considerations apply to the argument that treaties imposing partial bans on nuclear weapons must be interpreted as a current acceptance, by implication, of their legality.

This argument is not well founded. Making working arrangements within the context of a situation one is powerless to avoid is neither a consent to that situation, nor a recognition of its legality. It cannot confer upon that situation a status of recognition of its validity. Malaysia offered in this context the analogy of needle exchange programmes to minimize the spread of disease among drug users. Such programmes cannot be interpreted as rendering drug abuse legal (Written Comments, p. 14). What is important is that, amidst the plethora of resolutions and declarations dealing with nuclear weapons, there is not one which sanctions the use of such weapons for any purpose whatsoever.

A legal rule would be inconceivable that some nations alone have the right to use chemical or bacteriological weapons in self-defence, and others do not. The principle involved, in the claim of some nations to be able to use nuclear weapons in self-defence, rests on no different juristic basis.

Another feature to be considered in this context is that the community of nations is by very definition a voluntarist community. No element in it imposes constraints upon any other element from above. Such a structure is altogether impossible except on the basic premise of equality. Else "the danger is very real that the law will become little more than the expression of the will of the strongest"[164]

If the corpus of international law is to retain the authority it needs to discharge its manifold and beneficent functions in the international community, every element in its composition should be capable of being tested at the anvil of equality. Some structural inequalities have indeed been built into the international constitutional system, but that is a very different proposition from introducing inequalities into the corpus of substantive law by which all nations alike are governed.

It scarcely needs mention that whatever is stated in this section is stated in the context of the total illegality of the use of nuclear weapons by any powers whatsoever, in any circumstances whatsoever. That is the only sense in which the principle of equality which underlies international law can be applied to the important international problem of nuclear weapons.

5. The Logical Contradiction of a Dual Regime in the Laws of War

If humanitarian law is inapplicable to nuclear weapons, we face the logical contradiction that the laws of war are applicable to some kinds of weapons and not others, while both sets of weapons can be simultaneously used. One set of principles would apply to all other weapons and another set to nuclear weapons. When both classes of weapons are used in the same war, the laws of armed conflict would be in confusion and disarray.

Japan is a nation against which both sets of weapons were used, and it is not a matter for surprise that this aspect seems first to have caught the attention of Japanese scholars. Professor Fajita, in an article to which we were referred, observed:

---

[164] Weston, *op. cit.*, p. 254.

"this separation of fields of regulation between conventional and nuclear warfare will produce an odd result not easily imaginable, because conventional weapons and nuclear weapons will be eventually used at the same time, and in the same circumstances in a future armed conflict"[165]

Such a dual regime is inconsistent with all legal principle, and no reasons of principle have ever been suggested for the exemption of nuclear weapons from the usual regime of law applicable to all weapons. The reasons that have been suggested are only reasons of politics or of expediency, and neither a court of law nor any body of consistent juristic science can accept such a dichotomy.

It is of interest to note in this context that even nations denying the illegality of nuclear weapons *per se* instruct their armed forces in their military manuals that nuclear weapons are to be judged according to the same standards that apply to other weapons in armed conflict[166].

6. *Nuclear Decision-Making*

A factor to be taken into account in determining the legality of the use of nuclear weapons, having regard to their enormous potential for global devastation, is the process of decision-making in regard to the use of nuclear weapons.

A decision to use nuclear weapons would tend to be taken, if taken at all, in circumstances which do not admit of fine legal evaluations. It will in all probability be taken at a time when passions run high, time is short and the facts are unclear. It will not be a carefully measured decision, taken after a detailed and detached evaluation of all relevant circumstances of fact. It would be taken under extreme pressure and stress. Legal matters requiring considered evaluation may have to be determined within minutes, perhaps even by military rather than legally trained personnel, when they are in fact so complex as to have engaged this Court's attention for months. The fate of humanity cannot fairly be made to depend on such a decision.

Studies have indeed been made of the process of nuclear decision-making and they identify four characteristics of a nuclear crisis[167]. These characteristics are:

(1) the shortage of time for making crucial decisions. This is the fundamental aspect of all crises;
(2) the high stakes involved and, in particular, the expectation of severe loss to the national interest;
(3) the high uncertainty resulting from the inadequacy of clear information, for example, what is going on ?, what is the intent of the enemy?; and
(4) the leaders are often constrained by political considerations, restricting their options.

If such is the atmosphere in which leaders are constrained to act, and if they must weigh the difficult question whether it is legal or not in the absence of guidelines, the risk of illegality in the use of the weapon is great.

The weapon should in my view be declared illegal in *all* circumstances. If it is legal in some circumstances, however improbable, those circumstances need to be specified (or else a confused situation is made more confused still).

---

165 *Kansai University Review of Law and Political Science*, 1982, Vol. 3, p. 77.
166 See Burns H. Weston, *op. cit.*, p. 252, footnote 105.
167 See Conn Nugent, "How a Nuclear War Might Begin", in Proceedings of the Sixth World Congress of the International Physicians for the Prevention of Nuclear War, *op. cit.*, p. 117.

VI. The Attitude of the International Community Towards Nuclear Weapons

Quite apart from the importance of such considerations as the conscience of humanity and the general principles of law recognized by civilized nations, this section becomes relevant also because the law of the United Nations proceeds from the will of the peoples of the United Nations; and ever since the commencement of the United Nations, there has not been an issue which has attracted such sustained and widespread attention from its community of members. *Apartheid* was one of the great international issues which attracted concentrated attention until recently, but there has probably been a deeper current of continuous concern with nuclear weapons, and a universally shared revulsion at their possible consequences. The floodtide of global disapproval attending the nuclear weapon has never receded and no doubt will remain unabated so long as those weapons remain in the world's arsenals.

1.. The Universality of the Ultimate Goal of Complete Elimination

The international community's attitude towards nuclear weapons has been unequivocal — they are a danger to civilization and must be eliminated. The need for their complete elimination has been the subject of several categorical resolutions of the General Assembly, which are referred to elsewhere in this opinion.

The most recent declaration of the international community on this matter was at the 1995 Non-Proliferation Treaty Review Conference which, in its "Principles and Objectives for Nuclear Non-Proliferation and Disarmament", stressed "the ultimate goals of the complete elimination of nuclear weapons and a treaty on general and complete disarmament". This was a unanimous sentiment expressed by the global community and a clear commitment by every nation to do all that it could to achieve the complete elimination of these weapons.

The NPT, far from legitimizing the possession of nuclear weapons, was a treaty for their liquidation and eventual elimination. Its preamble unequivocally called for the liquidation of all existing stockpiles and their elimination from national arsenals. Such continued possession as it envisaged was not absolute but subject to an overriding condition — the pursuit in good faith of negotiations on effective measures relating to the cessation of the nuclear arms race at an early date. Inherent in this condition and in the entire treaty was not the acceptance of nuclear weapons, but their condemnation and repudiation. So it was when the NPT entered into force on 5 March 1970 and so it was when the NPT Review and Extension Conference took place in 1995[168].

The NPT Review Conference of 1995 was not new in the universality it embodied or in the strength of the commitment it expressed, but merely a reiteration of the views expressed in the very first resolution of the United Nations in 1945. From the formation of the United Nations to the present day, it would thus be correct to say that there has been a universal commitment to the elimination of nuclear weapons — a commitment which was only a natural consequence of the universal abhorrence of these weapons and their devastating consequences.

---

168 Article 4 of Decision No. 2 on the Principles and Objectives for Nuclear Non-Proliferation and Disarmament, adopted by that Conference, stipulated as an obligation of States parties, which was inextricably linked to the extension of the treaty, the following goal, *inter alia*:

"The determined pursuit by the nuclear-weapon States of systematic and progressive efforts to reduce nuclear weapons globally, with the ultimate goals of eliminating those weapons." (Para. 4 (c).)

Also the Conference on Disarmament was to complete the negotiations for a Comprehensive Nuclear-Test-Ban Treaty no later than 1996 (para. 4 (a)).

2. Overwhelming Majorities in Support of Total Abolition

This view, which cannot be more clearly expressed than it has been in numerous pronouncements of the General Assembly, provides a backdrop to the consideration of the applicable law, which follows.

It is beyond dispute that the preponderant majority of States oppose nuclear weapons and seek their total abandonment.

The very first resolution of the General Assembly, adopted at its Seventeenth Plenary Meeting on 24 January 1946, appointed a Commission whose terms of reference were, *inter alia*, to make specific proposals "for the elimination from national armaments of atomic weapons and of all other major weapons adaptable to mass destruction".

In 1961, at Belgrade, the Non-aligned Heads of State made a clear pronouncement on the need for a global agreement prohibiting all nuclear tests. The non-aligned movement, covering 113 countries from Asia, Africa, Latin America and Europe, comprises within its territories not only the vast bulk of the world's population, but also the bulk of the planet's natural resources and the bulk of its bio-diversity. It has pursued the aim of the abolition of nuclear weapons and consistently supported a stream of resolutions[169] in the General Assembly and other international forums pursuing this objective. The massive majorities of States calling for the Non-Use of Nuclear Weapons can leave little doubt of the overall sentiment of the world community in this regard.

States appearing before the Court have provided the Court with a list of United Nations resolutions and declarations indicating the attitude towards these weapons of the overwhelming majority of that membership. Several of those resolutions do not merely describe the use of nuclear weapons as a violation of international law, but also assert that they are a crime against humanity.

Among these latter are the resolutions on Non-Use of Nuclear Weapons and Prevention of Nuclear War, passed by the General Assembly to this effect in 1978, 1979, 1980 and 1981, were passed with 103, 112, 113 and 121 votes respectively in favour, with 18, 16, 19 and 19 respectively opposing them, and 18, 14, 14 and 6 abstentions respectively. These can fairly be described as massive majorities (see Appendix IV of Malaysian Written Comments).

Resolutions setting the elimination of nuclear weapons as a goal are legion. One State (Malaysia) has, in its Written Comments, listed no less than 49 such resolutions, several of them passed with similar majorities and some with no votes in opposition and only 3 or 4 abstentions. For example, the resolutions on conclusion of effective international arrangements to assure non-nuclear weapon States against the use or threat of use of nuclear weapons of 1986 and 1987 were passed with 149 and 151 votes in favour, none opposed and 4 and 3 abstentions respectively. Such resolutions, adopting a goal of complete elimination, are indicative of a global sentiment that nuclear weapons are inimical to the general interests of the community of nations.

The declarations of the world community's principal representative organ, the General Assembly, may not themselves make law, but when repeated in a stream of resolutions, as often and as definitely as they have been, provide important reinforcement to the view of the impermissibility of the threat or use of such weapons under customary international law. Taken in combination with all the other manifestations of global disapproval of threat or use, the confirmation of the position is strengthened even further. Whether or not some of the General Assembly resolutions are themselves "law making" resolutions is a matter for serious consideration, with not inconsiderable scholarly support for such a view[170].

Although the prime thrust for these resolutions came from the non aligned group,

---

169 See footnote 99, above.
170 For example, Brownlie, *Principles of Public International Law*, 4th ed., 1990, p. 14, re resolution 1653 (XVI) of 1961, which described the use of nuclear and thermonuclear weapons as such a "law-making resolution".

there has been supportive opinion for the view of illegality from States outside this group. Among such States contending for illegality before this Court are Sweden, San Marino, Australia and New Zealand. Moreover, even in countries not asserting the illegality of nuclear weapons, opinion is strongly divided. For example, we were referred to a resolution passed by the Italian Senate, on 13 July 1995, recommending to the Italian Government that they assume a position favouring a judgment by this Court condemning the use of nuclear weapons.

It is to be remembered also that, of the 185 Member States of the United Nations, only five have nuclear weapons and have announced policies based upon them. From the standpoint of the creation of international custom, the practice and policies of five States out of 185 seem to be an insufficient basis on which to assert the creation of custom, whatever be the global influence of those five. As was stated by Malaysia:

> "If the laws of humanity and the dictates of the public conscience demand the prohibition of such weapons, the five nuclear-weapon States, however powerful, cannot stand against them." (CR 95/27, p. 56.)

In the face of such a preponderant majority of States' opinions, it is difficult to say there is no *opinio juris* against the use or threat of use of nuclear weapons. Certainly it is impossible to contend that there is an *opinio juris* in favour of the legality of such use or threat.

3. World Public Opinion

Added to all these official views, there is also a vast preponderance of public opinion across the globe. Strong protests against nuclear weapons have come from learned societies, professional groups, religious denominations, women's organizations, political parties, student federations, trade unions, NGOs and practically every group in which public opinion is expressed. Hundreds of such groups exist across the world. The names that follow are merely illustrative of the broad spread of such organizations: International Physicians for the Prevention of Nuclear War (IPPNW); Medical Campaign Against Nuclear Weapons; Scientists Against Nuclear Arms; People for Nuclear Disarmament; International Association of Lawyers against Nuclear Arms (IALANA); Performers and Artists for Nuclear Disarmament International; Social Scientists Against Nuclear War; Society for a Nuclear Free Future; European Federation against Nuclear Arms; The Nuclear Age Peace Foundation; Campaign for Nuclear Disarmament; Children's Campaign for Nuclear Disarmament. They come from all countries, cover all walks of life, and straddle the globe.

The millions of signatures received in this Court have been referred to at the very commencement of this opinion.

4. Current Prohibitions

A major area of space on the surface of the planet and the totality of the space above that surface, and of the space below the ocean surface, has been brought into the domain of legal prohibition of the very presence of nuclear weapons. Among treaties accomplishing this result are the 1959 Antarctic Treaty, the 1967 Treaty of Tlatelolco in respect of Latin America and the Caribbean, the 1985 Treaty of Rarotonga in regard to the South Pacific, and the 1996 Treaty of Cairo in regard to Africa. In addition, there is the Treaty prohibiting nuclear weapons in the atmosphere and outer space, and the 1971 Treaty on the Prohibition of the Emplacement of Nuclear Weapons and Other Weapons of Mass Destruction on the Seabed and the Ocean Floor and in the Subsoil Thereof (see CR 95122, p. 50). The major portion of the total area of the space afforded for human activity by the planet is thus declared free of nuclear weapons — a result which would not have been achieved but for universal agreement on the uncontrollable danger of these weapons and the need to eliminate them totally.

5. Partial Bans

The notion of partial bans and reductions in the levels of nuclear arms could not, likewise, have achieved their current results but for the existence of such a globally shared sentiment. Important among these measures are the Partial Test Ban Treaty of 1963 prohibiting the testing of nuclear weapons in the atmosphere, and the Nuclear Non-Proliferation Treaty of 1968. These treaties not only prohibited even the testing of nuclear weapons in certain circumstances, but also provided against the horizontal proliferation of nuclear weapons by imposing certain legal duties upon both nuclear and non-nuclear States. The Comprehensive Test Ban Treaty, now in the course of negotiation, aims at the elimination of all testing. The START agreements (START I and START II) aim at considerable reductions in the nuclear arsenals of the United States and the Russian Federation reducing their individual stockpiles by around 2,000 weapons annually.

6. Who Are the States Most Specially Concerned ?

If the nuclear States are the States most affected, their contrary view is an important factor to be taken into account, even though numerically they constitute a small proportion (around 2.7 per cent) of the United Nations membership of 185 States.

This aspect of their being the States most particularly affected has been stressed by the nuclear powers.

One should not however rush to the assumption that in regard to nuclear weapons the nuclear States are necessarily the States most concerned. The nuclear States possess the weapons, but it would be unrealistic to omit a consideration of those who would be affected once nuclear weapons are used. They would also be among the States most concerned, for their territories and populations would be exposed to the risk of harm from nuclear weapons no less than those of the nuclear powers, if ever nuclear weapons were used. This point was indeed made by Egypt in its presentation (CR 95/23, p. 40).

For probing the validity of the proposition that the nuclear States are the States most particularly affected, it would be useful to take the case of nuclear testing. Suppose a metropolitan power were to conduct a nuclear test in a distant colony, but with controls so unsatisfactory that there was admittedly a leakage of radioactive material. If the countries affected were to protest, on the basis of the illegality of such testing, it would be strange indeed if the metropolitan power attempted to argue that because it was the owner of the weapon, it was the State most affected. Manifestly, the States at the receiving end were those most affected. The position can scarcely be different in actual warfare, seeing that the radiation from a weapon exploding above ground cannot be contained within the target State. It would be quite legitimate for the neighbouring States to argue that they, rather than the owner of the bomb, are the States most affected.

This contention would stand, quite independently of the protests of the State upon whose territory the weapon is actually exploded. The relevance of this latter point is manifest when one considers that of the dozens of wars that have occurred since 1945, scarcely any have been fought on the soil of any of the nuclear powers. This is a relevant circumstance to be considered when the question of States most concerned is examined.

A balanced view of the matter is that no one group of nations — nuclear or non-nuclear — can say that its interests are most specially affected. Every nation in the world is specially affected by nuclear weapons, for when matters of survival are involved, this is a matter of universal concern.

7. Have States, by Participating in Regional Treaties, Recognized Nuclear Weapons as Lawful?

The United States, the United Kingdom and France have in their written statements taken up the position that by signing a regional treaty such as the Treaty of Tlatelolco prohibiting the use of nuclear weapons in Latin America and the Caribbean, the signatories indicated by implication that there is no general prohibition on the use of nuclear weapons. The signatories to such treaties are attempting to establish and strengthen a non-proliferation regime in their regions, not because they themselves do not accept the general illegality of nuclear weapons, but because the pro-nuclear States do not.

The position of the regional States is made quite clear by the stance they have adopted in the numerous General Assembly resolutions wherein several of them, for example, Costa Rica, have voted on the basis that the use of nuclear weapons is a crime against humanity, a violation of the United Nations Charter and/or a violation of international law.

Indeed, the language of the Treaty itself gives a clear indication of the attitude of its subscribing parties to the weapon, for it describes it as constituting "an attack on the integrity of the human species", and states that it "ultimately may even render the whole earth uninhabitable".

VII. Some Special Aspects

1. The Non-Proliferation Treaty

An argument has been made that the NPT, by implication, recognizes the legality of nuclear weapons, for all participating States accept without objection the possession of nuclear weapons by the nuclear powers. This argument raises numerous questions, among which are the following:

- (i) As already observed, the NPT has no bearing on the question of *use* or *threat of use* of nuclear weapons. Nowhere is the power given to use weapons, or to threaten their use.
- (ii) The Treaty was dealing with what may be described as a "winding down situation". The reality was being faced by the world community that a vast number of nuclear weapons were in existence and that they might proliferate. The immediate object of the world community was to wind down this stockpile of weapons.

  As was stressed to the Court by some States in their submissions, the Treaty was worked out against the background of the reality that, whether or not the world community approved of this situation, there were a small number of nuclear States and a vast number of non-nuclear States. The realities were that the nuclear States would not give up their weapons, that proliferation was a grave danger and that everything possible should be done to prevent proliferation, recognizing at the same time the common ultimate goal of the elimination of nuclear weapons.
- (iii) As already observed, an acceptance of the inevitability of a situation is not a consent to that situation, for accepting the existence of an undesirable situation one is powerless to prevent is very different to consenting to that

situation.

(iv) In this winding-down situation, there can be no hint that the right to possess meant also the right of use or threat of use. If there was a right of possession, it was a temporary and qualified right until such time as the stockpile could be wound down.

(v) The preamble to the Treaty makes it patently clear that its object is:

> "the cessation of the manufacture of nuclear weapons, the liquidation of all existing . . . stockpiles, and the elimination from national arsenals of nuclear weapons and the means of their delivery".

That Preamble, which, it should be noted, represents the unanimous view of all parties, nuclear as well as non-nuclear, describes the use of nuclear weapons in war as a "the devastation that would be visited upon all mankind".

These are clear indications that, far from acknowledging the legitimacy of nuclear weapons, the Treaty was in fact a concentrated attempt by the world community to whittle down such possessions as there already were, with a view to their complete elimination. Such a unanimous recognition of and concerted action towards the elimination of a weapon is quite inconsistent with a belief on the part of the world community of the legitimacy of the continued presence of the weapon in the arsenals of the nuclear powers.

(vi) Even if possession be legitimized by the Treaty, that legitimation is temporary and goes no further than possession. The scope and the language of the Treaty make it plain that it was a temporary state of possession *simpliciter* and nothing more to which they, the signatories, gave their assent — an assent given in exchange for the promise that the nuclear powers would make their utmost efforts to eliminate those weapons which *all* signatories considered so objectionable that they must be eliminated. There was here no recognition of a *right*, but only of a *fact*. The legality of that fact was not conceded, for else there was no need to demand a *quid pro quo* for it — the *bona fide* attempt by all nuclear powers to make every effort to eliminate these weapons, whose objectionability was the basic premise on which the entire Treaty proceeded.

2. Deterrence

Deterrence has been touched upon in this opinion in the context of the NPT. Yet, other aspects also merit attention, as deterrence bears upon the threat of use, which is one of the matters on which the Court's opinion is sought.

(i) Meaning of deterrence

Deterrence means in essence that the party resorting to deterrence is intimating to the rest of the world that it means to use nuclear power against any State in the event of the first State being attacked. The concept calls for some further examination.

(ii) Deterrence — from what ?

Deterrence as used in the context of nuclear weapons is deterrence from an act of *war* — not deterrence from *actions which one opposes*[171].

One of the dangers of the possession of nuclear weapons for purposes of deterrence is the blurring of this distinction and the use of the power the nuclear

---
171 John Polanyi, *Lawyers and the Nuclear Debate, op. cit.*, p. 19. [in Cohen, and Gouin, 1988]

weapon gives for purposes of deterring unwelcome actions on the part of another State. The argument of course applies to all kinds of armaments, but *a fortiori* to nuclear weapons. As Polanyi observes, the aspect of deterrence that is most feared is the temptation to extend it beyond the restricted aim of deterring war to deterring unwelcome actions[172].

It has been suggested, for example, that deterrence can be used for the protection of a nation's "vital interests". What are vital interests, and who defines them? Could they be merely commercial interests? Could they be commercial interests situated in another country, or a different area of the globe?

Another phrase used in this context is the defence of "strategic interests". Some submissions adverted to the so-called "sub-strategic deterrence", effected through the use of a low-yield "warning shot" when a nation's vital interests are threatened (see, for example, Malaysia's submission in CR 95/27, p. 53). This opinion will not deal with such types of deterrence, but rather with deterrence in the sense of self-defence against an act of war.

(iii) The degrees of deterrence

Deterrence can be of various degrees, ranging from the concept of maximum deterrence, to what is described as a minimum or near-minimum deterrent strategy[173]. Minimum nuclear deterrence has been described as:

> "nuclear strategy in which a nation (or nations) maintains the minimum number of nuclear weapons necessary to inflict unacceptable damage on its adversary even after it has suffered a nuclear attack".[174]

The deterrence principle rests on the threat of *massive* retaliation, and as Professor Brownlie has observed:

> "If put into practice this principle would lead to a lack of proportion between the actual threat and the reaction to it. Such disproportionate reaction does not constitute self-defence as permitted by Article 51 of the United Nations Charter."[175]

In the words of the same author, "the prime object of deterrent nuclear weapons is ruthless and unpleasant retaliation — they are instruments of terror rather than weapons of war"[176].

Since the question posed is whether the use of nuclear weapons is legitimate in any circumstances, minimum deterrence must be considered.

(iv) Minimum deterrence

One of the problems with deterrence, even of a minimal character, is that actions perceived by one side as defensive can all too easily be perceived by the other side as threatening. Such a situation is the classic backdrop to the traditional arms race, whatever be the type of weapons involved. With nuclear arms it triggers off a nuclear arms race, thus raising a variety of legal concerns. Even minimum deterrence thus leads to counter-deterrence, and to an ever ascending spiral of nuclear armament testing and tension. If, therefore, there are legal objections to deterrence, those objections are

---

172 *Ibid.*
173 R. C. Karp (ed.), *Security Without Nuclear Weapons? Different Perspectives on Non-Nuclear Security*, 1992, p. 251.
174 *Ibid.*, p. 250, citing Hollins, Powers and Sommer, *The Conquest of War: Alternative Strategies for Global Security*, 1989, pp. 54-55.
175 "Some Legal Aspects of the Use of Nuclear Weapons", *op. cit.*, pp. 446-447.
176 *Ibid.*, p. 445.

not removed by that deterrence being minimal.

(v) The problem of credibility

Deterrence needs to carry the conviction to other parties that there is a real intention to use those weapons in the event of an attack by that other party. A game of bluff does not convey that intention, for it is difficult to persuade another of one's intention unless one really has that intention. Deterrence thus consists in a real intention[177] to use such weapons. If deterrence is to operate, it leaves the world of make-believe and enters the field of seriously intended military threats.

Deterrence therefore raises the question not merely whether the threat of use of such weapons is legal, but also whether use is legal. Since what is necessary for deterrence is assured destruction of the enemy, deterrence thus comes within the ambit of that which goes beyond the purposes of war. Moreover, in the split second response to an armed attack, the finely graded use of appropriate strategic nuclear missiles or "clean" weapons which cause minimal damage does not seem a credible possibility.

(vi) Deterrence distinguished from possession

The concept of deterrence goes a step further than mere possession. Deterrence is more than the mere accumulation of weapons in a store-house. It means the possession of weapons in a state of readiness for actual use. This means the linkage of weapons ready for immediate take-off, with a command and control system geared for immediate action. It means that weapons are attached to delivery vehicles. It means that personnel are ready night and day to render them operational at a moment's notice. There is clearly a vast difference between weapons stocked in a warehouse and weapons so readied for immediate action. Mere possession and deterrence are thus concepts which are clearly distinguishable from each other.

(vii) The legal problem of intention

For reasons already outlined, deterrence becomes not the storage of weapons with intent to terrify, but a stockpiling with *intent to use*. If one intends to use them, all the consequences arise which attach to *intention* in law, whether domestic or international. One *intends* to cause the damage or devastation that will result. The intention to cause damage or devastation which results in total destruction of one's enemy or which might indeed wipe it out completely clearly goes beyond the purposes of war[178]. Such intention provides the mental element implicit in the concept of a threat.

However, a secretly harboured intention to commit a wrongful or criminal act does not attract legal consequences, unless and until that intention is followed through by corresponding conduct. Hence such a secretly harboured intention may not be an offence. If, however, the intention is announced, whether directly or by implication, it then becomes the criminal act of threatening to commit the illegal act in question.

Deterrence is by definition the very opposite of a secretly harboured intention to use nuclear weapons. Deterrence is not deterrence if there is no communication, whether by words or implication, of the serious intention to use nuclear weapons. It is therefore nothing short of a threat to use. If an act is wrongful, the threat to commit it

---

177 For further discussion of the concept of intention in this context, see *Just War, Non violence and Nuclear Deterrence*, D. L. Cady and R. Werner (eds.), 1991, pp. 193-205.
178 For the philosophical implications of deterrence, considered from the point of view of natural law, see Cady and Werner, *op. cit.*, pp. 207-219. See, also, John Finnis, Joseph Boyle and Germain Grisez, *Nuclear Deterrence, Morality and Realism*, 1987. Other works which present substantially the same argument are Anthony Kenny, *The Logic of Deterrence*, 1985, and *The Ivory Tower*, 1985; Roger Ruston, *Nuclear Deterrence — Right or Wrong ?*, 1981, and "Nuclear Deterrence and the Use of the Just War Doctrine", in Blake and Pole (eds.), *Objections to Nuclear Defense*, 1984.

and, more particularly, a publicly announced threat, must also be wrongful.

(viii) The temptation to use the weapons maintained for deterrence

Another aspect of deterrence is the temptation to use the weapons maintained for this purpose. The Court has been referred to numerous instances of the possible use of nuclear weapons of which the Cuban Missile Crisis is probably the best known. A study based on Pentagon documents, to which we were referred, lists numerous such instances involving the possibility of nuclear use from 1946 to 1980[179].

(ix) Deterrence and sovereign equality

This has already been dealt with. Either all nations have the right to self-defence with any particular weapon or none of them can have it — if the principle of equality in the right of self-defence is to be recognized. The first alternative is clearly impossible and the second alternative must then become, necessarily, the only option available.

The comparison already made with chemical or bacteriological weapons highlights this anomaly, for the rules of international law must operate uniformly across the entire spectrum of the international community. No explanation has been offered as to why nuclear weapons should be subject to a different regime.

(x) Conflict with the St. Petersburg principle

As already observed, the Declaration of St. Petersburg, followed and endorsed by numerous other documents (see Section III.3 above) declared that weakening the military forces of the enemy is the only legitimate object which States should endeavour to accomplish during war (on this aspect, see Section V.2 above). Deterrence doctrine aims at far more — it aims at the destruction of major urban areas and centres of population and even goes so far as "mutually assured destruction". Especially during the Cold War, missiles were, under this doctrine, kept at the ready, targeting many of the major cities of the contending powers. Such policies are a far cry from the principles solemnly accepted at St. Petersburg and repeatedly endorsed by the world community.

3. Reprisals

The Court has not in its Opinion expressed a view in regard to the acceptance of the principle of reprisals in the corpus of modern international law. I regret that the Court did not avail itself of this opportunity to confirm the unavailability of reprisals under international law at the present time, whether in time of peace or in war.

I wish to make it clear that I do not accept the lawfulness of the right to reprisals as a doctrine recognized by contemporary international law.

Does the concept of reprisals open up a possible exception to the rule that action in response to an attack is, like all other military action, subject to the laws of war?

The Declaration concerning Principles of Friendly Relations and Cooperation among States (resolution 2625 (XXV) of 1970) categorically asserted that "States have a duty to refrain from acts of reprisal involving the use of force".

Professor Bowett puts the proposition very strongly in the following passage:

> "Few propositions about international law have enjoyed more support than the proposition that, under the Charter of the United Nations, the use of force by way of reprisals is illegal. Although, indeed, the words 'reprisals' and 'retaliation' are not to be found in the Charter, this proposition was

---

179 Michio Kaku and Daniel Axelrod, *To Win a Nuclear War*, 1987, p. 5; CR 95/27, p. 48.

generally regarded by writers and by the Security Council as the logical and necessary consequence of the prohibition of force in Article 2 (4), the injunction to settle disputes peacefully in Article 2 (3) and the limiting of permissible force by states to self-defense."[180]

While this is an unexceptionable view, it is to be borne in mind, further, that nuclear weapons raise special problems owing to the magnitude of the destruction that is certain to accompany them. In any event, a doctrine evolved for an altogether different scenario of warfare can scarcely be applied to nuclear weapons without some re-examination.

Professor Brownlie addresses this aspect in the following terms:

"In the first place, it is hardly legitimate to extend a doctrine related to the minutiae of the conventional theatre of war to an exchange of power which, in the case of the strategic and deterrent uses of nuclear weapons, is equivalent to the total of war effort and is the essence of the war aims."[181]

These strong legal objections to the existence of a right of reprisal are reinforced also by two other factors — the conduct of the party indulging in the reprisals and the conduct of the party against whom the reprisals are directed.

The action of the party indulging in the reprisals needs to be a measured one, for its only legitimate object is as stated above. Whatever tendency there may be to unleash all its nuclear power in anger or revenge needs to be held strictly in check. It is useful to note in this connection the observation of Oppenheim who, after reviewing a variety of historical examples, concludes that :

"reprisals instead of being a means of securing legitimate warfare may become an effective instrument of its wholesale and cynical violation in matters constituting the very basis of the law of war"[182].

The historical examples referred to relate, *inter alia*, to the extreme atrocities sought to be justified under the principle of retaliation in the Franco-German War, the Boer War, World War I and World War II[183] They all attest to the brutality, cynicism and lack of restraint in the use of power which it is the object of the laws of war to prevent. Such shreds of the right to retaliation as might have survived the development of the laws of war are all rooted out by the nature of the nuclear weapon, as discussed in this opinion.

If history is any guide, the party indulging in reprisals will in practice use such "right of reprisal" — if indeed there is such a right — in total disregard of the purpose and limits of retaliation — namely, the limited purpose of ensuring compliance with the laws of war.

Turning next to the conduct of the party against whom the right is exercised — a party who already has disregarded the laws of war — that party would only be stimulated to release all the nuclear power at its disposal in response to that retaliation — unless, of course, it has been totally destroyed.

In these circumstances, any invitation to this Court to enthrone the legitimacy of nuclear reprisal for a nuclear attack is an invitation to enthrone a principle that opens the door to arbitrariness and lack of restraint in the use of nuclear weapons.

The sole justification, if any, for the doctrine of reprisals is that it is a means of securing legitimate warfare. With the manifest impossibility of that objective in relation to nuclear weapons, the sole reason for this alleged exception vanishes.

---

180 D. Bowett, "Reprisals Involving Recourse to Armed Force", *American Journal of International Law*, 1972, Vol. 66, p. 1, quoted in Weston, Falk and D'Amato, *International Law and World Order*, 1980, p. 910.
181 "Some Legal Aspects of the Use of Nuclear Weapons", *op. cit.*, p. 445.
182 *Op. cit.*, Vol. II, p. 565.
183 *Ibid*, pp. 563-565.

Cessante ratione legis, cessat ipsa lex.

4. Internal Wars

The question asked of the Court relates to the use of nuclear weapons in any circumstance. The Court has observed that it is making no observation on this point. It is my view that the use of the weapon is prohibited in all circumstances.

The rules of humanity which prohibit the use of the weapon in external wars do not begin to take effect only when national boundaries are crossed. They must apply internally as well.

Article 3 which is common to the four Geneva Conventions applies to all armed conflicts of a non-international character and occurring in the territory of one of the Powers parties to the Convention. Protocol II of 1977 concerning internal wars is couched in terms similar to the Martens Clause, and refers to "the principles of humanity and to the dictates of public conscience".

Thus international law makes no difference in principle between internal and external populations.

Moreover, if nuclear weapons are used internally by a State, it is clear from the foregoing analysis of the effects of nuclear weapons that the effects of such internal use cannot be confined internally. It will produce widespread external effects, as Chernobyl has demonstrated.

5. *The Doctrine of Necessity*

Does the doctrine of necessity offer a principle under which the use of nuclear weapons might be permissible in retaliation for an illegitimate act of warfare?

There is some support for the principle of necessity among the older writers, especially those of the German school[184] who expressed this doctrine in terms of the German proverb *"Kriegsraeson geht vor Kriegsmanier"* ("necessity in war overrules the manner of warfare"). However, some German writers did not support this view and in general it did not have the support of English, French, Italian and American publicists[185].

According to this doctrine, the laws of war lose their binding force when no other means, short of the violation of the laws of war, will offer an escape from the extreme danger caused by the original unlawful act.

However, the origins of this principle, such as it is, go back to the days when there were no *laws* of war, but rather usages of war, which had not yet firmed into laws accepted by the international community as binding.

The advance achieved in recognition of these principles as binding laws, ever since the Geneva Convention of 1864, renders untenable the position that they can be ignored at the will, and in the sole unilateral judgment, of one party. Even well before World War I, authoritative writers such as Westlake strenuously denied such a doctrine[186] and, with the new and extensive means of destruction — particularly submarine and aerial — which emerged in World War I, the doctrine became increasingly dangerous and inapplicable. With the massive means of destruction available in World War II, the desuetude of the doctrine was even further established.

Decisions of war crimes tribunals of that era attest to the collapse of that doctrine, if indeed it had ever existed. The case of the *Peleus*[187] relating to submarine warfare, decided by a British military court; the *Milch* case[188] decided by the United States

---

184 See the list of German authors cited by Oppenheim, *op. cit.*, Vol. II, p. 231, foot note 6.
185 *Ibid.*, p. 232.
186 Westlake, *International Law*, 2nd ed., 1910-1913, pp. 126-128; *The Collected Papers of John Westlake on Public International Law*, ed. L. Oppenheim, 1914, p. 243.
187 *War Crimes Reports*, 1946, i, pp. 1-16.
188 *War Crimes Trials*, 1948, 7, pp. 44, 65.

Military Tribunal at Nuremberg; and the *Krupp* case[189], where the tribunal addressed the question of grave economic necessity, are all instances of a judicial rejection of that doctrine in no uncertain terms[190].

The doctrine of necessity opens the door to revenge, massive devastation and, in the context of nuclear weapons, even to genocide. To the extent that it seeks to override the principles of the laws of war, it has no place in modern international law.

In the words of a United States scholar:

"where is the military necessity in incinerating entire urban populations, defiling the territory of neighboring and distant neutral countries, and ravaging the natural environment for generations to come ...? ... If so, then we are witness to the demise of Nuremberg, the triumph of Kriegsraison, the virtual repudiation of the humanitarian rules of armed conflict ... The very meaning of 'proportionality' becomes lost, and we come dangerously close to condoning the crime of genocide, that is, a military campaign directed more towards the extinction of the enemy than towards the winning of a battle or conflict."[191]

6. *Limited or Tactical or Battlefield Nuclear Weapons*

Reference has already been made to the contention, by those asserting legality of use, that the inherent dangers of nuclear weapons can be minimized by resort to "small" or "clean" or "low yield" or "tactical" nuclear weapons. This factor has an important bearing upon the legal question before the Court, and it is necessary therefore to examine in some detail the acceptability of the contention that limited weapons remove the objections based upon the destructiveness of nuclear weapons.

The following are some factors to be taken into account in considering this question:

(i) No material has been placed before the Court demonstrating that there is in existence a nuclear weapon which does not emit radiation, does not have a deleterious effect upon the environment, and does not have adverse health effects upon this and succeeding generations. If there were indeed a weapon which does not have any of the singular qualities outlined earlier in this opinion, it has not been explained why a conventional weapon would not be adequate for the purpose for which such a weapon is used. We can only deal with nuclear weapons as we know them.

(ii) The practicality of small nuclear weapons has been contested by high military [192] and scientific[193] authority.

(iii) Reference has been made (see Section IV above), in the context of self-defence, to the political difficulties, stated by former American Secretaries of State, Robert McNamara and Dr. Kissinger, of keeping a response within the ambit of what has been described as a limited or minimal response. The assumption of escalation control seems unrealistic in the context of nuclear attack.

(iv) With the use of even "small" or "tactical" or "battlefield" nuclear weapons, one crosses the nuclear threshold. The State at the receiving end of such a nuclear response would not know that the response is a limited or tactical

---

189 *Ibid.*, 1949, 10, p. 138.
190 See, on these cases, Oppenheim, *op. cit.*, pp. 232-233.
191 Burns H. Weston, "Nuclear Weapons versus International Law: A Contextual Reassessment", *McGill Law Journal*, 1983, Vol. 28, p. 578.
192 General Colin Powell, *A Soldier's Way*, 1995, p. 324:
"No matter how small these nuclear payloads were, we would be crossing a threshold. Using nukes at this point would mark one of the most significant military decisions since Hiroshima .... I began rethinking the practicality of those small nuclear weapons."
193 See *Bulletin of the Atomic Scientists,* May 1985, p. 35, at p. 37, referred to in Malaysian Written Comments, p. 20.

one involving a small weapon and it is not credible to posit that it will also be careful to respond in kind, that is, with a small weapon. The door would be opened and the threshold crossed for an all-out nuclear war.

The scenario here under consideration is that of a limited nuclear response to a nuclear attack. Since, as stated above,

(a) the "controlled response" is unrealistic; and
(b) a "controlled response" by the nuclear power making the first attack to the "controlled response" to its first strike is even more unrealistic,

the scenario we are considering is one of all-out nuclear war, thus rendering the use of the controlled weapon illegitimate.

The assumption of a voluntary "brake" on the recipient's full scale use of nuclear weapons is, as observed earlier in this opinion, highly fanciful and speculative. Such fanciful speculations provide a very unsafe assumption on which to base the future of humanity.

(v) As was pointed out by one of the States appearing before the Court:

"it would be academic and unreal for any analysis to seek to demonstrate that the use of a single nuclear weapon in particular circumstances could be consistent with principles of humanity. The reality is that if nuclear weapons ever were used, this would be overwhelmingly likely to trigger a nuclear war." (Australia, Gareth Evans, CR 95/22, pp. 49-50.)

(vi) In the event of some power readying a nuclear weapon for a strike, it may be argued that a pre-emptive strike is necessary for self-defence. However, if such a pre-emptive strike is to be made with a "small" nuclear weapon which by definition has no greater blast, heat or radiation than a conventional weapon, the question would again arise why a nuclear weapon should be used when a conventional weapon would serve the same purpose.

(vii) The factor of accident must always be considered. Nuclear weapons have never been tried out on the battlefield. Their potential for limiting damage is untested and is as yet the subject of theoretical assurances of limitation. Having regard to the possibility of human error in highly scientific operations — even to the extent of the accidental explosion of a space rocket with all its passengers aboard — one can never be sure that some error or accident in construction may deprive the weapon of its so-called "limited" quality. Indeed, apart from fine gradations regarding the size of the weapon to be used, the very use of any nuclear weapons under the stress of urgency is an area fraught with much potential for accident [194] The UNIDIR study, just mentioned, emphasizes the "very high risks of escalation once a confrontation starts"[195].

(viii) There is some doubt regarding the "smallness" of tactical nuclear weapons, and no precise details regarding these have been placed before the Court by any of the nuclear powers. Malaysia, on the other hand, has referred the Court to a United States law forbidding "research and development which could lead to the production . . . of a low-yield nuclear weapon" (Written Comments, p. 20), which is defined as having a yield of less than 5 kilotons (Hiroshima and Nagasaki were 15 and 12 kilotons, respectively)[196]. Weapons of this firepower may, in the absence of evidence to the contrary, be presumed to be fraught with all the dangers

---

194 See the UNIDIR Study, *Risks of Unintentional Nuclear War*, supra.
195 *Ibid.*, p. 11.
196 National Defense Authorization Act for Fiscal Year (FY) 1944, *Public Law*, 103- 160, 30 November 1993.

attendant on nuclear weapons, as outlined earlier in this opinion.

(ix) It is claimed a weapon could be used which could be precisely aimed at a specific target. However, recent experience in the Gulf War has shown that even the most sophisticated or "small" weapons do not always strike their intended target with precision. If there should be such error in the case of nuclear weaponry, the consequence would be of the gravest order.

(x) Having regard to WHO estimates of deaths ranging from one million to one billion in the event of a nuclear war which could well be triggered off by the use of the smallest nuclear weapon, one can only endorse the sentiment which Egypt placed before us when it observed that, having regard to such a level of casualties: "even with the greatest miniaturization, such speculative margins of risk are totally abhorrent to the general principles of humanitarian law" (CR 95/23, p. 43).

(xi) Taking the analogy of chemical or bacteriological weapons, no one would argue that because a small amount of such weapons will cause a comparatively small amount of harm, therefore chemical or bacteriological weapons are not illegal, seeing that they can be used in controllable quantities. If, likewise, nuclear weapons are generally illegal, there could not be an exception for "small weapons". If nuclear weapons are intrinsically unlawful, they cannot be rendered lawful by being used in small quantities or in smaller versions. Likewise, if a State should be attacked with chemical or bacteriological weapons, it seems absurd to argue that it has the right to respond with small quantities of such weapons. The fundamental reason that all such weapons are not permissible, even in self-defence, for the simple reason that their effects go beyond the needs of war, is common to all these weapons.

(xii) Even if — and it has not been so submitted by any State appearing before the Court — there is a nuclear weapon which *totally* eliminates the dissemination of radiation, and which is not a weapon of mass destruction, it would be quite impossible for the Court to define those nuclear weapons which are lawful and those which are unlawful, as this involves technical data well beyond the competence of the Court. The Court must therefore speak of legality in general terms.

The Court's authoritative pronouncement that all nuclear weapons are not illegal (i.e., that every nuclear weapon is not illegal) would then open the door to those desiring to use, or threaten to use, nuclear weapons to argue that any particular weapon they use or propose to use is within the rationale of the Court's decision. No one could police this. The door would be open to the use of whatever nuclear weapon a State may choose to use.

It is totally unrealistic to assume, however clearly the Court stated its reasons, that a power desiring to use the weapon would carefully choose those which are within the Court's stated reasoning.

VIII. Some Arguments against the Grant of an Advisory Opinion

1. *The Advisory Opinion Would be Devoid of Practical Effects*

It has been argued that, whatever may be the law, the question of the use of nuclear weapons is a political question, politically loaded, and politically determined. This may be, but it must be observed that, however political be the question, there is always value in the clarification of the law. It is not ineffective, pointless and inconsequential.

It is important that the Court should assert the law as it is. A decision soundly based on law will carry respect with it by virtue of its own inherent authority. It will assist in building up a climate of opinion in which law is respected. It will enhance the authority of the Court in that it will be seen to be discharging its duty of clarifying and developing the law, regardless of political considerations.

The Court's decision on the illegality of the *apartheid* regime had little prospect of compliance by the offending Government, but helped to create the climate of opinion which dismantled the structure of *apartheid*. Had the Court thought in terms of the futility of its decree, the end of *apartheid* may well have been long delayed, if it could have been achieved at all. The clarification of the law is an end in itself, and not merely a means to an end. When the law is clear, there is a greater chance of compliance than when it is shrouded in obscurity.

The view has indeed been expressed that, in matters involving "high policy", the influence of international law is minimal. However, as Professor Brownlie has observed in dealing with this argument, it would be "better to uphold a prohibition which *may* be avoided in a crisis than to do away with standards altogether"[197].

I would also refer, in this context, to the perceptive observations of Albert Schweitzer, cited at the very commencement of this opinion, on the value of a greater public awareness of the illegality of nuclear weapons.

The Court needs to discharge its judicial role, declaring and clarifying the law as it is empowered and charged to do, undeterred by considerations that pertain to the political realm, which are not its concern.

2. Nuclear Weapons Have Preserved World Peace

It was argued by some States contending for legality that such weapons have played a vital role in support of international security over the last fifty years, and have helped to preserve global peace.

Even if this contention were correct, it makes little impact upon the legal considerations before the Court. The threat of use of a weapon which contravenes the humanitarian laws of war does not cease to contravene those laws of war merely because the overwhelming terror it inspires has the psychological effect of deterring opponents. This Court cannot endorse a pattern of security that rests upon terror. In the dramatic language of Winston Churchill, speaking to the House of Commons in 1955, we would then have a situation where, "Safety will be the sturdy child of terror and survival the twin brother of annihilation." A global regime which makes safety the result of terror and can speak of survival and annihilation as twin alternatives makes peace and the human future dependent on terror. This is not a basis for world order which this Court can endorse. This Court is committed to uphold the rule of law, not the rule of force or terror, and the humanitarian principles of the laws of war are a vital part of the international rule of law which this Court is charged to administer.

A world order dependent upon terror would take us back to the state of nature described by Hobbes in *The Leviathan*, with sovereigns "in the posture of Gladiators; having their weapons pointing and their eyes fixed on one another ... which is a posture of Warre"[198].

As international law stands at the threshold of another century, with over three centuries of development behind it, including over one century of development of humanitarian law, it has the ability to do better than merely re-endorse the dependence of international law on terror, thus setting the clock back to the state of nature as described by Hobbes, rather than the international rule of law as visualized by Grotius. As between the widely divergent world views of those near contemporaries, international law has clearly a commitment to the Grotian vision; and this case has provided the Court with what future historians may well describe as a "Grotian moment" in the history of international law. I regret that the Court has not availed itself of this opportunity. The failure to note the contradictions between deterrence

---

197 "Some Legal Aspects of the Use of Nuclear Weapons", *op. cit.*, p. 438, emphasis added.
198 Thomas Hobbes, *The Leviathan*, ed. James B. Randall, Washington Square Press, 1970, p. 86.

and international law may also help to prolong the "posture of Warre" described by Hobbes, which is implicit in the doctrine of deterrence.

However, conclusive though these considerations be, the weakness of the argument that deterrence is valuable in that it has preserved world peace does not end here. It is belied by the facts of history. It is well documented that the use of nuclear weapons has been contemplated more than once during the past 50 years. Two of the best-known examples are the Cuban Missile Crisis (1962) and the Berlin Crisis (1961). To these, many more could be added from well-researched studies upon the subject[199]. The world has on such occasions been hovering on the brink of nuclear catastrophe and has, so to speak, held its breath. In these confrontations, often a test of nerves between those who control the nuclear button, anything could have happened, and it is humanity's good fortune that a nuclear exchange has not resulted. Moreover, it is incorrect to speak of the nuclear weapon as having saved the world from wars, when well over 100 wars, resulting in 20 million deaths, have occurred since 1945[200]. Some studies have shown that since the termination of World War II, there have been armed conflicts around the globe every year, with the possible exception of 1968[201], while more detailed estimates show that in the 2,340 weeks between 1945 and 1990, the world enjoyed a grand total of only three that were truly war-free[202].

It is true there has been no global conflagration, but the nuclear weapon has not saved humanity from a war-torn world, in which there exist a multitude of flashpoints with the potential of triggering the use of nuclear weapons if the conflict escalates and the weapons are available. Should that happen, it would bring "untold sorrow to mankind" which it was the primary objective of the United Nations Charter to prevent.

IX. Conclusion

1. *The Task before the Court*

Reference has been made (in Section VI.3 of this opinion) to the wide variety of groups that have exerted themselves in the anti-nuclear cause — environmentalists, professional groups of doctors, lawyers, scientists, performers and artists, parliamentarians, women's organizations, peace groups, students' federations. They are too numerous to mention. They come from every region and every country.

There are others who have maintained the contrary for a variety of reasons.

Since no authoritative statement of the law has been available on the matter thus far, an appeal has now been made to this Court for an opinion. That appeal comes from the world's highest representative organization on the basis that a statement by the world's highest judicial organization would be of assistance to all the world in this all-important matter.

This request thus gives the International Court of Justice a unique opportunity to make a unique contribution to this unique question. The Opinion rendered by the Court has judicially established certain important principles governing the matter for the first time. Yet it does not go to the full extent which I think it should have.

In this opinion I have set down my conclusions as to the law. While conscious of the magnitude of the issues, I have focused my attention on the law as it *is* — on the numerous principles worked out by customary international law, and humanitarian law in particular, which cover the particular instances of the damage caused by nuclear

---

199 For example, *The Nuclear Predicament: A Sourcebook*, D. U Gregory (ed.), 1982. [1986?]
200 Ruth Sivard, in *World Military and Social Expenditures, World Priorities*, 1993, p. 20, counts 149 wars and 23 million deaths during this period.
201 See Charles Allen, *The Savage Wars of Peace: Soldiers' Voices 1945-1989*, 1989.
202 Alvin and Heidi Toffler, *War and Anti-War: Survival at the Dawn of the 21st Century*, 1993, p. 14.

weapons. As stated at the outset, my considered opinion on this matter is that the use or threat of use of nuclear weapons is incompatible with international law and with the very foundations on which that system rests. I have sought in this opinion to set out my reasons in some detail and to state why the use or threat of use of nuclear weapons is absolutely prohibited by *existing law* — *in all circumstances and without reservation.*

It comforts me that these legal conclusions accord also with what I perceive to be the moralities of the matter and the interests of humanity.

2. The Alternatives before Humanity

To conclude this opinion, I refer briefly to the Russell-Einstein Manifesto, issued on 9 July 1955. Two of the most outstanding intellects of this century, Bertrand Russell and Albert Einstein, each of them specially qualified to speak with authority of the power locked in the atom, joined a number of the world's most distinguished scientists in issuing a poignant appeal to all of humanity in connection with nuclear weapons. That appeal was based on considerations of rationality, humanity and concern for the human future. Rationality, humanity and concern for the human future are built into the structure of international law.

International law contains within itself a section which particularly concerns itself with the humanitarian laws of war. It is in the context of that particular section of that particular discipline that this case is set. It is an area in which the concerns voiced in the Russell-Einstein Manifesto resonate with exceptional clarity.

Here are extracts from that appeal:

> "No one knows how widely such lethal radioactive particles may be diffused, but the best authorities are unanimous in saying that a war with H-bombs might possibly put an end to the human race ...
> ... We appeal, as human beings, to human beings: Remember your humanity, and forget the rest. If you can do so, the way lies open to a new Paradise; if you cannot, there lies before you the risk of universal death."

Equipped with the necessary array of principles with which to respond, international law could contribute significantly towards rolling back the shadow of the mushroom cloud, and heralding the sunshine of the nuclear-free age.

No issue could be fraught with deeper implications for the human future, and the pulse of the future beats strong in the body of international law. This issue has not thus far entered the precincts of international tribunals. Now that it has done so for the first time, it should be answered — convincingly, clearly and categorically.

(Signed) Christopher Gregory WEERAMANTRY.

Appendix

(Demonstrating danger to neutral States)

Comparison of the Effects of Bombs

A - Lethal area from the blast wave of the blockbusters used in the Second World War.
B - Lethal area from the blast wave of the Hiroshima bomb.
C - Lethal area from the blast wave of a 1-Mt bomb.
D - Lethal area for fallout radiation from a 1-Mt bomb.

Chapter 11

Initiatives Since ICJ Advisory Opinions

The London Nuclear Warfare Tribunal (LNWT), World Court Project (WCP), and International Court of Justice (ICJ) have been discussed in earlier chapters. The results have been remarkable, and they have certainly helped to achieve progress in understanding the positions of various parties concerning the lawfulness of the possession, threat and use of nuclear weapons.

The LNWT provided one of the building blocks, and some substantive thinking, for the WCP to take the ideas forward, and lobby members of the UN General Assembly (UNGA), and WHO, to request Advisory Opinions from the ICJ.

The LNWT was not the only building block. By way of brief diversion, I mention the example of the determination and sincerity of those protesters who became known as the 'Greenham Women'. Those interested in legal issues arising from nuclear weapons and the peace movement can find more information in Dewar et al. (1984). Of specific legal relevance is the case of the 'Greenham Women Against Cruise Missiles v. Reagan' (Greenham, 1984; Hickman, 1986) held in the Southern District Court of New York, the first Court set up in the US in 1789 before the US had its Supreme Court. Sadly, the merits of the case against Cruise Missiles were never considered properly, because the case was dismissed as non-justiciable; so the US is also plagued by matters of the utmost concern to mankind outside legal control because they are 'non-justiciable'. We shall see that again shortly in relation to Trident and Scotland. So, whoever can use the electoral system to hijack the country, has acquired profound non-justiciable powers over the destiny of mankind (a recent example of that is the UK 2015 general election which resulted in a Conservative government even though 63.1% of the electorate voted for someone else — and that government has control over decisions concerning the UK's nuclear weapons).

As noted earlier, the WHO request for an Advisory Opinion was declined by the ICJ on the grounds of jurisdiction (matters of relevance to WHO). The ICJ agreed to provide an Advisory Opinion to the UN

General Assembly — that agreement was almost unanimous (13:1), but following the definitive paragraph 105 (2)E of the UNGA Advisory Opinion, some of the Judges commented subsequently that it may have been better for the ICJ to have declined to provide an Advisory Opinion in that case also. However, those comments were too late, and the proceedings took place.

The Advisory Opinion paragraph 2E resulted in an evenly split vote, resolved only by the President's casting vote in favour.

The legal reasoning presented by several Judges in their supplementary documents (Declarations, Separate Opinions, and Dissenting Opinions) is far more substantial than the Advisory Opinion itself.

Some Judges, and many commentators, have taken to mean that as far as 2E is concerned, there is a *non liquet*. No applicable law to deal with the question posed? Answering that question has prompted a great deal of legal academic writing. However, the remaining question in the minds of many, about that part of the ICJ Advisory Opinion is simple — did it do its job completely? It is very much in the interests of mankind that this very unsatisfactory situation is resolved somehow by the ICJ. What remains a total mystery, is to know what a lawful use of nuclear weapons could actually look like? So far, nobody has produced a satisfactory answer to that question. So, keep asking it of the nuclear weapons apologists and promoters. I would like those judges who voted in favour of that part of the decision to give the world good, solid legal reasoning — we know far too little of what was in their minds at the time, and they bear a very heavy burden. Of course, the other judges were convinced they could not imagine any use of nuclear weapons that could be consistent with the laws of war, and international humanitarian law. Notwithstanding all the subsequent debate, the first paragraph of 2E makes the illegality of nuclear weapons clear. The effects of that potential faultline in the Advisory Opinion have been an important factor in activities since 1996. It is not possible to discuss everything since 1996, therefore discussion in this Chapter will be limited to:

1. the establishment of the International Criminal Court;
2. Trident and Scotland;
3. ICAN, NAPF, Mayors for Peace and PICAT;
4. The Humanitarian Pledge;
5. cases of the Republic of the Marshall Islands Applications to the International Court of Justice against the world's known nuclear powers.

11.1 International Criminal Court

On 17th July 1998, many countries got together and signed a new treaty, the 'Rome Statute' (ICC,1998) setting up an International Criminal Court. Unlike the International Court of Justice (ICJ), the ICC is not a formal part of the UN. At the time of writing this book, there were 123 countries party to the Rome Statute.

The ICC is another international institution subject to the whims of a world order dominated by sovereign states, because accepting the jurisdiction of the ICC is voluntary. Of the 9 known nuclear weapons states, only France and the UK have signed up to the Rome Statute. Needless to say, there have been no cases yet before the ICC related to nuclear weapons, or to test some of the World War II victors' actions (such as the bombing of Hiroshima, Nagasaki, and Dresden).

We can only hope that more countries become subject to the jurisdiction of the ICC, particularly nuclear weapons states, some of which should in any case be indicted and charged with war crimes because of some of their military adventures that have not involved nuclear weapons.

11.2 Trident and Scotland

1998 was a significant year for another reason, which still has a long way to run; the foundation of Trident Ploughshares (2nd May, 1998). Trident Ploughshares started with a number of 'pledgers'; people who make a personal pledge to try to disarm the nuclear weapons system themselves. That is a powerful call to action.

Of particular relevance for nuclear weapons and international law, three pledgers decided to empty a research barge, the *Maytime*, that was used for research about the detection and cloaking of Trident submarines. The barge was anchored in Loch Goil in Scotland, near the Trident submarines. A lot of computer and related equipment was thrown into the loch. The three pledgers became known as the 'Trident Three' (Angela Zelter, Bodil Roder, and Ellen Moxley). This happened on 8th June, 1999.

Of course, the Trident Three were arrested. They appeared at Greenock Sheriff Court starting on 27th September, 1999, effectively charged with wilful and malicious damage. Their trial finished on 21st October, 1999. During the trial, there was little dispute as to the facts; the defendants essentially agreed they did what they had been accused of, but raised issues related to Trident nuclear weapons and customary international law, arguing that what they did was necessary and justifiable given the UK Government's unlawful activity in having Trident nuclear missiles.

Somewhat unexpectedly, on 21st October 1999, the Sheriff held that the accused had acted without the criminal intent required for the constitution of the crime of malicious mischief and directed the jury to acquit the pannels of the charges of malicious mischief. This they did, so the Trident Three walked free, not guilty as charged.

It came as no surprise that a nuclear weapon state would not be happy about a court dismissing a case against defendants who had set out to damage or destroy material related to the operations of their nuclear weapons, particularly with international humanitarian law at the heart of the defence. The state was not able to appeal the decision of the Sheriff Court, so it needed some other device by which legal matters raised during the original trial could be considered by a higher court. Such a device was found[1] whereby the Lord Advocate could refer points of law arising in a case where a person is tried on indictment and acquitted or convicted, to the High Court of Judiciary for an Opinion about those points of law.

The Lord Advocate did make such a reference (21st January, 2000) and in the literature about the Trident Three case, it is often referred to as the Lord Advocate's Reference, or LAR[2].

The LAR asked 4 questions of the High Court:

1. In a trial under Scottish criminal procedure, is it competent to lead evidence as to the content of customary international law as it applies to the United Kingdom?
2. Does any rule of customary international law justify a private individual in Scotland in damaging or destroying property in pursuit of his or her objection to the United Kingdom's possession of nuclear weapons, its action in placing such weapons at locations within Scotland or its policies in relation to such weapons?
3. Does the belief of an accused person that his or her actions are justified in law constitute a defence to a charge of malicious mischief or theft?
4. Is it a general defence to a criminal charge that the offence was committed in order to prevent or bring to an end the commission of an offence by another person?

---

1 Criminal Procedure (Scotland) Act 1995, s. 123.
2 Technically, it was the Lord Advocate's Reference No. 1 of 2000.

This is a very narrow set of questions on which an opinion was sought, but understandable given the nature of the charges against the Trident Three. In the event, the High Court became bogged down in the same main issue that had troubled the ICJ Judges about their Advisory Opinion; *disposatif* section 2E. The Appeal Court, High Court of Judiciary, handed down their opinion on 30th March, 2001 (LAR, 2001).

The opinion handed down displays a total absence of knowledge or understanding about what a nuclear weapon will do. This is evidenced by their astonishing statement in paragraph 93 that "We are not persuaded that even upon the respondents' description of, or hypothesis as to, the characteristics of Trident it would be possible to say *a priori* that a threat to use it, or its use, could never be seen as compatible with the requirements of international humanitarian law". Astonishingly, the Judges decided they would not investigate what nuclear weapons can do: "...it is not for us to make factual findings as to the characteristics or destructive potential of Trident" — para. 62. At least the ICJ had no such problem. There is no mechanism for appeal in Scotland or the UK from that Opinion. If there was, there are very clear reasons to argue substantial grounds of appeal. This was certainly not a legal decision that could be relied on safely, and is certainly not a decision that the judges or the High Court can be proud of.

The High Court dealt with the first questions with a clear, unambiguous response: "A rule of customary international law is a rule of Scots law" (LAR, 2001, para. 23). As a result, they made the obvious point that as this is a point of law, evidence was not needed about such international law. However, that is a major point of great significance in any future legal considerations about the law of nuclear weapons and Trident in Scotland. It is reminiscent of the arguments raised in the *Shimoda* case in Japan, that international law should be included as domestic law (see Falk, 1965, for a discussion of the *Shimoda* case).

The opinion does have a helpful discussion about the Scottish law of necessity. It addresses the question of justiciability, with a consideration of matters for which it asserts as matters for the prerogative. The court is trying to keep its cake and eat it at the same time; the key question they were dwelling on, as far as the defendants' motives were concerned, are either justiciable or they are not.

Looking at obvious potential grounds of appeal (but appeal was not possible), the opinion says it sets out the International Court of Justice Advisory Opinion's *disposatif* of section 105 at the opinion's paragraph 79 - except that it doesn't - clause 2F is missing. In addition to that, the judges made what I consider to be a fundamental error by not considering the *disposatif* paragraph 2C — after going through the opinion we have no idea what the Court thought about 2C. That by itself would normally give good grounds for appeal. Other grounds of appeal could based on failures to balance their construction of 2E with the other points made in the body of the ICJ Advisory Opinion. The very brief discussion of the effects of nuclear weapons (paragraphs 63 and 64) demonstrates that the court had no idea about the reality of the risks and threats the Trident Three were complaining about — therefore, most of the following judicial commentary must be considered to be too abstract for the case that resulted in the Lord Advocate requesting the High Court opinion.

That opinion to the Lord Advocate is certainly an opinion that cannot be relied on. It is not possible in the scope of this book to put all the detailed arguments placed before the court when considering the Lord Advocate's request for an opinion. There are other sources that present considerable detail for the interested researcher or individual, such as the Trident Ploughshares website[3], such as Moxley's response.

The High Court opinion for the Lord Advocate raises the question of what were all the motives of the judges when they put together their opinion?

The questions about Trident and Scotland are not likely to go away until Trident goes away from Scotland. In the UK's 2015 general election, the leader of the Scottish National Party explained on many occasions total objection to the presence of Trident on Scottish soil. The SNP hold almost all the Scottish Parliamentary seats in Parliament. If the UK government does not remove Trident from Scotland, serious constitutional problems arise, in addition to the more general problem of the UK government going against the right of self determination of the people of Scotland.

In February 2009 a conference, "Trident and International Law: Scotland's Obligations", was organized jointly by the Acronym Institute for Disarmament Diplomacy, the Edinburgh Peace and Justice Centre, and Trident Ploughshares. This brought back memories of the London Nuclear Warfare Tribunal held almost quarter of a century earlier.

Five key points were reported from that Edinburgh Conference:

    1. The launching of a nuclear-armed Trident missile would be

---

[3] available at: http://tridentploughshares.org/lord-advocates-reference/ [June 2015].

unlawful in any conceivable circumstance;
2. The deployment, renewal, and modernisation of nuclear weapons and the application of deterrence doctrines based on the use or threat of use of nuclear weapons, including the Trident nuclear weapons system, violate existing international law;
3. Scotland's obligations and responsibilities under international law are not nullified by the 1998 devolution settlement;
4. Citizens have a lawful right to protest the deployment of nuclear weapons and breaches of international law by governments and State authorities;
5. In addition to national obligations to cease deploying, developing and renewing nuclear weapons, there is an international law obligation to conclude multinational negotiations to achieve the total abolition of nuclear weapons, encompassing future prohibitions on the acquisition, deployment and use of nuclear armaments and the progressive elimination of all existing arsenals.
(Johnson and Zelter, 2011; pp19-28)

It is noteworthy that point 1 above was reinforced by Judge Bedjaoui who was the President of the International Court of Justice when it delivered its Advisory Opinion for the UN General Assembly. Point 2 was also reinforced by Judge Bedjaoui, and Judge Weeramantry, another of the ICJ AO judges.

The interested reader should have access to the book edited by Johnson and Zelter (2011). It contains several essential chapters about the issues raised in the Edinburgh conference. It is a collection of observations and writings of many eminent people. Among the authors, can be recognized the World Court Project, the International Court of Justice Advisory Opinion, the Trident Three, and several eminent practicing lawyers and legal academics.

Given the current focus and activities in Scotland about Trident, it is probably only a matter of time before Trident must be removed — the only issues are when, and all the noise and hot air that will be raised by politicians and judiciary before that happens. Keep up the political, judicial and public conscience pressure, and Trident will be gone.

11.3 ICAN, NAPF, Mayors for Peace and PICAT

This section presents very brief information about NGOs that are active currently with major and international programs. The NGOs discussed are not the only NGOs active at present (2015). The selection of these NGOs should not be taken as any implicit statement by this book of relative importance. A selection was made for the simple pragmatic reason of space in a single book that is also loaded with a great deal of legal commentary and doumentation. A separate book dedicated to current NGOs working for nuclear disarmament would be an excellent publication. There are other NGOs that should be considered by activists and scholars, some of which are identified in other parts of this book.

The NGOs selected for this section have very different programs and activities, illustrating a variety of ways in which people, NGOs, civil administrations and governments can contribute to working towards nuclear disarmament.

11.3.1 ICAN

"The International Campaign to Abolish Nuclear Weapons (ICAN)[4] is a global campaign coalition working to mobilize people in all countries to inspire, persuade and pressure their governments to initiate negotiations for a treaty banning nuclear weapons." (from http://www.icanw.org)

In 2006, the International Physicians for the Prevention of Nuclear War (IPPNW), at their Helsinki world congress, adopted ICAN as a priority. ICAN opened its first office in Melbourne, Australia. ICAN was firmly on the nuclear disarmament map. Since 2006 it has gone from strength to strength.

One key goal for ICAN is to persuade governments around the world to sign up to a Humanitarian Pledge (set out in the next section). At the time of writing this book, 112 countries have endorsed the Pledge (as at 2nd July 2015): Afghanistan, Andorra, Angola, Antigua and Barbuda, Argentina, Austria, Bahamas, Bahrain, Barbados, Belize, Benin, Bolivia,Botswana, Brazil, Brunei, Burundi, Cabo Verde, Central African Republic, Chad, Chile, Colombia, Congo, Cook Islands, Costa Rica, Côte d'Ivoire, Cuba, Cyprus, Djibouti, Dominica, Dominican Republic, Ecuador, Egypt, El Salvador, Eritrea, Ethiopia, Fiji, Grenada, Guatemala, Guinea, Guinea-Bissau, Guyana,

---
4 See: http://www.icanw.org.

Haiti, Indonesia, Iran, Iraq, Ireland, Jamaica, Jordan, Kenya, Kiribati, Kuwait, Kyrgyzstan, Lebanon, Lesotho, Liberia, Libya, Liechtenstein, Macedonia, Madagascar, Malawi, Malaysia, Malta, Marshall Islands, Mauritania, Mauritius, Mexico, Nicaragua, Niger, Nigeria, Niue, Palau, Palestine, Panama, Papua New Guinea, Paraguay, Peru, Philippines, Qatar, St. Kitts and Nevis, St. Lucia, St. Vincent and the Grenadines, Samoa, São Tomé and Príncipe, San Marino, Saudi Arabia, Senegal, Serbia, Seychelles, Sierra Leone, Singapore, Somalia, South Africa, Sri Lanka, Suriname, Swaziland, Tajikistan, Thailand, Timor-Leste, Togo, Trinidad and Tobago, Tunisia, Tuvalu, Uganda, United Arab Emirates, Uruguay, Vanuatu, Venezuela, Vietnam, Yemen, Zambia, Zimbabwe.

Guess what? Not a single nuclear weapons state has signed yet!

11.3.2 NAPF

The Nuclear Age Peace Foundation (NAPF)[5] was formed in 1982, pre-dating the LNWT. Their Mission is "To educate and advocate for peace and a world free of nuclear weapons, and to empower peace leaders.", and their Vision is "Our vision is a just and peaceful world, free of nuclear weapons.". One of their programs is the Nuclear Zero Lawsuits. These are the cases of the Republic of the Marshall Islands against the world's nuclear weapons states in the International Court of Justice. The last pages of this chapter set out the Application of the RMI v UK. Richard Falk and David Krieger who wrote the Foreword for this edition of the book, and contributed Chapter 12 are members of the Board of NAPF.

In addition to the Nuclear Zero Lawsuits, NAPF have an education program that includes training peace activists. As they point out accurately and correctly, military personnel have extensive training available; peace activists will also benefit from training. The education program has other activities — further information is available from their website.

Briefing booklets are available from NAPF about the Nuclear Zero lawsuits, issues related to NPT negotiations, and additional topics.

11.3.3 Mayors for Peace

Mayors for Peace are aiming for the total abolition of nuclear weapons by 2020. That is a very ambitious goal, but if enough people can apply enough pressure to the hidden faces behind the nuclear weapon states,

---
[5] See: https://www.wagingpeace.org.

considerable progress can be made.

They have been very successful in their reach around the globe: in July 2015 they have 6,733 cities in 160 countires and regions.

Following the UN Special Session on Disarmament in 1982, the Mayors of Hiroshima and Nagasaki started work to bring together Mayors around the world who would also like to see nuclear disarmament. The spread of membership around the world is extensive.

Current (2015) Executive cities are in Japan, Germany, Russia, France, Philippines, UK, US, Belgium, Croatia, Spain, Iraq, Cameroon, Mexico and Norway.

To illustrate the reach of Mayors for Peace, here is the basic data[6] about membership as at 1st July 2015:

Area	Countries and Regions	Cities
Africa	46	359
Asia	30	2,696
Europe	47	2,572
Latin America and the Carribean	25	671
North America	3	307
Oceania	9	128
TOTALS	160	6,733

11.3.4 PICAT

PICAT is 'Public Interest Case Against Trident'. This is a new initiative coordinated by Trident Ploughshares 'hot off the press' at the time of writing (July 2015). Because of the focus on Trident, it is primarily of concern in the UK, but of course others may use similar ideas elsewhere.

The aim of PICAT is to bring the crimes around Trident and its renewal before the courts and to secure a judgement that will lead to the ending of these crimes through the disarming of the UK's nuclear weapons system. If the case is stopped by the Attorney General, or it is deemed to be vexatious litigation, or if there is any other attempt to prevent these crimes from being addressed seriously by the courts, the people involved in the project shall consider taking it to the International Criminal Court instead, which has international jurisdiction over these

---
6 From: http://www.mayorsforpeace.org/english/membercity/map.html.

crimes. At the very least the attempts to bring the matter before the courts will inform more people about the illegality of weapons of mass destruction and help provide the public pressure needed to de-legitimise the UK's nuclear weapons.

The people who initiated the project were Angie Zelter, George Farebrother (unfortunately now deceased), and Robbie Manson, a lawyer and author of 'Pax Legalis'. Angie and Robbie are now co-ordinating the campaign and have been assisted by David Mackenzie.

11.4 Humanitarian Pledge

Given the failure of the nuclear weapons states to enter into meaningful negotiations leading to full and complete nuclear disarmament, the people of the world are left with having, yet again, to organize the public conscience and put pressure on governments to take effective and immediate steps to rid the world of those weapons. As mentioned above, many countries have now signed the Humanitarian Pledge. There are many missing countries, and doubtless with more organization and pressure, those missing countries can be informed about the Pledge and be encouraged to sign it.

Humanitarian Pledge

In light of the important facts and findings that have been presented at the international conferences in Oslo, Nayarit and Vienna, and after careful consideration of the evidence, We, the States supporting and/or endorsing this pledge, have come to the following inescapable conclusions and make the subsequent pledge to take them forward with interested parties in available fora, including in the context of the NPT and its 2015 Review Conference:

Mindful of the unacceptable harm that victims of nuclear weapons explosions and nuclear testing have experienced and recognising that that the rights and needs of victims have not yet been adequately addressed,

Understanding that the immediate, mid- and long-term consequences of a nuclear weapon explosion are significantly graver than it was understood in the past and will not be constrained by national borders but have regional or even global effects, potentially threatening the survival of humanity,

Recognizing the complexity of and interrelationship between these consequences on health, environment, infrastructure, food security, climate, development, social cohesion and the global economy that are systemic and potentially irreversible,

Aware that the risk of a nuclear weapon explosion is significantly greater than previously assumed and is indeed increasing with increased proliferation, the lowering of the technical threshold for nuclear weapon capability, the ongoing modernisation of nuclear weapon arsenals in nuclear weapon possessing states, and the role that is attributed to nuclear weapons in the nuclear doctrines of possessor states,

Cognisant of the fact that the risk of nuclear weapons use with their unacceptable consequences can only be avoided when all nuclear weapons have been eliminated, Emphasizing that the consequences of a nuclear weapon explosion and the risks associated with nuclear weapons concern the security of all humanity and that all states share the responsibility to prevent any use of nuclear weapons,

Emphasizing that the scope of consequences of a nuclear weapon explosion and risks associated raise profound moral and ethical questions that go beyond debates about the legality of nuclear weapons,

Mindful that no national or international response capacity exists that would adequately respond to the human suffering and humanitarian harm that would result from a nuclear weapon explosion in a populated area, and that such capacity most likely will never exist,

Affirming that it is in the interest of the very survival of humanity that nuclear weapons are never used again, under any circumstances,

Reiterating the crucial role that international organisations, relevant UN entities, the Red Cross and Red Crescent Movement, elected representatives, academia and civil society play for advancing the shared objective of a nuclear weapon free world,

We regard it as our responsibility and consequently pledge to present the facts-based discussions, findings and compelling evidence of the Vienna Conference, which builds upon the previous conferences in Oslo and Nayarit, to all relevant fora, in particular the NPT Review Conference 2015 and in the UN framework, as they should be at the centre of all deliberations, obligations and commitments with regard to nuclear disarmament,

We pledge to follow the imperative of human security for all and to promote the protection of civilians against risks stemming from nuclear weapons,

We call on all states parties to the NPT to renew their commitment to the urgent and full implementation of existing obligations under Article VI, and to this end, to identify and pursue effective measures to fill the legal gap for the prohibition and elimination of nuclear weapons and we pledge to cooperate with all stakeholders to achieve this goal,

We call on all nuclear weapons possessor states to take concrete interim measures to reduce the risk of nuclear weapon detonations, including reducing the operational status of nuclear weapons and moving nuclear weapons away from deployment into storage, diminishing the role of nuclear weapons in military doctrines and rapid reductions of all types of nuclear weapons,

We pledge to cooperate with all relevant stakeholders, States, international organisations, the International Red Cross and Red Crescent Movements, parliamentarians and civil society, in efforts to stigmatise, prohibit and eliminate nuclear weapons in light of their unacceptable humanitarian consequences and associated risks.

11.5 Marshall Islands Cases Before the ICJ - the Nuclear Zero Lawsuits

On 25th April 2014, the Marshall Islands (the Republic of the Marshall Islands - RMI) filed applications against what they believe to be the current nuclear weapons states: China, Democratic People's Republic of Korea (North Korea), France, India, Israel, Pakistan, the Russian Federation, the UK, and the USA.

By doing this, the Marshall Islands have exposed real weaknesses in the current world order with respect to nations exercising their sovereignty: not all states have accepted under Article 36 of the ICJ Statute, compulsory jurisdiction of the ICJ. Indeed, it was not until 24th April 2013 that the Marshall Islands accepted compulsory jurisdiction, this making it possible to make an application to the ICJ in respect of those nuclear weapons states that have also accepted compulsory jurisdiction of the ICJ — India (1974), Pakistan (1960), and UK (2004).

The consequence of that, is that the cases lodged by the Marshall Islands can only proceed in the ICJ against those countries that have accepted jurisdiction of the ICJ. Before the cases can be entered against the other states, those states must also accept the jurisdiction of the ICJ. Therefore the cases lodged in the ICJ against China, North Korea, France, Israel, the Russian Federation and the USA will remain on file at the ICJ until such time as the country accepts ICJ jurisdiction.

The RMI cases are based primarily on Article VI of the Non-Proliferation Treaty. The ICJ 1996 Advisory Opinion is used in places in support of the Applications.

There is a great deal of material prior to 2014, to understand why RMI have suffered a great deal from nuclear weapons tests. See, for example, Grief (1987).

11.6 UK Renewal of Trident

In terms of the timing of the publication of this book, and given that in the coming months, or a small number of years, the UK is expected to have Parliamentary debates and a vote concerning the renewal or updating of its Trident nuclear weapons system, the decision has been taken to include on the following pages, the text of the Application in the International Court of Justice by the Republic of the Marshall Islands against the United Kingdom. The reason for doing that, is that the Application contains a great deal of interesting and useful information about UK nuclear weapons policy and action. This can help to inform the debate that will be taking place in the coming months.

Given the likely Parliamentary debate (coming after the preparation of this book in 2015) about Trident renewal, it is important to provide access to the evolution of practices and policies of the UK towards nuclear weapons.

For this reason, the decision has been taken to include the full text of the RMI Application. It follows on the next 33 pages (or so). The text has been reformatted for the purposes of this book, and anyone who needs a copy of the original version should apply for that (RMI, 2014) from the International Court of Justice. A paper that is also very useful for this issue, is Grief (2011).

11.7 Application Instituting Proceedings against the United Kingdom

submitted on 24 April 2014 by
THE REPUBLIC OF THE MARSHALL ISLANDS to
THE INTERNATIONAL COURT OF JUSTICE re
obligation to pursue in good faith and conclude negotiations leading to nuclear disarmament

To the Registrar, International Court of Justice.

The Undersigned, being duly authorized by the Government of the Republic of the Marshall Islands, state as follows:

I. Introduction and Summary

1. It is a most fundamental legal and moral principle that bargains should be kept. This is embedded in international law through the principle of *pacta sunt servanda*[7]. The bargain which this Application concerns is that embodied in the 1968 Treaty on the Non-Proliferation of Nuclear Weapons (hereafter "the Treaty" or "the NPT")[8], whereby the non-nuclear-weapon States have agreed not to acquire nuclear weapons and the NPT nuclear-weapon States have agreed to negotiate their elimination.

2. This Application is not an attempt to re-open the question of the legality of nuclear weapons addressed by this Court in its Advisory Opinion of 8 July 1996 on the Legality of the Threat or Use of Nuclear Weapons[9]. Rather, the focus of this Application is the failure to fulfil the obligations enshrined in Article VI of the NPT and customary international law; and particularly the failure of the NPT nuclear-weapon States to keep their part of the strategic bargain and do what the Court unanimously called for based on its analysis of Article VI, namely "pursue in good faith and bring to a conclusion negotiations leading to nuclear disarmament in all its aspects under strict and effective international control"[10].

3. In its Advisory Opinion, the Court observed that "[t]he destructive power of nuclear weapons cannot be contained in either space or time" and that such weapons "have the potential to destroy all

---
7 Expressed in Article 26 of the Vienna Convention on the Law of Treaties 1969.
8 729 UNTS 161.
9 *L C.J Reports 1996*, p. 226.
10 *Id.*, para. 105, point 2F.

civilization and the entire ecosystem of the planet"[11]. It acknowledged "the unique characteristics of nuclear weapons, and in particular their destructive capacity, their capacity to cause untold human suffering, and their ability to cause damage to generations to come"[12].

4. Unless the required negotiations, aimed at reaching the required conclusions, take place, we shall continue to face the very real prospect of the 'devastation that would be visited upon all mankind by a nuclear war'[13]. We shall also continue to face the possibility, even the likelihood, of nuclear weapons being used by accident, miscalculation or design[14], and of their proliferation. As Nobel Peace Laureate Sir Joseph Rotblat pointed out: "If some nations - including the most powerful militarily -say that they need nuclear weapons for their security, then such security cannot be denied to other countries which really feel insecure. Proliferation of nuclear weapons is the logical consequence of this nuclear policy"[15].

5. In its Advisory Opinion, the Court observed: "In the long run, international law, and with it the stability of the international order which it is intended to govern, are bound to suffer from the continuing difference of views with regard to the legal status of weapons as deadly as nuclear weapons" [16]. A coherent legal system cannot countenance its own destruction or that of the community whose activities it seeks to regulate[17]. That is why fulfilment of the obligation "to pursue in good faith and bring to a conclusion negotiations leading to nuclear disarmament in all its aspects under strict and effective international control" is so important.

6. Equally, a coherent and civilized legal system cannot tolerate

---

[11] *Id.*, para. 35.
[12] *Id.*, para. 36.
[13] NPT preamble, 2nd recital.
[14] In 1996 Lord Carver, former UK Chief of the Defence Staff (the professional head of the UK's armed forces and the principal military adviser to the Secretary of State for Defence and to the UK Government) stated that "the indefinite deployment of nuclear weapons carries a high risk of their ultimate use - intentionally, by accident or inadvertence". See Hansard, HL Deb, 28 October 1996, vol. 575, col. 134.
[15] Joseph Rotblat, "Science and Nuclear Weapons: Where Do We Go From Here?" The Blackaby Papers, No. 5, December 2004, p. 7. In February 2007, Mohamed ElBaradei, then Director General of the IAEA, said that Britain cannot "modernise its Trident submarines and then tell everyone else that nuclear weapons are not needed in the future". See David Blair, 'UN nuclear watchdog: Trident is hypocritical', *Daily Telegraph,* 20 February 2007.
[16] *Supra,* n. 3, para. 98.
[17] As B.S. Chimni has stated, "No legal system can confer on any of its members the right to annihilate the community which engenders it and whose activities it seeks to regulate". B.S. Chirnni, "Nuclear Weapons and International Law: Some Reflections", in International Law in Transition: Essays in Memory of Judge Nagendra Singh, 1992, p. 142. Quoted by Judge Weeramantry in Section V.1 of his Dissenting Opinion in the Advisory Opinion in *Legality of the Threat or Use of Nuclear Weapons, supra,* n. 3, at p. 522; see also the Dissenting Opinion of Judge Shahabuddeen, id., p. 393: "Thus, however far-reaching may be the rights conferred by sovereignty, those rights cannot extend beyond the framework within which sovereignty itself exists; in particular, they cannot violate the framework. The framework shuts out the right of a State to embark on a course of action which would dismantle the basis of the framework by putting an end to civilization and annihilating mankind".

unacceptable harm to humanity. A lawful and sustainable world order is predicated on a civilizational right to survival rooted in "the principles of humanity" [18] and "elementary considerations of humanity" [19] which help to shape an emerging "law of humanity"[20], the international law for humankind of which the nuclear disarmament obligation is a key element. Yet it is now 68 years since the very first United Nations General Assembly Resolution sought to put in motion the elimination from national arsenals of nuclear weapons and other weapons of mass destruction[21], almost 45 years since the NPT entered into force and nearly 20 years since the Court delivered its Advisory Opinion. The long delay in fulfilling the obligations enshrined in Article VI of the NPT constitutes a flagrant denial of human justice[22].

7. Inspired and guided by these principles and values, this is an Application instituting proceedings against the United Kingdom ("UK"), an NPT nuclear-weapon State. The underlying claims, described in more detail herein, are that the UK is: (i) in continuing breach of its obligations under Article VI of the NPT, including specifically its obligation to pursue in good faith negotiations to cease the nuclear arms race at an early date, as well as to pursue in good faith negotiations leading to nuclear disarmament in all its aspects under strict and effective international control; (ii) in continuing breach of customary international law with respect to the same obligations; and (iii) in continuing breach of its obligation to perform its international legal obligations in good faith.

8. The Applicant herein is The Republic of the Marshall Islands (the "Marshall Islands", "RMI" or "Applicant). The Applicant is a non-nuclear-weapon State Party to the NPT. The Marshall Islands acceded to the Treaty on 30 January 1995 and has continued to be a Party to it since that time.

---

18 From the Martens Clause as expressed in Article 1, paragraph 2 of Protocol 1 1977 Additional to the Geneva Conventions 1949: "In cases not covered by this Protocol or by other international agreements, civilians and combatants remain under the protection and authority of the principles of international law derived from established custom, from the principles of humanity and from the dictates of public conscience".
19 *Corfu Channel case, Judgment of April <Jh, 1949, J C.J Reports 1949*, p. 22.
20 See e.g. the Opinion of the Tribunal in the *Einsatzgruppen case* (1948): "[An] evaluation of international right and wrong, which heretofore existed only in the heart of mankind, has now been written into the books of men as the law of humanity. This law is not restricted to events of war. It envisages the protection of humanity at all times". *United States of America v. Otto Ohlendorf, et al,* Military Tribunal II, Case No. 9 (1948), in *Trials of War Criminals Before the Nuremberg Military Tribunals Under Control Council Law No. 10*, Vol. IV, Nuremberg, October 1946 -April 1940 (U.S. Government Printing Office, 1950-872486), p. 497, *available at* http://www.loc.gov/rr/frd/Military _Law/pdfi'NT_war-criminals_ Vol-IV.pdf.
21 AIRES/I (I), 24 January 1946.
22 Cf Judge Cancado Trindade's remarks in Section XIII of his Separate Opinion in *Questions Relating to the Obligation to Prosecute or Extradite (Belgium v. Senegal), !CJ Reports 2012*, pp. 544-548; especially at para. 145 where he contrasts "the brief time of human beings (vita brevis) and the often prolonged time of human justice".

9. While cessation of the nuclear arms race and nuclear disarmament are vitally important objectives for the entire international community, the Marshall Islands has a particular awareness of the dire consequences of nuclear weapons. The Marshall Islands was the location of repeated nuclear weapons testing from 1946 to 1958, during the time that the international community had placed it under the trusteeship of the United States ("U.S".)[23]. During those 12 years, 67 nuclear weapons of varying explosive power were detonated in the Marshall Islands, at varying distances from human population[24]. According to the 3 September 2012 Report of Calin Georgescu, a Special Rapporteur to the UN Human Rights Council, the devastating adverse impact on the Marshall Islands of those nuclear substances and wastes continues to this day[25]. The Special Rapporteur concludes that "the harm suffered by the Marshallese people has resulted in an increased global understanding of the movement of radionuclides through marine and terrestrial environments," and urges the international community to "learn from the Marshallese experience with nuclear contamination, particularly the ...understanding of the relationship between radioiodine and thyroid cancer"[26].

10. With regard to the RMI's interest in bringing this Application to the Court, the following should be added. It is well known that over recent years the RMI has been preoccupied with combating the extremely harmful consequences that the effects of climate change have for its very survival. While focusing on the problem of climate change, the RMI has come to realize that it cannot ignore the other major threat to its survival: the ongoing threat posed by the existence of large arsenals of nuclear weapons the use of which, according to the Court, "seems scarcely reconcilable with respect for [...] requirements [of the principles and rules of law applicable in armed conflict]"[27]. It is obvious that the RMI's participation in the common struggle against climate change needs to lead to firm commitments by all States, which commitments must include not only moral, but also legal obligations aimed at realizing concrete, clear-cut goals in order to remove the threat of devastation caused by continued reliance on the use of fossil fuel energy sources. It is from this perspective of striving to reach agreement

---

[23] Report of the Special Rapporteur on the implications for human rights of the environmentally sound management and disposal of hazardous substances and wastes, Calin Georgescu; Addendum, Mission to the Marshall Islands (27-30 March 2012) and the United States of America (24-27 April 2012): 3 September 2012, Doc. A/HRC/21/48/Add. I.
[24] *Id.*, paras. 1-18.
[25] *Id.*, para. 19.
[26] *Id.*, para. 66(b).
[27] *Supra*, n. 3, para. 95

on such commitments in the struggle against climate change that the RMI has concluded that it is no longer acceptable simply to be a party to the NPT while total nuclear disarmament pursuant to Article VI and customary international law remains at best a distant prospect. This Application seeks to ensure that the legal obligations undertaken 44 years ago by the UK in the context of the NPT do indeed deliver the promised result.

11. One of the reasons why the RMI became a Party to the NPT is that this Treaty is the key instrument of the international community for ridding the world of nuclear weapons[28]. The Treaty contains the solemn promise and legal obligation of the nuclear weapon States to sit down and negotiate towards total nuclear disarmament. That promise has been broken and that obligation has not been met.

12. Article VI of the Treaty states, in its entirety, as follows:

> "Each of the Parties to the Treaty undertakes to pursue negotiations in good faith on effective measures relating to cessation of the nuclear arms race at an early date and to nuclear disarmament, and on a treaty on general and complete disarmament under strict and effective international control."

13. As previously stated, the Court concluded its Advisory Opinion of 8 July 1996 by unanimously holding that "[t]here exists an obligation to pursue in good faith and bring to a conclusion negotiations leading to nuclear disarmament in all its aspects under strict and effective international control"[29].

14. More than four decades after signing and ratifying the NPT, the UK maintains and continuously modernizes its nuclear arsenal.

15. The UK has not pursued in good faith negotiations to cease the nuclear arms race at an early date through comprehensive nuclear disarmament or other measures, and instead is taking actions to improve its nuclear weapons system and to maintain it for the indefinite future.

16. Similarly, the UK has not fulfilled its obligation to pursue in good faith negotiations leading to nuclear disarmament in all its aspects under strict and effective international control and instead has opposed the efforts of the great majority of States to initiate such negotiations.

17. These obligations are not limited to the States Parties to the Treaty, but also apply to all States as a matter of customary international

---

[28] At the UN High-Level Meeting on Nuclear Disarmament, 26 September 2013, Hon. Mr. Phillip Muller, Minister of Foreign Affairs, Republic of the Marshall Islands, stated that the RMI's "deeper purpose" is "that no nation and people should ever have to bear witness to the burden of exposure to the devastating impacts of nuclear weapons",
http://www.un.org/en/ga/68/meetings/nucleardisarmament/pdf/MH_en.pdf.
[29] *Supra*, n. 3, para. 105, point 2F.

law.

18. Further, the obligation of a State to perform its legal obligations in good faith, whether arising under a treaty or pursuant to customary international law, is itself a legal obligation which the UK has breached.

II. Facts

A. *The Five Nuclear Weapon States Parties to the NPT*

19. The U.S. was the first country in the world to develop and test nuclear weapons. The U.S. used nuclear weapons in warfare on the Japanese cities of Hiroshima and Nagasaki on 6 August 1945 and 9 August 1945 respectively[30]. The U.S. was the sole possessor of nuclear weapons in the world until the Soviet Union tested its first nuclear weapon on 29 August 1949. In 1952, the UK tested its first nuclear weapon. In 1960, France tested its first nuclear weapon. In 1964, China tested its first nuclear weapon.

20. In the 1960s, the UK negotiated with other countries, including the U.S. and the Soviet Union, both possessors of nuclear weapons, and States not possessing nuclear weapons, to reach agreement on what became the Nuclear Non-Proliferation Treaty. The U.S., Russia, the UK, France and China, all Parties to the NPT, are the only States meeting the Treaty's definition of a "nuclear-weapon State" for "the purposes of this Treaty"[31].

21. The Treaty was opened for signature on 1 July 1968, and entered into force on 5 March 1970. The UK signed the NPT on 1 July 1968 in London, Moscow and Washington and ratified it on 27 November 1968 in London and Washington and on 29 November 1968 in Moscow. The UK is one of the Treaty's three Depositary Governments[32].

B. *The Nine States Possessing Nuclear Weapons*

22. In addition to the five NPT nuclear-weapon States, four non-NPT States are known to possess nuclear weapons: India, Pakistan, Israel and Democratic People's Republic of Korea ("DPRK")[33].

---

[30] On 1 July 1945, Prime Minister Winston Churchill gave the UK's approval for atomic bombs to be dropped on Japan. See Peter Hennessy, *Cabinets and the Bomb* (The British Academy, 2007), p. 8.
[31] Article IX.3 of the ·NPT provides: "For the purposes of this Treaty, a nuclear-weapon State is one which has manufactured and exploded a nuclear weapon or other nuclear explosive device prior to 1 January 1967".
[32] The others are the Russian Federation and the U.S. See http://disarmament.un.org/treaties/t/npt.
[33] Regarding the DPRK, see *infra*, n. 126.

23. According to the Stockholm International Peace Research Institute ("SIPRI"), the individual and collective world nuclear forces as of January, 2013, were as follows:

World nuclear forces, January 2013[34]
(All figures are approximate)

Country	Year of first nuclear test	Deployed Warheads[a]	Other Warheads[b]	Total Inventory
United States	1945	2,150[c]	5,550	~7,700[d]
Russia	1949	~1,800	6,700[e]	~8,500[f]
United Kingdom	1952	160	65	225
France	1960	~290	~10	~300
China	1964		~250	~250
India	1974		90-110	90-110
Pakistan	1998		100-120	100-120
Israel			~80	~80
North Korea	2006			6-8?
Total		~4,400	~12,865	~17,270

[a] 'Deployed' means warheads placed on missiles or located on bases with operational forces.

[b] These are warheads in reserve, awaiting dismantlement or that require some preparation (e.g. assembly or loading on launchers) before they become fully operationally available.

[c] In addition to strategic warheads, this figure includes nearly 200 non-strategic (tactical) nuclear weapons deployed in Europe.

[d] This figure includes the U.S. Department of Defense nuclear stockpile of c. 4650 warheads and another c. 3000 retired warheads that are awaiting dismantlement.

[e] This figure includes c. 700 warheads for nuclear-powered ballistic missile submarines (SSBNs) in overhaul and bombers, 2000 non-strategic nuclear weapons for use by short-range naval, air force and air defense forces, and c. 4000 retired warheads awaiting dismantlement.

[f] This includes a military stockpile of c. 4500 nuclear warheads and another c. 4000 retired warheads await dismantlement.

---

34 *See* Shannon N. Kile, "World Nuclear Forces", SIPRI Yearbook 2013 (Oxford University Press: Oxford, 2013). The question mark (?) against North Korea's total inventory is in the original.

C. The UK and the Nuclear Arms Race

1. Early Nuclear History[35]

24. On 3 October 1952, the first British atomic device was detonated in the Monte Bello Islands off north-western Australia. On 7 November 1953, the UK's first operational atomic bomb, the Blue Danube, arrived at RAF Wittering from AWE Aldermaston[36].

25. On 26 July 1954 the Cabinet agreed to the manufacture of a much more powerful British hydrogen bomb and on 15 May 1957 the UK tested a thermonuclear device at Christmas Island in the Pacific[37].

26. On 4 August 1958, the U.S. and UK governments concluded the Agreement for Co-operation on the Uses of Atomic Energy for Mutual Defence Purposes (the "Mutual Defence Agreement" or "MDA")[38].

27. On 3 January 1963, the Cabinet authorized the purchase of Polaris C3 submarine- launched ballistic missiles and re-entry vehicles from the U.S. Government. On January 25, 1965, the decision was taken to build four Resolution-class submarines to carry the Polaris missiles, partly to ensure that one boat would always be on station when the Royal Navy assumed the main nuclear weapons system role in the late 1960s. HMS Resolution, the first of the four Polaris missile-carrying submarines, was commissioned on 30 October 1967[39] and on June 14, 1969, Polaris submarines formally took over the primary strategic nuclear weapons deployment role from the RAF's 'V' bomber force[40].

28. The development of the Super Antelope (later known as Chevaline) re-entry body for the UK's Polaris warheads was approved on 30 October 1973. This was because the UK could no longer be certain that a sufficient number of Polaris warheads would penetrate Soviet ABM defences to cause the damage required to exert a credible deterrent effect. In November 1982 the Ministry of Defence announced

---

35 See Hennessy, *supra*, n. 24, pp. 7-20. (Hennessy, 2007)

36 58 Blue Danube bombs were produced. They were in service with the RAF until 1961.

37 The device yielded 300 kilotons, 30% of the megaton target. On 8 November 1957 Britain's first megaton hydrogen bomb exploded off Christmas Island, yielding 1.8 megatons. See Hennessy, *supra*, n. 24, p. 10.

38 Treaty Series No.41 (1958) Cmnd 537. *See* Hennessy, *id.*, p. 11. The MDA has been renewed from time to time, most recently in 2004.

39 The other three Polaris submarines were HMS Repulse, HMS Renown and HMS Revenge.

40 *See* Hennessy, *supra*, n. 24, p. 14. The four nuclear-powered submarines were each equipped with 16 Polaris missiles, with three 200-kiloton warheads on each missile. Polaris was modernized with the Chevaline upgrade to have a number of dummy or decoy warheads on each missile as well, but each missile could only be used against one target.

that Chevaline-equipped missiles were operational at sea[41].

29. In July 1980, the UK government announced the decision to buy the U.S. Trident C4 missile system as a replacement for the Polaris system, which was due to reach the end of its service life in the early 1990s. In March 1982, however, the order was changed to the Trident II D5, a new missile announced by the U.S. in October 1981. This ensured missile commonality between the U.S. Navy and the Royal Navy. The UK defence establishment wanted to ensure that any future UK nuclear system remained in step with U.S. nuclear hardware and weapon programmes after the difficult experience with the indigenous Chevaline upgrade. Former Permanent Under Secretary at the Ministry of Defence, Sir Michael Quinlan, stated in 2004 that "Purely in weight of strike potential the United Kingdom could have been content with less than Trident could offer, even in the C4 version originally chosen (let alone D5 version to which the United Kingdom switched in early 1982, when it had become clear that the United States was committed to proceed with its acquisition and deployment). The original choice and the switch were driven in large measure by the long-term financial and logistic benefits of commonality with the United States"[42].

2. The UK's Current Nuclear Arsenal[43]

30. The UK's nuclear weapons system is based upon the submarine-launched Trident D5 missile. It is the UK's third-generation strategic nuclear weapon system. Trident was procured during the final decade of the Cold War and was brought into service to replace Polaris over a six-year period beginning in December 1994[44]. It is now the UK's only nuclear weapons system, the UK having retired its air-launched WE177 free-fall nuclear bombs and repatriated forward-deployed US tactical nuclear weapons operated by UK forces under dual-key arrangements in the 1990s[45].

31. The Trident nuclear weapons system has three technical components[46].

---

41 *Id.*
42 Michael Quinlan, "The British Experience", in Henry Sokolski (ed.), *Getting MAD: mutual assured destruction, its origins and practice* (Strategic Studies Institute, Anny War College: Carlisle, PA, November 2004), p. 271.
43 See House of Commons Defence Committee, 'The Future of the UK's Nuclear Deterrent: the White Paper' (HC 225-1), Vol. 1, ch. 2.
44 HMS Vanguard, the first Trident missile-carrying submarine, was commissioned on 14 August 1993 and sailed on the first Trident operational patrol in December 1994. HMS Repulse returned to Faslane on 13 May 1996 at the end of the final Polaris operational patrol, marking the end of Polaris' 27 years of continuous patrols. *See* Hennessy, *supra*, n. 24, p. 18.
45 *See supra*, n. 37, Vol.1, para. 8.
46 *Id.*, paras. 9-10.

a) The Vanguard-class nuclear-powered ballistic submarines (SSBN), of which the UK has four: HMS Vanguard, HMS Victorious, HMS Vigilant and HMS Vengeance, designed and built in the UK by Vickers Shipbuilding and Engineering Ltd (VSEL), now BAE Systems, in Barrow-in-Furness, Cumbria. Refit and maintenance are carried out by Devonport Management Limited in Devonport, Plymouth, UK.

b) The Trident D5 submarine-launched intercontinental ballistic missile (ICBM), manufactured in the US by Lockheed Martin. Under the Polaris Sales Agreement as modified for Trident[47], the UK has title to 58 missiles[48]. Aside from those currently deployed, the missiles are held in a communal pool at the US Strategic Weapons facility at King's Bay, Georgia, US. Each submarine is capable of carrying up to 16 Trident D5 missiles.

c) The components for the nuclear warheads, including qualitative improvements to them, are made in the UK at the Atomic Weapons Establishment (AWE) Aldermaston, Berkshire, and assembled at nearby AWE Burghfield. There is extensive collaboration between the UK and the US on the production of the UK's warheads under the Mutual Defence Agreement, "which provides for extensive cooperation on nuclear warhead and reactor technologies, in particular the exchange of classified information concerning nuclear weapons to improve 'design, development and fabrication' capability and the transfer of nuclear warhead-related materials"[49] As a result, some components of the UK warheads are manufactured, and undergo qualitative improvements, in the U.S[50].

32. The submarine fleet is supported by an extensive onshore infrastructure. The Vanguard submarines are based at HM Naval Base Clyde, Faslane, Scotland. Nuclear warheads are fitted to the D5

---

[47] The Polaris Sales Agreement was signed in Washington DC on 6 April 1963. On 30 September 1980 an exchange of diplomatic notes incorporated the Trident sale into the Polaris Sales Agreement.

[48] House of Commons Defence Committee, Session 2005-06, Eighth Report, para. 21.

[49] N. Ritchie, "A Nuclear Weapons-Free World? Britain, Trident and the Challenges Ahead", Palgrave Macmillan 2012, p. 92. Ritchie goes on to state that "Britain remains highly dependent on the US for nuclear weapon systems, technology, and support": *id.*, p. 95.

[50] John Ainslie, "United Kingdom", in Ray Acheson, ed., Assuring Destruction Forever: Nuclear Weapon Modernization Around the World (Reaching Critical Will -a project of the Women's International League for Peace and Freedom, 2012), pp. 68-71, http://www.reachingcriticalwill.org/images/documents/Publications/modemization/assuring-destruction forever.pdf.

missiles at the Royal Naval Armaments Depot Coulport (part of HM Naval Base Clyde). The warheads are transported by road from AWE Burghfield to Coulport, where they are placed in underground bunkers in the Trident Area. When required they are taken to the Explosive Handling Jetty where they are fitted onto the missiles on the Trident submarines.

33. The Strategic Defence Review, published on 8 July 1998[51], affirmed the Government's commitment to maintaining a nuclear weapons system but made a number of changes to it. The warhead stockpile was to be cut from the ceiling of up to 300 warheads maintained by the previous government to fewer than 200 operationally available warheads. The patrol cycle of the Trident submarines was also relaxed with normally only one submarine on patrol at any one time. As with pre-Chevaline Polaris[52], each submarine would now carry a maximum of 48 warheads, rather than the ceiling of up to 96. The Trident submarine's alert status was also to be reduced. Missiles had not been targeted for some years but, in addition, submarines would normally now be at several days' rather than 15 minutes' notice to fire[53]. A requirement for an additional seven Trident missile bodies was cancelled, leaving a new total of 58.

34. The Strategic Defence and Security Review, published on 19 October 2010[54], reaffirmed the UK's commitment to a submarine-launched nuclear weapons system on continuous alert based on the Trident missile delivery system, and announced that: the number of warheads on board each deployed submarine would be reduced from 48 to 40; the requirement for operationally available warheads would be reduced from fewer than 160 to no more than 120; the number of operational missiles on the Vanguard class submarines would be reduced to no more than 8; and the UK's overall nuclear weapons stockpile would be reduced from not more than 225 to no more than 180 by the mid-2020s[55]

---

51 Strategic Defence Review 1998 (Cm 3999), *available at* http://webarchive.nationalarchives.gov. uk/20121026065214/www.mod.uk/NR/rdonlyres/65F3D7AC- 4340-4119-93A2-20825848E50E/O/sdr1998 _complete. pdf
52 *see supra*, para. 27.
53 Strategic Defence Review, *supra*, n. 45, para. 68.
54 Securing Britain in an Age of Uncertainty: The Strategic Defence and Security Review, October 2010 (Cm 7948), *available at*
http://www.direct.gov. uk/prod_consum_dg/groups/dg_digitalassets/@dg/@en/ documents/digitalasset/d g_191634.pdf
55 *Id.*, para. 3.11.

3. Nuclear Policy, Doctrine and Expenditure

35. The Royal Navy has maintained unbroken nuclear weapon patrols since 1968. The 1998 Strategic Defence Review stated that the UK would continue to maintain these continuous-at-sea nuclear armed patrols. This means that one of the four Vanguard-class submarines is on patrol at any given time[56].

36. Trident is the UK's most advanced nuclear weapon system to date. With a range of between 6,500 kilometres and 12,000 kilometres, depending on payload, Trident's greater speed, accuracy and multiple independently targetable warheads distinguish it from, and enable it to reach more targets than, its predecessor, Polaris Chevaline.

37. As the Defence Select Committee noted in 1994:

> Trident's accuracy and sophistication in other respects does - and was always intended to - represent a significant enhancement of the UK's nuclear capability. We have invested a great deal of money to make it possible to attack more targets with greater effectiveness using nominally equivalent explosive power[57].

38. Trident was originally designed as a strategic nuclear system with respect to threats posed by the Soviet Union. In 1993, however, following the end of the Cold War, the then Secretary of State for Defence announced that in future Trident's role would be to deter "potential aggressors" from threatening UK "vital interests". In order to do this, Trident was assigned an additional "sub-strategic" role[58]:

> The ability to undertake a massive strike with strategic systems is not enough to ensure deterrence. An aggressor might, in certain circumstances, gamble on a lack of will ultimately to resort to such dire action. It is therefore important for the credibility of our deterrent that the United Kingdom also possesses the capability . to undertake a more limited nuclear strike in order to induce a political decision to halt aggression by delivering an unmistakable message of our willingness to defend our vital interests to the utmost[59].

---

56 Strategic Defence Review, *supra*, n. 45, para. 66.
57 HC 297 of Session 1993-94, p. xiv.
58 Hansard, HC Deb, 18 October 1993, col. 34. The UK's sub-strategic capability was at that time provided by the soon to be retired WEI 77 bomb carried on Tornado aircraft.
59 Malcolm Rifkind, 'UK Defence Strategy; A Continuing Role for Nuclear Weapons', 16 November 1993, Centre for Defence Studies, King's College London; see also the Strategic Defence Review 1998, para. 63: "The credibility of deterrence also depends on retaining an option for a limited strike that would not automatically lead to a full scale nuclear exchange. Unlike Polaris and Chevaline, Trident must also be capable of performing this 'sub-strategic' role".

263

39. As part of the agreement under which the UK procured Polaris and subsequently Trident missiles from the US, UK Trident forces are assigned to NATO to be used for the defence of the Alliance "except where the UK government may decide that supreme national interests are at stake"[60]. The UK is therefore committed to NATO's nuclear policy, which since the mid-1960s has been based on a doctrine of "flexible response"[61]. One of the key elements of NATO's nuclear doctrine is that the Alliance refuses to rule out the first use of NATO nuclear weapons, thereby allowing its nuclear planners to prepare for that option[62].

40. Similarly, the UK has always refused to rule out the first use of its nuclear weapons, especially in cases where biological or chemical weapons may have been used. For example, shortly after the 1997 general election, the then Minister of State Dr John Reid stated:

> The role of deterrence ...must not be overlooked. Even if a potential aggressor has developed missiles with the range to strike at the United Kingdom, and nuclear, biological or chemical warheads to be delivered by those means, he would have to consider - he would do well to consider - the possible consequences of such an attack ...It seems unlikely that a dictator who was willing to strike another country with weapons of mass destruction would be so trusting as to feel entirely sure that that country would not respond with the power at its disposal[63].

41. Following the terrorist attacks on the U.S. in September 2001, a new chapter of the Strategic Defence Review extended the role of nuclear weapons further to include allegedly deterring terrorist organisations:

> The UK's nuclear weapons have a continuing use as a means of deterring major strategic military threats, and they have a continuing role in guaranteeing the ultimate security of the UK. But we also want it to be clear, particularly to the leaders of states of concern and terrorist organisations, that all our forces play a part in deterrence, and that we have a broad range of responses available[64].

42. The implication is that the UK is willing, if deemed to be necessary, to use its nuclear weapons against States of concern and

---

[60] The British Strategic Nuclear Force: Text of Letters exchanged between the Prime Minister and the President of the United States and between the Secretary of State for Defence and the US Secretary of Defense. The letters are reproduced in 'Polaris Sales Agreement between the United States and the United Kingdom' signed in Washington on 6 April 1963.
[61] "The Alliance's Strategic Concept", NATO Press Release NAC-S(99)65, 24 April 1999.
[62] In 2006 the then Defence Secretary, Des Browne, stated: "A policy of no first use of nuclear weapons would be incompatible with our and NATO's doctrine of deterrence", Hansard, HC, 22 May 2006, col. 1331W.
[63] Hansard, HC Deb, 4 December 1997, cols. 576-577.
[64] Strategic Defence Review, New Chapter, 18 July 2002, Vol.1, para. 21, *available at* http://indianstrategicknowledgeonline.com/web/sdr _a_new_chapter_cm5566_vol1.pdf.

terrorist organisations[65].

43. The 2010 Strategic Defence and Security Review states that the UK "would only consider using nuclear weapons in extreme circumstances of self-defence, including the defence of our NATO allies", adding: "we remain deliberately ambiguous about precisely when, how and at what scale we would contemplate their use"[66].

44. The Strategic Defence and Security Review reaffirms in modified form existing assurances to non-nuclear-weapon States Parties to the NPT. It states "that the UK will not use or threaten to use nuclear weapons against non-nuclear weapon states parties to the NPT" but notes that "this assurance would not apply to any state in material breach of those non-proliferation obligations". It also notes that "while there is currently no direct threat to the UK or its vital interests from states developing capabilities in other weapons of mass destruction, for example chemical and biological, we reserve the right to review this assurance if the future threat, development and proliferation of these weapons make it necessary"[67].

45. The UK has continued to maintain and modernize its nuclear forces with annual expenditure on capital and running costs at around 5 to 6 per cent of the UK defence budget[68]. This does not include costs for recapitalising the Trident system estimated to be £25 billion at outturn prices[69].

4. Current Plans for Modernization and Qualitative Improvements of the UK's Nuclear Arsenal

46. In December 2006 the UK Government published a White Paper which formally opened the process to replace the UK's Trident nuclear weapons system[70]. The White Paper was endorsed by the

---

[65] The 2006 White Paper on *The Future of the United Kingdom's Nuclear Deterrent* stated, at 3-11: "We know that international terrorists are trying to acquire radiological weapons. In future, there are risks that they may try to acquire nuclear weapons. While our nuclear deterrent is not designed to deter non state actors, it should influence the decision-making of any state that might consider transferring nuclear weapons or nuclear technology to terrorists".

[66] Strategic Defence and Security Review, *supra*, n. 48, para. 3.5.

[67] *Id.*, 3.7.

[68] House of Commons Defence Committee, *The Future of the UK's Nuclear Deterrent: the White Paper*, Ninth Report of Session 2006-07, paras. 149, 152; see also Hansard, HL, 7 June 2010, col. WA28; HC, 20 December 2012. col. 908W. In 2010-11 the defence resource budget was c £28bn: Public Expenditure Statistical Analysis 2011, Departmental Budgets, HM Treasury, table 1 .3a, *available at* http://www.hm-treasury.gov.uk/d/pesa_201 I_chapter I.pdf. A recent analysis by Scientists for Global Responsibility has revealed that the UK Government spent an average of £327 million per year on nuclear weapons research and development over the three years from 2008 to 2011. See *UK nuclear weapons R&D spending: Addendum AA1 to Offensive Insecurity*, February 2014, *available at* http://www.sgr.org.uk/publications/uk-nuclear-weapons-rd-spending.

[69] Ministry of Defence (2011) *Initial Gate Parliamentary Report* (London: Ministry of Defence), p. 10.

[70] Ministry of Defence and Foreign and Commonwealth Office, *The Future of the United Kingdom's Nuclear Deterrent*, Cm 6994.

House of Commons on 14 March 2007 when the following motion was carried by 409 votes to 161:

> That this House supports the Government's decisions, as set out in the White Paper The Future of the United Kingdom's Nuclear Deterrent (Cm 6994), to take the steps necessary to maintain the UK's minimum strategic nuclear deterrent beyond the life of the existing system and to take further steps towards meeting the UK's disarmament responsibilities under Article VI of the Non-Proliferation Treaty[71].

47. According to British Pugwash, the effect of that vote and its present and future consequences are as follows:

> Parliament voted to authorize the initial 'Concept' phase of the Trident replacement system. The next major milestone, known as the 'Initial Gate' decision, was to move to the 'Assessment' phase, involving further detailed refinement of a set of design options to enable selection of a preferred solution. The government announced the Initial Gate decision on May 18, 2011. The next big decision to move to the 'Demonstration and Manufacture' phase is the Main Gate' decision, now scheduled for 2016 (delayed from 2014 in October 2010). That is supposed to be the key decision-point when the finalized submarine design is adopted; contracts to build the new boats are then tendered, and billions more pounds will be irrevocably committed to construction of a new generation of nuclear weapons[72].

48. The Strategic Defence and Security Review 2010 states:

> Under the 1958 UK-US Agreement for Cooperation on the Uses of Atomic Energy for Mutual Defence Purposes (the 'Mutual Defence Agreement') we have agreed on the future of the Trident D5 delivery system and determined that a replacement warhead is not required until at least the late 2030s. Decisions on replacing the warhead will not therefore be required in this Parliament. This will defer £500 million of spending from the next 10 years[73].

49. Under the UK-US Mutual Defence Agreement, a new "arming, fusing and firing system" developed by the US is to be used in current UK warheads[74]. The system would improve the nuclear warhead's effectiveness against hardened targets. The Trident II D5 missile can carry two types of re-entry vehicle that house each nuclear warhead: the Mark 4 for the U.S. W76 warhead and the Mark 5 for the more

---

[71] Hansard, HC Deb, 14 March 2007, cols. 298-407.
[72] Briefings on Nuclear Security, 'Trident: The Initial Gate Decision', *available at* http://www.britishpugwash.org/documents/Briefing%203%20-%20Initial%20Gate.pdf.
[73] *Supra*, n. 48, para. 3.12.
[74] Richard Norton-Taylor, "Trident more effective with US arming device, tests suggest," The Guardian, 6 April 2011, *available at* http://www.theguardian.com/uk/2011/apr/06/trident-us-arming-system-test; see also Hans M. Kristensen and Robert S. Norris, "British Nuclear Forces," Bulletin of the Atomic Scientists, September/October 2011 vol. 67 no. 5 89-97, *available at* http://bos.sagepub.com/ content/67/5/89.full#ref-24.

modern and higher yield W88 warhead. The UK purchased the Mark 4 RV and designed a warhead to meet Mk4 RV specifications in terms of weight, size, shape, centre of gravity, and centre of inertia. The U.S. is modernizing its W76 warheads and Mk4 re-entry vehicles, including launcher, navigation, fire control, guidance, and re-entry systems[75]. The modernized W76-1 and Mk4A RV have improved the accuracy of the warheads[76]. These improvements have cascaded through to the UK's Trident warhead and re entry vehicle[77]. The UK government has acknowledged procurement of the Mk4A RV[78].

Preliminary work on a successor warhead is also underway under the Nuclear Warhead Capability Sustainment Programme at AWE Aldermaston[79]. The replacement submarine will be quieter and stealthier[80]. All of these efforts confirm that the UK continues to be actively engaged in qualitative improvements to its nuclear weapons system.

50. On 2 November 2010, the UK and France concluded a bilateral Treaty for Defence and Security Cooperation[81]. Article 1 of the Treaty provides, *inter alia*:

> The Parties, building on the existing strong links between their respective defense and security communities and armed forces, undertake to build a long-term mutually beneficial partnership in defense and security with the aims of:
> ...
> 4. ensuring the viability and safety of their national deterrents, consistent with the Treaty on the Non-Proliferation of Nuclear Weapons[82].

51. On 18 May 2011, when informing Parliament that the Government had approved the 'Initial Gate' for the nuclear weapons system successor programme, the Secretary of State for Defence explained:

---

[75] Ainslie, *supra*, n. 44, at pp. 71-72.
[76] *Id.*, at p. 72; Hans Kristensen, 'Administration Increases Submarine Nuclear Warhead Production Plan', FAS Blog, Federation of American Scientists, 30 August 2007, *available at* http://www.fas.org/blog/ssp/2007 /08/us_!ripples_submarine_ warhead.php.
[77] Ainslie, *id.; see also* Hans Kristensen, 'British Submarines, to Receive Upgraded US Nuclear Warhead', FAS Strategic Security Blog, I April 2011, *available at* http://www.fas.org/blog/ssp/20 I 1/04/britishw76- l.php.
[78] Ainslie, *id* , pp. 68-69; Hansard, HC, 8 December 2009, col. 214W.
[79] Ainslie, *id* , pp. 70-71; Hansard, HC Deb, 28 November 2012, col. 353W.
[80] Ainslie, *id* , at pp. 72-73.
[81] France No. 01 (2010), *available at* http://www.ukdf.org.uk/assets/downloads/UKFranceDefenceCooperationTreaty.pdf#search="defence and security cooperation".
[82] he UK and France also signed a Treaty on Joint Radiographic/Hydrodynamics Facilities to build joint nuclear warhead diagnostic and development facilities at the Valduc site of the Commissariat it l'Energie Atomique et aux Energies Alternatives -Direction des Applications Militaires (CEA-DAM) and at AWE Aldermaston. See http://www.ukdf.org.uk/assets/downloads/UKFranceNuclearTreaty.pdf.

> We have now agreed the broad outline design of the submarine, made some of the design choices-including the propulsion system and the common US-UK missile compartment-and the programme of work we need to start building the first submarine after 2016. We have also agreed the amount of material and parts we will need to buy in advance of the main investment decision. ... Between now and main gate we expect to spend about 15% of the total value of the programme[83].

52. Although the Secretary of State for Defence denied that the Government was "locked into any particular strategy before main gate in 2016" and stated that he would "assist the Liberal Democrats in making the case for alternatives"[84] he declared:

> I am absolutely clear that a minimum nuclear deterrent based on the Trident missile delivery system and continuous-at-sea deterrence is right for the United Kingdom and that it should be maintained, and that remains Government policy[85].

53. On the same day, the Prime Minister told Parliament: "the Government's policy is absolutely clear: we are committed to retaining an independent nuclear deterrent based on Trident"[86].

54. On 30 April 2012, at the First Preparatory Committee for the Ninth Review Conference of the NPT, the Head of the UK Delegation stated:

> As long as large arsenals of nuclear weapons remain and the risk of nuclear proliferation continues, the UK's judgment is that only a credible nuclear capability can provide the necessary ultimate guarantee to our national security. The UK Government is therefore committed to maintaining a minimum national nuclear deterrent, and to proceeding with the renewal of Trident and the submarine replacement programme[87].

55. On 5 March 2013, in a Statement on Nuclear Disarmament, the UK's Permanent Representative to the Conference on Disarmament declared:

---

83 Hansard, HC Deb, 18 May 2011, col. 352.
84 In order to satisfy Liberal Democrat concerns, the government's Coalition Agreement negotiated after the 2010 general election stated that "we will maintain Britain's nuclear deterrent, and have agreed that the renewal of Trident should be scrutinized to ensure value for money. Liberal Democrats will continue to make the case for alternatives". In May 2011 agreement was reached that the government would conduct a formal 18-month assessment of "credible alternatives" to a like-for-like replacement led by the Cabinet Office.
85 *Supra*, n. 77, col. 352.
86 *Id.*, col. 338; *see also* the Prime Minister's statement at a press conference on 2 November 2010 after the UK-France summit at which the Treaty for Defence and Security Cooperation was concluded: "while we will always retain an independent nuclear deterrent, it is right that we look for efficiencies in the infrastructure required to develop and sustain our separate deterrents ...", *available at* http://www.number10.gov.uk/news/uk-france-summit-press-conference/.
87 *Available at* http://www.reachingcriticalwill.org/images/documents/Disarrnament fora/npt/prepcom 12/statements/30April_UK.pdf.

In 2007, the United Kingdom Parliament debated, and approved by a clear majority, the decision to continue with the programme to renew the UK's nuclear deterrent. The Government set out in the 20 I 0 Strategic Defence and Security Review that the UK would maintain a continuous submarine based deterrent and begin the work of replacing its existing submarines which are due to leave service in the 2020s. This remains the UK Government's policy[88].

56. On 5 June 2013, in response to a question in Parliament, the Prime Minister stated: "I am strongly committed to the renewal of our deterrent on a like-for-like basis. I think that is right for Britain"[89].

57. The Trident Alternatives Review[90] was published on 16 July 2013[91]. It had been tasked to answer three questions:

> a. Are there credible alternatives to a submarine-based deterrent?
> b. Are there credible submarine-based alternatives to the current proposal, *e.g.* Astute with cruise missiles?
> c. Are there alternative nuclear postures, i.e. non-continuous-at-sea deterrence ("CASD"), which could maintain credibility?

58. The Trident Alternatives Review concluded: "None of these alternative systems and postures offers the same degree of resilience as the current posture of Continuous at Sea Deterrence, nor could they guarantee a prompt response in all circumstances"[92].

D. *The UK and Nuclear Disarmament*

1. History and General Policy Regarding Negotiation of Nuclear Disarmament

59. As set forth in more detail below, the UK has refused to enter the Trident system (or its predecessors) into nuclear disarmament

---

88 *Available at* http://www.reachingcriticalwill.org/images/documents/Disarmament-fora/cd/2013/Statements/5March_UK.pdf.
89 Hansard, HC Deb, 5 June 2013, col. 1518.
90 *See supra*, n. 78.
91 *Available at*
https://www.gov.uk/government/uploads/system/uploads/attachment_data/file/212745/2013 0716_Trident_Alternatives_Study.pdf. For a commentary on the review, *see* http://www.basicint.org/sites/default/files/ingramcommentary-tar-jul2013.pdf.
92 Trident Alternatives Review, *supra*, n. 85, Executive Summary, para 32. The Review also concluded that "transitioning to any of the realistic alternative systems is now more expensive than a 3 or 4-boat Successor SSBN fleet": *id* , para. 34.

negotiations despite requests to do so.

60. During the 1970s and 1980s, the UK repeatedly refused to enter its nuclear weapon systems into the disarmament negotiations of that time. During the SALT I and SALT II talks in the 1970s, the UK's refusal to allow Polaris to be considered caused problems during negotiations. The Soviet Union repeatedly called for the ballistic missile submarines of US allies in NATO to be taken into consideration and argued that if "US allies in NATO should increase the number of their modem submarines ... the Soviet Union will have the right to a corresponding increase in the number of its submarines"[93].

61. When the UK government first announced its decision to procure the Trident I C4 nuclear weapon system in 1980, it argued that Trident was compatible with the UK's arms control obligations on the grounds that it was: "fully consistent with the terms of the SALT II Treaty"; that "the scale of our new capability will in no way disturb existing and prospective East/West relativities"; and that "Britain's strategic SLBM force lies outside the category of those United States and Soviet long-range, land-based theatre nuclear forces about whose limitation the United States... invited the Soviet Union to negotiate"[94].

62. Similarly, when the UK announced that it was changing to procure the Trident II D5 system in 1982, it argued that the deployed Polaris system and planned Trident system were not relevant to the INF and START negotiations. The government argued that its strategic nuclear weapon systems were not relevant because these negotiations were "bilateral", aimed at achieving a "level of strategic parity" between the U.S. and the Soviet Union. The UK argued that the "British strategic force will account for no more than a very small fraction of the total size of the strategic nuclear forces maintained by the United States and the Soviet Union"[95].

63. During the 1980s, the end of the Cold War resulted in massive cuts to Soviet/Russian military capabilities, in particular reductions in nuclear weapons. However, the UK Government would not allow the UK's nuclear weapons to be included in the negotiations on reductions. In 1987, the INF Treaty was signed by Presidents Reagan and Gorbachev. The Soviet Union had tried to involve UK nuclear weapons in the INF negotiations, but the UK, backed by its NATO allies,

---

[93] "Interim Agreement between the United States of America and the Union of Soviet Socialist Republics on Certain Measures with respect to the Limitation of Strategic Offensive Arms", Unilateral Statement by Minister Semenov, 17 May 1972.
[94] "The Future United Kingdom Strategic Nuclear Deterrent Force", Defence Open Government Document 80/23, Ministry of Defence, July 1980.
[95] "The United Kingdom Trident Programme", Defence Open Government Document 82/1, Ministry of Defence, Cmnd 8517, March 1982.

opposed this. Prime Minister Margaret Thatcher's response to INF was that she believed that nuclear arms cuts in Europe had gone far enough: "I will never give up Britain's independent nuclear deterrent", she told the media[96].

64. According to the Defence Select Committee, as US and Soviet nuclear reductions gathered pace, Mrs. Thatcher "sought and received assurances from the United States that the supply of Trident missiles to the UK will in no way be affected by any future arms control agreement"[97].

65. The Strategic Defence Review 1998 stated: "The Government wishes to see a safer world in which there is no place for nuclear weapons. Progress on arms control is therefore an important objective of foreign and defence policy"[98]. However, the UK Government continued to make negotiations on nuclear disarmament a long-term aspiration rather than an immediate policy objective. The Strategic Defence Review continued: "while large nuclear arsenals and risks of proliferation remain, our minimum deterrent remains a necessary element of our security"[99]. It essentially ruled out any further reductions in UK nuclear weapons until further reductions had been made by the US and Russia.

66. This has remained the UK Government's position. In his speech to the 2004 NPT PrepCom, the UK Ambassador stated:

> We have consistently stated that when we are satisfied that sufficient progress has been made - for example, in further deep cuts in their nuclear forces by the US and Russia - to allow us to include the UK's nuclear weapons in any multilateral negotiations, without endangering our security interests, we will do so[100].

67. On 17 March 2009, after observing that between them the US and Russia retained around 95% of the nuclear weapons in the world and that the START Treaty, "the mainstay of their bilateral arms control effort", would expire later that year, the then Prime Minister, Gordon Brown stated: "For our part - as soon as it becomes useful for our arsenal to be included in a broader negotiation, Britain stands ready to participate and to act"[101].

---

96 Nicholas Ashford and Alexander Chancellor, "Arms reduction accord threatens UK deterrent", *The Independent*, 22 September 1987.
97 "Progress of the Trident Programme", 422 of 1987-88, HMSO, 11 May 1988.
98 *Supra*, n. 45, para. 60.
99 *Id.*
100 Statement by Ambassador David Braucher, NPT Preparatory Committee 2004, Cluster I, 3 May 2004.
101 10 Downing Street, Press Notice, Speech on Nuclear Energy and Proliferation, 17 March 2009, *available at* http://image.guardian.eo.uk/sys-files/Politics/documents/2009/03/1 7/PMSPEECH1 70309.pdf?guni= Article:manual-trailblock package: Position3.

68. On 6 July 2010, the then Secretary of State for Defence, Dr Liam Fox, reiterated the previous government's position that "as soon as it becomes useful for the UK to include its nuclear stockpiles in broader disarmament negotiations, we stand ready to participate and to act"[102].

69. On 3 January 2012, the UN General Assembly decided to establish an Open-Ended Working Group (OEWG) to develop proposals to take forward multilateral nuclear disarmament negotiations for the achievement and maintenance of a world without nuclear weapons[103]. However, the UK voted against the resolution[104] and did not attend any of the Working Group's meetings[105].

70. In a statement made jointly with France and the U.S. in the UN General Assembly First Committee on 6 November 2012, the UK declared that it was "unable to support this resolution, the establishment of the OEWG and *any outcome it may produce*" (emphasis added)[106].

2. Opposition to Negotiation of a Nuclear Weapons Convention

71. Similarly, the UK has always voted against the UN General Assembly's Resolution on "Follow-up to the advisory opinion of the International Court of Justice on the Legality of the Threat or Use of Nuclear Weapons". The Resolution, adopted every year since 1996[107], underlines the ICJ's unanimous conclusion that there is an obligation to pursue negotiations leading to nuclear disarmament and calls on States to immediately fulfil that obligation by commencing multilateral negotiations leading to the early conclusion of a Nuclear Weapons Convention.

72. In 1997, at the request of Costa Rica, the UN Secretary-General circulated to all UN Member States a Model Nuclear Weapons Convention[108]. Costa Rica submitted the Model Convention as "an effective and helpful instrument inthe deliberative process for the implementation of 'the annual resolution on follow-up to the

---

102   Hansard, HC Deb, 6 July 2010, col. 159W. *See also* the Statement by Ambassador John Duncan to the 2010 Non-Proliferation Treaty Review Conference, *available at* http://www.un.org/en/confinpt/201 O/statements/pdf/uk_en.pdf.
103   UNGA Resolution AIRES/67/56, "Taking forward multilateral nuclear disarmament negotiations for the achievement and maintenance of a world without nuclear weapons" (147-4-31).
104   Along with France, the Russian Federation and the US: UN Doc N67/PV.48, pp. 20-21.
105   Hansard, HL Deb, 15 July 2013, col. WA93.
106   *Available at* http://www.reachingcriticalwill.org/images/ documents/Disarmament - fora/1com/!com]2/eov/L46_France-UK-US.pdf
107   Most recently on 5 December 2013 (AIRES/68/42).
108   *See* Letter dated 31 October 1997 from the Charge d'affaires a.i. of the Permanent Mission of Costa Rica to the United Nations Addressed to the Secretary-General, U.N. Doc. AIC .115217 (17 November 1997).

ICJ Advisory Opinion[109]. In 2008, at the request of Costa Rica and Malaysia, the Secretary-General circulated an updated version of the Model Convention[110]. The Secretary-General later described the Model Convention as "a good point of departure" for negotiation of a Nuclear Weapons Convention[111].

73. The Model Convention applies the approach taken by the Chemical Weapons Convention. The Model Convention provides general obligations regarding the non-use and non possession of nuclear weapons and their verified dismantlement; sets out phases of elimination; provides for multiple means of reporting, monitoring and verification, from declarations of states to satellite observation; prohibits production of fissile material for nuclear weapons; requires national implementation measures; provides for prosecution of individuals accused of committing crimes proscribed by the convention; establishes an implementing agency; and establishes mechanisms for dispute resolution and compliance inducement and enforcement. The Model also builds upon existing nuclear non-proliferation and disarmament regimes and verification and compliance arrangements, including the NPT, International Atomic Energy Agency safeguards, the International Monitoring System for the CTBT, regional nuclear weapon-free zones, UN Security Council Resolution 1540, the International Convention for the Suppression of Acts of Nuclear Terrorism, and bilateral nuclear force reduction agreements between Russia and the United States.

74. Despite the annual UN General Assembly resolution discussed above, however, there have been no inter-governmental negotiations or deliberations in any official forum leading toward adoption of a Nuclear Weapons Convention, except in the above-mentioned Open-Ended Working Group in which the UK and the other NPT nuclear weapon States refused to participate.

75. In February 2008, the UN High Representative for Disarmament Affairs, Sergio Duarte, condemned the great powers' "refusal to negotiate or discuss even the outlines of a nuclear-weapons convention" as "contrary to the cause of disarmament"[112].

---

109 *Id.*
110 Letter dated 17 December 2007 from the Permanent Representatives of Costa Rica and Malaysia to the United Nations Addressed to the Secretary-General, U.N. Doc. A/62/650 (18 January 2008).
111 Press Release, Secretary-General Ban Ki-moon, The United Nations and Security in a Nuclear Weapon-Free World, U.N. Doc. SG/SM/11881 (24 October 2008), *available at* http://www.un.org/N ews/Press/docs/2008/sgsm11881.doc.htm.
112 *Nuclear Disarmament and the NPT- The Responsibility of the Nuclear-Weapon States*, at "Global Summit for a Nuclear Weapon-Free World: Laying the Practical, Technical, and Political Groundwork", Campaign for Nuclear Disarmament and Acronym Institute for Disarmament Diplomacy, London, 16 February 2008, *available at*
http://www. un.org/disarmament/Home Page/HR/docs/2008/2008Feb16_London.pdf.

76. The UK Government officially expresses opposition to a Nuclear Weapons Convention. A 2009 policy paper provided that while a Nuclear Weapons Convention will "likely be necessary to establish the final ban on nuclear weapons", it is "premature and potentially counter-productive" to prioritise such a Convention "when the many other conditions necessary to enable a ban have yet to be put in place"[113].

77. In June 2010, Lord Howell of Guildford (Minister of State, Foreign and Commonwealth Office). stated: "The idea of a nuclear weapons convention is a fine one, but ... [a] whole series of things need to be done before one comes to the happy situation where the nuclear world is disarmed and a convention could then get full support"[114].

78. In August 2011, the Prime Minister stated that he disagreed "that negotiations now on a nuclear weapons convention should be the immediate means of getting us to a world free of nuclear weapons"[115]. While he acknowledged that a Nuclear Weapons Convention "could ultimately form the legal underpinning for this end point", he considered that the prospects of reaching agreement on a Convention "are remote at the moment"[116].

79. The first-ever UN General Assembly High-Level Meeting on Nuclear Disarmament was held on September 26, 2013, pursuant to a 2012 resolution which was opposed by the UK[117]. At that meeting the UK representative delivered a statement on behalf of the UK, France and the U.S. in which they welcome "the increased energy and enthusiasm around the nuclear disarmament debate" but "regret that this energy is being directed toward initiatives such as this High-Level Meeting, the humanitarian consequences campaign, the Open-Ended Working Group and the push for a Nuclear Weapons Convention"[118].

80. The UK subsequently voted against a new UN General Assembly resolution following up the High-Level Meeting[119]. The resolution calls for "the urgent commencement of negotiations, in the Conference on Disarmament, for the early conclusion of a comprehensive convention" to prohibit and eliminate nuclear weapons.

---

113 Foreign and Commonwealth Office, *Lifting the Nuclear Shadow*, 2009, p. 34.
114 Hansard, HL Deb, 9 June 2010, col. 641: answer to a question by Baroness Williams of Crosby (Liberal Democrat), who had pointed out that "the great bulk of non-nuclear powers decided to press for a nuclear weapons convention to abolish nuclear weapons completely by 2025".
115 Letter from the Prime Minister to Jeremy Corbyn MP, 15 August 2011.
116 *Id.*
117 A/RES/67/39, 3 December 2012.
118 *Available at* http://www.reachingcriticalwill.org/images/documents/Disarmament fora/HLM/26Sep_UKUSFrance.pdf.
119 A/RES/68/32, 5 December 2013.

III. The Law

A. *Article VI of the NPT*

81. Article VI provides:

> Each of the Parties to the Treaty undertakes to pursue negotiations in good faith on effective measures relating to cessation of the nuclear arms race at an early date and to nuclear disarmament, and on a treaty on general and complete disarmament under strict and effective international control.

82. The drafting history of the NPT demonstrates that the treaty constitutes a "strategic bargain": the non-nuclear-weapon States agreed not to acquire nuclear weapons and the NPT nuclear-weapon States agreed to negotiate their elimination[120]. This has been confirmed by NPT Review Conferences. In particular, the 2010 Review Conference noted that the overwhelming majority of States entered into their legally binding commitments not to acquire nuclear weapons "in the context, inter alia, of the corresponding legally binding commitments by the nuclear weapon states to nuclear disarmament in accordance with the Treaty"[121].

83. Article VI is "the single most important provision of the treaty ... from the standpoint of long-term success or failure of its goal of proliferation prevention"[122].

84. In its Advisory Opinion on the Legality of the Threat or Use of Nuclear Weapons, the Court declared that Article VI involves "an obligation to achieve a precise result - nuclear disarmament in all its aspects -by adopting a particular course of conduct, namely, the pursuit of negotiations on the matter in good faith"[123]. The Court went on to conclude, *unanimously*, that "[t]here exists an obligation to pursue in good faith and bring to a conclusion negotiations leading to nuclear disarmament in all its aspects under strict and effective control"[124]. This "recognizes that the provisions of Article VI...go beyond mere obligations of conduct - to pursue nuclear disarmament negotiations in good faith - and actually involve an obligation of result, i.e., to conclude

---

[120] Thomas Graham, Correspondence, "The Origin and Interpretation of Article VI", 15 *Nonproliferation Review* 7, 9 (2008), *available at* http://cns.miis.edu/npr/pdfs/151_correspondence.pdf.
[121] 2010 Review Conference of the Parties to the Treaty on the Non-Proliferation of Nuclear Weapons, Final Document, Vol. I, "Review of the operation of the Treaty," p. 2, para. 2, *available at* http://www.un.org/ga/search/view_doc.asp?symbol=NPT/CONF.2010/50 (VOL.I).
[122] E. Firmage, 'The Treaty on the Non-Proliferation of Nuclear Weapons', 63 *American Journal of International Law* (1969) 711, 732.
[123] *Supra*, n. 3, para. 99.
[124] *Id*, para. 105, point 2 F.

those negotiations"[125].

85. The Court observed that "fulfilling the obligation expressed in Article VI ... remains without any doubt an objective of vital importance to the whole of the international community today"[126]. The Court has long emphasized the importance of obligations *erga omnes,* owed to the international community as a whole[127]. Its conclusion in the Advisory Opinion was tantamount to declaring that the obligation in Article VI is an obligation *erga omnes*[128]. Every State has a legal interest in its timely performance, therefore[129], and a corresponding legal obligation to help bring it about[130].

B.   Customary International Law

86. The obligations enshrined in Article VI of the NPT are not merely treaty obligations; they also exist separately under customary international law[131].

87. In its Advisory Opinion, after noting that the twofold obligation in Article VI to pursue and to conclude negotiations *formally* concerns the (now 190[132]) States Parties to the NPT, the Court added that "any realistic search for general and complete disarmament, especially nuclear disarmament, necessitates the cooperation of all States"[133].

88. In point 2F of the *dispositif,* moreover, not confining its remarks to the States Parties to the NPT, the Court unanimously declared: 'There exists an obligation to pursue in good faith and bring to a conclusion negotiations leading to nuclear disarmament in all its aspects under strict and effective international control"[134].

89. The Court's declaration is an expression of customary international law as it stands today. *All* States are under that obligation,

125 M. Marin Bosch, "The Non-Proliferation Treaty and its Future," in L. Boisson de Chazournes and P. Sands, eds, *International Law, the International Court of Justice and Nuclear Weapons* (1999), p. 375.
126 *Supra,* n. 3, para. 103.
127 *Barcelona Traction, Light and Power Company, Limited, Judgment, I.C.J Reports 1970,* p. 3, para. 33.
128 See President Bedjaoui's Declaration in the *Nuclear Weapons Case, supra,* n. 3, at pp. 273-274, para. 23: "As the Court has acknowledged, the obligation to negotiate in good faith for nuclear disarmament concerns the 182 or so States parties to the Non-Proliferation Treaty. I think one can go beyond that conclusion and assert that there is in fact a twofold *general obligation,* opposable *erga omnes,* to negotiate in good faith and to achieve the desired result".
129 *See supra,* n. 121, para 33.
130 *Cf Legal Consequences of the Construction of a Wall in the Occupied Palestinian Territory,Advisory Opinion, I.C.J Reports 2004,* p. 136, paras. 154-159.
131 In *Military and Paramilitary Activities in and against Nicaragua (Nicaragua v. United States of America), Jurisdiction and Admissibility, Judgment, I.C.J Reports 1984,* p. 392, at para. 94, the ICJ held that the fact that principles of customary international law are enshrined in multilateral conventions does not mean that they cease to exist and to apply as principles of customary law.
132 There are 190 States Parties including the DPRK. Although the DPRK announced its withdrawal from the NPT on 10 January 2003, States Parties continue to express divergent views regarding its status under the Treaty. See UN Office for Disarmament Affairs, Treaty on the Non-Proliferation of Nuclear Weapons, Status of the Treaty, *available at* http://disarmament.un.org/treaties/t/npt.
133 *Supra,* n. 3, para. 100.
134 *Id.,* para. 105.

therefore. This is consistent with the view expressed by President Bedjaoui in his Declaration: "Indeed, it is not unreasonable to think that, considering the at least formal unanimity in this field, this twofold obligation to negotiate in good faith and achieve the desired result has now, 50 years on, acquired a *customary character*"[135].

90. As the Court itself noted, the UN General Assembly has been deeply engaged in working for universal disarmament of weapons of mass destruction since its very first resolution in 1946[136]. The UN Security Council also has repeatedly called for the implementation of Article VI by all States[137], not only Parties to the NPT. In Resolution 1887 of 24 September 2009, after calling upon States Parties to the NPT to implement Article VI, the Council called on "all other States to join in this endeavour"[138]. The Council has also described the proliferation of weapons of mass destruction as a threat to international peace and security[139].

91. Regarding the obligation of cessation of the nuclear arms race at an early date set forth in Article VI, it stands on its own as a customary international law obligation based on the very widespread and representative participation of States in the NPT and is inherent in the customary international law obligation of nuclear disarmament.

92. The UN General Assembly has declared the necessity of cessation of the nuclear arms race. In the Final Document of its first Special Session on Disarmament, held in 1978, the General Assembly stated that it is "imperative . .. to halt and reverse the nuclear arms race until the total elimination of nuclear weapons and their delivery systems has been achieved"[140].

C. Good Faith

93. That good faith constitutes a "fundamental principle" of

---

135 *Supra*, n. 3, at p. 274, Declaration of President Bedjaoui, para. 23. President Bedjaoui was referring to the 50 years that had then elapsed since the adoption of the UN General Assembly's first resolution in 1946 and the normative language repeatedly reiterated in its resolutions on nuclear weapons and in other instruments since then.
136 A/RES/1(I) of 24 January 1946, cited by the Court in para. 101 of the Advisory Opinion.
137 *E.g.*, Resolution 984 of 11 April 1995, cited by the Court in para. 103, and Resolution 1887 of 24 September 2009.
138 Operative para. 5.
139 *E.g.*, Resolution 1887, 2009.
140 Final Document of the Tenth Special Session of the General Assembly, adopted by A/RES/S-10/2, 30 June 1978, without a vote, para. 20; *see also, e.g.*, paras. 47, 50. *See* http://www.un.org/disarmament/HomePage/SSOD/ssod4-documents.shtml. The 1978 Special Session established UN disarmament machinery in its current form, with the Conference on Disarmament devoted to negotiations, the Disarmament Commission devoted to deliberation, and the First Committee of the General Assembly devoted to agenda-setting. The Special Session thus was a quasi-constitutional assembly with respect to disarmament.

international law is beyond dispute[141]. Not only is it a general principle of law for the purposes of Article 38(1)(c) of the Statute of the International Court of Justice[142] and a cardinal principle of the Law of Treaties[143], it also encapsulates the essence of the Rule of Law in international society[144] and is one of the Principles of the United Nations.

94. Article 2, paragraph 2 of the UN Charter provides: "All Members, in order to ensure to all of them the rights and benefits resulting from membership, shall fulfil in good faith the obligations assumed by them in accordance with the present Charter". The Declaration on Principles of International Law 1970 makes it clear that this duty applies not only to obligations arising under the Charter but also to those arising "under the generally recognized principles and rules of international law" and "under international agreements valid under the generally recognized principles and rules of international law"[145].

95. In the *Nuclear Tests* cases, the ICJ declared: "One of the basic principles governing the creation and performance of legal obligations, whatever their source, is the principle of good faith. Trust and confidence are inherent in international cooperation, in particular in an age when this co-operation in many fields is becoming increasingly essential"[146].

96. In the Final Document of the first Special Session on Disarmament, the General Assembly called upon all States to meet requirements of good faith, declaring:

> In order to create favourable conditions for success in the disarmament process, all States should strictly abide by the provisions of the Charter of the United Nations, *refrain from actions which might adversely affect efforts in the field of disarmament, and display a constructive approach to negotiations and the political will to reach agreements*[147].

97. As set forth above, Article VI of the NPT requires both conduct and result: States must not only negotiate in good faith with serious efforts to achieve the elimination of nuclear weapons, but must also

---

141 See Robert Kolb, *La bonnefoi en droit international public: Contribution a l'etude des principes generaux du droit*, pp. 112-13 (2001).
142 Cf *The Free Zones of Upper Savoy and the District of Gex*, Second Phase (1930) PCIJ, Series A, No.24, p. 12; *and see* J. Crawford, *Brownlie's Principles of Public International Law*, Oxford, 8th edition, 2012, pp. 36-37.
143 Articles 26 and 31(1) of the Vienna Convention on the Law of Treaties 1969.
144 V. Lowe, *International Law*, Oxford, 2007, p. 116.
145 Declaration on Principles of International Law concerning Friendly Relations and Cooperation among States in Accordance with the Charter of the United Nations, U.N.G.A. Res. 2625 (XXV), 24 October 1970.
146 *Nuclear Tests (Australia v. France), Judgment, I.C.J Reports 1974*, p. 253, at p. 268, para. 46; *Nuclear Tests (New Zealand v. France), Judgment, id.*, p. 457, at p. 473, para. 49.
147 *Supra*, n. 134, para. 41. Emphasis added.

actually achieve that result[148].

98. The Court has stated that the "principle of good faith obliges the Parties to apply [a treaty] in a reasonable way and in such a manner that its purpose can be realized"[149]. Conduct that prevents the fulfilment of a treaty's object and purpose is proscribed[150]. Further, conduct that calls into question a State's commitment to the achievement of agreed objectives undermines the trust necessary for successful cooperation towards their achievement. All of this applies equally to the obligation to fulfil customary international law obligations in good faith[151].

IV. Obligations Breached By the UK

99. Part II of this Application has outlined the facts that are relevant for an assessment of the Respondent's non-compliance with its international obligations with respect to nuclear disarmament and the cessation of the nuclear arms race. Part III has outlined the legal basis for this case. The conduct of the Respondent will now be analyzed very briefly in light of the relevant law.

A. Breach of Article VI of the NPT

100. Two of the obligations entailed by Article VI are relevant for the present case: the obligation with regard to nuclear disarmament and the obligation with regard to the cessation of the nuclear arms race at an early date.

Nuclear disarmament

101. As set forth above, the Court has provided an authoritative analysis of the nuclear disarmament element of the obligations laid down by Article VI. It has held that "the obligation involved here is

---
148 *See supra*, para. 84.
149 *Case Concerning the Gabcikovo-Nagymaros Project (Hungary v. Slovakia), I.C.J Reports 1997*, p. 7, para. 142.
150 *Report of the International Law Commission Covering its 16th Session, 727th Meeting*, 20 May 1964: Pursuant to the VCLT Article 26 obligation that every treaty in force must be performed by the parties in good faith, the duty of the parties is "not only to observe the letter of the law but also to abstain from acts which would inevitably affect their ability to perform ...."; Antonio Cassese, *The Israel-PLO Agreement and Self-Determination,* 4 Eur. J. Int'l. L. 567 (1993), available at http://www.ejil.org/journal/Vol4/No4/ (when there is an obligation of good faith negotiation, "both Parties are not allowed to (I) advance excuses for not engaging into or pursuing negotiations or (2) to accomplish acts which would defeat the object and purpose of the future treaty"); *see also* Judge Mohammed Bedjaoui, "Good Faith, International Law, and Elimination of Nuclear Weapons," Keynote Address, 1 May 2008, *available at* http://www.lcnp.org/disarmament/2008May01eventBedjaoui.pdf , pp. 24-29 (in the NPT context, good faith proscribes "every initiative the effect of which would be to render impossible the conclusion of the contemplated disarmament treaty").
151 *See supra,* para. 94.

an obligation to achieve a precise result - nuclear disarmament in all its aspects - by adopting a particular course of conduct, namely, the pursuit of negotiations on the matter in good faith"[152]. In the *dispositif* of its Advisory Opinion the Court concluded *unanimously*: "There exists an obligation to pursue in good faith and bring to a conclusion negotiations leading to nuclear disarmament in all its aspects under strict and effective international control"[153].

102. The Respondent has stated that "it is premature and potentially counter productive" to prioritise a Nuclear Weapons Convention[154] and opposes UN General Assembly resolutions calling for negotiations to begin[155].

103. The Respondent also refused to support the establishment of the Open-Ended Working Group and even declared preemptively that it would not support "any outcome it may produce"[156].

104. As set forth herein, including in Part II of this Application, the UK clearly has not actively pursued "negotiations leading to nuclear disarmament in all its aspects under strict and effective international control". On the contrary, it has opposed the efforts of the great majority of States to initiate such negotiations. Accordingly, the Respondent has breached and continues to breach its nuclear disarmament obligations under Article VI of the NPT.

Cessation of the nuclear arms race at an early date

105. With regard to the cessation of the nuclear arms race at an early date, the Respondent's conduct is similarly negative and obstructive.

106. Its conduct, set forth in Part II of this Application, in (i) continuing engagement in material efforts to qualitatively improve its nuclear weapons system; (ii) continuing efforts to maintain and extend that system indefinitely; and (iii) opposing negotiations on comprehensive nuclear disarmament or other measures in multilateral forums, including the Open-Ended Working Group and the UN General Assembly, is clear evidence of the UK's ongoing breach of its Article VI obligation regarding the cessation of the nuclear arms race at an early date[157].

107. Despite having been a party to the NPT for 44 years, therefore, the Respondent has breached and continues to breach its obligation

---
152 *Supra*, n. 3, para. 99.
153 *Id.*, para.105, point 2F.
154 *See supra*, para. 76.
155 *See supra*, para. 78.
156 *See supra*, para. 70.
157 *See supra*, Part II.C.4 and II.D.

under Article VI regarding the cessation of the nuclear arms race at an early date.

B, Breach of Customary International Law

108. For the reasons set out above, the obligations enshrined in Article VI of the NPT are not merely treaty obligations; they also exist separately under customary international law.

109. On the same grounds as those relied on in the preceding Section of this Application, the Respondent has breached and continues to breach its obligations under customary international law with regard to nuclear disarmament and the cessation of the nuclear arms race at an early date.

C. Breach of the Obligation to Perform its Obligations in Good Faith

110. In the previous two Sections, the Applicant has submitted that the Respondent has breached and continues to breach its obligations under both the NPT and customary international law regarding nuclear disarmament and cessation of the nuclear arms race at an early date. The Respondent is also failing to act in good faith as far as its performance of those obligations is concerned.

111. As set forth in Part II of this Application, the Respondent has been actively upgrading, modernizing and improving its nuclear arsenal. This constitutes qualitative vertical nuclear proliferation which clearly conflicts with the Respondent's fundamental commitment to nuclear disarmament and cessation of the nuclear arms race at an early date. It also encourages other States possessing nuclear weapons to follow suit and may induce non-nuclear-weapon States to reconsider their non-nuclear posture.

112. The Respondent has also repeatedly declared its intention to rely on its nuclear arsenal for decades to come[158].

113. In short, by not actively pursuing negotiations in good faith on effective measures relating to cessation of the nuclear arms race at an early date and to nuclear disarmament, and instead engaging in conduct that directly conflicts with those legally binding commitments, the Respondent has breached and continues to breach its legal duty to perform its obligations under the NPT and customary international law in good faith.

---

158 The May 2011 Initial Gate report states that the submarines will be operational "until the 2060s". See *The United Kingdom's Future Deterrent: The Submarine Initial Gate Parliamentary Report,* May 2011, para 3.1; cited by Ainslie, *supra,* n. 44, at p. 75.

V. Jurisdiction of the Court

114. In accordance with the provisions of Article 36, paragraph 2, of the Statute, jurisdiction exists by virtue of the operation of the Declaration of the Applicant dated 15 March 2013 (and deposited 24 April 2013) and the Declaration of the United Kingdom dated 5 July 2004, each Declaration without pertinent reservation.

VI. Final Observations

115. Pursuant to Article 31 of the Statute of the Court and Article 35, paragraph 1 of its Rules, the Applicant will exercise the power conferred by Article 31 of the Statute and choose a person to sit as judge ad hoc and will so inform the Court in due course.

116. The Applicant reserves the right to modify and extend the terms of this Application, the grounds invoked and the Remedies requested.

REMEDIES

On the basis of the foregoing statement of facts and law, The Republic of the Marshall Islands requests the Court

to adjudge and declare

   a) that the United Kingdom has violated and continues to violate its international obligations under the NPT, more specifically under Article VI of the Treaty, by failing to pursue in good faith and bring to a conclusion negotiations leading to nuclear disarmament in all its aspects under strict and effective international control;
   b) that the United Kingdom has violated and continues to violate its international obligations under the NPT, more specifically under Article VI of the Treaty, by taking actions to qualitatively improve its nuclear weapons system and to maintain it for the indefinite future, and by failing to pursue negotiations that would end nuclear arms racing through comprehensive nuclear disarmament or other

measures;

c) that the United Kingdom has violated and continues to violate its international obligations under customary international law, by failing to pursue in good faith and bring to a conclusion negotiations leading to nuclear disarmament in all its aspects under strict and effective international control;

d) that the United Kingdom has violated and continues to violate its international obligations under customary international law, by taking actions to qualitatively improve its nuclear weapons system and to maintain it for the indefinite future, and by failing to pursue negotiations that would end nuclear arms racing through comprehensive nuclear disarmament or other measures;

e) that the United Kingdom has failed and continues to fail to perform in good faith its obligations under the NPT and under customary international law by modernizing, updating and upgrading its nuclear weapons capacity and maintaining its declared nuclear weapons policy for an unlimited period of time, while at the same time failing to pursue negotiations as set out in the four preceding counts; and

f) that the United Kingdom has failed and continues to fail to perform in good faith its obligations under the NPT and under customary international law by effectively preventing the great majority of non-nuclear-weapon States Parties to the Treaty from fulfilling their part of the obligations under Article VI of the Treaty and under customary international law with respect to nuclear disarmament and cessation of the nuclear arms race at an early date.

In addition, The Republic of the Marshall Islands requests the Court

to order

the United Kingdom to take all steps necessary to comply with its obligations under Article VI of the Treaty on the Non-Proliferation of Nuclear Weapons and under customary international law within one year of the Judgment, including the pursuit, by initiation if necessary, of negotiations in good faith aimed at the conclusion of a convention on nuclear disarmament in all its aspects under strict and effective international control.

DATED this 24th of April 2014

Tony A. deBrum
Co-Agent of the
Republic of the Marshall Islands
and Minister of Foreign Affairs of
the Republic of the Marshall Islands

Phon van den Biesen
Co-Agent of the
Republic of the Marshall Islands

[this page is left blank intentionally]

Chapter 12

Falk and Krieger Dialogue

Nuclear Weapons and International Law

Krieger: In the aftermath of World War II, people throughout the world understood the terrible consequences of the use of nuclear weapons, instruments of mass annihilation whose force had been tragically demonstrated first at Hiroshima and then at Nagasaki. When Allied leaders agreed in the Nuremberg Charter to hold Axis leaders to account for crimes against peace, war crimes, and crimes against humanity, there was no consideration of nuclear weapons. These weapons, after all, had been used not by the Axis powers but by the United States, an Allied power. The Allies were not placing themselves or the weaponry they had developed and used on trial. Ironically, Hiroshima was bombed on August 6, 1945, the Nuremberg Charter was signed on August 8, 1945, and Nagasaki was bombed on August 9, 1945. In other words, Allied war crimes took place immediately before and after the Allies agreed to hold Axis leaders accountable for their crimes.

Even before Hiroshima was bombed, there were prohibitions in international humanitarian law, the law of warfare, against using weapons that did not discriminate between soldiers and civilians, that caused unnecessary suffering, or that constituted a disproportionate response to a prior attack. These prohibitions did not stop either the Allied or the Axis militaries from carpet bombing cities in Europe and Japan; nor did they prevent the use of the atomic bombs by the United States at the first opportunity in Japan.

Falk: There was, as you suggest, no willingness by the victorious powers in World War II to accept any accountability for their departures from the law of war, the most extreme instance of which was, of course, the atomic bombings at a time when Japan seemed ready, according to many reports, to accept defeat. More than this, led by the United States, there has been a consistent reluctance to allow questioning of the legal status of nuclear weaponry. The United States vigorously opposed referral of the issue to the International Court of Justice (ICJ) by the UN General Assembly.

But beyond resisting efforts to have these weapons considered formally unlawful and their threat or use declared a crime against humanity, as the UN General Assembly asserted in Resolution 1653 (XVI) back in 1961, the U.S. government has been very touchy about acknowledging the suffering endured by the people in Hiroshima and Nagasaki. In a much publicized incident, for instance, politically powerful forces brought so much pressure to bear that an exhibit depicting the suffering of the civilian population in Japan, put together by the respected Smithsonian Institution in Washington, DC, to commemorate the fiftieth anniversary of these events, was cancelled. And shockingly, no U.S. president has seen fit to visit either Japanese city that experienced atomic devastation, although many American leaders have made it a point to visit Nazi death camps. Of course, the latter is entirely appropriate in memory of the Holocaust, but to avert our eyes from the devastation of Hiroshima and Nagasaki is to be guilty of a particularly serious form of denial, one that tends to withdraw stigma from the bombings and the weaponry.

Let me make the point differently. It is hard to imagine even the most cynical realist political leader setting forth a justification for genocide, while it is perfectly respectable in the media or in think tanks to propose strategic roles for nuclear weapons, including their use against cities.

The Nuremberg Promise

Falk: We should not forget what Justice Robert Jackson, the American chief prosecutor at Nuremberg, said in his extraordinary statement to the tribunal on that historic occasion in 1945: "And let me make clear that while this law is first applied against German aggressors, the law includes, and if it is to serve any useful purpose it must condemn, aggression by any other nation, including those which sit here now in judgment. We are able to do away with domestic tyranny and violence and aggression by those in power against the rights of their own people only when we make all men [sic] answerable to the law. This trial represents mankind's desperate effort to apply the discipline of law to statesmen who have used their powers of state to attack the foundations of world peace." (Jackson, 1946; p172). There is no doubt that this noble Nuremberg Promise has been broken many times by World War

II's victors and that we have grown accustomed to living in a world of double standards: accountability for the weak and geopolitically vulnerable; impunity for the strong and geopolitically protected.

Krieger: Justice Jackson had wisdom and foresight. He could see clearly the need to make universal the application of the Nuremberg principles, holding to account all leaders who commit serious crimes under international law. The failure of the Allied powers to live up to the Nuremberg Promise in the aftermath of World War II is one of the great tragedies and certainly one of the lost opportunities of our time. The Nuremberg Promise was to end impunity for serious crimes under international law for all. So far, the promise hasn't been realized. Instead, powerful states and their leaders have sought to override the Nuremberg principles and build double standards of law and justice into the international system. A prime example of the application of double standards is found in the NonProliferation Treaty (NPT).

When the United States, United Kingdom, and Soviet Union sought to create the NPT in 1968, they agreed in Article VI to a provision calling for nuclear disarmament but phrased it ambiguously: "Each of the parties to the Treaty undertakes to pursue negotiations in good faith on effective measures relating to cessation of the nuclear arms race at an early date and to nuclear disarmament, and on a treaty on general and complete disarmament under strict and effective international control." (NPT, 1968). Since the NPT's entry into force in 1970, there has been little, if any, attempt at "good faith" negotiations on nuclear disarmament.

The World Court Pronounces on the Legality of Nuclear Weapons

Krieger: Not until twenty-six years later, in 1996, did the International Court of Justice address this issue by providing an advisory opinion, requested by the UN General Assembly, titled *The Legality of the Threat or Use of Nuclear Weapons*. After hearings and deliberations, the ICJ issued a multipart opinion and voted separately on each part. It found unanimously that there was in neither customary nor conventional international law any specific authorization of the use of or threat to use nuclear weapons (ICJ, 1996b; para 105 (2)A - and *supra*) It also found, by a vote of eleven to three, that there was no comprehensive and universal prohibition of such threat or use (ICJ, 1996b; para 105 (2)B - and *supra*) Three judges believed there was a comprehensive and universal prohibition. The ICJ went on to state unanimously that any threat or use that did not comply with the UN Charter would be unlawful (ICJ, 1996b; para 105 (2)C - and *supra*)

The ICJ agreed unanimously that any use of or threat to use nuclear weapons needed to be compatible with international humanitarian law. It stated, "A threat or use of nuclear weapons should also be compatible with the requirements of the international law applicable in armed conflict, particularly those of the principles and rules of international humanitarian law, as well as with specific obligations under treaties and other undertakings which expressly deal with nuclear weapons." (ICJ, 1996b; para 105 (2)D - and *supra*)

The ICJ then split seven to seven, with the president's vote deciding the central conclusion of the advisory opinion:

> It follows from the above-mentioned requirements that the threat or use of nuclear weapons would generally be contrary to the rules of international law applicable in armed conflict, and in particular the principles and rules of humanitarian law;
>
> However, in view of the current state of international law, and of the elements of fact at its disposal, the Court cannot conclude definitively whether the threat or use of nuclear weapons would be lawful or unlawful in an extreme circumstance of self-defense, in which the very survival of a State would be at stake. (ICJ, 1996b; para 105 (2)E - and *supra*).

In this latter section of the opinion, the ICJ introduced some doubts. It used the fudge word "generally" before the words "be contrary to the rules of international law." It went on to explain this by stating that the current state of international law didn't allow a conclusion as to whether "an extreme circumstance of self-defense, in which the very survival of a State would be at stake," would be lawful or unlawful. It is important to note that the ICJ did not say that the use of or threat to use nuclear weapons would be lawful in such a circumstance, only that the law was unclear. Three of the judges who voted against this position thought the law was in fact clear and that it was possible to conclude that any use of or threat to use nuclear weapons would be a violation of international law. The three were Judge Christopher G. Weeramantry of Sri Larika, vice president of the ICJ; Judge Mohammed Shahabuddeen of Guyana; and Judge Abdul Koroma of Sierra Leone. The three judges wrote important dissenting opinions. Judge Weeramantry wrote, "My considered opinion is that the use or threat of use of nuclear weapons is illegal *in any circumstances whatsoever.*" (Weeramantry, 1996: p 211 - and *supra* - emphasis preserved). He also strongly challenged the word "generally" in the opinion, which modified "unlawful."

The ICJ concluded its opinion by stating, "There exists an obligation to pursue in good faith and bring to a conclusion negotiations leading to nuclear disarmament in all its aspects under strict and effective international control." (ICJ, 1996b; para 105 (2)F - and *supra*) This was the ICJ's interpretation of Article VI of the NPT. It affirmed, in essence, an obligation not only to negotiate nuclear disarmament in good faith but also to conclude those negotiations and achieve nuclear disarmament in all its aspects.

Since the ICJ released its advisory opinion in 1996, there has been scant change on the part of the nuclear weapon states. The United States and Russia have negotiated to reduce the size of their nuclear arsenals, but they have not taken seriously the obligation set forth by the ICJ to pursue disarmament negotiations. Between the two countries, there still remain some 20,000 nuclear weapons. Both states have unfortunately demonstrated a gross indifference to international law, which I fear will have serious consequences for humanity.

Falk: You have provided an excellent summary of what the ICJ decided. I would add just a few observations. If read fairly, the majority opinion, although leaving some room for exceptional claims in the event that a state's survival is credibly at stake, goes a long way toward viewing nuclear weapons as unlawful. This view is inconsistent with the unwillingness of the United States and other nuclear weapon states to configure their weaponry and doctrine for defensive uses in survival situations. At minimum, this should lead all nuclear weapon states to make an unconditional declaration renouncing the option to use such weapons first. It would also preclude the development of so-called tactical nuclear weapons with battlefield missions.

A second observation is that, although the conclusions of the ICJ took the form of an advisory opinion, the legal assessments were the most authoritative attainable within the world legal system. These assessments of the relationship of the weaponry to the law were made by distinguished jurists from the world's major legal systems and would seem to deserve appropriate respect from all governments that purport to uphold adherence to the rule of law. The decision was also endorsed in a UN General Assembly resolution by a large majority of the membership of the United Nations.

A third observation relates to the failure of the United States and other nuclear weapon states to alter their approach to nuclear weaponry in response to this historic legal appraisal. In this regard, the imperatives of geopolitics, which continue to treat this weaponry as essential for national security, have taken precedence over respect for international law. Even the more modest unanimous finding among the fourteen participating judges regarding the obligation to pursue nuclear disarmament in good faith, as declared in NPT Article VI, had produced no appropriate initiative in the subsequent sixteen years. True, calls for nuclear disarmament and visions of a world without nuclear weapons are set forth from time to time, but there has been no concrete willingness to establish a mechanism at the national and global levels to frame a disarmament process that could guide intergovernmental negotiations.

Failure to Act on the ICJ's Opinion

Falk: This is not only a shocking disregard of the ICJ's clear finding but also a material breach of the Non-Proliferation Treaty that casts legal doubt on its continuing validity. It may be time for the General Assembly to put this question to the ICJ: What legal consequences arise from the persistent failure of the nuclear weapon states to fulfill their obligations under Article VI of the NPT? In my view, the nonnuclear states have also been irresponsible in not insisting on mutuality of respect in the nonproliferation setting. It may be up to civil society actors to bring wider attention to this pattern of disrespect for vital norms of international law bearing on the status of nuclear weaponry and the irresponsibility of governments in failing to seek compliance.

Krieger: I agree with you that the ICJ's advisory opinion goes a long way toward making the use of or threat to use nuclear weapons unlawful, particularly by concluding that any such act that violates international humanitarian law is illegal. It is almost impossible to imagine a scenario in which the use of or threat to use nuclear weapons would not violate the laws of war, even when "the very survival of a state" was at stake. It is not enough, though, to declare the use of or threat to use the weapons illegal. It is also necessary to declare their possession illegal and to eliminate them altogether if we are to ensure we prevent either threat or use. Possession alone can be construed as an implicit threat to use, and reliance on, nuclear deterrence makes the threat explicit.

As we have discussed before, a declaration of No First Use of nuclear weapons would be a step in the right direction, but it is only a step and not sufficient. So long as the weapons are held in the arsenals of states, a pledge of No First Use can be quickly overridden. Such a pledge must be followed by negotiations for a nuclear weapons convention for the total elimination of all nuclear weapons.

The ICJ's advisory opinion is all the more remarkable when one considers that the Court's composition included judges from the five initial nuclear weapon states, those that are defined as nuclear weapon states in the NPT: the United States, Russia, the United Kingdom, France, and China. Without these five countries represented, the ICJ would quite likely have gone even further and ruled, as Judge Weeramantry expressed in his dissent, that the weapons were illegal "*in any circumstances whatsoever.*" ICJ president Mohammed Bedjaoui of Algeria wrote in his declaration that nuclear weapons were "the ultimate evil". He found the existence of nuclear weapons to be "*a challenge to the very existence of humanitarian law,* not to mention their long-term effects of damage to the human environment, in respect to which the right to life can be exercised". (Bedjaoui, 1996; para 20, p 50 - emphasis retained).

Judge Bedjaoui pointed out the irony of the ICJ's conclusion regarding its inability to find the threat or use of nuclear weapons illegal when "the very survival of a state" is at stake. He wrote, "The fact remains that the use of nuclear weapons by a State in circumstances in which its survival is at stake risks in its turn endangering the survival of all mankind, precisely because of the inextricable link between terror and escalation in the use of such weapons. It would thus be quite foolhardy unhesitatingly to set the survival of a State above all other considerations, in particular above the survival of mankind itself." (Bedjaoui, 1996; para 22, p 51). For this reason, the law as it stands is not sufficient, and it is necessary for states to fulfill the advisory opinion's final unanimous directive "to pursue in good faith and bring to a conclusion negotiations leading to nuclear disarmament in all its aspects." I think those who have looked carefully at the behavior of the NPT nuclear weapon states would share widespread agreement that they have not engaged in "good faith" negotiations on nuclear disarmament and thus have not fulfilled their obligations under international law, specifically under Article VI of the NPT.

I'm not sure how it would help move nuclear disarmament forward to ask the ICJ for another advisory opinion, inasmuch as the nuclear weapon states have been largely unresponsive to the existing advisory opinion. The status of international law seems insufficient to bring the most powerful states into line with its dictates. The politics of power in the international system evidently takes precedence over the power of the law. In some respects, since the ICJ issued its advisory opinion, the nuclear weapon states have used international law cynically to justify their nuclear arsenals on the basis of their potential need in the event of "the very survival of a state" being at stake. In other words, powerful states have treated the ICJ's opinion as an excuse for relying on nuclear weapons for geopolitical purposes. Of course, in doing so, these states continue to put at risk, as Judge Bedjaoui pointed out, "the survival of mankind itself".

Civil Society and the Enforcement of International Law

Krieger: I believe it is incumbent on civil society to point out the dangers of nuclear weapon states failing to fulfill their obligations under international law with regard to nuclear disarmament. It is also incumbent upon civil society to push governments to take greater action: to push nuclear weapon states to engage in the good faith negotiations for nuclear disarmament required of them and also to push the non-nuclear weapon states to put serious pressure on the nuclear weapon states to fulfill these obligations. With no enforcement mechanism available to hold the nuclear weapon states to account, the law loses its power. Perhaps only civil society, if seriously engaged, would have the capacity to restore this power to the law by pressing its demands to end the risk that nuclear weapons pose to the human future.

Falk: I agree with your observation that significant progress toward nuclear disarmament will depend on the mobilization of civil society around this issue to a greater extent than has occurred in the past. How to make this imperative a viable political project is the great unanswered question hanging over all efforts to proceed in an atmosphere that is definitely not receptive at present to a serious movement either in the United States or elsewhere. In the past, movements only formed during those periods of the Cold War when there was widespread public anxiety about the possible use of nuclear weapons.

I hope that the new doubts raised about the expansion of and reliance on nuclear energy will foster a wider debate that links these concerns with those that we have focused on involving the weaponry, past, present, and future.

In these regards, I think you undervalue the continuing role of international law and the ICJ in challenging the legality and legitimacy of nuclear weaponry. In my view, we need to understand this role as a process not an event. Recall that the ICJ was asked four times to pronounce on the legality and legitimacy of the racist apartheid regime that prevailed in South Africa and was extended to Southwest Africa (now Namibia) in their role as administering mandatory power. The experience in the ICJ was not entirely favorable, and the case involving Southwest Africa perversely endorsed apartheid as a legal and legitimate means for South Africa to carry out its responsibilities. The composition of the IC] at the time had some peculiarities that made it much more conservative on human rights issues than the general international climate. The decision outraged many governments and world public opinion, which accelerated rather than undermined the global antiapartheid campaign, leading the General Assembly to terminate South Africa's role as a mandatory power. International law was symbolically important even when perversely invoked to validate reactionary policies.

With respect to nuclear weaponry, another General Assembly resolution seeking to clarify the legal obligations of states to implement the earlier advisory opinion would have important educative and consciousness-raising implications. It would reinforce the impression that the nuclear weapon states have twisted the outcome of the 1996 advisory opinion to serve their essentially nuclearist purposes and paid little attention to their obligations under the NPT regime. It would not be expected to transform the behavior of these governments, especially the United States, but it could reinforce the idea that they are openly defiant toward international law on this issue of ultimate significance for the future of humanity.

Finally, I believe we in civil society should make maximum use of international law and global legal institutions to wage a legitimacy war against the possession and normalization of nuclear weaponry. Without such an orientation, I see little hope that educational efforts on their own can produce the sort of political outcomes we favor. As I have suggested at various stages in our conversations, the greatest challenge antinuclear activists face is converting their fervent concerns into a viable political project. At present, we are still operating as a prepolitical movement, that is, without a plan that we have any reason to believe will be implemented by leaders, will enlist widespread-enough support on the part of citizens, or will be given priority in the policy agenda of global civil society. There exist widespread dormant antinuclear fears and sentiments but insufficient will to achieve political relevance. I think, in this dialogue, we need further commentary on whether the struggle for nuclear disarmament can be waged, as I have suggested in passing, as a legitimacy war and the precise role we can assign to international law.

International Law versus Deterrence Theory

Krieger: I appreciate your point about looking at international law, as it pertains to nuclear weapons, as a process rather than an event. The process must involve the establishment of norms so strong that their violation would engage the public and cause a mass uprising. The problem as it exists now is that the public does not widely know about or understand the applicable international law related to the use of or threat to use nuclear weapons. This law also, and importantly, fails to go to the heart of the matter, which is possession of the weapons. So long as possession is deemed legal, at least for the five NPT nuclear weapon states and the four nuclear weapon states outside the treaty, the threat of use will be implicit, and the possibility of actual use will remain close at hand.

The possession of nuclear weapons is intertwined with nuclear deterrence theory, which posits that the threat of nuclear retaliation by country x will prevent the use of nuclear weapons and other proscribed behavior against country x. Many people believe that nuclear deterrence has prevented nuclear war and thus is beneficial. If leaders of a country believe that nuclear weapons are a shield against attack, they will be reluctant to give up the weapons regardless of their understanding of international law or the state of the law as expressed by the ICJ. In the "legitimacy war" to which you refer, nuclear deterrence is a major obstacle to delegitimizing the possession of nuclear weapons. Thus, we must call into question the legitimacy of nuclear deterrence. As we have discussed, nuclear deterrence theory has many flaws, including that it is subject to communication failures, requires rational leaders, and is not effective against nonstate extremists. Another real danger of nuclear deterrence lies in its undermining of international law by its justification of possession of the weapons.

The final portion of the ICJ's opinion on the legality of the use of or threat to use nuclear weapons refers to "an obligation to pursue in good faith and bring to a conclusion negotiations leading to nuclear disarmament in all its aspects." This element of the opinion, which rests upon Article VI of the NPT, goes to possession of the weapons, saying, in essence, that the nuclear weapon states must negotiate to end possession of the weapons, that is, to achieve "nuclear disarmament in all its aspects." It is not possible both to engage in good faith negotiations to achieve nuclear disarmament and to retain nuclear weapons for deterrence. The nuclear weapon states have thus far chosen nuclear deterrence and failed to engage in good faith negotiations for the elimination of their nuclear arsenals. Perhaps this situation is too esoteric to engage the man on the street. That must change. We must drive home, not only to leaders but to the public at large, the dangers of the nuclear status quo based on nuclear deterrence and convey the importance of international law as a way out of the dilemma.

Mobilization and Motivation

Falk: I would situate the failure of mobilization somewhat differently. In my view, the primary failure relates to the inability of antinuclear activists and intellectuals to mobilize those who would support nuclear disarmament, even with enthusiasm, but are unmoved to demand such a result or to engage actively in the struggle to attain antinuclear goals. This shallowness of motivation makes the concern seem to have a low priority. This undoubtedly reflects many different considerations: a sense of despair about challenging such an entrenched national security posture, a false partial acceptance of the relative stability of the present nuclear regime because of the absence of use in sixty-six years, and a rather irrational concern that perhaps giving up nuclear weapons would make the country vulnerable to nuclear terrorism and to a government that "cheated" during the disarming process. As I have stressed throughout these conversations, no rational closure is possible on these issues as the uncertainties are too pervasive. This means that our attitude toward nuclear weapons involves weighing essentially incalculable risks, and when it comes to national security, citizens have a broad willingness to defer to the views of the government, even when they collide with ethical convictions and political preferences. In the end, only competing views of human nature and values count, whether they see human nature as essentially aggressive or only conditionally so. It seems to me that those who say that the path of legality is a dead end when it comes to nuclear weaponry-the Kissingerian mentality-always prefer the risks of nuclear possession to those of nuclear disarmament. In contrast, those who say that nuclearism leads toward the apocalypse-the Kriegerian mentality-always prefer the risks associated with nuclear disarmament and believe that the international order can be transformed ultimately, by stages, from reliance on political violence to peaceful forms of conflict resolution.

Krieger: There is no doubt that a lack of motivation among the general public and policy makers keeps the abolition of nuclear weapons a low priority. In addition to the reasons for this that you suggest, there are also psychological reasons for avoiding the issue, as well as a sense of more pressing day-to-day economic and social concerns. Deference to the authority of government officials' views may prove the greatest obstacle to ridding the world of nuclear weapons. But the people of the United States, the country that most needs to lead, have become too invested in patriotic songs and presidential elections. And they are too removed from critical thinking and conscientious objection to dangerous government policies, including not only nuclear weapons policies but many other policies related to weaponry and war. The widespread passivity of the U.S. citizenry is not a force for change and makes it difficult to create the conditions that would bring about change on issues of war and nuclear disarmament.

I am honored to be placed in your perspective as holding a contrasting viewpoint to "the Kissingerian mentality." But, of course, even Henry Kissinger himself now seems to believe that the risks of nuclear deterrence are roo great to be borne indefinitely and favors moving, albeit far too slowly for me, toward a nuclear weapon-free world. You are right about my position. I think it is a foolish manifestation of hubris to continue to tempt fate by relying on nuclear weapons for security. I believe we need to move carefully from where we are today to a world without nuclear weapons, but we need to do so with serious and unwavering commitment. This will require leadership. One tool available to aid in that leadership is international law, including the ICJ's advisory opinion.

I agree with you that the ICJ's opinion is the most authoritative source of international law that exists on the issue of nuclear weapons. The problem is that the law alone does not seem to be sufficient to move the nuclear weapon states to action. I view international law as an element in the "legitimacy war" that needs to be reinforced and is not at present sufficiently powerful to prevent reliance by some states on nuclear weapons. The weakness of the law at present lies in its not directly challenging possession of nuclear weapons. So long as nuclear deterrence justifies possession, nuclear catastrophe is just the push of a button or a mishap away.

I believe the possession of the weapons themselves must be delegitimized and made illegal. This could be done with a negotiated nuclear weapons convention, which would, in effect, supersede the NPT and change the law with regard to nuclear weapons. It must be made illegitimate not only to use or threaten to use the weapons but also to possess them. Any possession of nuclear weapons should be viewed as illegitimate under strengthened provisions of international law and made a global taboo.

Falk: For this type of issue, legality is at best an instrument of persuasion helpful in mobilizing popular support, especially if law is seen as congruent with justice and human well-being, as is the case with nuclear weaponry. But in an atmosphere where political influence is heavily weighted in support of bureaucratic, strategic, and economic interests that favor lawlessness, the tendency will be to dismiss the relevance of law to the shaping of policy. The outcome of the ICJ process should have at least challenged the approach taken by the nuclear weapon states, but they took almost no notice of it after failing in trying to prevent the issue from ever being referred to the World Court. What is more, the non-nuclear weapon states might have seized upon the outcome to challenge the viability of the nonproliferation regime, putting forth a common position demanding that a disarmament process be implemented in good faith and without further delay. But these ;overnments were essentially silent and, in a profound way, became complicit with the damaging view that international law is basically irrelevant in the context of nuclear weaponry.

At the same time, it would be wrong to conclude that in the setting of nuclear weaponry, international law is irrelevant. It should be remembered that the United States used its geopolitical muscle in a failed effort to dissuade the General Assembly from referring the issue to the ICJ. The American judge on the Court wrote a dissent that went along with the view that deterrence plus nonproliferation was the best way to mitigate the harmful effects of nuclear weaponry and that existing international law was incapable of prescribing the conditions under which a use of or threat to use nuclear weaponry might be lawful. In other words, the debate about nuclear weapons has a lawfare dimension, and the ICJ is the most respected arbiter of this debate. For this reason, the U.S. government responded quasi-officially with criticisms of the majority opinion that narrowed the occasions on which it would be lawful to use or threaten to use nuclear weapons and simply claimed, disingenuously in my view, that its arms control initiatives from time to time satisfy its legal obligations under the NPT, which were reaffirmed by the ICJ, including the fundamental legal duty to pursue nuclear disarmament in good faith.

Krieger: The nuclear weapon states approached the ICJ's advisory opinion from the perspective of damage control, seeking to prevent limitations on their freedom to use or threaten to use nuclear weapons. Rather than embracing the opinion as moving toward a safer and more secure world, they fought hard to resist or limit any statements of law that intruded on their ability to use or threaten to use the most powerful weapons yet created by man. This approach has always seemed shortsighted to me in light of the fact that these states and their citizens also remain threatened by these weapons. In many respects, the arms control agreements that the nuclear weapon states have reached are also a form of damage control, achieving incremental steps that disarm public opinion more effectively than they disarm the weapons themselves. The nuclear weapon states have promoted these steps in lieu of the good faith negotiations for nuclear disarmament called for by the NPT and reinforced by the ICJ's advisory opinion.

Falk: Civil society activists and educators who study the ICJ advisory opinion as indicative of the proper approach to nuclearism often go further and single out the long dissent of Judge Weeramantry as the basis of both law and justice — and even political sanity — in the context of nuclear weaponry. For a small number of people, this legal condemnation of nuclear weaponry is reinforced by, and reinforcing of, a preexisting ethical repudiation of the whole idea of weaponry of mass destruction and induces political action of various kinds: civil disobedience at facilities relating to the production and possession of the weaponry, initiatives seeking to terminate the relationship between universities and weapons labs engaged in research and development of the weaponry, and initiation of citizen tribunals (e.g., the London Nuclear Weapons Tribunal) that pronounce upon the criminality of doctrines proposing use of the weaponry. But this is fringe activity.

Krieger: Judge Weeramantry's dissent in the ICJ's advisory opinion is a well-reasoned argument for the illegality of nuclear weapons under any circumstance. Like all good law, it is rooted in justice — and justice not only for those alive on the planet today but for future generations as well. I find it one of the most important statements of the illegality of nuclear weapons to date and all the more valuable for having been made in the official context of the ICJ's advisory opinion. As important as his dissent is, however, it is little known, and its importance little understood, by either the public or by government officials.

Falk: Why, we must ask ourselves, is such an authoritative assessment of nuclear weapons as is contained in Judge Weeramantry's dissent so little known? A superficial explanation would be that the length, density, and complexity of his argument; covering some eighty pages, discourages reading by all except the most devoted antinuclearists. Also, much of his discussion focuses on the historical and cultural context that informs a legal analysis of nuclear weaponry. There is beyond this a Western jurisprudential bias against nonpositivistic styles of analysis, which is further reinforced by a reluctance to give much intellectual traction to viewpoints that question the underlying morality of Westcentrism, which, in important respects, is culminated by the advent, use, development, and possession of nuclear weaponry. I am also reminded of the great dissent by Judge Radhabinod Pal, the Indian member of the Tokyo War Crimes Tribunal convened after World War II to impose criminal accountability on surviving Japanese political and military leaders. The scholarship of international criminal law virtually ignores Pal's dissent, although it questions in a detailed and impressive manner the self-righteous construction of international law to demonstrate that Japan was the aggressor exclusively responsible for the Asian carnage of World War II. Pal's dissent is an exemplary instance of anticolonial jurisprudence, and not only does the Western academic literature ignore it, but it is not published in a text that is readily available in most libraries (but those interested could look at Boister and Cryer, 2008).

We need to remember that the expansion of Europe at the expense of the non-Western world rested on violence and the superiority of European weaponry and strategic logistics, including naval power. This link between Western militarism and its historical ascendancy is, in my view, one of the deep reasons why there is such a seemingly irrational attachment to nuclear weaponry, making it very difficult to renounce as the supreme expression of political violence. It also suggests that critiques of militarism and what I call "violent geopolitics" need to be an integral part of any movement .. that mounts an effective challenge to nuclearism. In this regard, I find it encouraging that military approaches to political conflict have had an increasingly poor record in shaping political outcomes, and, particularly since Vietnam, the American reliance on its military superiority, a posture of unprecedented global military dominance, has proven dysfunctional in drawn out conflicts, as well as costly in lives, resources, and reputation. I believe we should call attention to the Weeramantry position in this wider geopolitical setting.

Krieger: You set forth a number of possible reasons why Judge Weeramantry's dissent is not known to the general public or even to political leaders. I would add that there is a general orientation in much of Western society to subordinate international law to geopolitical desire — in other words, not to allow international law to be a limiting factor in seeking geopolitical advantage. International law is thus applied when useful and ignored when self-interest and convenience dictate. This is a striking manifestation of the double standards that have served the interests of the powerful in both the colonial and postcolonial worlds. I think you are right that the West links its military prowess with its historical ascendancy. This may be a psychological factor in the reluctance of the West to give up its nuclear capability and thus put at risk its dominant economic position. The irony, of course, is that by subordinating the universality of international law to the achievement of short-term economic advantage, the West puts itself at risk of nuclear proliferation, nuclear terrorism, and nuclear war. The application of international law to nuclear weapons, nuclear threat, and nuclear war would create conditions that would make all peoples, including the people of the West, more secure.

Falk: What would it take to make the demand for a lawful approach to nuclear weaponry an effective challenge to existing policies? It would seem to require a much greater fear among the public that the weaponry would be used in the near future. or a reaction to use that would renew the feeling of urgency that followed immediately upon the use of atomic bombs in 1945. That is, at this point, only a pre- or postcatastrophe surge of public anxiety seems capable of mobilizing enough people to have political weight. Now, possibly an antinuclear Rosa Parks will come along and surprise us. It should be remembered, as has often been pointed out, that Rosa Parks did not act in a vacuum, that a civil rights movement had been growing in the preceding years, and that there was present a Martin Luther King Jr. who knew how to seize an opportunity to move in more peaceful directions.

Krieger: You ask an important question, but one that may not be answerable at present. In essence, you are asking, What conditions would lead to law being given preference over geopolitics with regard to nuclear policies? If we look to the past, one example stands out for me. The nuclear weapon states, at least the United States, United Kingdom, and Soviet Union, agreed initially to the NPT because they believed that international law would keep them safer and relatively more powerful by preventing the spread of nuclear weapons to other countries. They favored international law in this instance because they understood it to be in their geopolitical interests. They even agreed to the clause on pursuing good faith negotiations on nuclear disarmament, but they have never followed the law with regard to this clause. At least in this instance, we can see that the nuclear weapon states have supported, even promoted, the law when they have seen it as undergirding their power but opposed it when perceiving it to limit their power. In this regard, they have played a very dangerous game, moving humanity to the nuclear precipice and putting their own citizens at risk of nuclear annihilation.

An antinuclear Rosa Parks would be a wonderful catalyst for giving the nuclear abolition movement higher prominence, but this is difficult to imagine at the present moment. There are perhaps only two ways in which the movement couid be ignited: first) by widespread fear of nuclear annihilation; second, by an awakening to the moral implications of the threat of omnicide posed by nuclear weapons. The former route seems more likely than the latter, but after sixty-six years of the Nuclear Age, most people appear numb to the fear of nuclear annihilation or even a lesser nuclear catastrophe.

An Unequal Treaty

Falk: In retrospect, I believe the NPT was from the outset an example of an unequal treaty that reflected the predominant interests of the rich and powerful. Such treaties have always been viewed with favor by those who benefit and have generally remained effective as long as the power ratio has held up. Throughout the colonial era, unequal treaties formed the basis of many economic relationships that exploited the natural resources of the countries of the global South. I believe it is important to recognize the NPT as an unequal treaty whose lack of mutuality of obligations and benefits casts its validity into doubt. Many nations held in colonial captivity repudiated such unequal treaties in their attempts to couple political independence with economic sovereignty over natural resources. It is questionable whether this effort has succeeded_ in this present era of economic globalization in which new procedures sustain exploitative economic relationships, most prominently in the resource-rich, yet impoverished, least developed countries of sub-Saharan Africa.

I understand the difficulties that you pointed out earlier with regard to casting doubt on the NPT, and I realize that encouragement of additional nuclear weapons acquisition would be a step backward. Perhaps, a more modest version of my position would be a determined call for the renegotiation of the NPT to ensure that it would be implemented on a more symmetrical basis to include monitoring mechanisms and procedures for mounting legal challenges to noncompliance by nuclear weapon states. Now, only the nuclear weapon states have the will and capabilities to challenge supposed noncompliance by nonnuclear states. The confrontation with Iran that includes UN-backed severe sanctions illustrates this one-sided enforcement regime.

Krieger: I think there is a mutuality of obligations in the NPT, but there has been a lack of mutuality in the implementation of the treaty. The obligation of the non-nuclear weapon states not to develop or acquire nuclear weapons has been largely realized up to this point. On the other hand, the obligation of the nuclear weapon states to pursue good faith negotiations for nuclear disarmament has not been realized. The ICJ advisory opinion made it clear that this was an obligation for nuclear disarmament in all its aspects. The nuclear weapon states have made the NPT an unequal treaty by failing to fulfill their obligations. In doing so, they are devaluing and abrogating a treaty of critical importance to themselves and the world.

I doubt that the NPT can be renegotiated because its amendment process is very difficult, but I believe it is time for a new treaty, a nuclear weapons convention, that would replace the NPT. That treaty should require the elimination of nuclear weapons by a certain date and should set up phases to assess progress along the way. If the nuclear weapon states continue to drag their feet on negotiating such a new treaty, the non-nuclear weapon states should begin the negotiating process without them. The non-nuclear weapon states should make it clear that more than forty years of one-sided implementation of the NPT is far too long, and they should move forward in demanding that the nuclear weapon states achieve new goals and markers. Without such serious commitment on the part of the non-nuclear weapon states, I think there will be drift toward breakdown of the NPT, resulting in nuclear chaos.

Falk: I generally agree with your comment here as applied to the text of the NPT, but I do think the expectations about compliance from the outset were asymmetrical in the sense that the nonproliferation obligations were meant to be taken seriously as duties, whereas the disarmament commitment was always viewed differently, as essentially aspirational rather than obligatory in character. I would argue that this interpretation explains the naming of the treaty as the "Nuclear Non-Proliferation Treaty" rather than the "Nuclear Non-Proliferation and Disarmament Treaty." I do not mean to belabor this issue, but it does bear on my argument that the NPT was, from the time of its drafting, viewed as principally dealing with nonproliferation and only nominally as addressing the imperative of nuclear disarmament.

I would say that the challenge to the antinuclear community of educators and activists is to make international law matter in public attitudes toward nuclear weaponry. Leaders from time to time envision a world without nuclear weapons as a utopia sustained by law that might ultimately be attained but is never credibly pursued. These leaders never acknowledge the dubious legality of current possession of and policies toward the weaponry, and they generally reaffirm, as Barack Obama did at Prague, commitments to rely on a regime of nuclear deterrence until the promised day arrives on wings of unseen angels. In other words, the affirmation is here and now, while the realization is beyond the horizon of feasibility, so far as even the more unconditional repudiations of nuclearism are concerned.

Krieger: Your characterization of the NPT is a fair one. The treaty's predominant focus, particularly from the side of the nuclear weapon states, was nonproliferation. While there was an obligation to pursue good faith negotiations for nuclear disarmament, this has never been met, leading to the conclusion that there has been a decided lack of good faith on the part of the nuclear weapon states. This lack of good faith is causing the treaty to fray and undermining the nonproliferation obligations it imposes.

The Need to Make International Law Visible

Krieger: The great problem that we confront today, which gives rise to public complacency, is the invisibility of both nuclear weapons and the law pertaining to them to most people. Neither appears in the foreground of public consciousness. Our educational systems, even in the most advanced countries, do not concern themselves either with issues of global survival or with critical thinking. Young people are brought up today in a world oriented toward a culture of war rather than peace. Nuclear weapons are often viewed as useful tools in a culture of war. Few people any where are even aware of either the ICJ's advisory opinion on nuclear arms or any other aspect of international law pertaining to nuclear weapons. International law is invisible because we do not educate the young or the broader public to know that international law pertaining to nuclear weapons exists and matters. This should not be particularly surprising when the weapons themselves have become invisible.

The challenge for those of us working on these issues in the nuclear abolition movement is to educate the public so that the weapons and their potential for annihilation become visible, as does the international law making the use of or threat to use them illegal. Breaking through the thick walls of public complacency remains our most difficult challenge. The rationality of law, particularly law rooted in justice, is important, but it is not sufficient. If I could wave a magic wand, I would require classes in human survival to be offered in every high school and college throughout the world, and I would make Judge Weeramantry's dissenting opinion required reading and a subject of study. Discussing his dissent in such a course would not only awaken new generations to the importance of the issue of nuclear weapons abolition and the role of international law but also provide for young people a model of critical thinking in action. Of course, establishing such classes would be an extremely difficult task in itself, and it is not sufficient to educate only the young. The most pressing task is to awaken a complacent public and to engage them in transforming public attitudes toward nuclear dangers and the need to fulfill existing legal obligations to achieve nuclear disarmament in all its aspects.

Falk: Basically, I share this perspective. I would only reiterate the point that the invisibility of law is a direct consequence of the geopolitical repudiation of a law-oriented approach to the regulation of hard power. Law is quite visible when it serves geopolitical interests, which explains the relative success of the NPT with respect to countering proliferation impulses. International law, whether in trade or diplomacy or on the oceans, is respected when it serves either the mutual interests of all political actors or facilitates the ambitions and projects of the powerful.

This chapter is concluded by two of David Krieger's poems from a recent book of poetry by him (Kreiger, 2010).

Eisenhower's View

*"It wasn't necessary to hit them
with that awful thing"*
                        -- General Dwight D. Eisenhower

We hit them with it, first
at Hiroshima and then at Nagasaki –
the old one-two punch.

The bombings were tests really, to see
what those "awful things" would do.

First, of a gun-type uranium bomb, and then
of a plutonium implosion bomb.

Both proved highly effective
in the art of obliterating cities.

It wasn't necessary.

David Krieger
(from Krieger, 2010)

Hibakusha Do Not Just Happen

For every *hibakusha*
there is a pilot

for every *hibakusha*
there is a planner

for every *hibakusha*
there is a bombardier

for every *hibakusha*
there is a bomb designer

for every *hibakusha*
there is a missile maker

for every *hibakusha*
there is a missileer

for every *hibakusha*
there is a targeter

for every *hibakusha*
there is a commander

for every *hibakusha*
there is a button pusher

for every *hibakusha*
many must contribute

for every *hibakusha*
many must obey

for every *hibakusha*
many must be silent

David Krieger
(from Krieger, 2010)

Chapter 13

Epilogue

Writing this 2nd edition of the book, particularly given the objective of adding material reflecting activities since 1985, has required a lot of research, and has raised some issues that may help readers, and other issues that require further exploration.

One aim of this book is to make available in one book, all the key legal issues likely to be encountered in discussions and legal argument about nuclear weapons and international law — and at a reasonable cost. Many law books are very expensive, and this will not be one of them!

Given the need for economy, decisions had to be taken to leave out of the book, much important and helpful material that can add more depth to different aspects of law and nuclear weapons. The concerned reader may well wish to explore further, so in this chapter I identify additional material that may help. Inclusion here is not a statement about the importance or otherwise of other useful material that I have not yet mentioned — and there is a lot of it: this book and this chapter make no claims to include reference to everything or every organization that is important. However, it should give a good indication of all the key legal angles you are likely to encounter.

13.1 Nuclear Weapons - and their Effects

Judicial deliberations, such as the ICJ case, and the LAR, have gone some way to discussing the nature of nuclear weapons, the effects of their use (Hiroshima, Nagasaki, and nuclear weapons tests), and the probable consequences of future use.

It is not necessary for the purpose of this book to go further into the characteristics of nuclear weapons. Similarly, it is not necessary to go further into the effects of the nuclear weapons used on Hiroshima and Nagasaki — a lot of material is available beyond references to witnesses and materials used in the various official (such as ICJ, LAR, and Greenham Women v Reagan) and unofficial legal proceedings (such as LNWT and Edinburgh Conference). However, the interested reader may wish to find out more. Two websites that I have found to be particularly useful are the Nuclear Weapons Archive (Sublette, 2007) and the Trinity Atomic Website (Walker, 2005) (Trinity is the name of the site in New Mexico, USA, where the world's first nuclear explosion took place on 16th July, 1945 — another key atomic event from 70 years ago).

There are many books and websites available to find out more information about what nuclear weapons have done when used — Hiroshima, Nagasaki, and the many tests carried out since 1945.

Available books include: Brown and MacDonald (1977); Committee for the Compilation of Materials on Damage Caused by the Atomic Bombs in Hiroshima and Nagasaki (1981); Ehrlich et al., (1984); Glasstone et al. (1950); Greene et al. (1982); Jungk (1958; 1961); Manhattan Engineer District (1946); Nagai (1951); Pacific War Research Society (1972); SIPRI (1984 and the many other years their handbooks assess the world's nuclear weapons); and, Thompson et al. (1987).

Many images of the effects of nuclear explosions are available on the internet. There are also books available, for example see O'Brian (2015).

Related to the effects of nuclear weapons, are more general discussions about nuclear weapons, associated policies, and observations about. For example, see: Calder, (1968).

13.2 Tokyo Tribunal

The vast majority of legal commentary about nuclear weapons and international law is based, in part, on legal principles derived from the Nuremberg trials. To some extent this is understandable. Even though there was controversy at the time about the Nuremberg Principles acting to give effect to what some strict legal scholars considered to be establishing and trying people under retrospective law, there is no such controversy today as those Nuremberg Principles (see Appendix A) have become an established part of international law.

However, let us not forget that following the end of the war in 1945, there was also a Tokyo International Military Tribunal. It took more than 2 years, eventually delivering its judgment in November 1948.

One fact did not help lawyers and legal academics, was that there was a dissenting opinion by Justice Pal from India. That dissenting opinion became very rare and difficult to study because the USA and the UK rendered circulation of the opinion to be illegal — because it did not say what the victorious powers controlling the Tribunal wanted to be said. It is absolutely astonishing that a dissenting opinion from one of the Tribunal judges should have been prohibited from circulation. It was several years before copies could be obtained more easily, but only after Japan formally accepted the Tribunal and its results, even though the dissenting opinion was very critical of the legal basis of the Tribunal. This incident is of great discredit to the US and UK and the other countries providing Tribunal judges.

Material is now available for those who would like to understand the Tribunal, the evidence put before it, the charges, the procedures, and the judgment (with dissenting opinions). The interested reader might like to consider a variety of sources, including: Boister and Cryer (2008); Brackman (1989); and, Minear (1971).

There are slight echoes of Pal's Tokyo dissenting judgment in the equivocation of the ICJ in its UNGA Advisory Opinion. Pal (who was probably the most experienced international lawyer sitting as one of the judges in Tokyo) took a very traditional approach by limiting his sources of international law primarily to law established by treaties, and some precedents set by international case law. Weeramantry, in his ICJ dissenting opinion, does not take the same narrow view as Pal, deriving some of his sources of international law, back to some ancient texts. Some of the lawyers' approaches in the Tokyo trial were based on "of course the defendants knew that the things they were accused of, were wrong things to do" whatever the niceties of formal international law as it stood then.

Notwithstanding his dissenting judgment, Pal was in no doubt about the unacceptable atrocities that had been committed on a massive scale in the war in the Far East — even though he characterized the fundamental Tokyo Tribunal judgment as "victors' justice".

There is also little doubt that the US should also have faced a trial to deal with the bombings of Hiroshima and Nagasaki, which were almost inevitably war crimes.

Hopefully, more scholarship will emerge as the Tokyo Tribunal receives more attention from scholars of international law.

13.3 Alternatives to deterrence

A common apologist approach of the nuclear weapons states is based on 'deterrence'. Therefore, it is not surprising that some writers have put their minds to the point that deterrence based on nuclear weapons is unlawful, and there are credible alternatives (Alternative Defence Commission, 1983; Green, 2014).

Of course, the history of warfare since 1945 is sufficient to show that nuclear weapons have been singularly ineffective in preventing the many wars that have taken place. It is more common these days for states to create an excuse and go to war, without what used to be the formality of a declaration of war.

13.4 Peace and War

There are many writers who present different perspectives on nuclear weapons: nuclear war happening unintentionally (Frei, 1982); difficulties getting rid of nuclear weapons (Goldblat, 2000); flexible response (Legge, 1983); could anyone benefit from nuclear war? (Ground Zero, 1982); political and psychological reasons to be anti-nuclear (Lifton and Falk, 1983).

Going beyond the concept of nuclear war, there are studies of war more generally (Wright, 1965), and difficulties of getting to a peaceful state (Etzioni, 1962). A seminal book discussing how the nuclear arms race can be represented as a set of differential equations is Richardson (1960a). That book is also important for showing why it may be necessary for the nuclear weapons states to go beyond 'mere' nuclear disarmament.

Much of the war-peace discussion operates with what can be seen as a 'single' war-peace dimension; peace is the absence of war — war is the breakdown of peace. A much more radical view is that war and peace are not on one dimension, but are actually orthogonal; the elimination of war does not *ipso facto* lead to peace (Darnton, 1971). Further discussion of general ideas of 'peace' is for another book.

13.5 Religion and Morality

Weeramantry's Dissenting Opinion makes reference to several sources relevant for considering the position of various religions with respect to conduct in war, and there are additional sources that may prove helpful, such as Church of England Board for Social Responsibility (1982), Jayatilleke (1967), and, Khadduri (1955).

Further information is available in various religious texts. Richardson (1960b) has looked at the participation of religious adherents in war.

13.6 More legal Commentary

Other books about law which have been useful in putting this book together, include: Dewar et al. (1986); Grotius (1682); Mayer (2002) - about the Trident Three; Mettraux (2008); Motherson (1992) - about the World Court Project, Nanda and Krieger (1998); Pathak and Dhokalia (1992); Pictet (1952, 1958, and 1960) - commentary on the Geneva Conventions; Pogany (1987) Roberts and Guelff (1982); United Nations War Crimes Commission (1947-9) - Nuremberg Trials; Wright (1950) - review of Nuremberg and Tokyo Tribunals, and US chief prosecutor's comments about the Tokyo Tribunal.

13.7 Psychological and Sociological State of Mass Murder Killers

Nuclear weapons only exist because there are people willing to contemplate and plan for killing and mass murder on an existentialist scale. People who display such a tendency and willingness should not be in any position of government or decision making — they are simply not mentally fit enough to govern or have any position of power over others. They must be removed; they are a fundamental threat to mankind and the planet.

Much more research is needed to understand the sociological and psychological conditions that produce people who are capable of mass killing. Nuclear weapons are an extreme of this. Of course, the phenomenon includes people who are willing to kill others simply because those others think or believe differently from the killers.

Ultimately these killers or planners of mass killing know that what they are doing is fundamentally wrong — that's why they must have some kind of excuse such as 'deterrence' or even religion. There are some people who are just 'power junkies'.

People who are willing to plan and allocate resources for nuclear weapons grew up in some milieu that was ineffective in controlling or suppressing such mental tendencies, and worse, may have encouraged them. This needs to be understood.

Anybody who is willing to plan for or allocate resources towards such weapons or related behaviour needs to have a very clear understanding of the potential consequences of what they are doing. How is it possible for anyone to think it reasonable to cause such massive suffering on others so indiscriminately and disproportionately. Do they not understand the fundamental laws of war, or international humanitarian law, let alone basic humanity independently of formal legal systems?

13.8 Taking this Book Forward

It has now been 40 years between the London Nuclear Warfare Tribunal and this 2nd edition of the book about it, and its follow-on. It will not be another 40 years until the next edition.

This book is compact in presenting the key arguments about the legal situation of nuclear weapons. There are sections which deserve much more detail. Consideration is being given to additional supplementary information, although the reader looking for supplementary information will find much in the books referred to above and elsewhere in this book.

Consideration is also being given to internet resources that can supplement this book. This includes a general news channel, a discussion forum, an educational facility, and perhaps accreditation.

13.9 Register of Nuclear Weapons Advocates, Decision-Takers, etc.

There is an initiative likely to go 'live' in 2015 or 2016 to create a public register of people known to advocate, decide upon, deploy, or operate nuclear weapons systems.

This will make it easier for future war crimes tribunals, or tribunals set up for indicted people who advocate and support breaches of international humanitarian law, to know who may be indicted. It will also help members of the public to know who is willing to put in place weapons systems that pose an existentialist threat to mankind, or the planet. It is of fundamental public interest to know who are the people behind the existentialist threats facing the world.

13.10 Errors, Omissions, and, Comments

It is inevitable that a major new edition such as this will contain errors. Also, you may consider something is missing. You may wish to comment. Please send comments, suggestions, and information about errors and omissions. These will be considered for the next edition or be made available by the book associated website: nwil.xyz.

Appendix A

Nuremberg Principles

The Nuremberg Principles of International Law

Principle I

Any person who commits an act which constitutes a crime under international law is responsible therefore and liable to punishment.

Principle II

The fact that internal law does not impose a penalty for an act which constitutes a crime under international law does not relieve the person who committed the act from responsibility under international law.

Principle III

The fact that a person who committed an act which constitutes a crime under international law acted as Head of State or responsible government official does not relieve him from responsibility under international law.

Principle IV

The fact that a person acted pursuant to order of his government or of a superior does not relieve him from responsibility under international law, provided a moral choice was in fact possible to him.

Principle V

Any person charged with a crime under international law has the right to a fair trial on the facts and law.

Principle VI

The crimes hereinafter set out are punishable as crimes under international law:

- a. Crimes against peace:
  - i Planning, preparation, initiation or waging of a war of aggression or a war in violation of international treaties, agreements or assurances;
  - ii Participation in a common plan or conspiracy for the accomplishment of any of the acts mentioned under (i)

- b. War Crimes:
  Violations of the laws or customs of war which include, but are not limited to, murder, ill-treatment of prisoners of war or persons on the seas, killing of hostages, plunder of public or private property, wanton destruction of cities, towns, or villages, or devastation not justified by military necessity.

- c. Crimes against humanity:
  Murder, extermination, enslavement, deportation and other inhuman acts done against any civilian population, or persecutions on political, racial or religious grounds, when such acts are done or such persecutions are carried out in execution of or in connection with any crime against peace or any war crime.

Principle VII

Complicity in the commission of a crime against peace, a war crime, or a crime against humanity as set forth in Principle VI is a crime under international law.

Appendix B

McCloy-Zorin Accords

JOINT STATEMENT OF AGREED PRINCIPLES
FOR DISARMAMENT NEGOTIATIONS
20th September 1961

The United States and the USSR have agreed to recommend the following principles as the basis for future multilateral negotiations on disarmament and to call upon other states to cooperate in reaching early agreement on general and complete disarmament in a peaceful world in accordance with these principles:

1. SECURE DISARMAMENT AND PEACEFUL SETTLEMENT OF DISPUTES...WAR NO LONGER.

The goal of negotiations is to achieve agreement on a programme which will ensure:

a. That disarmament is general and complete and war is no longer an instrument for settling international problems, and
b. That such disarmament is accompanied by the establishment of reliable procedures for the peaceful settlement of disputes and effective arrangements for the maintenance of peace in accordance with the principles of the Charter of the United Nations.

2. RETENTION OF NON-NUCLEAR FORCES FOR DOMESTIC ORDER AND A UN PEACE FORCE

The programme for general and complete disarmament shall ensure that States have at their disposal only such nonnuclear armaments, forces, facilities, and establishments as are agreed to be necessary to maintain internal order and protect the personal security of citizens;

and that States shall support and provide manpower for a United Nations peace force.

3. ALL MILITARY FORCES, BASES, STOCKPILES, WEAPONS, AND EXPENSES TO BE ENDED

To this end, the programme for general and complete disarmament shall contain the necessary provisions, with respect to the military establishment of every nation for:

a. The disbanding of armed forces, the dismantling of military establishments, including bases, the cessation of the production of armaments as well as their liquidation or conversion to peaceful uses;
b. The elimination of all stockpiles of nuclear, chemical, bacteriological, and other weapons of mass destruction, and the cessation of the production of such weapons;
c. The elimination of all means of delivery of weapons of mass destruction;
d. The abolition of organizations and institutions designed to organize the military efforts of States, the cessation of military training, and the closing of all military training institutions; and
e. The discontinuance of military expenditures.

4. IMPLEMENTATION BY TIMED STAGES WITH COMPLIANCE AND VERIFICATION AGREED TO AT EVERY STAGE

The disarmament programme should be implemented in an agreed sequence, by stages, until it is completed, with each measure and stage carried out within specified time-limits. Transition to a subsequent stage in the process of disarmament should take place upon a review of the implementation measures included in the preceding stage and upon a decision that all such measures have been implemented and verified and that any additional verification arrangements required for measures in the next stage are, when appropriate, ready to operate.

5. EQUITABLE BALANCE AT EVERY STAGE SO NO ADVANTAGE TO ANYONE AND SECURITY FOR ALL

All measures of general and complete disarmament should be balanced so that at no stage of the implementation of the treaty could any State or group of States gain military advantage and that security is ensured equally for all

6. STRICT CONTROL TO MAKE SURE OF COMPLIANCE BY ALL PARTIES AND CREATION OF AN INTERNATIONAL DISARMAMENT ORGANIZATION WITH INSPECTORS HAVING UNRESTRICTED ACCESS EVERYWHERE WITHOUT VETO FOR FULL VERIFICATION

All disarmament measures should be implemented from beginning to end under such strict and effective international control as would provide firm assurance that all parties are honoring their obligations. During and after the implementation of general and complete disarmament, the most thorough control should be exercised, the nature and extent of each control depending on the requirements for verification of the disarmament measures being carried out in each stage. To implement control over and inspection of disarmament, an international disarmament organization including all parties to the agreement should be created within the framework of the United Nations. This international disarmament organization and its inspectors should be assured unrestricted access without veto to all places, as necessary for the purpose of effective verification.

7. DISARMAMENT PROCESS MUST BE ACCOMPANIED BY MEASURES TO MAINTAIN PEACE AND SECURITY AND A UNITED NATIONS PEACE FORCE STRONG ENOUGH TO DETER OR SUPPRESS ANY THREAT OR USE OF ARMS IN VIOLATION OF THE UNITED NATIONS CHARTER

Progress in disarmament should be accompanied by measures to strengthen institutions for maintaining peace and the settlement of international disputes by peaceful means. During and after the implementation of the programme of general and complete disarmament, there should be taken, in accordance with the principles of the United Nations Charter, the necessary measures to maintain international peace and security, including obligations of States to place at the disposal of the United Nations agreed manpower necessary for an international peace force to be equipped with agreed types of armaments. Arrangements for the use of this force should ensure that the United Nations can effectively deter or suppress and threat or use of arms in violation of the purposes and principles of the United Nations.

8. STATES SHOULD SEEK WIDEST AGREEMENT AT EARLIEST DATE WHILE CONTINUING TO SEEK MORE LIMITED AGREEMENTS WHICH WILL FACILITATE AND FORM PART OF THE OVERALL PROGRAM FOR SECURED GENERAL AND COMPLETE DISARMAMENT IN A PEACEFUL WORLD

States participating in the negotiations should seek to achieve and implement the widest possible agreement at the earliest possible date. Efforts should continue without interruption until agreement upon the total programme has been achieved, and efforts to ensure early agreement on and implementation of measures of disarmament should be undertaken without prejudicing progress on agreement on the total programme and in such a way that these measures would facilitate and form part of that programme.

Appendix C

Baden Consultation

SODEPAX Report of the Baden Consultation
3–9 April 1970, Rights and World Peace

The Rights of Conscientious Objectors

"The consultation considers that the exercise of conscientious judgment is inherent in the dignity of human beings and that accordingly, each person should be assured the right, on grounds of conscience or profound conviction, to refuse military service, or any other direct or indirect participation in wars or armed conflicts:

The right of conscientious objection also extends to those who are unwilling to serve in a particular war because they consider it unjust or because they refuse to participate in a war or conflict in which weapons of mass destruction are likely to be used.

The consultation also considers that members of armed forces have the rights and even the duty, to refuse to obey military orders which may involve the commission of criminal offences, or of war crimes or of crimes against humanity.

It is urged that the Churches should use their best endeavour to secure the recognition of the right of conscientious objection as hereinbefore defined under national and international law.

Governments should extend the right of asylum to those refusing to serve in their country for reasons of conscience".

Appendix D

Interim Declaration

This Appendix presents the Interim Declaration which was issued by the Members of the Tribunal on the last day of hearings at the London Nuclear Warfare Tribunal.

**Interim Declaration
of the
London Nuclear Warfare Tribunal
6th January 1985**

After listening to expert testimony for the past four days and considering very extensive written submissions, the London Nuclear Warfare Tribunal issues this Interim Declaration of its main conclusions and recommendations. A reasoned Judgment will be prepared and published in due course. The Tribunal also plans to publish a volume that will contain the evidence and the main documentation on which the Judgment was based.

The Tribunal has been organised and arranged by the British group, Lawyers for Nuclear Disarmament, together with the following supporting organisations: Architects for Peace; Campaign for Nuclear Disarmament; Ecology Party; Haldane Society of Socialist Lawyers; Journalists Against Nuclear Extermination; Medical Campaign Against Nuclear Weapons; National Peace Council; National Union of Public Employees; Scientists against Nuclear Arms; Scottish Lawyers for Nuclear Disarmament; Society of Friends (Quakers); Teachers for Peace; United Nations Association. It has been from start to finish a private initiative, operating with complete political independence, and without influence from any government. The organisers did make diligent efforts to obtain the participation of government representatives from the main nuclear powers, but without success. The intention was to present the Judges of the Tribunal with the arguments about nuclear weapons policy in as realistic and careful form as possible. To offset the absence of participation by current political and military leaders, each witness appearing before the Tribunal was cross-examined by a trained and prepared lawyer from a viewpoint that incorporated official thinking, especially prevailing ideas about the morality, legality, and reliability of deterrence as an acceptable way to live with nuclear weapons.

The expert commentary presented to the Tribunal can be divided into four main sections:

1. evidence relating to the medical and environmental effects of nuclear warfare, including information about the secondary effect of "nuclear winter";
2. evidence relating to the history of the growth of nuclear arms and of proposals for their use in the last forty years, the concepts of deterrence and counterforce and current weaponry and strategy and their bearing on the overall risk of nuclear war now confronting humanity;
3. evidence relating to the moral and religious implications of nuclear war preparations, and their consequences for citizen accountability;
4. evidence relating to the legal character of nuclear weapons, prevailing strategies and potential patterns of use, as well as the consequences for the individual legal responsibility of leaders and others associated with the use and production of this weaponry.

Preliminary Conclusions

At this stage of its deliberations the Tribunal is prepared to release the following preliminary conclusions. These conclusions might be modified or extended on the basis of the further reflection required to produce a Tribunal Judgment.

1. It is now established beyond any reasonable doubt that any major nuclear exchange would be an unprecedented human and environmental catastrophe, posing a serious threat to the survival of all life on the planet. One aspect of this threat has been dramatized by the experimental findings that soot and dust from nuclear explosions totalling no more than 100 megatons could produce a "nuclear

winter" of at least several months' duration.

2. The evidence presented overwhelmingly convinced the Tribunal that current weapons developments and strategies for their use (such notions as "limited nuclear war", "first—strike options", and "winnable nuclear wars") are creating acute public anxiety and produce a set of tendencies in international affairs that make the outbreak of nuclear war virtually inevitable at some point in the years ahead.

3. The evidence established beyond reasonable doubt that governments of nuclear weapons states have preferable alternatives to their current reliance on deterrence and maintaining a favourable position in the nuclear arms race.

4. The evidence was overwhelmingly convincing that there is no acceptable way to reconcile these weapons developments and strategies with prevailing morality, either as interpreted by the main world religions or by the leading ideas of non—religious political ethics.

5. The Tribunal was satisfied that current and planned weapons developments, strategies, and deployments violate the basic rules and principles of international law both customary and conventional, the procurement and use of such weapons involve infringements of the Charter of the United Nations, the Hague Conventions of 1899 and 1907 on the Law of War, the Geneva Conventions of 1949 and the Geneva Protocols of 1977.

6. The evidence was convincing that the Principles of the Nuremberg Judgment (the "Nuremberg Principles"), unanimously endorsed by a resolution of the United Nations General Assembly, as well as the Genocide Convention, are being violated in the most extreme fashion by ongoing preparation to wage nuclear war, especially to the extent that plans include indiscriminate, poisonous and massive destruction of civilian populations, amounting to a conspiracy to wage aggressive war. It appears to the Tribunal that this is particularly true of newly-developed and highly accurate weaponry.

7. The evidence overwhelmingly established that war preparations

are undermining the maintenance of political democracy and constitutional government in the nuclear weapons states, and compromising the sovereign rights that non-nuclear states, especially for those states that adhere to a policy of neutrality.

8. The evidence established that resources devoted to war are excessive and wasteful, even given a commitment to military methods of self-defence, and that this circumstance greatly complicates the challenge of overcoming widespread poverty at home and abroad, an effect especially shocking at this time of massive famine in sub-Saharan Africa.

Recommendations

These conclusions lead the Tribunal at this stage of its deliberations to offer the following recommendations:

THAT official studies be undertaken by governments and international institutions to consider longer term alternative security policies to that of nuclear deterrence, including comprehensive disarmament (within the framework of the 1961 McCloy-Zorin Principles), non-provocative defence arrangements, and the strengthening of the United Nations and regional security organisations (as distinct from Alliances);

II THAT immediate steps be taken by governments to renounce unconditionally any reliance on weapons, doctrines, and manoeuvres being developed or possessed for potential first strike or first use roles;

III THAT lawyers and lawyers' groups throughout the world accept as a matter of professional responsibility an urgent obligation to create an awareness as to the vital importance of the issues involved and the role which lawyers should play;

IV THAT also, political and military leaders as well as scientists, engineers, soldiers, and workers consider their own moral and legal responsibility for participating directly or indirectly in preparations for nuclear war and to uphold their personal and collective obligations;

V THAT peace groups and individual tax-payers consider adopting extraordinary means of non-violent direct action to increase levels of public opposition to current preparations and plans for nuclear war;

VI THAT moral authorities, legal specialists, and educators, re-examine and extend notions of citizenship and conscientious objection to justify refusals of individuals in military or government service to participate in any way in nuclear war preparations.

dated this 6th day of January, 1985, at London, England Signed by the Members of the Tribunal,

**Sean MacBride,
Chairman of the Tribunal**

**Richard Falk, Dorothy Hodgkin, Maurice Wilkins,
Members of the Tribunal**

Appendix E

Tribunal Judges

This appendix lists the Members of the Tribunal who sat as Judges during the London Nuclear Warfare Tribunal, listened to the oral evidence and considered all the documents placed before the Tribunal during its four days of session.

Sean MacBride LL.D D.Litt - Chairman of the Tribunal

- Senior Counsel, Irish Bar
- Awarded Military Service Medal, 1935
- Minister for External Affairs, Eire, 1948-51
- President, Council of Foreign Ministers of Council of Europe, 1950
- Vice-President QEEC, 1948-51
- Member of European Round Table
- Chairman of Irish Association of Jurists
- One of the Founders of Amnesty International and Chairman of its International Executive, 1961-75
- Assistant Secretary General of the United Nations, 1973-77
- Nobel Peace Prize Winner, 1974
- Awarded Lenin International Prize for Peace, 1977
- American Medal of Justice, 1978
- International Institute of Human Rights Medal, 1978
- UNESCO Medal of Merit, 1980
- Present international positions (as at late 1984/early
- 1985)
    - President, UNESCO Commission for the Study of Communication
    - President, International Peace Bureau, Geneva
    - Hon. President, World Federation of UN Associations

Richard Falk B.Sc. LL.B. J.S.D.

- Albert G. Milbank Professor of International Law and Practice, Princeton University
- Vice President, American Society of International Law, 1969–71, 1974–75
- Research Director, North American Team, World Order Models Project, 1968—81
- Co-Director, Project on the Future of the International Legal Order, 1966-75
- Editorial Board of
    - *Foreign Policy Magazine*, 1970-80
    - *American Journal of International Law*, 1961-present
    - *Alternatives*, 1974-present
    - *The Nation*, 1978-present
    - *World Policy Journal*, 1983-present
    - *Coexisstence*, 1984-present
- Chairman, Consultative Council, Lawyers' Committee on American Policy Toward Vietnam, 1967-75
- Member, Executive Council, Federation of American Scientists, 1969—71
- Member, Board of Directors, Foreign Policy Association, 1969–72
- Senior Fellow, Institute for World Order, 1972-78
- Member, Consultative Council Lawyers' Committee on Nuclear Policy, 1981-present

Dorothy Hodgkin OM FRS

- Professor Emeritus and Fellow of Wolfson College at Oxford
- Currently an honorary Fellow of Somerville and Linacre Colleges at Oxford, and Girton and Newnham at Cambridge
- numerous fellowships worldwide, including
    Australian Academy of Science, 1968
    Academy Leopoldina, 1968
- Honorary Member of the US National Academy of Science, 1971
- Honorary Member of the USSR National Academy of Science, 1976

- Honorary degrees and doctorates from, inter alia,
    University of Leeds
    University of Manchester
    University of York
    University of Bristol
    University of Modena
    University of Zagreb
- Chancellor of Bristol University
- Nobel Prize winner for Chemistry, 1964
- Royal Medallist, Royal Society, 1956

Maurice Wilkins CBE MA PhD LLD FRS

- Emeritus professor of Biophysics and Fellow of Kings College, London
- Manhattan Project, University of California, 1944
- Lecturer in Physics, St. Andrews University, 1945
- MRC Unit, Kings College, London University: successively member of the scientific staff, Associate Director, and Deputy Director
- Professor of Molecular Biology, Kings College, London, 1963–70
- Honorary Member of the American Society for Biological Chemists, 1964
- President of British Society for Social Responsibility in Science, 1969–present
- Foreign Honorary member of the American Academy of Arts and Sciences, 1970
- President of Food and Disarmament International
- Member of British PUGWASH
- Albert Lasker Award, 1960
- Nobel Prize for Medicine, 1962
- Honorary LLD Glasgow 1972

Appendix F

Tribunal Supporting Organizations

This Appendix lists alphabetically those Organisations in Britain which supported the establishment and organisation of the London Nuclear Warfare Tribunal.

1. Architects for Peace
2. Campaign for Nuclear Disarmament
3. Green Party (formerly Ecology Party)
4. Haldane Society of Socialist Lawyers
5. Journalists Against Nuclear Extermination
6. Medical Campaign Against Nuclear Weapons
7. National Peace Council
8. National Union of Public Employees
9. Scientists Against Nuclear Arms
10. Scottish Lawyers for Nuclear Disarmament
11. Society of Friends (Quakers)
12. Teachers for Peace
13. United Nations Association

Appendix G

Convenors of the Tribunal

This Appendix lists alphabetically, the members of the Organising Committee who established, convened and organised the London Nuclear Warfare Tribunal on behalf of the supporting organizations. Not all persons listed participated for the whole time:

- Geoffrey Darnton
- Christine Kings
- Nick Kollerstrom
- Ross McKenzie
- Jonathon Porritt
- Edward Rees
- Elaine Steel
- Philip Webber
- Graeme Wilkinson

Appendix H

List of Evidence before the Tribunal

The Tribunal had before it the oral and written evidence submitted by the people shown in the following few pages. These pages list the witnesses and deponents, and show the titles of written evidence submitted to the Tribunal. This list of witnesses and deponents is then followed by discussions of the evidence itself. The list of witnesses is shown under the principal headings of:

1.   Moral Issues
2.   Medical and Environmental Effects
3.   Current Weaponry and Strategy
4.   Legal Implications

H.1 Moral Issues

Witness/Deponent	Title of Evidence (if written and submitted)
GREET, Kenneth V.	Statement
KENT, Bruce	Nuclear Weapons and Morality
OESTREICHER, Paul	• Morality and Nuclear Deterrence • see book - The Church and the Bomb
OHKAWA, Yoshiatsu	The dehumanising crime of the use of nuclear weapons
SATO, Gyotsu N.	Inquiry into the morality of alignment for war, under Modern Technology and Systems of Warfare

Table H-1: Witnesses and Evidence on Moral Issues

H.2 Medical and Environmental Effects

Witness/Deponent	Title of Evidence (if written and submitted)
ALCALAY, Glenn	• Maelstrom in the Marshall Islands: The Social Impact of Nuclear Weapons Testing • Marshall Islanders Exposed to Fallout: Summary of Evidence • United Nations General Assembly Special Committee on the situation with regard to the implementation of the Declaration on the Granting of Independence to Colonial Countries and People - 125th Meeting verbatim record pp 16—25
DAWSON, John D.	BMA Report - see section on books
GREENE, Owen, and, STEADMAN, Philip	Evidence on the effects of nuclear attack on Britain
HAINES, Andrew	• Medical Aspects of the Nuclear Arms Race. • Nuclear Weapons and Medicine: some ethical dilemmas • The role and effectiveness of civil defence and medical planning for nuclear war
IWASA, Mikiji	Testimony before London Tribunal
MYERS, Norman	Environmental Consequences of Nuclear War
PERCIVAL, I.C.	Evidence on Global Physical Effects of Nuclear War
PORRITT, Jonathon	The Impact of Nuclear War on the Biosphere
SAITO, Osamu	Environmental and Medical Effects of Atomic Bombing
THOMPSON, J.	Psychological Reactions to Disaster

H.3 Current Weaponry and Strategy

Witness/Deponent	Title of Evidence (if written and submitted)
ALDRIDGE, Robert C.	• Background Paper on Flexible Response Options and the Defense of Europe • Background Paper on Star Wars and First Strike
DANDO, Malcolm	see Books: (1) Death of Deterrence (2) Guide to Nuclear Weapons 84-85
HARBOTTLE, Michael N.	Submission to the Nuclear War Tribunal
KALDOR, Mary H.	[no written evidence]
PASTI, Nino	Evolution of the American Military Strategy
PENTZ, M.J.	• New Weapons and the Strategies for their Use • New Strategies for NATO? Conventional Deep Strikes or Nuclear War Fighting?
PRINS, Gwyn	• Nuclear Deterrence in its Historical Context • see book - The Nuclear Crisis Reader
ROGERS, Paul	see Books: (1) Death of Deterrence (2) Guide to Nuclear Weapons 84-85
SMITH, Dan	Notes on the Strategy of Nuclear Deterrence
VLASIKHIN, Vasily A.	To the question regarding the assessment of the lawfulness of the military and political strategy of the Warsaw Treaty Organisation
WEBBER, Philip R.	• Tribunal Evidence • NATO Strategy for the Defence of Europe
WILSON, Andrew	Evidence - no title

H.4 Legal Implications

Witness/Deponent	Title of Evidence (if written and submitted)
AKAMATSU, Koichi	• Use of Nuclear Weapons - Violation of International Law for a total ban on Nuclear Weapons • The Tokyo District Court ruled Atomic Bombing of Hiroshima and Nagasaki violates International Law
ARBESS, Daniel	U.S. Countervailing Nuclear Strategy and the International Law of Armed Conflict
BOYLE, Francis A.	• Nuclear Weapons and International Law: The Arms Control Dimension • The Relevance of International Law to the So-called "Paradox" of Nuclear Deterrence
CARTY, J.A.	The question of the legality of the use of nuclear weapons in accordance with existing nuclear power strategic policy and the 1st Protocol Additional to the 1949 Geneva Convention on the Laws of War
CASTELLINA, Luciana	Evidence - no title
GRIFFITH, John	The Illegality of Nuclear Weapons
HUTCHINSON, Jean	An Examination of the Legality of Nuclear Weapons
LAWYERS FOR NUCLEAR DISARMAMENT	The Illegality of Nuclear Warfare
MEYROWITZ, Elliott L.	• Prohibitions and Restraints on Nuclear Weapons in International Law since 1945 • The Laws of War and Nuclear Weapons

Witness/Deponent	Title of Evidence (if written and submitted)
RUSSBACH, Olivier	Nuclear Weapons: A Denial of Democracy and Law
SCOTTISH LAWYERS FOR NUCLEAR DISARMAMENT	Submission to the Nuclear War Tribunal 3rd-6th January 1985
STANIA, Peter	Some Aspects of Neutrality and the Nuclear Threat
TAIROV, T.	International Law and the use of Nuclear Weapons
TAKAMURA, Yoshiatsu	Testimony before London Tribunal
WRIGHT, David	An overview and assessment of possible peace/justice initiatives and the role of law therein: one Canadian's perspective

H.5 Books Submitted to the Tribunal

Several books were submitted to the Tribunal as part of the evidence given by witnesses and deponents. This section references the books which were referred to and used by the Tribunal in reaching their conclusions.

TITLE	AUTHOR(S)/EDITOR(S) and PUBLISHER
BMA Report - The Medical Effects of Nuclear War	British Medical Association Board of Science and Education, John Wiley & Sons, 1983
The Choice: Nuclear Weapons versus Security	Prince, Gwyn (ed.) (1984) Chatto & Windus
The Church and the Bomb	Hodder and Stoughton, 1982
Death of Deterrence	tbs
Defence without the Bomb	Alternative Defence Commission, Taylor and Francis, 1983
Defended to Death	Gwyn Prins (ed), Penguin Books, 1983
Documents on the Laws of War	Adam Roberts and Richard Guelff (eds.), Oxford University Press, 1982
Guide to Nuclear Weapons 84-85	Paul Rogers, University of Bradford School of Peace Studies, 1984
Hiroshima and Nagasaki	The Committee for the Compilation of Materials on Damage caused by the Atomic Bombs in Hiroshima and Nagasaki, Hutchinson, 1981
Nuclear Winter	Paul R. Ehrlich, Carl Sagan, Donald Kennedy, and Walter Orr Roberts, Sidgwick and Jackson, 1984
RAND Corporation Document	tbs

References

Preparing this list of references was particularly problematic because of the custom for writers of legal materials to use footnote referencing, and for writers in subjects like social sciences, business, and management, to use author-date referencing. This book has adopted a hybrid approach; footnote referencing has been retained for some legal sources, but some references to books have been repeated here as references. Full references have not yet been constructed for all footnotes. That will be a major task and is reserved for a future edition of this book. Hopefully, all in-text citations will be found here. Many references have been derived from the various legal document footnotes — for some books, there are later versions available but earlier versions are listed to have consistency with the legal documents reproduced in the book.

* * * * *

Allen, Charles (1990) *The Savage Wars of Peace: Soldiers' Voices, 1945-89*, London: Michael Joseph Ltd.
Alternative Defence Commission (1983) *Defence Without The Bomb*, London: Taylor & Francis.
Aristotle (4th C BC) *Politics*, many English translations.
Atomic Energy Commission (1950) The Effects of Atomic Weapons
Bach, Wilfrid (1986) "Climatic Consequences of Nuclear War", in *Proceedings of the Sixth World Congress of the International Physicians for the Prevention of Nuclear War* (IPPNW), Cologne, 1986.
Baher, H. W. (ed.) (1992) [Albert Schweizer] *Letters, 1905-65*, Prentice-Hall.
Bates, Don G. (1983) "The Medical and Ecological Effects of Nuclear War", *McGill Law Journal*, Vol. 28, p. 717.
Bedjaoui, Mohammed (1996) *Declaration of President Bedjaoui*, Hague: International Court of Justice.
Blake, Nigel P., and Pole, Kay (1984) *Objections to Nuclear Defence: Philosophers on Deterrence*, Law Book Co of Australasia.
BMA (1983) *BMA Report - The Medical Effects of Nuclear War*, Chichester: John Wiley & Sons.
Boister, Neil and Cryer, Robert (eds.) (2008) Documents on the Tokyo International Military Tribunal: Charter, Indictment, and Judgments, Oxford: Oxford University Press.
Brackman, Arnold C. (1989) *The Other Nuremberg: the untold story of the Tokyo war crimes trials*, Glasgow: William Collins Sons & Co. Ltd.

Brown, Anthony Cave and MacDonald, Charles B., (1977) *The Secret History of the Atomic Bomb*, New York: Dell Publishing.
Brownlie, Ian (1990) *Principles of Public International Law*, Oxford: Oxford University Press.
Brundtland, Gro Harlem (1987) For the 'Brundtland Commission' Report, see World Commission on Environment and Development.
Burroughs, John (1997) *The Legality of Threat or Use of Nuclear Weapons: A Guide to the Historic Opinion of the International Court of Justice*, LIT Verlag.
Butler, William E. (ed.) (1991) *Control over Compliance with International Law*, Kluwer Academic Publishers.
Cady, Duane L. and Werner, Richard (eds) (1992) *Just War, Nonviolence, and Nuclear Deterrence: Philosophers on War and Peace (Ethics, Violence and Peace)*, Longman Pub Group
Calder, Nigel (ed.) (1968) *Unless Peace Comes: A Scientific Forecast of New Weapons*, Harmondsworth: Allen Lane.
Castrén, Erik J. S (1954) *The present law of war and neutrality*, Suomalainev Tiedeakemia.
Chimni, B.S. (1992) "Nuclear Weapons and International Law: Some Reflections" in Pathak and Dhokalia (1992).
Church of England Board for Social Responsibility (1982) *Church and the Bomb*, Hodder & Stoughton
Churchill, Winston (1954) *Triumph and Tragedy: The Second World War, vol 6*, London: Cassell.
Cohen, Maxwell T. and Gouin, Margaret E. (eds.) (1988) *Lawyers and the Nuclear Debate*, University of Ottawa Press.
Committee for the Complation of Materials on Damage Caused by the Atomic Bombs in Hiroshima and Nagasaki (1981) *Hiroshima and Nagasaki: The Physical, Medical, and Social Effects of the Atomic Bombings*, London: Hutchinson.
Cooper, R.W. (1947) *The Nuremberg Trial*, Harmondsworth: Penguin Books.
Dando, Malcolm & Rogers, Paul (1982) *The Death of Deterrence*, London:Campaign for Nuclear Disarmament.
Darnton, Geoffrey (1971) "The Concept Peace" *in Proceedings of the International Peace Research Association Fourth General Conference*, Bled, Yugoslavia 22-25 October, 1971. Oslo: International Peace Research Association.
Darnton, Geoffrey (ed.) (1989) *The Bomb and the Law: London Nuclear Warfare Tribunal: Evidence, Commentary and Judgment*, Stockholm: Alva and Gunnar Myrdal Foundation & Swedish Lawyers Against Nuclear Arms. [1st edition of this book]
de Chazournes, Laurence Boisson, and Sands, Philippe (eds.) (1999) *International Law, the International Court of Justice and Nuclear Weapons*, Cambridge: Cambridge University Press.

Dewar, John; Paliwala, Abdul; Picciotto, Sol; and, Ruete, Matthias (eds) (1986) *Nuclear Weapons, the Peace Movement and the Law*, Basingstoke: Palgrave Macmillan, for Warwick Legal Defence Trust.

Dewes, C.F. (1998) *The World Court Project: the evolution and impact of an effective citizen's movement*, PhD Dissertation. Armidale, Australia: University of New England. Available at: https://e-publications.une.edu.au/vital/access/manager/Repository/une:17024. [May 2015].

Dias, R.W.M. (1976) *Jurisprudence* (4th ed.), London: Butterworth & Co Publishers Ltd. [other editions available]

Dutt, Romesh Chunder (trans) (n.d.) *Ramayana: Epic of Ram, Prince of India*, Rupa & Co

Ehrlich, Paul R.; Sagan, Carl; Kennedy, Donald; and, Roberts, Walter Orr (1984) *Nuclear Winter: The Cold and the Dark*, London: Sidgwick and Jackson.

Etzioni, Amitai (1962) *The Hard Way to Peace: A New Strategy*, Ney York: Collier Books.

Falk, Richard A. (1965) "The Shimoda Case: A Legal Appraisal of the Atomic Attacks Upon Hiroshima and Nagasaki", *The American Journal of International Law*, Vol. 59, No. 4, pp. 759-793.

Falk, Richard A. (1971) "Beyond Deterrence: The Quest for World Peace" in Falk, Richard A., *This Endangered Planet: Prospects and Proposals for Human Survival*, New York: Random House.

Falk, Richard and Krieger, David (eds.) (2008) *At the Nuclear Precipice: Catastrophe or Transformation?* New York: Palgrave Macmillan, 20

Falk, Richard A., and Krieger, David (2012) *The Path to Zero: Dialogues on Nuclear Dangers*, Boulder, CO: Paradigm Publishers.

Fenwick, Charles G. (1965) *International Law*, New York: Appleton-Century-Crofts.

Ferrari Bravo, L. (1996) *Declaration of Judge Ferrari Bravo*, Hague: International Court of Justice.

Finnis, John; Boyle, Joseph M.; and Grisez, Germain (1988) *Nuclear Deterrence, Morality and Realism*, Oxford: Oxford University Press.

Fleck, Dieter (ed.) (1995) *The Handbook of Humanitarian Law in Armed Conflicts*, Oxford: Oxford University Press.

Fleischhauer, Carl-August (1996) *Separate Opinion of Judge Fleischhauer* Hague: International Court of Justice.

Fleutry, Michel (1995) *Dictionnaire encyclopédique d'électronique Anglais-Français*, Paris: La Maison Du Dictionnaire.

Frei, Daniel (1982) *Risks of Unintentional Nuclear War*, Geneva: United Nations Institute for Disarmament Research.

Ginsberg, Robert (1969) *The Critique of War*, Chicago: Henry Regnery Company.

Glasstone, Samuel; Hirschfelder, Joseph O; Parker, David B; Kramish, Arnold; and, Smith, Ralph Carlisle (1950) *The Effects of Nuclear Weapons*, Washington, D.C.: US Government Printing Office.

Glasstone, Samuel, and, Dolan, Philip J. (1977) *The Effects of Nuclear Weapons* (3rd ed.), Washington, D.C.: US Department of Defense.

Goldblat, J. (ed.) (2000) *Nuclear Disarmament: Obstacles to Banishing the Bomb*, London: I.B. Tauris.

Goodchild, Peter (1980) *J. Robert Oppenheimer. 'Shatterer of Worlds'*, London: British Broadcasting Corporation.

Gore, Al (1992) *Earth in the Balance: Forging a New Common Purpose*, Earthscan Ltd

Green, Robert (2014) *Security Without Nuclear Deterrence* (2nd ed.), Christchurch, NZ: Disarmament & Security Centre

Greene, Owen; Rubin, Barry; Turok, Neil; Webber, Philip; Wilkinson, Graeme (1982) *London After the Bomb: What a Nuclear Attack Really Means*, Oxford: Oxford University Press.

Greenham (1984) "Greenham Women Against Cruise Missiles v. Reagan", in U.S. District Court for the Southern District of New York.

Gregory, Donna Uthus (ed.) (1986) *The Nuclear Predicament: A Sourcebook*, New York: St. Martin's Press.

Grief, Nicholas (1987a) "The Legality of Nuclear Weapons", *in* Pogany (1987).

Grief, Nicholas (1987b) "Nuclear Tests and International Law", *in* Pogany (1987).

Grief, Nicholas (1992) *The World Court Project on Nuclear Weapons and International Law*, Northampton, MA: Aletheia Press.

Grief, Nicholas (1993) *The World Court Project on Nuclear Weapons and International Law* (2nd ed.) Northampton, MA: Aletheia Press.

Grief, Nicholas (2011) "Nuclear Weapons: the Legal Status of Use, Threat and Possession" in *Nuclear Abolition Forum*, Issue No. 1, October 2011, pp. 7-13, London: Nuclear Abolition Forum. Available online at: http://www.abolitionforum.org/site/wp-content/uploads/2012/01/NAF-First-issue.online-version.pdf [July 2015].

Grotius, Hugo (1682) *Treating of the Rights of War & Peace. In the first is handled, Whether any War be Just. In the second is shewed, The Causes of War, both Just and Unjust. In the Third is declared, What in War is Lawful; that is, Unpunishabe.* London: Thomas Basset and Ralph Smith. [trans. William Evats].

Ground Zero (1982) *Nuclear War: What's in it for You?*, New York: Pocket Books.

Guillaume, Gilbert (1996) *Separate Opinion of Judge Guillaume*, Hague: International Court of Justice.

Guruswamy, Lakshman D.; Palmer, Geoffrey W. R.; Weston, Burns H. (1994) *International Environmental Law and World Order: A Problem-Oriented Coursebook*, West Group.

Hachiya, Michihiko (1955) *Hiroshima Diary: The Journal of a Japanese Physician, August 5-September 30, 1945*, University of North Carolina Press.

Hannikainen, Lauri (1988) *Peremptory norms (jus cogens) in international law: historical development, criteria, present status*, Finnish Lawyers' Pub. Co.
Hart, Herbert Lionel Adolphus (1961) *The Concept of Law*, Oxford: Oxford University Press.
Hassan, Syed Riazul (1974) *The Reconstruction of Legal Thought in Islam*, Idara Tarjuman al-Quran.
Hennessy, Peter. (2007) *Cabinets and the Bomb*, Oxford University Press for the British Academy.
Herczegh, Geza (1984) *Development of International Humanitarian Law*, Akademiai Kiado
Herczegh, Geza (1996) *Declaration of Judge Herczegh*, Hague: International Court of Justice.
Hersey, John (1946) *Hiroshima*, Harmonsworth: Penguin Books.
Hickman, Jane (1986) "Greenham Women Against Cruise Missiles and others v. Ronald Reagan and others", *in* Dewar et al. (1986).
Higgins, Rosalyn (1996) *Dissenting Opinion of Judge Higgins*, Hague: International Court of Justice.
Hobbes, Thomas (1651) *Leviathan, or the Matter, Forme, & Power of a Common-Wealth Ecclesiasticall and Civill*, London: Andrew Crooke. [there are many more modern editions of *Leviathan*].
Hollins, H.B.; Powers, A. L.; and Sommer, Mark (1989) *The Conquest of War: Alternative Strategies for Global Security*, Westview Press Inc.
Holm, E. (ed.) (1995) *Radioecology: Lectures in Environmental Radioactivity*, World Scientific Pub Co Inc
ICC (1998) *Rome Statute of the International Criminal Court*, The Hague: International Criminal Court.
ICJ (1996a) *Legality of the Use by a State of Nuclear Weapons in Armed Conflict Advisory Opinion of 8 July 1996*, Hague: International Court of Justice. [the 'WHO Advisory Opinion]
ICJ (1996b) *Legality of the Threat or Use of Nuclear Weapons Advisory Opinion of 8 July 1996*, Hague: International Court of Justice. [the 'UNGA Advisory Opinion]
International Court of Justice (1998) *Reports of Judgments, Advisory Opinions and Orders 1996: Legality of the Threat of Use of Nuclear Weapons: Advisory Opinion of 8 July 1996 (Reports of judgments, advisory opinions & orders, 1996)*, New York: United Nations.
IPB (1992) *World Court Project: International Launch Geneva, 14-15 May, 1992*, Geneva: International Peace Bureau.
Ishikawa, Eisei, and Swain, David L. (1981) translators - see Committee for the Complation of Materials on Damage Caused by the Atomic Bombs in Hiroshima and Nagasaki (1981).
Jackson, Robert (1946) "Opening Address for the United States" in Office of the United States Chief of Counsel For Prosecution of Axis Criminality, *Nazi Conspiracy and Aggression* (Vol 1), Washington DC: United States Government Printing Office. available at: http://www.loc.gov/rr/frd/Military_Law/pdf/NT_Nazi_Vol-I.pdf [July 2015].

Jayatilleke, Kulatissa Nanda (1967) "The principles of international law in Buddhist doctrine" *Volume 120 of Collected Courses of the Hague Academy of International Law*. Hague: The Hague Academy of International Law.
Johnson, R., and Zelter, A. (eds.) (2011) *Trident and International Law: Scotland's Obligations*, Edinburgh: Luath Press Ltd.
Jungk, Robert (1958) *Brighter than a Thousand Suns: A Personal History of the Atomic Scientists*, London: Victor Gollancz Ltd.
Jungk, Robert (1961) *Children of the Ashes: The People of Hiroshima*, London: William Heinemann Ltd.
Kaku, Michio and Axelrod, Daniel (1987) *To Win a Nuclear War: The Pentagon's Secret War Plans*, South End Press
Karp, Regina Cowen (1992) *Security Without Nuclear Weapons?: Different Perspectives on Non-Nuclear Security* (SIPRI Monographs), Oxford: Oxford University Press.
Kenny, Anthony J.P. (1985a) *The Logic of Deterrence*, University of Chicago Press.
Kenny, Anthony J.P. (1985b) *Ivory Tower: Essays in Philosophy and Public Policy*, Blackwell.
Khadduri, Majid (1955) *War and Peace in the Law of Islam*, Johns Hopkins University Press.
Kissinger, Henry (1957) *Nuclear Weapons & Foreign Policy*, New York: Harper & Brothers
Koroma, Abdul G. (1996) *Dissenting Opinion of Judge Koroma*, Hague: International Court of Justice.
Krieger, David, (ed.) (2009) The Challenge of Abolishing Nuclear Weapons. New Brunswick, NJ: Transaction Publishers.
Krieger, David, (2010) *God's Tears: Reflections on the Atomic Bombs Dropped on Hiroshima and Nagasaki*, Tokyo: Coal Sack Publishing Company.
Krieger, David. (2013) *Zero: The Case for Nuclear Weapons Abolition*. Santa Barbara, CA: Nuclear Age Peace Foundation, 2013.
Lapp, Ralph E. (1958) *The Voyage of the Lucky Dragon*, Harmonsworth: Penguin Books
LAR (2001) *Opinion of the Court in Lord Advocate's Reference No. 1 of 2000 by Her Majesty's Advocate*, Edinburgh: Appeal Court, High Court of Justiciary. Available at: https://www.scotcourts.gov.uk/opinions/11_00.html [June 2015].
Legge, J. Michael (1983) *Theater Nuclear Weapons and the NATO Strategy of Flexible Response*, Santa Monica, CA: RAND Corporation.
Lifton, Robert Jay, and, Falk, Richard A. (1983) *Indefensible Weapons: Political and Psychological Case Against Nuclearism*, Basic Books.
Lowe, Vaughan (2007) *International Law*, Oxford: Oxford University Press.
Manhattan Engineer District (1946) *The Atomic Bombings of Hiroshima and Nagasaki*, The Manhattan Engineer District of the United States Army.

Mayer, John (2002) *Nuclear Peace: the Story of The Trident Three*, London: Vision.
McDougal, Myres Smith, and Feliciano, F. P. (1961) *Law and Minimum World Public Order: The Legal Regulation of International Coercion*, Yale University Press.
Mettraux, Guénaël (2008) Perspectives on the Nuremberg Trial, Oxford: Oxford University Press.
Minear, Richard H. (1971) *Victors' Justice: The Tokyo War Crimes Trial*, Princeton, NJ: Princeton University Press.
Motherson, Keith (1992) *From Hiroshima to The Hague - -A guide to the World Court Project*, Geneva: Internationalo Peace Bureau.
Nagai, Takashi (1951) *We of Nagasaki: The story of survivors in an atomic wasteland*, London: The Harborough Publishing Co. Ltd.
Nanda, Ved and Krieger, David (1998) *Nuclear Weapons and the World Court*, New York: Transnational Publishers.
NPT (1968) Treaty on the Non-Proliferation of Nuclear Weapons (NPT), New York: United Nations Office for Disarmament Affairs (UNODA), available at: http://www.un.org/disarmament/WMD/Nuclear/NPTtext.shtml
Nuremberg (1945) *Agreement for the Prosecution and Punishment of the Major War Criminals of the European Axis, and Charter of the International Military Tribunal. London, 8 August 1945*, London: UK Foreign and Commonwealth Office.
Nuremberg (1946) *Judgment of the International Military Tribunal for the Trial of German Major War Criminals (with the dissenting opinion of the Soviet member), Nuremberg 30th September and 1st October 1946*, London: His Majesty's Stationery Office (Document Miscellaneous No. 12 (1946)).
Nussbaum, Arthur (1947) *A Concise History of the Law of Nations*, New York: Macmillan Co.
Nystuen, G.; Casey-Maslen, S.; and Bersagel, A.G. (eds.) (2014) *Nuclear Weapons under International Law*, Cambridge: Cambridge University Press.
O'Brian, John (ed.) (2015) *Camera Atomica*, London: Black Dog Publishing.
Oda, Shigeru (1996) *Dissenting Opinion of Judge Oda*, Hague: International Court of Justice.
OED (1987) *The Shorter Oxford English Dictionary*, (3rd ed.) Oxford: Oxford University Press.
Oppenheim, Lassa Francis Lawrence (1914) *The Collected Papers of John Westlake on Public International Law*, Cambridge: Cambridge University Press.
Oppenheim, Lassa Francis Lawrence (1952) *International Law: Vol. 2: Disputes, War, and Neutrality*, edited by H. Lauterpacht, London: Longmans, Green & Co.
Pacific War Research Society (1972) *The Day Man Lost: Hiroshima, 6 August 1945*, Tokyo: Kodansha International.

Pathak, R.S., and Dhokalia, R.P. (1992) *International Law In Transition: Essays In Memory of Judge Nagendra Singh*, Boston: Lancers Books in collaboration with Martinus Nijhoff Publishers.

Permanent People's Tribunal (1985) *Crime of Silence: Armenian Genocide*, London: Zed Books Ltd

Pictet, Jean S. (ed.) (1952) *I Geneva Convention for the Amelioration of the Conditions of the Wounded, and Sick in Armed Forces in the Field* (with commentary), Geneva: International Committee of the Red Cross.

Pictet, Jean S. (ed.) (1958) *IV Geneva Convention Relative to the Protection of Civilian Persons in Time of War*, (with commentary), Geneva: International Committee of the Red Cross.

Pictet, Jean S. (ed.) (1960a) *II Geneva Convention for the Amelioration of the Conditions of the Wounded ,Sick and Shipwrecked Members of Armed Forces at Sea* (with commentary) Geneva: International Committee of the Red Cross.

Pictet, Jean S. (ed.) (1960b) *III Geneva Convention Relative to the Treatment of Prisoners of War*, (with commentary), Geneva: International Committee of the Red Cross.

Pogany, Istvan (ed.) (1987) *Nuclear Weapons and International Law*, New York: St. Martin's Press.

Powell, Colin (1995) *A Soldier's Way*, Hutchinson.

Prins, Gwyn (ed.) (1983) *Defended to Death: Study of the Nuclear Arms Race*, London: Penguin Books

Prins, Gwyn (ed.) (1984) *The Choice: Nuclear Weapons Versus Security*, Chatto & Windus

Rahula, Walpola (1959) *What the Buddha Taught*, Everygreen Original/ Grove Press.

Ranjeva, Raymond (1996) *Separate Opinion of Judge Ranjeva*, Hague: International Court of Justice.

Rawls, John (1971) *A Theory of Justice*, Harvard University Press.

Richardson, Lewis Fry (1960a) *Arms and Insecurity: A Mathematical Study of the Causes and Origins of War*. London: Stevens & Sons Ltd.

Richardson, Lewis Fry (1960b) *Statistics of Deadly Quarrels* London: Stevens & Sons Ltd.

RMI (2014) *Application Instituting Proceedings against the United Kingdom*, Hague: International Court of Justice.

Roberts, Adam and Guelff, Richard (eds.) (1982) *Documents on the Laws of War*, Oxford: Oxford University Press. [later editions are available].

Rogers, Paul (1984) *Guide to Nuclear Weapons 84-85*, Bradford: University of Bradford School of Peace Studies.

Rotblat, Joseph (1981) *Nuclear Radiation in Warfare,* London: Taylor & Francis Ltd. for SIPRI.

Ruston, Roger (1981) *Nuclear deterrence, right or wrong?: A study of the morality of nuclear deterrence*, Catholic Information Service.

Schell, Jonathan (1982) *The Fate of the Earth*, Jonathan Cape Ltd.

Schell, Jonathan (1984) *The Abolition*, Basingstoke: Picador Books.

Schwarzenberger, Georg (1958) *The legality of nuclear weapons*, London: Stevens & Sons.
Schwebel, Stephen M. (1996) *Dissenting Opinion of Judge Schwebel*, Hague: International Court of Justice.
Shahabuddeen, Mohamed (1996) *Dissenting Opinion of Judge Shahabuddeen*, Hague: International Court of Justice.
Shi, Jiuyong (1996) *Declaration of Judge Shi*, Hague: International Court of Justice.
Singh, Nagendra and McWhinney, Edward (1989) *Nuclear Weapons and Contemporary International Law* Dordrecht: Martinus Nijhoff Publishers.
Singh, Nagendra (1973) *India and International Law*, S. Chand

Singh, Nagendra (1980) *Juristic Concepts of Ancient Indian Polity*, Vision Books.
SIPRI (1984) *World Armaments and Disarmament:* SIPRI Yearbook 1984, London: Taylor & Francis Ltd.
Sivard, Ruth Leger (1993) *World Military and Social Expenditures 1993*, World Priorities.
Spaight, James Molony (1947) *Air Power and War Rights* (3rd ed.), Longmans, Green.
Stone, Julius (1954) *Legal controls of international conflict : a treatise on the dynamics of disputes - and war-law*, London: Stevens.
Sublette, Carey (2007) The Nuclear Weapon Archive: A Guide to Nuclear Weapons, available at: http://nuclearweaponarchive.org/ [July 2015].
Tanaka, Toshiyuki (1996) *Hidden Horrors: Japanese War Crimes in World War II*, Westview Press Inc.
Thompson, E. P; Davis, Mike; Williams, Raymond; Bahro, Rudolf; Magri, Lucio; Balibar, Etienne; Medvedev, Roy and Zhores; Cox, John; Kugai, Saburo; Raskin, Marcus; Chomsky, Noam; Wolfe, Alan; Kaldor, Mary; and, Halliday, Fred (1987) *Exterminism and Cold War*, London: Verso Books.
Toffler, Alvin and Heidi (1993) *War & Anti-War In 21st Century: Survival at the Dawn of the 21st Century*, Little Brown.
UNIDIR - see Frei (1982).
United Nations War Crimes Commission (1947-9) *Law Reports of Trials of War Criminals* [15 volumes], London: Published for the United Nations War Crimes Commission by His Majesty's Stationery Office.
Vatican (1965) *Gaudium et Spes*, [joy and hope] Vatican: Roman Catholic Church.
Vereshchetin, Vladlen S. (1996) *Declaration of Judge Vereshchetin*, Hague: International Court of Justice.
Walker, Gregory (2005) *Trinity Atomic Web Site :Nuclear Weapons: History, Technology, and Consequences in Historic Documents, Photos, and Videos*, available at: http://www.abomb1.org/ [July 2015].

Webber, Philip; Wilkinson, Graeme; and Rubin, Barry (1983) *Crisis Over Cruise: A Plain Guide To The New Weapons*, Harmonsworth: Penguin.
Weeramantry, Christopher Gregory (1988) *Islamic Jurisprudence: An International Perspective*, Palgrave Macmillan
Weeramantry, Christopher Gregory (1996) *Dissenting Opinion of Judge Weeramantry*, Hague: International Court of Justice.
Weiss, Edith Brown (1989) *In Fairness to Future Generations: International Law, Common Patrimony and Intergenerational Equity*, Transnational Publishers Inc.
Wells, Herbert George (1913) *The First Men in the Moon and The World Set Free*, London: Literary Press.
Westlake, John (1910-13) *International Law, Part I - Peace, Part II - War*, Cambridge: Cambridge university Press.

Weston, Burns H. (1983) "Nuclear Weapons and International Law: Prolegomenon to General Illegality", *New York Law School Journal of International and Comparative Law*, 1982-1983, Vol. 4, p. 252,
Weston, Burns H.; Falk, Richard A.; D'Amato, Anthony (1990) *International Law and World Order: A Problem-Oriented Coursebook* West Group.
World Commission on Environment and Development (1987) *Our Common Future*, Oxford Paperbacks.
World Court Project (1995) *Implications of Advisory Opinions by the International Court of Justice on the Legal Status of Nuclear Weapons*, Twyford: UK Chair, World Court Project.
WHO (1984) *Effects of Nuclear War on Health and Health Services*, Geneva: World Health Organization
WHO (1987) *Effects of Nuclear War on Health and Health Services*, (2nd ed.) Geneva: World Health Organization
Wright, Quincy (1950) "Review of Law Reports of Trials of War Criminals by United Nations War Crimes Commission; History of the United Nations War Crimes Commission and the Development of the Law of War by United Nations War Crimes Commission; Report of Robert H. Jackson", *Journal of Criminal Law and Criminology* Vol. 40, No. 5 (Jan. - Feb., 1950), pp. 622-625.
Wright, Quincy (1965) *A Study of War : Second Edition with a Commentary on War since 1942*, Chicago: University of Chicago Press. {for relevance to nuclear weapons, it is the Commentary, pp 1499-1577 of particular relevance.]
Zelter, Angie (2001) *Trident on Trial: the case for people's disarmament*, Edinburgh: Luath Press Ltd.

Index

A

Abrams, Herbert 170, 176
Acronym Institute for Disarmament Diplomacy 242
Advisory Opinion
  to UN General Assembly
    full text 114–148
African humanitarian traditions 184
Aggressive war
  planning 8
Ago, Roberto 195
Agreement for Co-operation on the Uses of Atomic Energy for Mutual Defence Purposes
  UK and US agreement, 1958 258
Akamatsu, Koichi 56, 333
Alcalay, Glenn 23, 331
Aldridge, Robert C. 45, 51, 332
Allen, Charles 234, 337
Allied war crimes 285
Alternative Defence Commission 310, 337
Alva and Gunnar Myrdal Foundation 338
American Civil War 185
An Examination of the Legality of Nuclear Weapons 12
Antarctic Treaty, 1959 63
Antelope case 216
Anti-Ballistic Missile Treaty (ABM), 1972 (Salt I) 22, 87
  US unilateral withdrawal xii
Arbess, Daniel 81, 333
Archer, Colin xxi
Architects for Peace 320, 328
Aristotle 214, 337
Arjuna 184
Armenia 11
atomic bomb injury after-effects 27
Australia
  oral statement to ICJ 117
Austria 41
Axelrod, Daniel 227, 342

B

Bach, Wilfrid 169, 337
Bacteriological (Biological) and Toxin Weapons Treaty, 1971 21, 67
bacteriological weapons 19
Baden Consultation xxvi, 319
Baher, H. W. 156, 337
Bahro, Rudolf 345
Balibar, Etienne 345
Bates, Don G. 162, 165, 166, 171, 174, 337
Bedjaoui, Mohammed 276, 337
  ICJ Judge, President 115, 243
  Declaration 103–104, 276, 291
Bersagel, Annie Golden 113, 343
Bhagvadgita 158
Bikini Atoll 33
biological weapons 8
biosphere 34
Blake, Nigel P. 226, 337
blast 171
Blue Danube 258
BMA. *See* British Medical Association
Boister, Neil 299, 309, 337
Bosnia and Herzegovina
  written statement filed at ICJ 116
Boyle, Francis A. 39, 41, 44, 47, 53, 62, 73, 74, 78, 79, 80, 333
Boyle, Joseph M. 226, 339
Brackman, Arnold C. 309, 337
BRAVO test 1954 33
British Council of Churches
  MAD offensive to Christian conscience 68
British Medical Association 31, 337
Brown, Anthony Cave 308, 337
Brown, Gordon 270
Brownlie, Ian 197, 220, 338
Brundtland, Gro Harlem 167, 338
Brussels Conference, 1874 186
Buddhism 71
  traditions 185
Burroughs, John 338
Burundi
  written statement filed at ICJ 116
Butler, William E. 176, 338

C

Cady, Duane L. 226, 338
Calder, Nigel 308, 338
Cameron, David 273
Campaign for Nuclear Disarmament 320, 328
campaigning 71
Canada 73
  agreement over US nuclear weapons 56
Canadian Conference on Nuclear Weapons and the Law 159
cancer 27
Carty, J.A. 333
Carver, Lord 252
Casals, Pablo 156
Casey-Maslen, S. 113, 343
Castellina, Luciana 55, 333
Castrén, Erik J. S. 204, 338
Catholics 53
Charter of the United Nations xxiv
chemical
  warfare 8
  weapons 8
chemical weapons 19
  in Germany 56
  in Japan 56
Chernobyl 170
Chevaline 258
Chimni, B.S. 213, 252, 338
China 10, 49
  Republic of the Marshall Islands case against 249
Chomsky, Noam 345
Christian
  moral interpretations 68
  traditions 184
Churchill, Winston 179, 338
Church of England Board for Social Responsibility 310, 338
civil disobedience 89, 90
civilians 9, 17, 19
  injury to 4
  installations 20
  objects 20
  view of nuclear weapons use 53
civilised nations 14
civilised peoples 82
civil society 292–293
  activism xii
  mobilization and motivation 295–298
Clausewitz 215
Cohen, Maxwell T. 159, 224, 338
Cold War xi
collateral damage 192
Committee for the Complation of Materials on Damage Caused by the Atomic Bombs in Hiroshima and Nagasaki 308, 338
complicity in war crimes is a crime under international law 314
congenital deformities 171
conscientious objection xxvi
  rights 319
conspiracy
  to commit crimes 60
  to wage aggressive war 86
constitutional powers
  loss of 55
Convention for General and Complete Disarmament xxvii
Convention for the Respect of the Laws and Customs of War on Land xxiii
Convention on Maritime Neutrality, 1928 142
Convention on Prohibitions or Restrictions on the Use of Certain Conventional Weapons which may be Deemed to be Excessively Injurious or to have Indiscriminate Effects 64, 187
Convention on the Prohibition of Military or Any Other Hostile Use of Environmental Modification Techniques, 1977 126
Convention Respecting the Rights and Duties of Neutral Powers and Persons in Case of War on Land 16
Cooper, R.W. 338
Corbyn, Jeremy 273

Corfu Channel case 139, 188
Costa Rica
 oral statement to ICJ 119
countervailing strategy
 Nixon 47
Cox, John 345
Crimean War 185
crimes against humanity xxv, 17, 59, 86, 88, 220, 223, 285
 Nuremberg Principles definition 314
crimes against peace 8, 17, 58, 60, 88, 285
 Nuremberg Principles definition 314
Criminal Procedure (Scotland) Act 1995 240
criminal responsibility 87
 governments 88
 individuals 52, 59, 88
 personal 17, 63
Cryer, Robert 299, 309, 337
cultural
 monuments 9
 objects 20
 treasures 174
customary international law 4, 5, 7, 14, 17, 63, 85, 275
 is a rule of Scots law 241

D

D'Amato, Anthony 228, 346
Dando, Malcolm 38, 50, 332, 338
Darnton, Geoffrey xvii, xx, xxxi, 310, 329, 338
Davis, Mike 345
Dawson, John D. 23, 32, 331
decapitation 45, 49, 51
de Chazournes, Laurence Boisson 113, 275, 338
Declaration on the Prevention of Nuclear Catastrophe 179
Declaration Renouncing the Use, in Time of War, of Explosive Projectiles Under 400 grammes Weight, St. Petersberg 1868. 14
delegation
 battlefield 50

democracy 87
Democratic People's Republic of Korea (North Korea)
 Republic of the Marshall Islands case against 249
 withdrawal from NPT 275
 written statement filed at ICJ 116
deterrence 2, 86, 143
 alternatives 309
 chemical weapons 8
 degrees of 225
 doctrine of 43
 failure 46
 theory 294
 unstable system 46
detonation of a single weapon 37
Deuteronomy 184
Dewar, John 237, 311, 338
Dewes, C.F. xxi, 224, 338
Dhokalia, R.P. 311, 344
Dias, R.W.M. 193, 339
dictates of human conscience 82
dictates of the public conscience 189, 189–190
diminishing stability 39
disarmament negotiations
 agreed principles 315–318
Discrimination
 Principle of 5, 12, 62, 86, 104, 108, 150, 196, 197, 197–198, 207, 209, 211
doctrine of deterrence 43
Dolan, Philip J. 166, 340
double standards over application of international law 300–302
DPRK. *See* Democratic People's Republic of Korea (North Korea)
Duarte, Sergio
 UN High Representative for Disarmament Affairs 272
Dunant, Henri 160
Dutt, Romesh Chunder 183, 339

E

ecological disruption 5
Ecology Party xix, xxvii, 320, 328

economic structures 174
Ecuador
  written statement filed at ICJ 116
Edinburgh Conference 242, 308
Edinburgh Peace and Justice Centre xxi, 242
Egypt
  oral statement to ICJ 117
  written statement filed at ICJ 116
Ehrlich, Paul R. 308, 339
Eisenhower, Dwight D. 305
  massive retaliation policy 47
Eknilang, Lijon 172
electromagnetic pulse 175
environment 5, 20, 87, 199
environmental effects of nuclear war 321
Etzioni, Amitai 310, 339
Euphemisms Concealing the Realities of Nuclear War 164
Evats, William
  translator of Grotius, 1682 340
excessive state security 40
Exterminism 345

F

Falk and Krieger Dialogue 285–306
Falk, Richard A. xv, xxxii, 204, 228, 241, 310, 324, 326, 339, 342, 346
  dialogue with David Krieger 285, 285–306
Farebrother, George 247
Feliciano, F.P. 187, 343
Fenwick, Charles G. 216
Ferrari Bravo, L. 339
  ICJ Judge 115
  Declaration 106
Finland
  written statement filed at ICJ 116
Finnis, John 226, 339
first strike 8, 9, 10, 48, 49, 61, 86
Fleck, Dieter 187, 193, 339
Fleischhauer, Carl-August 339
  ICJ Judge 115
  Separate Opinion 108

Fleutry, Michel 176, 339
flexible response 44, 263
  Johnson policy 47
food productivity
  damage to 176
Fox, Liam 271
France
  oral statement to ICJ 117
  Republic of the Marshall Islands case against 249
  voted against UN Resolution 1653 79
  written statement filed at ICJ 116
Frei, Daniel 310, 339
fuel air explosive
  signature similar to nuclear weapon 51

G

Gaudium et Spes 69, 345
general and complete disarmament xxvi, 9, 87
General Grant 186
General Treaty for the Renunciation of War, 1928 xxiv
Geneva Convention on Wounded Persons, 1906 xxiii
Geneva Conventions, 1949 9, 42, 85, 322, 344
Geneva Gas Protocol, 1925 67, 131, 152, 204
Geneva Law 138
Geneva Protocol I 63
  Article 35 19, 126
  Article 36 19
  Article 48 19
  Article 51 19
  Article 52 20
  Article 53 20
  Article 54 20
  Article 55 20
  Article 56 20
  Article 59 20
Geneva Protocols I and II, 1977 9, 13, 20, 42, 78, 85, 87, 322
  reservations on nuclear weapons 21

genocide 199
  definition 16, 125
Genocide Convention, 1948 8, 322
geopolitical issues
  and NPT 300–302
German Constitution
  nuclear weapons and loss of constitutional powers 55
Germany
  oral statement to ICJ 117
  written statement filed at ICJ 116
Ginsberg, Robert 165, 339
Glasstone, Samuel 166, 308, 339
Goldblat, J. 310, 340
Goodchild, Peter 158, 340
good faith 276
  negotiations to be in xiii, 9, 18, 87, 89, 144, 291
  negotiations to date not in 82
Gorbachev, Mikhail 269
Gore, Al 200, 340
Gouin, Margaret E. 159, 224, 338
governments
  criminal responsibility 86
  implications for 88
Gratian 185
Greene, Owen 23, 28, 30, 308, 331, 340
Greenham Common 72, 237
Greenham Women Against Cruise Missiles v. Reagan 237, 307
Greenock Sheriff Court 239
Green Party xxvii, 328
  German 91
Greenpeace International xiv
Green, Robert xxi, 310, 340
Greet, Kenneth V. 68, 330
Gregory, Donna Uthus 234, 340
Grief, Nicholas xxi, 92, 250, 340
Griffith, John 41, 61, 79, 81, 333
Grisez, Germain 226, 339
Grotius, Hugo 1, 77, 186, 311, 340
Ground Zero 310, 340
Guelff, Richard 311, 344
Guillaume, Gilbert 340
  ICJ Judge 115
    Separate Opinion 107

Guruswamy, Lakshman D. 200, 340

H

Hachiya, Michihiko 161, 170, 340
Hague Convention IV Respecting the Laws and Customs of War on Land, 1907 7
Hague Conventions 15, 41, 42, 81, 85, 322
  1899 xxiii, 7, 131
  second, 1907 xxiii, 7, 77, 131, 152
Hague Law 138
Hague Peace Conference xxiii
Haines, Andrew 23, 32, 331
Haldane Society of Socialist Lawyers 320, 328
Halliday, Fred 345
Hannikainen, Lauri 195, 340
Harbottle, Miichael N. 38, 332
Hart, Herbert Lionel Adolphus 212, 341
Hartman, Robert S. 165
Hassan, Syed Riazul 185, 341
Hennessy, Peter 258, 341
Herczegh, Geza 168, 183, 341
  ICJ Judge 115
    Declaration 104–105
Hersey, John 170, 341
Hibakusha xiv, 25, 27, 172, 306
Hickman, Jane 237, 341
Higgins, Rosalyn 341
  ICJ Judge 115
    Dissenting Opinion 111
Hiroshima xiv, 3, 25, 26, 100, 161, 180, 285
  bombing illegal? 309
  eye-witness account 161
  injuries 26
  mortality 26, 28
Hirschfelder, Joseph O 339
Hobbes, Thomas 233, 341
Hodgkin, Dorothy 324, 326
Hollins, H.B. 225, 341
Holm, E. 167, 341
hotline 51
humanitarian law 7, 150, 159–162,

181–206, 195–202, 253
  views of Russian Federation, UK, and USA 181, 181–182
Humanitarian Pledge xiv
  countries pledged 244–245
  text of 247–249
humanity 202, 235
Humanity
  Principle of 5, 9, 12, 110, 111, 115, 139, 143, 157, 158, 159, 162, 164, 177, 179, 182, 186–187, 190, 215, 220, 229, 231
Hutchinson, Jean 73, 333
hyper-destructive weapons 183

I

IALANA 107
ICAN. *See* International Campaign to Abolish Nuclear Weapons
ICC. *See* International Criminal Court
ICJ. *See* International Court of Justice
illegality exists independently of specific prohibitions 192
India
  Republic of the Marshall Islands case against 249
  written statement filed at ICJ 116
individual criminal responsibility 17, 59, 86
  set out by Nuremberg Tribunal 72
Indonesia
  oral statement to ICJ 117
Initial Gate 266, 280
intention 59
  to breach Nuremberg Charter 63
Intermediate-Range Nuclear Forces (INF) Treaty, 1987 22
International Campaign to Abolish Nuclear Weapons xx, 244
International Committee of the Red Cross 344
International Court of Justice 88, 237, 307, 341
  Advisory Opinion xii, 243, 275, 287–289
    dispositif paragraph 2E 241
    dispositif paragraph 2F 275
    Judge voting 111, 146–147
    Advisory Opinion full text 114–148
    Advisory Opinion recommended by London Nuclear Warfare Tribunal 90, 91
    determinations 146
  Republic of Marshall Islands cases xiii, 249–284
  requests for Advisory Opinions 237
International Covenant on Civil and Political Rights 125
International Criminal Court 239, 341
international law
  customary 4, 5
  double standards in application 300
  public conscience 7
  relevance to nuclear weapons 1, 21
  as a process 294
  sources of 4
  treaty rules 6
  value of 77–84
International Law Commission xxv, 17
International Peace Bureau xxi, xxiii, xxvii, 341
  1981 Conference xxvi
  Nobel Peace prize, 1910 xxiii
International Physicians for the Prevention of Nuclear War 175, 179, 244
interpretation of international law 80
IPB. *See* International Peace Bureau
IPPNW. *See* International Physicians for the Prevention of Nuclear War
Iran, Islamic Republic of xii
  oral statement to ICJ 117
  written statement filed at ICJ 116
Ireland
  written statement filed at ICJ 116
Ishikawa, Eisei 341
Islamic traditions 185
Israel 40
  Republic of the Marshall Islands case against 249
Italy

Constitution 56
  nuclear weapons and loss of constitutional powers 55
  oral statement to ICJ 118
  written statement filed at ICJ 116
Iwasa, Mikiji 23, 25, 26, 331

J

Jackson, Robert 286, 341
  chief prosecutor at Nuremberg
  Nuremberg Promise 286–287
Japan
  oral statement to ICJ 118
  tribunals investingating nuclear weapons 71
  written statement filed at ICJ 116
Jayatilleke, K.N. 310
Jayatilleke, Kulatissa Nanda 185, 341
Johnson, Lyndon B.
  flexible response policy 47
Johnson, Rebecca xxi, 243, 342
Jonathan Schell 174
Journalists Against Nuclear Extinction 320, 328
Judgment and Recommendations of the London Nuclear Warfare Tribunal 85, 285
Judgment of the International Military Tribunal for the Trial of German Major War Criminals 16
Jungk, Robert 308, 342
justiciability 241
Just War Doctrine 4, 68, 70

K

Kaku, Michio 227, 342
Kaldor, Mary H. 38, 40, 332, 345
Karp, Regina Cowen 225, 342
Kauravas 184
Kelly, Petra 91
keloids 27
Kennedy, Donald 339
Kennedy, John F.
  MAD policy 47
Kenny, Anthony J.P. 226, 342
Kent, Bruce 69, 72

Khadduri, Majid 310, 342
Kier, Hiltrud 175
King, Martin Luther 300
Kings, Christine 329
Kissinger, Henry A. xi, 173, 209, 296, 342
Kollerstrom, Nick 329
Korea 79
Koroma, Abdul G. 342
  ICJ Judge 115
  Dissenting Opinion 111
Kramish, Arnold 339
Krieger, David xv, 96, 311, 339, 342, 343
  dialogue with Richard Falk 285–306
Krupp Trial 188
Kugai, Saburo 345

L

Lakshmana 183
land forces 9
Landmine Ban Treaty xiv
Lapp, Ralph E. 342
LAR. *See* Lord Advocate's Reference
Larkin, Brian xxi
Lateran Council
  Second, 1139 184
Latin America Nuclear-Free Zone Treaty, 1967 21
Lauterpacht, H. 343
Lawfulness
  Principle of 5, 12, 100, 108, 114
Law of Geneva 9
Law of the Hague 9
laws of humanity 10, 14. *See also* Humanity, Principle of
Laws of Manu 184
lawyers
  nuclear weapons xxvii
Lawyers Committee on Nuclear Policy xxvii
Lawyers for Nuclear Disarmament xxvii, 333
Legge, J. Michael 310, 342
Lesotho
  written statement filed at ICJ 116

leukaemia 27
Lieber Code 186, 196
Lieber, Francis 186
Lifton, Robert Jay 310, 342
Limited Test Ban Treaty, 1963 9, 87
Lincoln, Abraham 186
Loch Goil 239
London Nuclear Warfare Tribunal xi, 237, 308
  Convenors 329
  Interim Declaration 320–324
  Members 324
  Supporting Organizations 328
  Witnesses and Evidence 330–336
long-term effects
  global ecosphere 34
  nuclear injury 27
  radiation 33
Lord Advocate's Reference 240, 307, 342
Lotus Rationale 80, 81, 124, 194
  intended for use in peace time 80
  vs de Martens clause 80
Lowe, Vaughan 277, 342

M

MacBride, Sean xxviii, 324, 325
MacDonald, Charles B. 308, 338
Mackenzie, David 247
Magri, Lucio 345
Mahabharatha 183
Malaysia
  oral statement to ICJ 118
  written statement filed at ICJ 116
malicious mischief 240
Manhattan Engineer District 308, 342
Manhattan Project 177
Manson, Robbie 247
Manu
  Laws of 184
Marshall Islands, Republic of
  file cases against nuclear weapons states 249
  oral statement to ICJ 118
  site of nuclear weapons tests 254
  written statement filed at ICJ 116

Marshall Islands v United Kingdom 251–284
Martens, de 7, 10, 15, 53, 80, 85, 139, 186
  clause. acceptance by states 188
  comments at Hague Conference 163
  vs Lotus Rationale 80
Massive Interventions of Democracy 71
massive retaliation doctrine
  Eisenhower 47
Maurya, Chandragupta 184
Mayer, John 311, 343
Mayors for Peace xx, 245
Maytime 239
McCloy-Zorin Accords 315–318
McDougal, Myres Smith 187, 343
McKenzie, Ross 329
McNamara, Robert 174, 207
McWhinney, Edward 165, 169, 196, 206, 345
means of injury not unlimited 15, 138
Medical Campaign Against Nuclear Weapons 320, 328
medical effects
  nuclear war 321
  nuclear weapons 27
medical scientists xxvii
Medvedev, Roy and Zhores 345
Megasthenes 184
Merton, Thomas 165
Mettraux, Guénaël 343
Mexico
  oral statement to ICJ 117
  written statement filed at ICJ 116
Meyrowitz, Elliott L. 13, 39, 40, 48, 74, 81, 333
Military and Paramilitary Activities in and against Nicaragua (Nicaragua v. United States of America) 162
Minear, Richard H. 309, 343
Mobilization and Motivation 295–298
Model Nuclear Weapons Convention 271
Monte Bello Islands
  UK nuclear test 258

Moon Treaty, 1979 22, 63
moral and religious implications of nuclear war preparations 321
morality xxvii, 2, 4
Motherson, Keith 311, 343
Moxley, Ellen 239, 242
multicultural background to the humanitarian laws of war 183
mushroom cloud shadow 177
Mutually Assured Destruction (MAD)
  inconsistent with international law 48
  Kennedy policy 47
Myers, Norman 23, 35, 331

N

Nagai, Takashi 308, 343
Nagasaki xi, xiv, 3, 25, 100, 161, 180, 285
  bombing illegal? 309
  mortality 28
Nanda, Ved 96, 311, 343
NAPF. *See* Nuclear Age Peace Foundation
National Peace Council 320, 328
National Union of Public Employees 320, 328
NATO 10, 13, 38, 44, 49, 55
Nauru
  written statement filed at ICJ 116
Necessity
  Principle of 5, 12, 110, 111, 114, 127, 129, 130, 151, 229–230, 241
negiotiations
  to be in good faith xiii, 9, 18, 87, 89, 144
  to date, not done in good faith 82
  negotiate in good faith 291
Netherlands
  written statement filed at ICJ 116
Neutrality 55, 141
  Principle of 5, 12, 114, 131, 138, 141, 142, 207, 209–210
neutral powers 16, 41
New Zealand
  canvassing for ICJ AO 91
  oral statement to ICJ 118
  written statement filed at ICJ 116
New Zealand Foundation for Peace Studies 91
Nixon
  countervailing strategy policy 47
Nobel Women's Initiative xiv
No First Use xii
non-belligerent states 150. *See also* Neutrality, Principle of
Non-Proliferation Treaty, 1968 xiii, 9, 62, 63, 87
  Article VI 274, 287
  failure by nuclear weapons states to negotiate in good failth 251
  is an unequal treaty 301–302
Nuclear Age Peace Foundation xiv, xx, 245
Nuclear Ban Treaty xiv
nuclear blackmail 40
nuclear reactors
  damage to 176
Nuclear Tests cases 277
nuclear war 180
  survivable? 180
Nuclear War
  Euphemisms Concealing the Realities of 164
nuclear war and provision of health services 31
Nuclear Warhead Capability Sustainment Programme 266
Nuclear Weapon Archive 345
nuclear weapons
  accuracy 48
  counter-democratic 40
  ecological effects 35
  effects 26–27, 165–177
  environmental effects 35
  estimate of world stockpiles 257
  existential breaches of international law 99
  illegal in any circumstances whatsoever 152, 291
  limit situation 162
  loss of constitutional powers 55
  medical effects 27, 31

modernization xii
'nuclear' merely an adjective 81
outlawed in several world regions 190
possession 43–66, 162
psychological effects 32
radiation effects 27, 33
relevance of international law 20
simulated attack on UK 28
states supporting legality 163
threats to use 6
use 23–42
use or threat to use illegal in any circumstances whatsoever. 152
US policies on use 47
Nuclear Weapons Archive 308
Nuclear Weapons, Sea-Bed and Ocean Floor Treaty, 1971 21, 63, 64
nuclear weapons states xiii, 256
   approaches to ICJ Advisory Opinion 298
nuclear winter 25, 34, 36, 87, 168, 321
Nuclear Zero xiv, 249
Nugent, Conn 218
Nunn, Sam xi
Nuremberg 3, 11
Nuremberg Charter xxv, 16, 61, 285
   Article 6 59, 62
   Article 6a 58
   Article 6b 58
   Article 6c 59
   Article 7 59
   Article 8 59
   Britain xxv
   France xxv
   Soviet Union xxv
   United States xxv
Nuremberg Judgment xxv, 3, 77, 85
   Treaty of Paris basis xxiv
Nuremberg Principles, 1950 xxv, 3, 85, 308, 313–314, 322
   Principles I, II, III, IV, V 313
   Principles VI, VII 314
Nuremberg Promise 286
Nuremberg Tribunal xxiv, xxv, 3, 139, 343
   Charter xxv

set out individual responsibilities 72
Nussbaum, Arthur 184, 343
Nystuen, G. 113, 343

O

Obama, Barack xi
O'Brian, John 308, 343
Oda, Shigeru 343
   ICJ Judge 115
   Dissenting Opinion 109
Oestreicher, Paul 70, 330
Ohkawa, Yoshiatsu 70, 71, 330
one megaton bomb
   like a 200-mile train loaded with TNT 165
Open-Ended Working Group
   UK failed to attend meetings 271
Oppenheim 229
Oppenheimer, Robert 158
Oppenheim, Lassa Francis Lawrence 343
orders
   obligation to refuse to obey 53
Outer Space Treaty, 1967 21, 52, 63, 87
Oxford English Dictionary 153, 343
   definition of poison 204

P

Pacific War Research Society 308, 343
pacifism 70
Pact of Paris 8
Pakistan
   Republic of the Marshall Islands case against 249
Paliwala, Abdul 339
Palmer, Geoffrey W. R. 200, 340
Pal, Radhabinod
   Tokyo War Crimes Tribunal Judge 299
Pandavas 184
Parker, David B 339
Parks, Rosa 300
Pasti, Nino 50, 56, 332
Pathak, R.S. 311, 344
Pentz, M.J. 38, 49, 52, 71, 332

Percival, Ian C. 23, 35, 36, 331
Permanent Court of International Justice 80, 122
Permanent People's Tribunal 11, 344
permissive theory
  vs prohibitive theory 80
Perry, William xi
personal criminal responsibility 17, 52, 63
Philippines
  oral statement to ICJ 118
PICAT. *See* Public Interest Case Against Trident
Picciotto, Sol 339
Pictet, Jean S. 311, 344
places of worship 20, 175, 185
Pogany, Istvan 344
poison 15, 16
  weapons 8
Polanyi, John 224
Polaris 258
Pole, Kay 226, 337
Porritt, Jonathon 35, 329, 331
positive international law 4
possession, deployment and use contrary to intenational law 82
possession of an offensive weapon
  crime in many jurisdictions 60
possession of nuclear weapons 2, 43–66, 62
  intention to breach Nuremberg Charter 63
  unlawfulness 79
Powell, Colin 230, 344
Powers, A. L. 225, 341
prerogative 241
Prevention and Punishment of the Crime of Genocide 125
Principle of
  Discrimination 5, 12, 62, 86, 197. *See also* Discrimination, Principle of
  Humanity 5, 9, 12. *See also* Humanity, Principle of
  Lawfulness 5, 12. *See also* Lawfulness, Principle of
  Necessity 5, 12. *See also* Necessity, Principle of
  Neutrality 5, 12. *See also* Neutrality, Principle of
  Proportionality 5, 12, 62, 86, 197. *See also* Proportionality, Principle of
Prins, Gwyn 38, 332, 344
prisoners of war 9
prohibition against causing unnecessary suffering 196
prohibition against environmental damage 199
prohibition against genocide 199
prohibitive theory
  vs permissive theory 80
Proportionality 208
  Principle of 5, 12, 62, 86, 108, 114, 127, 129, 130, 150, 163, 196, 197, 207, 210, 230
Protocol for the Prohibition of the Use in War of Asphyxiating, poisonous or Other Gases, and of Bacteriological Methods of Warfare, 1925 8, 16
Protocol for the Prohibition of the Use of Asphyxiating, Poisonous and Other Gases, 1925 xxiii
psychological effects of nuclear weapons 32
public conscience 10, 11, 14, 15, 67–76, 158, 189, 189–190, 292–293, 307–312
  mobilization and motivation 295–298
  relevance in international law 10
Public Interest Case Against Trident xx, 246

Q

Qatar
  oral statement to ICJ 118
  written statement filed at ICJ 116
Quinlan, Michael 259

R

radiation

does it involve bodily contact with materials? 205
is it poisonous? 204
long-term effects 33
Rahula, Walpola 185, 344
Rama 183
Ramayana 183
RAND Corporation Report 39, 48
Ranjeva, Raymond 344
  ICJ Judge 115
  Separate Opinion 107-108
Raskin, Marcus 345
Rawls, John 214, 344
Reagan, Ronald xi, 183, 269
  hotline 51
Rees, Edward 329
refusal to obey unlawful orders 53
Reid, John 263
relevant international law 13-22
religious
  bodies 10
  groups
    genocide against 199
  ideas in humanitarian law 159
  leaders xxvii
  morality 4
  public opinion 221
reprisals 20, 127, 130, 151, 152, 155, 164, 227-228
Republic of the Marshall Islands
  cases against nuclear powers xiii, 249-284
  effects of atomic tests xiii, xiv
  v United Kingdom
    application to ICJ 251-284, 344
Requests for Advisory Opinions
  WHO and UNGA 237
Resolution-class submarines 258
Richardson, Lewis Fry 310, 344
Rifkind, Malcolm 262
Rights of Conscientious Objectors 319
Rio Declaration, 1992 126
Roberts, Adam 311, 344
Roberts, Walter Orr 339
Roder, Bodil 239
Rogers, Bernard William General, Commander of NATO forces 48
Rogers, Paul 38, 332, 338, 344
Roman Catholic Church 4, 69
Rome Statute 239, 341
Rotblat, Joseph 171, 177, 252, 344
Rubin, Barry 340, 346
Ruete, Matthias 339
Russbach, Olivier 73, 334
Russian Federation. *See also* USSR
  oral statement to ICJ 118
  Republic of the Marshall Islands case against 249
  view of humanitarian law 181
  written statement filed at ICJ 116
Ruston, Roger 226, 344

S

Sagan, Carl 23, 35, 339
Saito, Osamu 23, 25, 26, 71, 331
Samoa
  oral statement to ICJ 118
  written statement filed at ICJ 116
Sands, Philippe 113, 275, 338
San Marino
  oral statement to ICJ 118
  written statement filed at ICJ 116
Sato, Gyotsu N. 330
Schachter, Oscar 159
Schell, Jonathan 174, 201, 344
Schlesinger doctrine 47
Schwarzenberger, Georg 204, 206, 344
Schwebel, Stephen M. 345
  ICJ Judge, Vice-President 115
  Dissenting Opinion 108
Schweitzer, Albert 156
Scientists Against Nuclear Arms 320, 328
Scottish Lawyers for Nuclear Disarmament 320, 328, 334
Scottish National Party 242
Scott, J.B. 164
sea forces 9
self-defence 8, 16, 114, 127, 129, 133, 136, 142, 143, 146, 150, 177, 206-211

not an available defence in international law 60
shadow of the mushroom cloud 177
Shahabuddeen, Mohamed 252, 345
  ICJ Judge 115
    Dissenting Opinion 109–110
Shi, Jiuyong 345
  ICJ Judge 115
    Declaration 105
Shimoda case 156, 339
Shultz, George xi
Singh, Nagendra 165, 169, 183, 185, 196, 206, 214, 345
SIPRI 308, 345
Sivard, Ruth Leger 234, 345
Smith, Dan 38, 332
Smith, Ralph Carlisle 339
Smithsonian Institution
  cancel 50th anniversary of atomic bombings 286
SNP. *See* Scottish National Party
social institutions 174
Society of Friends (Quakers) 320, 328
SODEPAX Report
  Baden Consultation 319
Solferino 160
Solomon Islands
  oral statement to ICJ 119
  written statement filed at ICJ 116
Sommer, Mark 225, 341
sovereignty 4
Soviet Union 10. *See also* Russian Federation and USSR
  Zorin-McCloy Accords xxv
Spaight, James Molony 204, 345
Stania, Peter 334
START Treaty 270
Star Wars 24
statist positions 2, 7
Steadman, Philip 23, 28, 29, 331
Steel, Elaine 329
Stockholm Declaration, 1972 126
Stone, Julius 345
St. Petersberg Declaration, 1868 15, 186
strategic bombing 79
Strategic Defence Initiative (SDI) 24, 38, 39, 45, 52, 87
Sublette, Carey xxii, 308, 345
Super Antelope 258
survivability of nuclear war 180
Swain, David L. 341
Sweden
  written statement filed at ICJ 116
Swedish Lawyers Against Nuclear Arms 338
Switzerland 41

T

Tairov, T. 334
Takamura, Yoshiatsu 334
Teachers for Peace 320, 328
technology 6, 51
  evolution and deterrence 46
terrorization of the enemy 187
Test-Ban Treaty, 1963 52
Thatcher, Margaret 270
The Convention for the Pacific Settlement of International Disputes xxiii
Thompson, E.P. 308, 345
Thompson, Gordon 176
Thompson, J. 23, 32, 331
threat of force 215
Toffler, Alvin 234, 345
Toffler, Heidi 234, 345
Tokyo
  comments of Justice Pal 3, 308
  International Military Tribunal 308
  Judgment 85
  Tribunal 8, 100
Treaty between the United States of America and the Union of Soviet Socialist Republics on the Elimination of their Intermediate-Range and Short-Range Missiles, 1987 49
treaty law 5
Treaty of Paris, 1928 16
  Article 1 xxiv
  Article 2 xxiv
Treaty of Rarotonga, 1985 133, 143
Treaty of Tlatelolco, 1967 133, 143

Treaty on the Limitation of Anti-Ballistic Missile Systems, 1972 52
Treaty on the Limitation of Underground Nuclear Weapons Tests, 1974 22, 64
treaty rules 6
Tribunal Against First Strike and Mass Destructive Weapons', Nuremberg 1983 91
Trident 259
  C4 v D5 259
  renewal of 250
  stockpile reduction 261
  technical components 259–260
Trident Alternatives Review 268
Trident and International Law Edinburgh Conference, 2009 242
Trident and Scotland 239–243, 244–248, 247–251
Trident Ploughshares 239, 242
Trident Three 239, 243
Trinity Atomic Web Site 308, 345
TTAPS study 168, 179
Turok, Neil 340

U

UK. *See* United Kingdom
Ukraine xii
UK-US Mutual Defence Agreement, 265
undefended villages and towns 15
UNESCO 175
UNGA. *See* United Nations General Assembly
UNIDIR 208, 231, 345
uniqueness of nuclear weapons 178
Uniqueness of Nuclear Weapons
  uniqueness 178
United Kingdom 9
  casualty estimates 28
  Foreign Office 13
  health service provision in the event of nuclear attack 31
  oral statement to ICJ 119
  position on lawfulness of nuclear weapons 13

renewal of Trident 250
Republic of the Marshall Islands case against UK 249
reservation on Geneva 1977 Protocols 21
view of humanitarian law 182
voted against UN Resolution 1653 79
written statement filed at ICJ 116
United Nations
  and nuclear weapons 74
  Article 51 60, 80, 101
  Charter xxiv, 8, 14, 41, 79, 86, 158, 322
    Article 1 xxv, 153
    Article 2 101
    Article 2(4) 153, 215
    signed before Hiroshima and Nagasaki 157
  First Special Session of the General Assembly on Disarmament xxvi
  General and Complete Disarmament programme, 1961 xxvi
  General Assembly xxv
  Resolutions re nuclear weapons 115
  Resolution 1653 (XVI) 10, 79, 190, 286
United Nations Association 320, 328
United Nations Convention on the Prevention and Punishment of the Crime of Genocide 16
United Nations Convention on the Prohibition or Restriction on the Use of Certain Conventional Weapons which may be Deemed to be Excessively Injurious or to Have Indiscriminate Effects 21
United Nations General Assembly
  request to ICJ for an Advisory Opinion 97–148, 115–116
United Nations Institute of Disarmament Research (UNIDIR) 179, 339
United Nations War Crimes Commis-

sion 311, 345
United States of America 9, 88
  Army Field Manual 53
  Field Manual on the Laws of Land Warfare 52
  Navy Manual 54
  oral statement to ICJ 119
  policies on nuclear weapons use 47
  position on lawfulness of nuclear weapons 13
  Republic of the Marshall Islands case against 249
  reservation on Geneva 1977 Protocols 21
  view of humanitarian law 182
  voted against UN Resolution 1653 79
  written statement filed at ICJ 116
  Zorin-McCloy Accords xxv
unnecessary suffering 15
unstable system 46
use of nuclear weapons 23–42
USSR 45, 88. *See also* Russian Federation
  position on lawfulness of nuclear weapons 13
  voted for UN Resolution 1653 79

V

Valencia-Ospina, Eduardo
  ICJ Registrar 115
Vatican xxvi, 345
V bombers 258
Vereshchetin, Vladlen S. 345
  ICJ Judge 115
  Declaration 105
victors' justice 309
Vienna Convention on the Law of Treaties, 1969 21, 67
Vlasikhin, Vasily A. 13, 38, 45, 332

W

Walker, Gregory xxii, 308, 345
war as an instrument of national policy xxiv
war crimes xxv, 8, 58, 285

Nuremberg Principles definition 314
obeying orders 60
Ware, Alyn xxi
War of Secession 186
Warwick Legal Defence Trust 339
WE177 air-launched free-fall nuclear bomb 259
weapons of mass destruction 82
Webber, Philip R. 38, 329, 332, 340, 345
Weeramantry, Christopher Gregory 185, 252, 309, 346
  ICJ Judge 115
  Dissenting Opinion xii, 111, 149–236, 291
Weiss, Edith Brown 168, 346
Wells, Herbert George 181, 346
Werner, Richard 226, 338
Westlake, John 229, 346
Weston, Burns H. 190, 200, 204, 217, 218, 228, 230, 340, 346
WHO
  Request to ICJ for an Advisory Opinion 97
Wilkins, Maurice 324, 327
Wilkinson, Graeme 329, 340, 346
Williams, Raymond 345
Wilson, Andrew 38, 332
Wolfe, Alan 345
World Commission on Environment and Development 346
World Conference for Religion and Peace, 1970 xxvi
World Council of Churches xiv, xxvi
World Court Project 91–96, 107, 237, 243, 346
World Health Assembly (WHA). *See* World Health Organization
World Health Organization 346
  effects of nuclear war 173
  ICJ decline to give Advisory Opinion 98
  request to ICJ for Advisory Opinion 97, 156
World War III
  prevented by nuclear weapons? 2
worship

places of 20, 175, 185
Wright, David 334
Wright, Quincy 310, 311, 346

Z

Zelter, Angie xxi, 239, 243, 247, 342, 346
Zimbabwe
  oral statement to ICJ 119
Zorin-McCloy Accords xxv, 323. *See* McCloy-Zorin